A NECESSARY FANTASY?

CHILDREN'S LITERATURE AND CULTURE
VOLUME 18
GARLAND REFERENCE LIBRARY OF THE HUMANITIES
VOLUME 1873

CHILDREN'S LITERATURE AND CULTURE
JACK ZIPES, *Series Editor*

A NECESSARY FANTASY?

THE HEROIC FIGURE IN CHILDREN'S POPULAR CULTURE

edited by
DUDLEY JONES AND TONY WATKINS

GARLAND PUBLISHING, INC.
A MEMBER OF THE TAYLOR & FRANCIS GROUP
NEW YORK & LONDON / 2000

Published in 2000 by
Garland Publishing, Inc.
A member of the Taylor & Francis Group
29 West 35th Street
New York, NY 10001

10 9 8 7 6 5 4 3 2 1

Library of Congress Cataloging-in-Publication Data
A necessary fantasy? : the heroic figure in children's popular culture / edited
by Dudley Jones & Tony Watkins
        p. cm.—(Garland reference library of the humanities ; v. 1873 Children's
literature and culture ; v. 18)
        Includes bibliographical references and index.
        ISBN 0-8153-1844-8 (alk. paper)
        1. Children's mass media. 2. Heroes in mass media. 3. Popular
culture. I. Jones, Dudley. II. Watkins, Tony. III. Garland reference library
of the humanities ; vol. 1873. IV. Garland reference library of the humanities.
Children's literature and culture ; v. 18.

P94.5.C55 N43 2000
302.23'083—dc21   00-026505

J.S. Bratton: "British imperialism and the reproduction of femininity in girls' fiction, 1900–1930." From *Imperialism and Juvenile Literature,* edited by Jeffrey
Richards. Manchester, UK: Manchester University Press, 1989. Reprinted with
permission of J. S. Bratton.

To Jill and Barbara—thanks for all your love and patience

Contents

Series Editor's Foreword

Dedicated to furthering original research in children's literature and culture, the Children's Literature and Culture series includes monographs on individual authors and illustrators, historical examinations of different periods, literary analyses of genres, and comparative studies on literature and the mass media. The series is international in scope and is intended to encourage innovative research in children's literature with a focus on interdisciplinary methodology.

Children's literature and culture are understood in the broadest sense of the term *children* to encompass the period of childhood up through late adolescence. Because the notion of childhood has changed so much since the origination of children's literature, this Garland series is particularly concerned with transformations in children's culture and how they have affected the representation and socialization of children. Although the emphasis of the series is on children's literature, all types of studies that deal with children's radio, film, television, and art are included in an endeavor to grasp the aesthetics and values of children's culture. Not only have there been momentous changes in children's culture since the mid-twentieth century, but there have been radical shifts in the scholarship that deals with these changes. In this regard, the goal of the Children's Literature and Culture series is to enhance research in this field and, at the same time, point to new directions that bring together the best scholarly work throughout the world.

Jack Zipes

ix

A Necessary Fantasy?

Introduction

DUDLEY JONES AND TONY WATKINS

The contributors to this book address, from a variety of critical perspectives, the central issues of what constitutes heroism and the nature of the heroic figure in American, Australian, and British popular culture. They refer to a wide range of cultural forms including, film, television, comics and periodicals, books, and toys.

Until recently, a book focusing on heroic figures for young people would have been regarded as unfashionable, if not inappropriate. What makes the concept of heroism problematic is that it is "so irrevocably a gendered and 'raced' concept as to be practically unusable in any of its old forms" (Hall 1996, p. 116). We live, after all, in a post-heroic age: Heroes are for debunking and deconstructing. The gendered associations of the terms "hero" and "heroism"—macho posturing, manliness, celebrations of physical bravery (often in a context of imperial conquest), and a consequent devaluing of what are often seen as feminine qualities—have been analysed and condemned by such cultural critics as Barbara Taylor: "Virtually all discussions of heroism . . . have taken male heroes as the norm" (Taylor 1996, p. 120), and Stuart Hall: "There are heroines, but the very concept seems to operate on decisively masculine terrain" (Hall 1996, p. 116).

"Heroines," they maintain, are defined by their difference from heroes; in the 1970s and 1980s, it was argued that fairy tale heroines, for example, popularised by such artists as Disney, offered girls models of passivity and subordination: They were depicted as pretty adornments, enduring suffering passively and waiting to be rescued by the courageous actions of a handsome prince.[1] Feminist critics claimed that while many

1

folk and fairy tales *do* feature active heroines, these stories have failed to achieve popularity or recognition because their collection, publication, and dissemination has been controlled by male-dominated institutions. Critics of colonialism and post-colonialism shared the concern of feminists about the ways in which cultural values are assimilated and inculcated through stories of heroic figures in popular literature for children.[2]

As a result of these attacks on the concepts of "hero," "heroism," and "heroine," we must now accept that many of the best ideas seem to operate

> as Jacques Derrida put it, "under erasure." That is, with a line running through them, cancelling them in their old form, but still permitting them to go on being read, since we have no other, alternative, better concepts to put in their place, to think with. (Hall 1996, p. 117)

Thus the editors of the "Heroes & Heroines" issue of *Soundings* (Summer 1996), describe the contributors as

> post-heroic, or post-utopian because they are writing, so to speak, from the other side—the dark side—of heroism, idealisation and identification. Each is aware of the space in thinking and language which has to be negotiated before anything useful can be said, now, on this subject. (p. 117)

In this introduction we seek to contextualise the debate about heroes and heroism by (1) exploring the arguments put forward in the nineteenth and twentieth centuries regarding the value of heroes in children's education and the curriculum, and (2) examining two of the main theoretical approaches within which the hero, heroine and heroism have been conceptualised. One of these, the archetypal approach stemming from the work of the analytical psychologist, Carl Gustav Jung, emphasises the transhistorical, transcultural significance of the hero and his relationship with the collective unconscious. Some of Jung's ideas were developed in anthropology and the study of religion by Joseph Campbell, and in literary study by the critic Northrop Frye. The other approach, a more materialist one associated with cultural critics such as Richard Slotkin and Marina Warner, argues that the figures of the hero and heroine are constructed within history and that myths (including heroic myths) "are stories, drawn from history, that have acquired through usage over many generations a symbolizing function that is central to the cultural functioning of the society that produces them" (Slotkin 1985, p. 16). The emphasis in this approach on the constructed nature of the "hero" and "heroine" in history has opened up the possibilities of feminist intervention in the theoretical debate on heroism.

HISTORICAL HEROES AND THE SCHOOL CURRICULUM

The arguments of commentators such as Stuart Hall are only part of a debate that emerged in the 1990s over the role of heroic figures in children's education and popular culture. By the middle of the decade, there were attempts to re-affirm the traditional, positive role of heroes in education. For example, in 1995 Nicholas Tate, the British Government's Chief Advisor on the curriculum for schools, provoked a heated argument when he accused teachers of "selling Britain short." He argued that "Britain's sense of national identity was being eroded because history teachers were ignoring British heroes" (Samuel 1995, p. 27). Tate's belief in the exemplary value of heroes, and their role in defining landmarks in British history, sounds remarkably similar to the views put forward almost a century and a half earlier by Thomas Carlyle in his famous treatise, *On Heroes, Hero-worship and The Heroic in History*. Carlyle expresses regret that "hero-worship" has gone out of fashion: "this . . . is an age that, as it were, denies the existence of great men; denies the desirableness of great men" (for Carlyle, the terms "great men" and "heroes" are interchangeable) though earlier he asserts: "Hero-worship *is* nevertheless, as it was always and everywhere, and cannot cease till man himself ceases" (Carlyle 1903, p. 11). Carlyle rails against the tendency to diminish heroes, to see them simply as products of their time, shaped by historical circumstances rather than shaping those circumstances. "We cannot look upon a great man," he argues, "without gaining something by him" (p. 2). He goes on to formulate a biographical view of history: "The History of the World, I have said already, [is] the Biography of Great Men" (p. 12).

Later in the nineteenth century, a whole constellation of moral virtues was attributed to heroes. Henry Johnson's *A Book of Heroes Or Great Victories in the Fight for Freedom,* published by The Religious Tract Society, illustrates through a collection of stories of historical heroes, the qualities which constitute heroism. He points out that in nearly every story, "the motive of self interest [is] entirely absent." The true hero's qualities are "unselfishness, consideration for others' interests", and "a strong faith in right doing" (Johnson n.d., pp. 253–254).

Another late Victorian example gives a more nationalistic inflection to the notion of "hero." Edwin Hodder's *Heroes of Britain in Peace and War* begins by discussing the general virtues of heroism.[3] However, the nationalistic purpose of the heroic stories in his book becomes clear when the editor adds proudly:

> There is no country in the world where the deeds of great men are held in higher estimation than in Great Britain, and in no other country can there be found so many men and women whose lives have been devoted to energetic and praiseworthy works for the benefit of others. And it is good for us that we refresh our minds by dwelling on the deeds of great men, for, as Carlyle so well says, "no nobler feeling than this of admiration for one higher than himself dwells in the breast of man". (Hodder n.d., p. 14)

It is generally accepted that notions of the exemplary value of the heroic figure influenced children's literature throughout the nineteenth century and well into the twentieth century. However, it is clear that the moral virtues of the hero were always articulated through the ideological frameworks of gender, imperialism, and national identity. For example, several cultural critics have observed that late Victorian culture became sharply differentiated along lines of gender and that gender-related children's literature expanded greatly from the late 1870s with the rise of the new imperial fiction for boys.

> Stories of the colonial adventures of British soldiers, told and retold across many different narrative forms, constituted the very keystone of the hero-industry and constructed a new imperial tradition, a heroic pantheon of historical and contemporary heroes. (Dawson 1996, p. 149)

Further, from around 1900, the demand for history text-books based on the narratives of great men and women increased considerably. Such a demand reflected significant cultural changes in which a commercially produced children's culture allied itself to "evangelical, state and civic concerns about the propagation of gender-specific moral virtues." Commercial interests and youth organisations such as the Scouts and the Guides "worked to institute a comprehensive separation of the adventure worlds of boys and men from the domestic world of girls and women—a split inscribed . . . within juvenile narrative forms" (Dawson 1996, p. 151).

Jeffrey Richards suggests that the adventure tales of juvenile literature in the latter half of the nineteenth century and first half of the twentieth were "steeped in every aspect of imperialism," which functioned

> not just as a mirror of the age but an active agency constructing and perpetuating a view of the world in which British imperialism was an integral part of the cultural and psychological formation of each new generation of readers. (Richards 1989, p. 3)

He quotes Charlotte Yonge's advice in 1887 on the establishment of suitable libraries for boys in the home and at school:

> Boys especially should not have childish tales with weak morality or "washy" piety, but should have heroism and nobleness kept before their eyes . . . True manhood needs above all earthly qualities to be imposed on them, and books of example (not precept) with heroes, whose sentiments they admire, may also raise their tone, sometimes individually, sometimes collectively. (Yonge 1887, p. 6; in Richards 1989, p. 4)

The nineteenth-century tradition of teaching history to children through stories of "heroism and nobleness" undoubtedly lay behind some of the school curricular debates in the 1980s. The heroes cited by the Schools' Curriculum Advisor, Nicholas Tate, included Alfred the Great, Nelson, Livingstone, Florence Nightingale, and Churchill. Not surprisingly, he was attacked for his jingoism, for confusing British with English history and for failing to recognise that Britain's multi-cultural composition meant not all its citizens shared the same cultural identity and historical tradition. As one commentator observed, the call for national heroes begged the question of whose nation they represented: "William Wallace is a traditional hero in Scotland but not in England" (Samuel 1995, p. 27). However, the tabloids were quick to defend Tate. "Don't let them turn our heroes into zeroes!" declared Gary Bushnell in the *Sun* (never a newspaper to let a jingoistic opportunity go begging). Qualified support for Nicholas Tate came from a more unexpected quarter. In an article in the *Guardian,* the socialist historian Raphael Samuel, conceded that Carlyle's "great man theory of history" had proved a highly successful pedagogic device, embraced by Mechanics Institutes as well as public schools.

While admitting his professional commitment to the practice of "history from below," Samuel acknowledges that ordinary people have always been excited by the "*romance* of the past" (our emphasis). He also concedes that the representative hero of "penny history" chapbooks—"one of the great sources of knowledge about the past"—was generally an aristocratic figure such as Sir Guy of Warwick rather than a poor labourer. He emphasises the role of oral narratives in creating legendary figures heroes:

> The capacity to create legends is one of the primary forms of storytelling, confronting folklorists and anthropologists—the collectors of the oral tradition—in whatever sphere they work.

In our own time, he says, mass idols—the stars of cinema and popular music—form an inescapable part of historical narrative. Regardless of whether heroes and heroines are the creations of an oral tradition or are media constructions they satisfy a universal need.

> If heroes and heroines are myth, a projection of our longings, and if some of their most famous moments turn out to be apocryphal, they are nevertheless a necessary fantasy. We all need at some stage in life, mentors. We all seek out people to believe in, patterns to follow, examples to take up. (Samuel 1995, p. 27)

Carlyle and Tate are concerned primarily with historical heroes and heroines. But for many children and adults, fictional heroes have been as influential as "real-life" heroes. Both are constructed through popular narratives which frame them for public consumption and foreground particular attitudes and values.

MYTHIC, FOLK, AND FICTIONAL HEROES

Phillipe Sellier describes the rise of interest in heroic myths as a "strange phenomenon" which began to emerge in the early twentieth century:

> it became clear that narratives with striking similarities had appeared at different times almost everywhere on the planet. These were the "lives of heroes," of supermen, people halfway between the status of gods and ordinary human life. Two new sciences, psychoanalysis and mythology, established the previous century combined and intersected to explain these constants. (Sellier 1992, p. 557)

Sellier, in discussing these early developments within the study of psychoanalysis and mythology, draws attention to the contribution of cultural analysts like Freud, Rank, Jung, and Campbell.

In the 1930s and 1940s, several attempts were made—from different perspectives—to identify a common structural pattern which was said to underlie most mythic and legendary hero-narratives. Lord Raglan's now largely forgotten *The Hero: A Study in Tradition, Myth and Drama* (1936), took a dozen heroes from Classical and non-Classical sources and identified a ritual pattern of twenty-two incidents, corresponding to the three principal *rites de passage* of birth, initiation, and death.[4] He applied this pattern to mythic and legendary heroes such as Oedipus, Theseus, Arthur, and Robin Hood, and also to historical heroes. Significant differences emerged between the two groups of heroes, with the legendary heroes conforming far more closely to the pattern identified by Raglan than the historical heroes (Raglan 1936, p. 189).

But the dominant theoretical approach to mythic, legendary, and fictional heroes was developed from the psychoanalytical roots of the study of myth, and may be broadly labelled "archetypal." Jung argued that all myths, including the hero myth, are transcultural and transhistorical because they emerge from the collective unconscious and are common to all peoples in all times. Therefore, he argued, "the hero figure is an archetype, which has existed since time immemorial" and "the universal hero myth . . . always refers to a powerful man or god-man who vanquishes evil in the form of dragons, serpents, monsters, demons, and so on, and who liberates his people from destruction and death" (Jung 1964, pp. 73, 79). Joseph Campbell developed these ideas in such influential works as *The Hero With a Thousand Faces* (1975), which seeks to understand the relationship between the hero figure in myth and religion in different parts of the world, and the inner world of the psyche. For Campbell,

> Dream is the personalized myth, myth the depersonalized dream; both myth and dream are symbolic in the same general way of the dynamics of the psyche. (Campbell 1975, p. 24)

Campbell's research into comparative myth and religion convinced him that though hero myths varied enormously in detail, structurally they were very similar and exemplified what Campbell called "the monomyth." The heart of the classical monomyth is "a magnification of the formula represented in the rites of passage: *separation—initiation—return*" (p. 31).

Later analysts of contemporary hero-myths rely to a greater or lesser extent on this idea of the monomyth put forward by Campbell. For example, in their book, *The American Monomyth* (1977), Robert Jewett and John Shelton Lawrence contrast the classical monomyth as rites of passage with the American monomyth which is a story of redemption. In the classical monomyth

> A hero ventures forth from the world of common day into a region of supernatural wonder. Fabulous forces are there encountered and a decisive victory is won. The hero comes back from the mysterious adventure with the power to bestow boons on his fellow men. (Campbell 1975, p. 31)

But in the American monomyth:

> A community in a harmonious paradise is threatened by evil. Normal institutions fail to contend with this threat. A selfless hero emerges to renounce temptations and carry out the redemptive task, and, aided by fate, his decisive victory restores the community to its paradisal condition. The superhero then recedes into obscurity. (Jewett & Lawrence 1977, p. xx; cited in Lang & Trimble 1988, p. 158)

Such a concept as "the American monomyth" suggests that when we analyse the heroes of popular culture, pure archetypal theory is not enough. The archetypal pattern is modified by a sense of national identity. As Jeffrey S. Lang and Patrick Trimble argue, America created monomythic heroes that "personified the way Americans wished to see themselves".

> youthful, physically vigorous, morally upright, a people capable of existing in the melting pot of American technological society without sacrificing an individual sense of value. (Lang & Trimble 1988, p. 159)

Conflict is at the heart of the sense of national identity embodied in the American monomyth:

> As a frontier nation, the idea of struggle was inbred into the American monomyth; the hero's struggle was one of vertical mobility, raising himself from humble beginnings until he had forced society to recognize him as a successful individual. (Lang & Trimble 1988, p. 159)

The national monomyth is a concept that can be applied to both historical and fictional heroes. Just as British children were told stories of national heroes such as Nelson, Florence Nightingale, and Baden-Powell, American children heard tales of historical heroes like Paul Revere, George Washington, and Charles Lindbergh. But the concept works equally well when applied to comic book superheroes and other fictional heroic figures.

The theory of the national monomyth provides a bridge between the archetypal approach and an argument that myths and hero myths must be seen as constructions within history. This approach insists that the substance of myth is provided by human "authors," "men and women who fabricate or compose the stories, and promulgate them, who bring to the work their needs, intentions and concerns." However, conventional theories of myth deny "this premise of human authorship" (Slotkin 1985, p. 26). Richard Slotkin attacks the theory of archetypalism (including that of the hero and the concept of the monomyth), arguing that:

> Jung translated the doctrine into terms appropriate to psychoanalysis; Joseph Campbell and others adapted it to the concerns of students of literature and religion; Northrop Frye and more recently the various schools of structuralists have adapted the conceptual structures of archetypalism to the study of literary forms and genres . . . the weakness of the archetypal approach is that it must scant the historical particular in the search for the universal structure. (Slotkin 1985, pp. 26–28)

Marina Warner also insists on returning myth to history. She sees her work as differing "fundamentally from both Freudian and Jungian approaches" by arguing that "the meanings of rituals and images change in relation to the social structure with which they interact" (Warner 1994, p. xiii). She agrees with Roland Barthes that "myths are not eternal verities, but historical compounds which conceal their contingency, changes, and transitoriness" (Warner 1994, p. xiii). Barthes' insights "can give rise to newly told stories, can sew and weave and knit different patterns into the social fabric" (Warner 1994, p. xiv). However, although new cultural narratives of the heroic figure can be constructed, the task is not easy. For example, a feminist critic like Diane Purkiss argues that "the rewriting of myth cannot be limited to the rewriting of particular favoured or disliked figures." It must, rather, "extend to complex engagements with the very place of myth in literature, the place of the woman writer in relation to those discourses, and the displacement of myth as a buried truth of culture" (Purkiss 1992, p. 445). However, a task of this magnitude obviously requires radical new ways of conceptualising the mythic hero which, at present, lie beyond the scope of this collection of essays.

In considering the heroes of traditional popular culture, the epic hero of myth and legend can be distinguished from the trickster hero of folk tales, although as Marina Warner reminds us, the fairy tale elements of the trickster hero "are impossible to keep separate from the grandest of myths: when Oedipus . . . meets the Sphinx, it's a battle of wits" (Warner 1994, p. 25). The stories surrounding the heroes of ancient myth and legend—Jason, Gilgamesh, Cuchulain, and Beowulf—celebrated epic feats of bravery, loyalty, skill, and endurance. These heroes were often endowed with exceptional, superhuman powers that distinguished them from ordinary men: they were, quite literally, supermen who occupied a dominant position within the social hierarchy. However, a different group of traditional heroes—the peasant heroes of folklore and fairy tale—could embody a subversive potential. If the peasant boy embarked on a heroic quest and overcame the various obstacles that lay in his way, he could claim the hand of the princess and, in due course, become ruler of the kingdom. Although the revolutionary implications of this usurpation were undermined by the incorporation of the peasant boy figure within that order (i.e., he becomes a king or an aristocrat), the subversive potential of the story signified the utopian aspirations—the desire for a more egalitarian society—of the peasant culture from which the story sprang.[5] Oral narratives from many parts of the world which featured trickster heroes (both male and female), were less subject to this process of ideological recuperation. While remaining outside the ruling order, trickster heroes demonstrated how members of an oppressed class could use cunning and resourcefulness to outwit their masters and at least improve the material and economic conditions of their existence.

The fictional heroes of twentieth-century popular culture embody the qualities of the epic superhero of ancient myth. Figures like Superman, Spiderman, Batman, and Wonderwoman each possess some secret access to extraordinary, superhuman powers. As Marina Warner pointed out in her 1994 Reith lectures, the emphasis in the narratives of contemporary heroes—whether they are men like Sylvester Stallone and Arnold Schwarzenegger, or superhuman beings like Superman or Robocop—is usually upon physical strength and aggression. Warner deplores this trend "towards defining male identity and gender through visible, physical, sexualised signs of potency" rather than the cunning and mental agility that characterises trickster heroes.

Boys are not raised to be cozenors or tricksters—it'd be unthinkable to train the future men in lures and wiles and masks and tricks; they're brought up to play with Action Man, and his heavy duty, futuristic Star Wars arsenal; they're taught to identify with Ninja Turtles, as crusaders, vigilantes, warriors on behalf of the planet, to flick a transformer toy from a flash car into a heavy duty fighting exoskeleton, bristling with weapons, a monster of technological innovation—the Terminator, Robocop. There are even games with a create-your-own-deity option, in which, having chosen which god you want to be, you then acquire nearly thirty ways of "smiting your enemy." (Warner 1994, p. 26)

Warner's primary concern is with the appeal of these heroes to boys, the glamorisation of violent physical aggression. However, it is possible girls do not read these texts in the same way as boys and that what appeals to them are those moments when the hero is depicted as vulnerable and displays what might traditionally be regarded as feminine characteristics. As Sarland argues, discussing children's responses to David Morrell's novel, *First Blood* (later adapted into film), the girls "find things in the book that enable them to read it differently from the boys. They exploit, in other words, the *plurality* of the text" (Sarland 1991, p. 51).

This raises an important question. How do children read hero narratives? Clearly, attempts to propose some form of psychoanalytic theory must take into account what Dawson calls "the historical determination of psychic life." He suggests that a modification of Melanie Klein's work which argues that a reciprocal relationship exists between the psychic life and the social world, is required to take into account the importance of culture, language, and representation. Heroes are constructed through cultural narratives—

these narratives are not only shaped by imaginative investments derived from the psyche; they are also forms of representation, socially and culturally determined. (Dawson 1996, p. 160)

Heroes and villains may well be psychic requirements, but they assume particular forms with specific cultural values and qualities attached to them.

This generalisation, we would argue, is only a partial truth. There may be important psychoanalytical reasons why we need heroes. For example, Jonathan Rutherford maintains that:

> The myth of idealism, the desire inherent in hero-worship, is a belief in
> the possibility of our own completeness. It is a dream of becoming our
> idealised father. (Rutherford 1996, p. 143)

Even from a cultural studies perspective, it has been argued there may be
"trans-historical, perhaps universal, imaginative impulses" which
prompt us to value "desirable human qualities embodied in an idealised
object" (Dawson 1996, p. 152). But all the evidence from the analysis of
heroes and heroines leads us to hesitate from accepting too readily the
ahistorical nature of such statements which imply "a dubious universalism grounded in the psyche" (Dawson 1996, p. 152). Rather, we would
qualify any tendency towards "universalism" by arguing that

> heroes are cultural constructs, their ideal masculine virtues are the
> products of history, expressions not of some universal essence of man-
> liness but of ideological configurations of gender, class, "race" and na-
> tion, in which versions of "the masculine" are defined, propagated and
> contested. (Dawson 1996, p. 146)

This restores the concepts of "hero," "heroine," and "heroism" to history.
The ideological discourses operative at a particular historical moment
within a particular culture determine, in part, the way that culture defines
"heroism." The values inscribed within that definition, will, in turn, determine the selection and construction of heroes.

However, to ascribe the creation of heroic figures solely to history,
or ideology is to ignore those yearnings for transcendence, the manifest
need expressed by different peoples in different cultures and differing
periods, for inspirational and exemplary figures and if "some of their
most famous moments turn out to be apocryphal, they are nevertheless a
necessary fantasy" (Samuels, *Guardian,* 23 September 1995). If heroes
and heroines did not exist, we would have to invent them.

*   *   *

The first article in this collection focuses upon a pre-industrial form
of popular culture, described by some commentators as "folk" culture (as
opposed to "mass culture," or post-industrial popular culture). Nina
Mikkelsen explores the trickster hero in traditional tales for children. She
examines the trickster's manifestation across a range of cultures including African, American, and European, demonstrating the figure's subversive role in stories, and emphasising that trickster heroes are not confined
to males.

The other contributors to this book concentrate upon post-industrial popular culture, drawing upon a range of critical approaches derived from feminism, cultural history, and reception theory. Utilising concepts such as ideology and cultural appropriation, they explore a variety of themes and issues related to the diversity of heroic figures and their representation in popular culture, including gender and its representation in the spheres of home, work, sport, and adventure; cultural myths and national identity; and social hierarchy and its subversion.

One of the most popular fictional genres for children has been the adventure story, a genre generally associated with colonising pioneers and ethno-centric notions of racial superiority. The ways in which imperialist ideologies were mediated through the heroes of adventure narratives are illustrated in Dennis Butts' account of Capt. W. E. Johns' flying hero, Biggles. However, discussion of these ideologies has usually focused on fictions for boys and J. S. Bratton's article in this volume demonstrates the problems facing writers of girls' adventure stories in the first part of this century. They had to find a "balance in narrative romance between such opposite ideological constructs as spiritualism, disembodied femininity, and vigorous pioneering motherhood." In fact, it has always been difficult to overcome the inherent masculinist bias of the adventure story genre (one might include sporting narratives within this category) and prevent women being marginalised. This has led some feminist critics to reject the term "heroine," preferring to speak of the "female hero," or simply use "hero" to refer to either sex.

The articles by Haymonds, Phillips, and Christian-Smith, explore the ways in which this masculinist bias has been contested in narratives where the heroic protagonist is female. Linda Christian-Smith examines the career of Nancy Drew, an American female detective hero. Ethnographic research carried out by Christian-Smith reveals that though many black and working-class readers might have felt alienated by Drew's privileged racial and class background, the stories encouraged them to believe they could challenge race and class boundaries and that young women could be as knowledgeable, resourceful, intelligent, and brave as men. Similarly, Alison Haymonds in examining "the pony story," a popular fictional genre which has been sadly neglected by critics of children's literature, demonstrates how the pony empowers the central female character, enabling her to become the hero of her own story and fosters the reader's sense of self-worth. Deborah Phillips focuses on the way girls' career aspirations in the 1950s were addressed through literature that featured "socially responsible and active young women" in a range of texts including comics, career manuals, and Noel Streatfeild's ballet stories. Phillips traces the way these progressive developments were reversed in the 1960s and 1970s, when links with the fashion and cosmetic industry led to a preoccupation in girls' magazines like *Marty* and *Valentine* with physical appearance and the promotion of marriage and domesticity as their readers' future goal.

Representations of masculinity and heroism are explored in essays on four British heroes: Robin Hood, Biggles, Dan Dare, and Roy of the Rovers. Dudley Jones examines the Robin Hood legend through screen versions which highlight twentieth-century anxieties and preoccupations, while Dennis Butts argues that the heroic exploits of the stereotypically British hero Biggles must be seen in the light of changing political and cultural attitudes towards class, gender, race, and nationhood. Tony Watkins discusses the way the adventures of the comic-strip space hero, Dan Dare, with their positive visions of a technological future, came to symbolise national identity at a particular "moment" of post-war reconstruction. Alan Tomlinson and Christopher Young consider the career of the fictional sporting hero, Roy of the Rovers, and show how the discourses of "real" sport draw upon the narratives, conventions, and myths of football (soccer) fictions. As a result, the discourses associated with both "*fictional* and *lived* forms of football culture" coalesce to articulate a "patriarchal, nationalist ideology of male heroism in sport."

Militarist and sexist ideologies are reproduced, as Marina Warner reminds us, not only in popular cultural forms like literature, film, and television but also within the culture of toys. Jonathan Bignell examines the "Action Man" toy figure and its various commercial "spin-offs," including an Action Man comic, a comic-book annual, and an animated television series. Though parents are often concerned by the warlike aggression and gender-stereotyping of the Action Man figures and their accessories, Bignell warns against simplistic assumptions that children regard toys in similar ways as adults. The heroic meanings inscribed in Action Man, he argues, "depend on the narratives produced by the manufacturer and by the children themselves, into which the toys and the mythic figures are inserted."

Like Action Man, Spider-Man and the Teenage Mutant Turtles are heroes reproduced in a range of cultural mediums. The texts associated with these heroes, perhaps reflecting the influence of post-modernism, tend to make more use of parody and inter-textuality than Action Man toys and patriotic heroes.

Christine Stephens attributes the longevity of Spider-Man, who began his career in 1962, to the fact that a (predominantly male) adolescent audience was able to empathise so strongly with this realistically portrayed, flawed superhero. His creator Stan Lee declared that Spider-Man was "probably the first super-hero to wear his neuroses on his sleeve" (Lee 1997, p. 127), not only does he experience frequent identity crises and problems in relationships with relatives and girlfriends (in his human persona), but as Spider-Man he is often reviled by those closest to him.

The connections between Spider-Man and the Teenage Mutant Turtles are not dissimilar. Just as Spider-Man acquires his powers from the bite of a radio-active spider, four pet turtles are accidentally spilled into a radio-active drain and subsequently mutated into knights errant. David Lusted argues that, like Spider-Man, the Turtles were popular with children because "in significant ways [they] could be perceived by children as living out in fantasy the social and psychic conditions of childhood, what being a child 'feels' like." Similar to the Spider-Man stories, the Turtles' texts involve post-modern play with names, language, and intertextuality, whilst there is also "the absurdity of heroic *Turtles* . . .". Using the Turtles as an example of the way children's popular culture in Britain is controlled by a cultural elite imbued with Reithian notions of entertainment, Lusted traces some of the major developments in popular culture in America and Britain this century and argues that a text's popularity with children or adults cannot be guaranteed by a costly, vigorous, and efficient marketing campaign.

Christine Routh and Catriona Nicholson both examine authors whose work has achieved the status of "popular classics" for children. By analysing the illustrations in different editions of *Peter Pan,* Routh explores Peter's heroism in relation to that of figures such as Wendy and Captain Hook, and demonstrates how gender becomes a key issue in critical debates about the text. Nicholson concentrates on the way Roald Dahl, "a literary cult hero" and an international publishing phenomenon, re-works his own extraordinary life in the fantastic plots and characters of his novels. Like many popular writers for children, Dahl claimed that he remained a child at heart, and Nicholson suggests that the heroic figures in his novels can be seen as a way of overcoming the adult monsters of his childhood.

Like Dahl, Steven Spielberg has become one of the world's most popular storytellers. Douglas Brode argues that in films such as *E.T.* and the Indiana Jones trilogy, Spielberg testifies to the liberating power of the child's imaginative vision. Many of Spielberg's heroes have "a psychic connection with a child" and Brode suggests that the reason for the films' popularity is that they speak "to both the emergent man in any child viewer and the lost boy hidden deep inside any adult."

The final articles offer an Australian perspective on popular culture and return to the central issues of gender representations and national identity that surround the heroic figure.

Robyn McCallum and John Stephens examine the "masculine schemata and the modes of representation" in a sample of Australian novels and telemovies produced during the 1980s and early 1990s. They argue that during this period, these texts began to challenge the masculine stereotype of the "bronzed Aussie" hero and to replace it by alternative models such as the "anti-hero and the sensitive guy."

The concluding article focuses on Dr. Who, a figure who has achieved considerable popularity in the United States and Australia, though he may seem to be quintessentially English. Combining cultural-ideological and textual analysis with the analysis of the responses of Australian schoolchildren, John Tulloch discusses *Dr. Who* "in the light of its engagement with British popular culture and British nationalism at a time of major economic conflict" in the 1970s.

NOTES

1. Andrea Dworkin cited in Patricia Duncker: "Re-imagining the Fairy Tales: Angela Carter's Bloody Chambers," *Literature and History* Vol 10:1, 1984 p. 4, comments:

> "The lessons are simple, and we learn them well.
> Men and women are different, absolute opposites.
> The heroic prince can never be confused with Cinderella, or Snow-white, or Sleeping Beauty.
> She could never do what he does at all, let alone better . . .
> Where he is erect, she is supine. Where he is awake, she is asleep. Where he is active, she is passive."

> Duncker adds: "So the tales send the boys out into the world to seek their fortunes, create their wealth, possess their women. The boys must be taught courage. The girls must be taught fear."

2. In particular, see Dixon (1977)

3. The terms "hero" and "heroism" are defined as follows:

> A HERO may be defined as man of distinguished valour, intrepidity, or enterprise; HEROISM, as the qualities of a hero—bravery, gallantry,

intrepidity, daring, courage, boldness, magnanimity, self-sacrifice. (Hodder n.d., p. 2)

Like Johnson's book, this is a collection of historical heroes and heroines—many of them heroes of war and empire, but others explorers, scientists and reformers of prisons and of the slave trade. They are placed in such categories as: "Heroes of the Faith"; "Philanthropic Heroes"; "Conscientious Heroes", "Scientific Heroes"; and "Patriotic Heroes."

4. Lord Raglan's pattern (Raglan 1936, pp. 178–179) of twenty-two points applied to mythic and legendary heroes was as follows:

(1) The hero's mother is a royal virgin;

(2) His father is a king, and

(3) Often a near relative of his mother, but

(4) The circumstances of his conception are unusual, and

(5) He is also reputed to be the son of a god.

(6) At birth an attempt is made, usually by his father or his maternal grandfather, to kill him, but

(7) He is spirited away, and

(8) Reared by foster-parents in a far country.

(9) We are told nothing of his childhood, but

(10) On reaching manhood he returns or goes to his future kingdom.

(11) After a victory over the king and/or a giant, dragon or wild beast,

(12) He marries a princess, often the daughter of his predecessor, and

(13) Becomes king.

(14) For a time he reigns uneventfully, and

(15) Prescribes laws, but

(16) Later he loses favour with the gods and/or his subjects, and

(17) Is driven from the throne and city, after which

(18) He meets with a mysterious death,

(19) Often at the top of a hill.

(20) His children, if any, do not succeed him.

(21) His body is not buried, but nevertheless

(22) He has one or more holy sepulchres.'

5. Zipes, in *Breaking the Magic Spell*, says that "whereas it is true that change is realised in the tales, this change reflects the desire of the lower classes to move up in the world and seize power *as monarchs*, not necessarily the desire to alter social relations" (Zipes 1979, p. 28 [his italics]) and "the fact that the people [in fairy and folk tales] as carriers of the tales do not explicitly seek a total

revolution of social relations does not minimise the revolutionary and utopian aspect in the imaginative portrayal of class conflict" (p.30).

BIBLIOGRAPHY

Campbell, Joseph. *The Hero with a Thousand Faces*. London: Sphere Books, 1975 (orig. 1949).

Carlyle, Thomas. *On Heroes, Hero-Worship, and the Heroic in History*. London: Chapman and Hall, 1903 (orig. 1841).

Dawson, Graham. 1996. Heroes of history, heroes of phantasy: Idealisation, masculinity and the Soldiers of Empire. *Soundings* 3: 145–160.

Dixon, Bob. *Catching them Young, Volume 1: Sex, Race and Class in Children's Fiction*. London: Pluto Press, 1977.

———. *Catching them Young, Volume 2: Political Ideas and Children's Fiction*. London: Pluto Press, 1977.

Hall, Stuart. 1996. Editorial. *Soundings* 3: 116–118.

Hodder, Edwin (ed.). *Heroes of Britain in Peace and War*. London: Cassell and Co., (n.d.).

Jewett, Robert & John Shelton Lawrence. *The American Monomyth*. Garden City, NY: Anchor Press, 1977.

Johnson, Henry. *A Book of Heroes Or Great Victories in the Fight for Freedom*. London: The Religious Tract Society, n.d..

Jung, Carl G. *Man and His Symbols*. London: Aldus Books, 1964.

Lang, Jeffrey S. & Patrick Trimble. 1988. Whatever happened to the Man of Tomorrow? An examination of the American monomyth and the Comic Book Superhero. *Journal of Popular Culture* 22(3): 157–173).

Lee, Stan. *Origins of Marvel Comics*. New York: Marvel Comics, 1997 (orig. 1974).

Purkiss, Diane. Women's rewriting of myth. In *The Feminist Companion to Mythology*, Carolyne Larrington, ed. London: Pandora Press, pp. 441–457, 1992.

Richards, Jeffrey. *Imperialism and Juvenile Literature*. Manchester: Manchester University Press, 1989.

Rutherford, Jonathan. 1996. Heroes and mother's boys. *Soundings* 3: 137–144.

Samuel, Raphael. 1995. The people with stars in their eyes. *The Guardian,* 23 September p. 27.

Sellier, Phillipe. Heroism. In *Companion to Literary Myths, Heroes and Archetypes,* Pierre Brunel, ed. (transl. Wendy Allatson, Judith Hayward, Trista Selous). London and New York: Routledge, pp. 557–565, 1992.

Slotkin, Richard. *The Fatal Environment: The Myth of the Frontier in the Age of Industrialization 1800–1890.* New York: Athenaeum, 1985.

Taylor, Barbara. 1996. An impossible heroine? Mary Wollstonecraft and female heroism. *Soundings* 3: 119–135.

Warner, Marina. *Managing Monsters.* London: Vintage, 1994.

Yonge, Charlotte. *What Books to Lend and What to Give.* London: The National Society's Repository, 1887.

Strange Pilgrimages
Cinderella Was a Trickster—and Other Unorthodoxies of American and African-American Heroic Folk Figures

NINA MIKKELSEN

Recently in Ireland I met a man who was taking his family to Disney World. Thousands of dollars it was costing him, but he didn't mind a bit. It was something that must be done for his children, he said. I was astonished. "You have the real thing here!" I exclaimed. "Castles and as many folk characters as anyone could want." He replied that his children wanted no part of the *real* folk world. They wanted Disney. Or perhaps *he* did, he admitted. "There's a little boy in every grown man," this Irishman's eyes twinkled, "just waiting to get out!"

Wishing to save his family fortune, I mentioned Disney's Uncle Remus and the way African Americans felt about it. I recalled negative ethnic (and sexist) stereotypes in *Pocahontas* and almost every other famous Disney film (as well as how high the mercury soars in Florida during July, how many waterbugs, mosquitoes—or random bullets—he might encounter). He would have none of it.

I myself was headed for Paris a few days later, for a look at all the Chagall paintings but only one was being exhibited currently. I had to content myself with books about Chagall and was amazed to discover, in a little shop on Boulevard du Montparnasse, five children's picturebooks featuring this artist, with one devoted entirely to the painting then on exhibit at the Pompidou ("Double Portrait with Wineglass," 1917–1918). In this book, the painting had been "cut" into many little pictures, around which a story had been composed, the whole painting having been put back together again for the last page (and the story ending). Was the painting at the Pompidou a response to this book, I began wondering. Surely not; children's books never have such power. Was the book a response to the exhibited painting? Perhaps. Or was this merely a matter of a popular painting finding its way into the child's world, where art in this culture was of primary importance? American children, for example, would have little knowledge of any artist through their children's books, except the cartoonist's world of Disney; and surely they would have little knowledge of the pilgrimage Chagall made to Paris in 1910 or what this painting signified to him, confined to Russia as he was during the war, when the borders were closed.

I didn't purchase the book, however, preferring to keep Chagall's painting all in one piece. Why destroy, even for a moment, such perfectly balanced and rhythmical cubist design? Instead I found the perfect book to connect with my own museum experiences that week, Helme Heine's picturebook, *L'exposition des trois amis* (Gallimard, 1991), in which three animal friends make their way to an art gallery. The next day on the Euro Star I translated the book; the following day on British Airways, as scenes from *The American President* and *Get Shorty* flickered above me, I continued thinking about it. What do Heine's little friends have to tell us about the human propensity for strange pilgrimages? A great deal I de-cided—and a great deal also about art, popular culture, and being heroic.

HEROIC PICTUREBOOK FIGURES
AND POPULAR CULTURE

Heine's earlier picturebook about these three animals, entitled *Friends* (Verlag 1982) has now been translated from the German into seventeen languages. And it is not difficult to see why. Here Fat Percy, Charlie Rooster, and Johnny Mouse take off one morning on their bike to play, pretend, discover, sail, conquer the village pond, consume cherries, get tummy aches, recover, ride home, swear eternal friendship, attempt to spend the night together—to their great discomfort (a pig cannot perch in a hen house; a rooster cannot pass through a mousehole). So they end up simply dreaming of one another "as all true friends do."

What makes these animals so engaging? Capricious, vulnerable, and childlike, they are everyperson, in human terms. Courageous, noble, and inventive, they are also heroes, in children's terms. But it is in Heine's se-quel to *Friends* that the friends become what we might describe as heroic figures of popular culture. *L'exposition des trois amis* gives us a way of looking at life and art from a "populist" point of view. What is art really like to those untutored in the ways of art? We discover answers through the eyes of a rooster, a pig, and a mouse, these animal "children" that be-come, in essence here, heroic figures for the child's world of story.

The exposition itself is a compendium of paintings, in a variety of media and artistic styles, filled mostly with animals or scenes, in which humans sometimes appear. Sometimes the animals find themselves framed (as in the opening portraits, including one of the author-illustrator); sometimes they have stepped into a painting to assume an imagined role; most often they are seen, in small pen and ink drawings, scurrying about the museum commenting on the paintings that tower over them, even managing to discover the storage room where undisplayed paintings are kept (not impossible to visit if you are Johnny Mouse!). And sometimes they interpret life as art (the pig sees his snout in a wall outlet and discovers himself as an abstract painting: "Regardez!" he tells his friends, "C'est moi vu par un paintre abstrait").

There are intertextual artistic links (in one painting a man sits atop a cow playing a harp, suggesting Chagall's "The Rooster," 1929). There are links between the animals of the paintings: in one scene the polar bears hanging on one wall stare longingly at the animals on an adjacent wall (two giraffes bathed in golden light). But the most interesting pages reveal the ways life and art are connected in the minds of those who have natural and spontaneous responses to art. One museum-goer, a dog with sharp knife, takes home a slice of one painting (ducks floating on a pond), thinking it has obtained its dinner.

In another scene, a rabbit sits atop a collection of eggs painting each a different color. Is this a work of art? the mouse asks. No, the rooster replies, looking at one of the eggs that has slipped out of the picture onto the museum floor. It was Anna who produced the egg, he says. The pig ponders the question further, asking himself if it is a work of art to lay an egg? (Much food for thought here. Is life art? Is producing life art? What is art? Producing life? Imitating life? Producing a replica of life? Embellishing life? Is a natural object better "art" if left unembellished?)

In still another scene the friends ponder whether nature needs embellishment, or is nature itself art? "I think it is beautiful," Charlie Rooster says about a painting that shows two rabbit lovers sitting in the forest on a moonlit night, as a hunter plays his violin to heighten the romantic scene. But why does he play for them? the pig wonders. And the mouse explains that he "tames" them before shooting them.

The mouse knows well a trickster tactic; his tiny size has rendered him vulnerable to predators and he has learned many a survival scheme, as we see in a later scene in which the pig and the rooster lie resting against a museum bench. Hanging on a nearby large wall is a painting of blue-black, yellow-eyed cats looking eerily down on a mouse (our mouse?) resting comfortably on a bed of cheese, at the foot of which is a sawtoothed trap. Then in the museum cafeteria, Johnny Mouse imagines himself taking a bath in a teacup while reading a book, on the cover of which is one of these same cats holding a blood-tipped dagger.

Later, back in the room with the cat paintings, the pig stands holding the mouse who has fainted in the face of these cats, who, we now see, have yellow mice for eyes. Around the corner, in the next painting, the cats have changed to look more like polar bears, with closed eyes, except for one that is pale yellow (and looks like a man rather than a cat/bear). In the world, the pig tells the mouse, one man in three is Chinese. Nevertheless, the mouse sighs, there are more cats.

Still, he puts the knowledge to good use. And in the next to the last scene, when each animal is standing beneath a painting of his own imagining (one that could easily be entitled "Happiness is . . ."), the pig "dreams" of a pig who is sleeping and dreaming of food; the rooster envisions his Anna, having just laid a huge egg; and the mouse sees himself as a mouse standing on the head of a Chinese man. (Every third cat is a cat/bear/man who can save him.)

Best of all, art can save us too, especially if we are the creators of our own art (we find ways to save ourselves, as the mouse does in his cat and mouse imaginings). The last frame shows the mouse using his paws to make a shadow picture on the wall of the rooster's head, its beak open to make a great noise (to frighten away the cats, Johnny Mouse may hope). And the pig says: "Le mieux, c'est encore de peindre soi-meme."

The problem with art as mere entertainment (Disney or otherwise) is that it gives onlookers nothing to do for themselves, even to think for themselves, to question, to ponder, to enter more deeply as an interpretive experience (Johnny and Mickey are two very different mice). To paint for oneself is to create one's own vision of the world, and this is just what participants in folk cultures around the world have always done as a way of interpreting the world and being entertained by their own imaginings. Johnny Mouse thus stands in a long line of heroic folk figures who provide interpretive pleasure for children, not the least of which is the cultural hero as trickster. How does Heine's mouse friend take his place among these trickster-ancestors? What does the heroic figure look like when it takes on the role of "trickster?"

THE UR-TRICKSTER TEXT

Actually there is no such thing as a prototypical trickster; the trickster "text" is essentially a nontext—or it is a very open one that changes constantly as it crosses geographical, historical, and cultural (class, gender, and ethnic) lines. Yet for practical, explanatory purposes, folklore specialists often attempt to capture the trickster story in a simple framework of traits, motifs, and roles.

Traits of mischief-making, cleverness, and shape-shifting are often mentioned in connection with the trickster character. Also at times, he (note the "he"—tricksters are rarely described as female) may be vain, cruel, blundering, foolish, completely amoral, violent, rude, offensive, asocial, undisciplined, duplicitous, irresponsible, or self-destructive. At other times, and especially at those times when he assumes the role of popular culture hero, he is inspiring, benevolent, awesome, powerful, altruistic, a discoverer, or an inventor. He may be human, animal, or supernatural.

He may be a primary or secondary character in the story. As a primary character, he is often seen performing great tasks, surviving trials and tests (the questing, conquering hero), protecting members of his social community (the cultural hero) or outsmarting oppressors (the clever hero). Or sometimes he functions as both cultural and clever hero, a double role, (as exemplified by the African American trickster, John de Conquer/High John). As a secondary character, he might simply be frightening or coercive (the ogre that Jack found at the top of the beanstalk or the witch that Vasilisa meets in the Russian forest). And he may appear in stories ranging from aboriginal tellings, such as Native American and Caribbean tales, to folktales diffused worldwide through the oral tradition, to literary retellings and new creations in picturebooks and illustrated storybooks for children, as well as in unillustrated collections and highly sophisticated novels for adults, such as Toni Morrison's novel *Tar Baby*.

Motifs of trickster stories, as Stith Thompson (1946) explains, might include actors such as deities, deceivers, fools, seducers, licentious fathers, rascals, outcasts, and blunderers; background items such as magic objects, particular customs, or beliefs; and incidents such as transformations, thefts, deceptions, and tricks such as those depicted in Heine's modern picturebook. There a mouse settles carefully into a cheese-trap bed in order to outsmart the big cats that stare down upon him (later when one cats looms large in Johnny's imagination with yellow mice for eyes, the cats take on the role of shape-shifter). A dog steals a scene of a painting for its supper. And a violinist lures a pair of rabbit lovers into a mellow-passive state (also for a supper).

Heine's scene of the violinist recalls Chagall's painting "The Fiddler" (1912–13). In the one, the violinist-trickster is using his musical talent for a clever ruse (but since the small, harmless rabbits are not his oppressors, he assumes the role of ogre as well). In the other, the violinist as cultural folk hero stands as the central figure of his Russian village. His boot poised on the top of the small, snow-covered hut, Chagall's fiddler on the roof uses his transformative, artistic gifts to provide spiritual strength for the members of his Jewish community. Both men are tricksters in the broadest sense: one of destructive bent, the other of mystical, magical intent.

Trickster stories have always been told by adults to one another for amusement. But they have always been told to children both for entertainment and for cultural learning. African American children hearing about the most famous animal trickster, Brer Rabbit, learned a great deal about dealing with white oppressors from such stories. In fact, it is the condition of oppression that appears to produce a need or predilection for trickster stories in a society. As Greenway (1964) says, "It could be stated as a general rule and defended fairly well by ethnographic evidence that the occurrence of Trickster tales is directly proportional to the degree of oppressiveness of socio-religious and, we would add now, the socio-cultural restrictions. In such situations, Trickster is a cathartic to purge his audience of tensions built up by incest taboos, avoidance restrictions, and similar regulations of conduct" (Greenway 1964, pp. 89–90).

The oppressed in different cultures, in different eras (those regulated or restricted by the rich, the noble, the clergy, the white man, cultural insiders, and males or adults generally), include the poor, the peasant class, members of the church, people of color, outsiders/outcasts of all cultures, females, and children. "Psychologically," says Maria Leach (1950), "the role of the trickster seems to be that of projecting the insufficiencies of man in his universe onto a smaller creature who, in besting his larger adversaries, permits the satisfactions of an obvious identification to those who recount or listen to these tales" (p. 1123).

What makes Heine's Johnny Mouse a particularly interesting character (and a good trickster-model for our purposes here) is the way his behavior corresponds to tricksters of other times and places. "Trickster usually does not play willful tricks," says Greenway, but "blunders into situations that often result in his being rudely discomfited" (p. 72). We have seen the mouse fainting in the room that displays the angry cat portraits. And why? Simply fear—or something more?

Victor Barnouw (1950), in his study of the Wisconsin Chippewa culture, says that "the isolated individual anticipated emotional frustration and hostility, so that he became wary and developed paranoid or pseudo-paranoid fears of persecution" (p. 353). Johnny Mouse is, of course, surrounded in the museum by his friends the rooster and the pig. But the pig's size and the rooster's noise-making ability place each in a more powerful, therefore more secure position, which accounts for their greater psychic strength. Johnny, small and vulnerable in contrast, remains the outcast throughout. His condition has its bright side, however, and that is why Johnny (and so many "unpromising" heroes who file in and out of trickster stories worldwide) commands our attention and interest.

"Being frightened," says Greenway, speaking of Winnebago Indian symbolism, "is generally the indication of an awakening consciousness and sense of reality, indeed the beginning of a consciousness" (pp. 84–85). Johnny first "sees" a way to entrap the cat that pursues him in his fearful imagining (sees himself in the painting of the mouse in the cheese-trap bed). Then he sees himself in the cat's eyes (another way to be saved: to become the villain or his terrible fate). Such imagining causes him to faint. A better solution appears to be the help of a more powerful alliance (balancing himself on the Chinaman's head). And this position does give him greater insight. "Je sais très bien ce à quoi vous pensez . . ." he says to his friends as they all stand beneath three paintings that represent what happiness is for each of them (food for fat Percy; love of Anna for Charlie Rooster, and escape from the cat or safety for Johnny).

A greater sense of reality emerges, however, with Johnny's awakening to the meaning of art (or what emerges for him—and perhaps ideally for all pilgrims to *l'exposition*—that the best art is that which we create ourselves). Johnny creates his own way to escape the cat, and a fine trick it is too: a large shadow portrait of Charlie Rooster that will frighten the cat, as a mouse alone (without art) cannot do. And perhaps the cat, as the ogre figure of the story, serves its own important trickster purpose, too, especially if Johnny is assuming the double role of culture hero and trickster.

Says Greenway, "It is one of the regular duties of the Culture Hero to rid his people of ogres. Since the ogre has incomparably more strength than his human adversary, the hero must use man's unique possession, his guile, to overcome his stupid enemy . . . Fear is the universal emotion evoked by ogre tales, and since fear is a powerful source of psychic energy, ogres are used to coerce people into proper conduct" (p. 102). And it is one of the fascinating ironies of this fascinating picturebook that Johnny has found psychic energy to slay the "dragon"—and with conduct "proper"—in terms of the child's world, for solving a problem: to draw, paint, imagine, envision, create one's way out of difficulties.

Heroes of sophisticated literature, Greenway tells us, grow out of aboriginal and folk literature, the height of heroic development being, he says, in folk literature. And an analysis of these sophisticated heroes, he adds (and Johnny Mouse, of modern picturebook fame fits such a category), helps us to understand the unsophisticated characters from which they spring. Two such unsophisticated characters are the Jack and John figures of Appalachian stories collected by Richard Chase in *The Jack Tales* (1943) and *Grandfather Tales* (1948) and African American stories collected in central Florida by Zora Neale Hurston in *Mules and Men* (1935), folk collections very close to one another in time and, in the case of Hurston's, very close to what would eventually become the mecca for so many twentieth-century American and European pilgrims, Eatonville, Florida being less than twenty miles away from Disney World.

APPALACHIAN JACK

The Jack Tales evolved from Chase's chance encounter in 1935 with a man named Marshall Ward, in the mountains of western North Carolina. Ward told stories handed down in his family for generations about a boy who killed giants and scared away robbers in England (and did many of the same things in America—but not always in the same way). Such a trickster hero had been observed in the German Grimms' tales and also in Irish, Spanish, French, and Jamaican stories, but there were only a few such tales in Joseph Jacobs' English collections, compared to the many Chase was to discover in the American South and Appalachian Mountain regions. Apparently those bound for the New World years before had packed up Jack with other keepsakes and carried him along in their pilgrimage to America, to take on the traits and personality of his new relatives in the years ahead.

Chase (1943) describes Ward and his family of southern mountain people as "honest, industrious, and intelligent," with "rare qualities of kindliness and poise" (Chase 1943, viii). And if it is true that storytellers leave their own imprint on the stories they tell, it may be said that Appalachian Jack, as we come to know him in these stories, was a true kinsman of the Wards. Humor and rich imagination mark the stories, the teller, and Jack, as particularly American, and as one of the few American folk characters that can compare to his animal cousin, Brer Rabbit, in popularity. If Jack's English cousin, in Chase's words, was "the cock-

sure, dashing young hero of the 'fairy' tale," then the Jack that Chase uncovered was conversely the "easy-going, unpretentious rural American"
(ix), a trickster, as in Europe, and always the youngest-born underdog,
but self-propelled rather than dependent on supernatural magic—and
lucky primarily because he was shrewd and resourceful.

It is not only a natural storytelling style but also the wealth of understated mountain humor and imaginative detail Chase was able to capture
that sets these tales off from those of both Jacobs and the Grimms. Yet
there seems to be something more fundamental at stake, something particularly American in terms of cultural traits, if we compare "Jack and the
Robbers," an Appalachian story, with its counterparts in the Grimms
("The Bremen Town-Musicians") and Jacobs ("How Jack Went to Seek
His Fortune" in *English Fairy Tales*). In each of these stories a group of elderly animals enter a robbers' enclave and await the return of the robbers,
in order to stake their own claim. And the unlikely or "unpromising" animals win the day. In fact it is their ability to trick the robbers and surprise
us that leaves us laughing, humor being the hallmark of all three stories.
But there is more than just humor in Chase's version; there is a way for
the story to rise from mere entertainment into *interpretive* pleasure. And
that way is Jack himself, a strong character who does not appear in the
German version and has a less important role in the English one.

In both the English and American versions, Jack accompanies the
animals in their quest to seek a fortune. (And since he takes no actual
part in the fighting, the same emphasis holds in each tale: that the old can
still outwit the young.) But only in the American version do we hear any
more about Jack after the animals win their new home. Chase's story
concludes with the words, "The last time I was down that way, Jack had
gone on back home to his folks. He was out in the yard a cuttin' his
mother a big pile of stovewood." (The animals seem to have taught Jack a
lesson about hard work and responsibility. He has joined ranks with
them.) What seems to be running through the tale, therefore, is a trickster
hero and the impetus, an emotional readiness, that sends him out into the
world with the quest to succeed, and brings him back successful in the
end (having completed the "passage" from one stage of maturity to
the next).

Consider the story from a different perspective. In the German version, a donkey whose master forced him to carry corn-sacks to the mill
"for many a long year" (Chase 1943, p. 4), becomes in the American
story a boy who, even at twelve, refuses, as does the Grimms' donkey,
to be placed in the donkey's position. When whipped, he becomes

stubborn, as does a real donkey. But like the Grimms' literary donkey, he does not refuse to budge. He hits the road to seek his fortune and, as it turns out, wins it from the robbers. The Jacobs' version gives no motive for Jack's leaving home, except that he is seeking his fortune. English Jack is not learning responsibility; he is ready for it. German "Jack" (the donkey) has long known responsibility. Only American Jack seems to be in this position of initiate, as he is in almost every one of the stories.

Thus, unlike the English and German versions of this tale, three cultural symbols rise to importance here: the emergent adolescent crossing to adulthood, the trickster using initiative to gain his ends, and the road as passage to opportunity. Even when tellers record this same tale today, some fifty years later, the same three symbols are evident. Notice that Jackie Torrence, well-known, southern, African American storyteller, records this tale, extending Chase's introduction of one hundred words to seven hundred, in order to emphasize these same three elements of the original story: the adolescent standing at the crossroads of childhood play and adult responsibility; his finding a solution to his problem in trickster tactics; and his escape by the road. And although her ending is a little different from that of Chase, it still speaks of—actually emphasizes—the adolescent passage to adult responsibility:

> Jack went back home. His Mama and daddy gave him a little whippin' for runnin off there, not cuttin' the wood. But they also bought Jack a little ol' farm, put all those ol' useless animals on there. They tell me that Jack is takin' care of those animals to this day. And that's the end of that.

Of these three elements or symbols—the road, the adolescent crossing to sexual maturity, and trickster tactics—it is the road that appears early in the stories, to provide escape from home, unlimited opportunity, boundless, continuous movement, and to act as the supporting structure or impetus for the other two. Jack takes to the road to try his luck, make his fortune, find work, or win a wife. But he comes back each time, a responsible son, a wealthy man, or a new husband. As a young, or emergent, adolescent, he thus escapes responsibility for a time in order to grow into it, because the road leads to freedom and, at the same time, is a destination.

So the road is something of a microcosm for the American dream—not that the road as symbol is absent from the European tales of Hans or English Jack. There, as here, the road as setting, is the male counterpart to the female's traditional place by the hearth. European Jack walks it too: it is his path to adventure, prosperity, and locating a wife. But because America with so much land and opportunity has always been the land of roads, the road takes on greater importance in these tales. It is both springboard for daring action, and passage to manhood. It is also springboard to change in economic status, for it nearly always leads to wealth or the dream of it.

Money is an important factor in almost all of the stories: proving your worth with money before marriage, making your fortune, making the most of your money or increasing your wealth. The dream of wealth without hard work is also important in these stories, which were collected in the depression years of hard-to-come-by work. The phrase "independent rich" is a common one. Six stories end with the phrase "and he was doing real well."

The teaching responsibility of stories told for children is also obvious here. At the end of one story, Jack decides to go home and save his money instead of spending it. At the end of another, Little Jack (the wily trickster) pays the doctor bill of Big (brawn without brains) Jack, inculcating the value that in a society with, as yet, nonexistent social programs such as welfare or the dole, the more intelligent take care of the less able.

Yet as strongly as it is implied that money leads to happiness here, what the stories really say is that money is only the outer manifestation of something much more rudimentary—what money cannot buy, but what, if possessed, nearly always brings money: initiative, risk taking, facing a challenge, sometimes facing anything, with nothing for collateral but the bare facts. In "Jack and the Doctor's Girl," comedy arises from the blunt, deadpan "logic" in the "Ma Barker" gang that Jack encounters when he takes off over the mountain to make his fortune and marry the doctor's daughter:

> The old lady says, "No, not kill him while he's asleep. Wake him up first.
> I never did like to see nobody killed in their sleep."
> One of 'em shook Jack right good, says, "Wake up, stranger! What's your name?"
> Jack sort-a roused up, says, "My name's Jack."
> "Well, Jack, get up from there. We got to kill ye. That's our rules here. We don't want nobody messin' in our business" (p. 117).

Jack replies, "Well, you all can kill me if ye want. But I ain't got a thing except what clothes I got on. I got no money." This is the frontier ideal of raw courage in the face of danger. This is a *man* (a crazy man in his nonchalance, it seems, but still a man who wins laughter and applause for his constant willingness to attempt whatever task is given him). Here, with typical folktale impossibility, he is to steal three fat oxen for a good price, then twelve horses from under twelve men, a rabbit from the pot while everyone watches, and finally, sheets from under the sleepers, for the price of the girl. These are the terms. They also are the rites of passage to maturity and marriage, if he can meet them.

First, to be a provider in marriage, he must have money (be enterprising). He must earn one thousand dollars to win the girl. He meets this task by seizing opportunities as they present themselves. He uses what turns up in the road as a resource that tricks the farmer and helps him steal the oxen for the robbers. He has money then but the doctor wants something else. He sets up three more hurdles that Jack must jump before winning the girl (the unforeseen conflicts and challenges of adult life). Again Jack shows persistence, a willingness to try. Again he sees a way, perception rather than magic providing success for the American trickster. He drugs the twelve men, diverts the attention of those watching the rabbit so that he can retrieve it from the pot, and steals the sheets from the doctor's bed by impersonating the doctor.

"The Doctor's Girl" is significant for illustrating how trickster talents and tactics aid the protagonist in his passage to maturity—in the end Jack marries the girl and goes to work. In this story both of these cultural symbols, the trickster and the sexual passage, are equally powerful themes. Most of the stories of the book, however, fall into one of two categories: the tale of sexual initiation in which male trickster tactics may or may not be of primary importance (such as "Old Fire Dragaman"), and the pure trickster tale. Two stories in the latter category are the well known "Jack and the Giant's Newground" and the less well-known "Big Jack and Little Jack."

In the first, Jack is typically poor, "awful lazy sometimes," and off on a "fine smooth road" to try his luck in another part of the country. The giants, large, gullible, and stupid, are really simple for Jack to knock down one by one (and a sound business venture for a thousand dollars a head). The less familiar "Big Jack and Little Jack" is similarly based on a contrasting binary pattern of large/empty-headed: small/crafty, seen often in the Brer Rabbit tales. Here, as in the animal stories, the underlying meaning has more serious sociological implications. In this story, the king bargains with all who come to work for him that anyone who becomes angry with him can cut three strops from his back ("long enough to make shoestrings"), and that he can exact the same "justice." The king keeps control this way, maintains total power, for those who cannot voice disapproval cannot make trouble in this otherwise smooth operation.

The first one on the scene is Big Jack (big and stupid like the giants). He collects praise from the king for his honesty, but no wages and no food (in today's terms, benefits), and finally he is knifed in the back for feeling indignation. Enter Little Jack (small but wary) who sees what has happened to his less fortunate "brother" and goes as trickster to bring down the king. Once on the job, this Jack steals a sheep to feed himself, and it is significant that he steals on three occasions, not just one, and that the first and second time, the king tolerates it (it is economically more desirable for the powerful to live with occasional thievery than to promote fair wages and benefits at all times). It is also significant that even after the third time he is caught stealing, Jack is not fired, but merely transferred to a different line of work under this king; firing would indicate that the king had some standards. But his morals are remarkably fluid on this point. As long as everyone pretends to be happy (displaying good manners, positive attitude, no anger), breaking the law can be overlooked. The king is in good shape economically, too.

After Jack plays his second trick, however, and trades the king's horse for a mule (that is, he depletes the king's property to get even with him), the king's economics suffer a little. So he places Jack in a job of less responsibility, one which offers less possibility of Jack causing him an economic loss. As apple picker, Jack moves in for the kill—plays dumb, so that when the king climbs up the ladder to teach him how to pick, Jack takes the ladder away and strikes a bargain for food.

With stories such as this one, it is not difficult to see why African Americans, long submerged in a society that supported the code of subterfuge for maintaining power, might adapt the Jack tales for their own telling, as Jackie Torrence has done. Such tales show us how any group of people, locked into systems of *noblesse oblige,* may find the trickster tactic of lawbreaking an acceptable way, often the encouraged way, of survival. But it would be foolish to assume that Chase's "Jack" is the same trickster we see in all African American Jack and John characters. There are, of course, clear parallels in a story such as Hurston's "How Jack O'Lanterns Came to Be" (collected in Lakeland, Florida from a teller named Mack Ford for *Mules and Men*) and Chase's "Wicked John and the Devil" (collected in Charlottesville, Virginia from two tellers, Mrs. Jenning Yowell and her daughter Alois for *Grandfather Tales* [Chase 1948]). The question is, however, who heard the tales from whom?

JACK, JOHN, AND BIG SIXTEEN: DIFFUSION OR TRANSCULTURATION?

Where did stories like "Wicked John and the Devil" and "How Jack O'Lanterns Came to Be" originate? Did they spring up in America independently from one another? Or did one story pass into the culture of the other as a "borrowing?" If so, which culture did the borrowing? And how did the original story make its way into America? Did "Wicked John and the Devil," for example, travel from Europe to America and then to African American tellers who turned it into "How Jack O'Lanterns Came to Be?" Or did a Jack tale similar to "Wicked John and the Devil" travel from Europe to Jamaica to African American tellers who then passed it on to white listeners at some point? Did African American tellers adapt a European story to their own culture? Did white Appalachian tellers adapt an African American story to their own? Or was there mutual borrowing, or what Greenway describes as " 'cultural ping pong'—the bouncing back and forth of cultural items, the borrowing of something borrowed from the borrowers?" (Greenway 1964, p. 183), as seems to have occurred with the Tar Baby story?

Hurston's and Chase's stories have four motifs in common:

1. Saint Peter appears in both (at the end in Hurston's version; at the beginning in Chase's);
2. Each hero, Big Sixteen, the "Jack" character in Hurston's tale (named for his shoe size), and Wicked John in Chase's story, confronts the devil and either kills him (Hurston) or outsmarts him (Chase);
3. Each hero is rejected by both God and the devil; neither can enter heaven or hell at the end of the story, even though he has bested the devil (Hurston) or proved himself successful in his workplace (Chase);
4. Each hero becomes a wanderer in the world, and his Jack O'Lantern signifies his creation of a little hell of his own.

At the same time, the African American devil, as Hurston makes clear, is not the European one. "The devil," says Hurston, "is not the terror that he is in European folk-lore. He is a powerful trickster who often competes successfully with God. There is a strong suspicion that the devil is an extension of the story-makers while God is the supposedly impregnable white masters, who are nevertheless defeated by the Negroes"

(Hurston 1935, p. 248). The devil is neither intimidating to Big Sixteen in this story, nor a nuisance, as he is to Wicked John. He is just another hurdle, a test to get the day's work done when Ole Massa tells him to catch and bring him the devil.

And African American Jack or John is not linked to European Jack or German Hans, in Hurston's view. "Jack or John," says Hurston, "is the great human culture hero in Negro folklore. He is like Daniel in Jewish folklore, the wish-fulfillment hero of the race. The one who, nevertheless, or in spite of laughter, usually defeats Ole Massa, God and the Devil. Even when Massa seems to have placed him into a hopeless dilemma, he wins out by a trick. Brer Rabbit, Jack (or John) and the Devil are continuations of the same thing" (p. 247). And we see that Saint Peter in Chase's story does not have Jack in a vice, as Ole Massa has Big Sixteen in Hurston's tale. If anything, Saint Peter offers Wicked John a great gift (three wishes) and then he leaves him to use the wishes when he needs them. Hurston's Ole Massa keeps Big Sixteen in his power throughout the story (requires him to do hard labor, constantly tests him). Ole Massa remains always on one side, with Wicked John and the Devil on the other.

Hurston's views are much too iconoclastic, in European terms, for the Jack or John of her stories to be as thoroughly European as Chase's Jack supposedly is. In fact, a comparison of these two versions of the Jack O'Lantern story with one another, and with the European versions (German and Norwegian) casts doubt on just how European, Chase's Jack really is. Hurston's story is shorter and less elaborate than Chase's, with the stronger, more realistic, more memorable dialogue and narration. Ole Massa tests Big Sixteen and he wins each time, even managing finally to kill the devil. But he still cannot go to Heaven; he is too powerful to remain there (the power structure of *race* is reversed: a white god is threatened by the black man's abilities). So with nowhere to go (the Devil's wife is so angry with him for killing the Devil that she shuts him out of Hell), he has no choice but to remain on earth with his hot coal (his way to make an earthly hell of his own): "So she called 'im in de house and shet de door. When Sixteen got dere she handed 'im a li'l piece of fire and said, 'You ain't comin' in here. Here, take dis hot coal and g'wan off and start you a hell uh yo' own' " (p. 164).

Chase's version is a longer, more elaborate story with stronger characterization and stronger motivation for the character's actions than Hurston's. Here as in the European versions, the story begins with a visit of Saint Peter to a blacksmith who is finally given three wishes by the

Saint. Because the smith is troubled by people taking his possessions (his rocker, his sledge hammer, switches from his thornbush) he wishes that anyone taking these items will remain fixed in a certain position until he releases them (since the switches are always taken by fox hunters or "high falutin fellas," Chase's story reverses the power structure of *class*). When his wife tells him three times to go to the devil and the devil appears, Wicked John is able to put his three wishes to good use. But later when he is locked out of heaven for being irreligious, the treatment of the devils comes back to haunt him: the devil fears his craftiness and he, like Big Sixteen, is given hot coals to start a hell of his own on earth.

Here, as in so many of the stories Chase retells, the emphasis is on business or the capitalistic notion of having or starting a business of your own (even if it is called Hell). Even John's wishes become "credit" in the "bank of life" to sustain him if his possessions are threatened. Big Sixteen is not his own master (like Wicked John is, in his smithy); therefore he simply wants to survive the tasks that are foisted upon him. John wants to promote his business (and his rest after a hard day's work); his entire "agenda" is based on the moral "slogan": "work hard and you will reap the benefits of your work."

In the Grimms' version, "Brother Lustig," Saint Peter appears at the beginning, as he does in the Chase version. In both versions there is also the hero's confrontation with, and outwitting of, the devil. And both heroes are rejected from hell by the devil who feels threatened by them, and from heaven by Saint Peter who now knows how worthless they are. But unlike the Chase version, here in the Grimms' version, the Jack figure (Brother Lustig) tricks the saint and jumps into heaven at the last because he is a quick thinker (and quicker than the reader who is, like Saint Peter, caught by surprise at the final turn of events). The Grimms' version is thus the most clever of the three and the strongest in terms of narrative strategies—and wit.

The Norwegian story (George Dasent's translation of "The Smith and the Devil") is a close parallel of the Grimms, but it lacks the narrative strength, the humor, and thus the impact of the German story. The hero is memorable, however, and more familiar here in America now that the frontier days of openness and opportunity have somewhat dimmed: This smith is a prudent, political hypocrite, working all the angles to win power and fame on earth and a safe place in heaven too. But he forces his way physically into heaven at the last, rather than using his intellect to trick the saint, as the smith in the German story does.

Each story, then, has a strength not present in the others; differences rather than similarities remind us why we continue to study these stories, and it is the differences between the American and the German versions that stand out most.

Unlike Wicked John—self-employed, "well-heeled," and resourceful—who doesn't need Saint Peter's money and who couldn't care less about the wishes he gains from the saint (although they come in handy for him later), Brother Lustig, improvident and jobless, manipulates Saint Peter to get the money, then squanders it (he wants money but doesn't want to do any work to earn it). He tries to bring a dead princess back to life as he saw Saint Peter do, but fails (he is neither pure of heart nor an attentive student of the Saint's teaching). He is particularly clever, however, and manages to trick his way into heaven or, ultimately to best Saint Peter. So in this case, a trickster story does what trickster stories do best: It overturns the solid values of the culture from which it springs. European religious values teach that the lazy cheat cannot get into heaven, but Brother Lustig manages to do so (thus reversing the power structure of the church).

The American and African American versions overturn or reverse values of the cultural power structure also, but the values are different from those of the Grimms' story. Here, since members of each culture telling the story (the Appalachian, white one and the southern, African American one) had, from necessity, produced a strong and independent female population, the American stories reverse our expectations about *gender*. It is Wicked John's wife who sends him to the devil each time (she is so powerful that he needs to utilize his three wishes to escape *her* wish—that the devil should "take" him). And it is the devil's wife in Hurston's story who keeps Big Sixteen out of her own territory. (She is as powerful in Hell as Ole Massa is in Heaven; both she and Ole Massa consider Big Sixteen too powerful to be allowed onto their "turf" and both manage to keep him out.) In the European versions, there is no wife (of either the devil or the hero), so no wife's anger or negative wishes enters into the plot. The only females in these versions are the dead princess (German version) or an old woman (Norwegian version) brought back to life by Saint Peter (in each case the female is passive and helpless, rather than assertive and powerful as in the American versions).

Where women have participated more or less equally with men (socially, politically, economically), different story characters, different cultural heroines have tended to emerge. And among these heroines we find something that male scholars, folklorists, and critics, in something of a cultural time lag, have failed to note or investigate—the female trickster.

HER-TRICKSTERS

Consider Chase's "Old Fire Dragaman" (*The Jack Tales*). Although the story has received attention because of its supposed link with *Beowulf,* a connection Chase admits may be far-fetched, what is perhaps more important, from a feminist perspective, is the fact that the trickster in this case is not so much Jack, as the girl who saves him from the dragon. In this tale, a giant called Old Fire Dragaman comes and goes above ground and inadvertently leads Jack down to a place below the ground where he also keeps three girls as prisoners (a parallel version is Grimm's "The Gnome" in which there is both a dwarf and a dragon—the dwarf, serving as mental capacity or knowledge, leads the youngest son, Hans, underground to a dragon lair).

Above ground, the Grimms' Hans and Chase's Jack (both youngest brothers) work in similar ways to show their readiness for destroying the dragon. In the Grimms' tale, two older brothers of Hans are cowardly, each giving the dwarf just what he wants to avoid confrontation. Hans stands up to him, refusing to serve him and finally even beating him. Then he attains the knowledge needed to find the dragon and slay him. In the Chase story, each of the older brothers crouch in fear before the giant who then takes their dinner. When Jack offers him dinner, however, he refuses it (generosity conquers brute force; cowardice plays into its hands). Thus the male character becomes in essence a male Cinderella figure, in traditional, orthodox terms: that is, an unpromising character who succeeds through luck, hard work, magic, or the condition of goodness or humbleness, rather than through duplicity, guile, or intellect.

In both stories, the older brothers plot against the younger one, suggesting that cowardice (insecurity) breeds selfish behavior, but the younger still succeeds in finding his way down to the imprisoned maidens underground. In the Grimms' version, the dwarf (possessor of psychic or intellectual power) leads Hans down into the well; in the Chase story, Jack follows the giant (the hated ogre figure) and discovers the underground place for himself. In both stories, the older brothers leave the younger one trapped underground, and in each case the youngest is best able to rise to the surface (to find his way back to consciousness and win his mate) through psychic power, symbolized in the Grimms' story by the elves that seize Hans by the hair and fly him back up to the earth again.

In the Chase story, however, it is the girl who gives Jack a wishing ring before she is taken above ground by the older brothers *(she* is the clever one—or the trickster—who produces the magical object), and he later uses this ring to transport himself home magically, when he suddenly wishes to be home. But it is significant that his wish is not a consciously intended strategy to get back home or even to get back to the girl. He notices the ring when he wonders how much weight he has lost during a week underground and then he suddenly wishes to be back home "in his mother's chimley corner smokin' my old chunky pipe" (Chase 1943, p. 113). And not only does this girl produce the ring that saves them both, she shows Jack the chest with the sword to kill the giant, and the magic ointment to protect him from the giant's blows (in the Grimm story, Hans kills the dragon with his own hunting knife).

Chase's female character is thus seen playing a larger and more decisive role in her own destiny and in Jack's than he himself plays, and because she also is an oppressed youngest daughter who succeeds through humility, goodness, and magic, she appears as something of a "Cinderella" figure. But because she is one who succeeds through cleverness, she shows us, in addition, that Cinderella can be a trickster. This girl, not the elves, gives Jack the wishing ring, thereby emphasizing her consent and her desire. Thus her sexual maturity precedes his and for a good reason: In presenting him with the sword, she can transfer her allegiance from the oedipal father, represented by the dragaman/ogre/giant figure, to the prospective mate; then she can help Jack do the same, as he takes the dragon's blows (but protected by the magic ointment, they are light) and deals them out *for her.*

We do not easily forget this youngest daughter of "Old Fire Dragaman." There is a simple grace in this girl who, with timeless knowledge, shows Jack how to save them from the dragon, and with quiet charm gives him the ribbon at last to weave through her hair. Forthright and unaffected, she compares well to her female counterpart in the Grimms' tale and is the perfect partner for Jack who, in this particular tale, above all the others, shows us the Southern Mountain traditions of his people and his own rare qualities of kindliness and poise. But, in fact, many clever females appear in these stories, as well as in the African-American tellings of Hurston's *Mules and Men.*

Consider the Devil's daughter in a story John French, of Eatonville, Florida, tells for Hurston: "How Jack Beat the Devil," recorded in *Mules and Men.* In this story, it is difficult to see that Jack does anything at all to "beat" the Devil. Luck, chance, and a magical helper (the Devil's daughter) save him, when he is caught in the Devil's grip after a gambling match in which Jack agrees to the Devil's wager of all the money on the table against his life. When Jack loses the match, the Devil gives him another chance: to arrive at the Devil's house across the sea before sunrise. An old man helps him to find the way and once there, the Devil's daughter helps him to master the three tasks the Devil sets for him.

And later, after the Devil has offered Jack the daughter for his wife, it is again the daughter who saves him by giving him a magic formula to escape the Devil (when the Devil comes one night to kill him): "drag yo' feet backwards nine steps, throw some sand over yo' shoulders." At this point, she turns herself and the horses into goats and tells Jack to hide in a hollow log. When the Devil arrives and Jack saves himself, he does so not by conscious guile, but merely by chance. He cries, "O Lawd, have mercy," and the Devil becomes so angry that he jumps on his bull, the bull turns too fast, and he breaks his neck.

In this case, Jack fits more the pattern of the Cinderella or Unpromising Hero than the Clever or Conquering Hero, categories that Orrin Klapp (1949) devised for studying the cultural distribution of heroes in narrative literature. Greenway, in describing Klapp's categories, comments:

> The Conquering Hero demonstrates an extraordinary power in performing Feats, in winning Contests, surviving Tests, and accomplishing Quests . . . Clever Heroes are Tricksters, primarily, who accomplish their goals by clever ruses, and Klapp is astute enough to appreciate that the Clever Hero is perilously close to being a Villain. The Cinderella or Unpromising Hero is: a) "an unpromising person (b) derided or persecuted by rivals (c) before his unexpected, brilliant triumph. By way of contrast to the unexpected victories of the clever hero, the unpromising hero succeeds by some other means than cleverness, usually luck, miraculous assistance, or modest toil." (Greenway 1964, p. 105)

And since the Devil's daughter fits more the pattern of the Clever Hero, we might say that either males and females in folktales exchange roles more often than scholars notice, or that these categories are more fluid—and unorthodox at times—than they suppose. If we study the stories that Chase records, we find that the Appalachian Cinderella was often a trickster and a conquering heroine too. Consider "Rush Cape" (in Chase's *American Folk Tales and Songs*), collected from tellers in Abingdon, Virginia, Kentucky, and Tennessee. This version, categorized most often now as Type 510b, the King Lear version, or by the motif of the outcast heroine, has parallels in Joseph Jacobs' "Cap o' Rushes" (*English Fairy Tales*) and Andrew Lang's "The Shepherdess" (*The Green Fairy Book*), but it is so much richer in detail and characterization that it is surprising that Jane Yolen (1977) calls it "an exact parallel" of Jacobs' story. And it is equally surprising that Rosemary Minard chooses the Jacobs' version for her feminist collection of folktales (*Womenfolk and Fairy Tales,* 1975).

In the English version the father asks for proof of his daughters' love. The eldest says she loves him "as she loves her life"; the second daughter says "better than all the world"; the third says "as fresh meat loves salt." He drives her out of his house at this point, finding little in her response to gratify his ego. The contrast is less subtle in the Chase version. Here the eldest daughter says she loves him more than silver and gold; the second daughter adds diamonds and jewels; the youngest says "as bread loves salt." What money can buy is contrasted with what parent and child each need and can give the other (the concept of mutual dependency). In addition, the youngest daughter adds, with great honesty, that someday she will love a young man better than him "and that's the dyin' truth" she adds. The truth stings; he turns his back on her, and so she must take to the road, or in Chase's words, she "went to seek her fortune."

The words imply some sense of adventure stronger than we find in the English version when Jacobs says, "she went on and on till she came to a great house" where she asked for "any sort of work" and "no wages." Seeking one's fortune, in the American story, suggests greater pride, greater initiative, and independence, however. Significant in both stories is that at this time she gathers rushes and weaves a cloak and hood that covers her hair and hides her fine clothes. Making something to wear in order to seek one's fortune, in the Chase story, places Cinderella a little closer to her male counterparts of these stories, who also strike out to seek their fortunes, as clever tricksters. For them, the road stands as springboard for daring action and passage to manhood.

For most Cinderellas, however, all roads usually lead to a ball. It is the only place that provides her with daring action. A man is always a man if he faces challenge: death, danger, wild animals, bandits, increasing his wealth and thus his independence. A woman is a woman if her dress is the best at the ball. The importance of Chase's story is that we see Cinderella for the first time moving a little closer to what men have always had—a wider life of action. The suppression of her wealth (the covering of her beauty and fine clothes as a definite choice on her part) points to a Cinderella of greater independence. She doesn't have to search for a dress. She was clever enough to make it for herself, out of nature (she doesn't rely on magic; she is her own resource). She doesn't even have to get to the ball. There are no stepsisters chiding her in this story, thus no feeling of being left behind or of competing. She isn't desperately yearning to go because they go; instead in Chase's words, "She decided she'd go." Choice.

There is no shoe in this story either, although there is a dance. The King's son slips a ring on her finger at the third dance, and when she wants at last to be recognized, she slips the ring back into the soup she sends him from the kitchen of his house, where she now works. The English version ends with the father's return and his recognition of her at last—*after* she tells him who she is. Chase's story comes full circle too, but in different ways. The older daughters have cast out the father now. He is a beggar, as Rush Cape was at the beginning. And just as she made her own clothing of rushes, he has woven himself a crown of weeds. When she brings the salt for his bread, "he looked at her and knew who she was," without being told, just as when she brought the soup to the King's son, he knew her before she removed her cape. (In the English version, he does not recognize her until afterward.)

Thus the Prince of Chase's American story proves he is no trickster placing tar on the castle steps to trap the female, as in the Grimms' version. Yet he is as clever as she is, with greater perception than the Grimms' Prince who goes about trying shoes and errs in the choosing, or the Prince of another Chase story ("Ashpet" in *Grandfather Tales,* told by Nancy Shores of North Carolina), who is tricked by the girl. This version reveals the ill-treated heroine and the shoe test characteristic of the most well-known Cinderella stories (Type 510a), but it certainly takes its own cultural path, and quite a distant one from Perrault's "Cendrillon," Grimm's "Aschenputte," or Basile's "Zezolla."

Here, deep in the southern mountains, Ashpet's godmother is a witch, a trickster herself, who sets Ashpet's luck in motion. Thus, because the ogre/witch figure is a trickster and the Cinderella figure receives her help, Ashpet succeeds as a trickster too. What is interesting, however, is how she receives the witch's help—and why.

CINDERELLA AND THE WITCH:
TRICKSTER CONNECTIONS

Ashpet is the hired girl of a woman with two daughters in this story ("rich folks"). But she is prettier than the daughters, so when anyone comes to visit, the daughters shove her under the washtub. She is also kind and without pretensions. When the daughters must go to the old witch-woman to borrow hot coals, they refuse to comb the old woman's hair, but Ashpet is not too proud to do so. In return, the witch-woman offers to fix things so that Ashpet can go to "meetin' " (church). She recites a charm that washes the dishes and scours the pots and pans for Ashpet (sends them rolling down to the creek and bumping back to the hearth).

She then makes Ashpet a fine mare, with bridle and saddle, from scraps of leather, a rag, and a mouse (just as Perrault's godmother makes the horses for her coach from mice). Finally, she tells the girl to wish for the dress and slippers she would wear to "meetin'," and soon Ashpet is off to the church in a pretty red dress and shoes, where nobody knows her but the king's son, who is smitten and follows her home. Since the witch-woman has warned Ashpet to get back home "quick as meetin' breaks," she must either find a way to leave a trace of herself (if she wants to see him again), or be caught.

An unpromising heroine would have to be tricked or caught, if the Prince were to succeed. But a trickster heroine would find her own way to have what *she* wanted and still not be caught—and Ashpet does. On the way home, "she eased off one of her slippers and kicked it in[to] the bresh [brush or thicket]; rode on a little piece farther, says 'I've lost one of my slippers, sure's the world!'." When the king's boy goes to look for it, she escapes. When he comes to all the houses, to try on the slipper, the daughters trim their heels and toes to fit the shoe (as in the Grimm version), but a bird warns the boy to look under the washtub, and the story ends happily for Ashpet.

Or almost ends. In this version, a new "coda" emerges with the sisters one day taking Ashpet to the "swimmin' place . . . [where] Old Hairy Man lived . . . and when Ashpet went in, he got her." But she proves to be not only courageous and "savvy," but also able to save herself. She listens to Hairy Man's bragging about his thick hide and learns where his vulnerable spot is, so that when the king's men arrive, she can direct them to shoot him in the back of his left shoulder. The story ends with a joke: When Hairy Man yells that the king's son has "his woman," the king's boy arrests the rich family and throws them in the swimmin' place, "Says, 'Here's ye *three* women!' " And "they're down there yet, I reckon," says the narrator.

Ashpet wins our respect as a strong female (a clever trickster too, for the way she dispenses with her shoe in the nick of time) but the witch-woman is also a character worthy of some attention. One of the regular duties of the Culture Hero, as Greenway says, "is to rid his people of ogres" (p. 102). So it follows that the such a hero also must be a trickster, since, as Greenway also points out, "the ogre has incomparably more strength than his human adversary, [and] the hero must use man's unique possession, his guile, to overcome his stupid enemy" (ibid.). Such tales, concludes Greenway, are of necessity unpleasant and frightening, since the hero must act with cruelty, but the benefit or reason for such tales is their ability to frighten listeners into proper conduct, fear being, in his words, "a powerful source of psychic energy" (ibid.).

The obvious ogre in this story is Old Hairy Man, but no one in the story is able to rid the world of him. The less obvious ogres are those who are thrown to Hairy Man (the old woman and her daughters or the "rich folks"'). And who has been responsible for ridding the world of them? The king's son again. But the witch-woman, before him, was a clever adversary of the old woman and her daughters when she helped Ashpet get to the church meeting. So one of the more unorthodox duties of the witch-trickster character, it seems, is to rid the world of (or at least to outsmart) the oppressor. Chase's story leads us to see more about witches as female subversives, power figures, or power brokers, rather than simply as wicked crones, as the daughters felt about the witch-woman in this story, or as victimizing creatures—what many European fairy tales such as "Hansel and Gretel" show and what the Disney Corporation has promoted to an ever greater extent in its version of "Snow White."

> In how many folktales would the entire meaning of the story change if we regarded the witch differently, as Ashpet does, as a protective force for females, one who uses her abilities to free females from oppressors—male or female? The witch here is the first cause in a chain of events that leads to the Cinderella character being victorious (becoming a culture heroine and a trickster—or both). And the same is true of another Cinderella story, this time of the African American tradition, uncovered recently by Virginia Hamilton, which she entitles "Catskinella" for her collection *Her Stories* (1995).

For this story, Hamilton changed the "original similar title and used a footnote title" (letter from Hamilton; 11 March 1996):

> I did not change the original story [the literary source is unnamed by Hamilton] in any essential meaning. Most all of the elements of the

original story remain in my recast versions. What I did was simplify the story, remove the so-called black dialect in favor of my written/spoken colloquial speech to make it easier for young readers, smooth out the language, add language touches that I felt were there but had not come to the surface of the material.

She also replaced the licentious father motif with the woodsman character because of the child audience. The story is a Cinderella variant of the Type 510b, according to Thompson, "The dress of gold, of silver, and of stars" (Thompson 1946, p. 283), with parallel versions in Grimms' "Allerleirauh" ("All Fur") and Jacobs' "Catskin" in *More English Fairy Tales*.

The full "formula" for this tale-type, as Jacobs explains in the end notes of *More English Fairy Tales*, involves a death-bed promise, the dead mother's resemblance to the daughter, which promotes the unnatural father motif (father desiring to marry his daughter), magic dresses, heroine flight and disguise, menial heroine (heroine in a menial job as seen in the "Rush Cape" story above), meeting place or dance, token object (a ring), flight from the dance, lovesick prince, his recognition of a ring, and marriage to the prince or king's son. The two most important motifs are the unnatural father (often transformed to an ogre) and the heroine's need for hasty departure, in some cases actual *flight.*

Hamilton's story utilizes only seven of these motifs: the unnatural father (turned into a woodsman here), magic dresses, heroine flight and disguise, menial heroine, meeting place, recognition of a ring, and happy marriage. The story is therefore tighter and more economical for the child reader. But what makes the story interesting is the heroine herself who sets her own luck in motion, and the use of a witch figure who is so competent a trickster that the girl succeeds as a trickster too, and largely because here, as an added motif, is a magic object—a talking mirror. When Ella learns that she must marry, she requests a looking-glass that can talk (a delaying tactic since she doesn't "take to" the woodsman). But the woodsman obtains the mirror ("Talking as big as it pleased"), so Ella then must appeal to her godmother, Mattie, who advises that she tell her father to kill a cat and have the hide made into a dress. "Skintight and shimmery" it appears. There also is a ring from the woodsman. When the wedding day arrives, Ella escapes by the window while the mirror goes on talking behind the door, as if she is there.

At the king's castle, Ella finds refuge and love. The king's son sees her beautiful face rather than "that scary, skintight catskin." He finds her work "minding the chickens" and "a little cabin all her own." He spies on her too, sees her shake the catskin gown and pretty dresses that fall from it, and becomes sick with love. All the maidens of the kingdom are commanded to bake cakes, with the best baker entitled to marry the ailing prince. The prince requests a cake from Ella, who drops her ring into the batter. Later, her finger is the only one to fit the ring, and the motif of the happy marriage follows.

Both the catskin dress and the talking mirror produce trickster power. Since the woodsman replaces the licentious father, it is the father who would have been the one to obtain the mirror, which very likely belonged to the mother. Thus the mirror allows the ghost-mother's voice to speak directly to the daughter she would help. Mirrors occur in African American folktales as one way for the ordinary person to see ghosts (according to Puckett), if the person is looking into the mirror "with another person" (Puckett 1926, p. 139). And since, in the Catskin formula, the licentious father desired the daughter because she so strongly resembled the mother, we can assume that the other person looking into the mirror with Catskinella here *was* the mother (she and the daughter being the same person, in the father's eyes).

The ring the girl drops into the cake batter is also the power of the mother working for her, since it is probably the mother's ring, as well as the mirror, that the woodcutter/father has given the girl. As for the dress made of catskin, it enables her to pass unobstructed through a dangerous world. As Hamilton says in her endnote, "Probably, the Cinderella motif was mixed in with that of the cat as woman/witch. African American tellers often utilized cats in their stories, and other animals that were common where they lived. Witches became cats and vice versa. They shed their skins and flew away" (Hamilton 1995, p. 27).

In a parallel "Catskin" story that Chase records ("Catskins" in *Grandfather Tales*), there is no old woman witch/helper as in the Hamilton story (or no henwife, as in the Jacobs version, who advises the girl to have a catskin coat made). The girl is already wearing a ragged dress of old cat hides, as the story begins (thus her name, "Catskins"). So she is already in role as a witch, since, as Puckett explains, "the English witch most commonly takes the form of a cat" (p. 149). And she becomes her own trickster, requesting a widowed neighbor (the hated-father substitute) for the magic dresses. After receiving them, she asks for his "flyin' box," which she promptly uses to escape from him, by reciting a charm that takes her up into the sky and across the country to a big house (certainly a strange pilgrimage, but an important one).

Like Rush Cape who "went to seek her fortune," she tells them at the big house that she wants to work, and she does find work—with the "poor folks" in the kitchen. And like Hamilton's Catskinella, her magic dresses cause the king's boy to fall in love with her. But here in Chase's story, the prince gives her a ring at the third dance and later she drops his ring into the cake she makes for him (the same clever trick that Catskinella uses, but this time he recognizes his own gift rather than her face or her dress, as in Hamilton's story). She will not marry him, however, until she is wearing her dress the color of all the flowers in the world. So a witch who becomes her own trickster, saving herself from her oppressors, has thus freed herself to become the conquering heroine (the "flower" of her culture). And the story, like so many of these truly American Cinderella stories, helps all females know they can be heroes, too.

STRANGE PILGRIMAGES: WHAT DO THEY MEAN?

The real heroic figures for children, as we see, are not found in a Disney theme park filled with plastic creatures parading around for tourists who flock to the gates because of extensive advertising by an entertainment industry. Plastic creatures have no ties to real people; their ties are simply to plastic places. But there are real heroes still around, as there have always been. African American heroes like Brer Rabbit, Jack, and John are alive and well only ten miles away from Orlando in Eatonville, as Hurston showed us, and as Steve Sanfield discovered more recently when he began collecting stories for *The Adventures of High John the Conqueror* (1989). And they are alive outside Eatonville too, as Virginia Hamilton has shown in her fascinating trickster recreations of *The Magical Adventures of Pretty Pearl* (1983), set in Georgia and the Midwest, and *The People Could Fly* (1985), and *Her Stories* (1995), which draw on heroic black characters from all parts of America, as well as the Caribbean.

Scotch-Irish heroes are still living alongside their transplanted English cousins in the Appalachian Mountains of Virginia, North Carolina, and Kentucky, as Richard Chase revealed and as Gail Haley has given us in so many of her vibrant and inventive picturebooks. Native American heroes are living on the Plains and on the North Pacific Coast, in the Central Woodlands and the Southwest, as Stith Thompson revealed and as Joseph Bruchac is now portraying for children in the rich imagery of his poems and stories. They are living in family stories and cultural memories, as storytellers like Jackie Torrence and Marshall Ward show us.

They are found in bookstores and libraries, in many languages and settings as Helme Heine reveals. They are seen in art galleries, in the theater, and in films we see, if we consider the strange pilgrimage of Marc Chagall's fiddler on the roof. They are present in stories about females and males, children and adults, animal and humans. They spring up in all ethnicities and nationalities.

All people are their own heroes. Every hero is the shadow figure on the wall, as Johnny Mouse shows us, in the pictures we make for ourselves—of ourselves, for heroes are tied to personal and family cultures, ancestors, a sense of place. My mother's Irish grandmother, weaving a Cinderella story of her own in the Appalachian Mountains, brought stories like the Jack tales all the way from the city of Cork. My mother's German mother made shadow pictures on the wall, just like the one Johnny Mouse made of Charlie Rooster, to occupy my sister the night I was born. My mother never stopped telling all these stories to me, and my father never stopped telling stories of his first home in Lithuania, on the Russian border. I can't go there to see it; his village, and others like it, simply aren't there anymore—except in paintings like those of Chagall. My father called himself a twentieth-century pilgrim, having made his way, at age three, from the Old World to the New, then striking out like Jack, at age twelve, to make his fortune in the Appalachian Mountains. And probably because of him, I never stay in one place very long.

Back home from Paris now, and not very far from those same mountains, I am at this moment reading about the opening of a new exhibit of Chagall's paintings in New York City, not so many blocks from where my father spent his childhood. And two of those paintings have been shipped from the Pompidou, which, it turns out, wasn't hoarding—it was sharing. In a few weeks I'll see them too.

Strange pilgrimages; things come around.

BIBLIOGRAPHY

Barnouw, Victor. *Acculturation and Personality Among the Wisconsin Chippewa.* Menasha, Wisconsin: American Anthropological Association, Memoir 72, 1950.

Basile, Giambattista. *The Pentamerone.* Tr. Sir Richard Burton. London: Spring Books, 1958.

Chase, Richard. *American Folk Tales and Songs.* New York: Dover, 1971.

———. *Grandfather Tales.* Boston: Houghton Mifflin, 1948.

———. *The Jack Tales.* Boston: Houghton Mifflin, 1943.

Dasent, George, translator. "The Smith and the Devil" in *Scandinavian Folk and Fairy Tales*. Ed. Claire Booss. New York: Crown, 1984.

Disney Corporation. *The Complete Story of Walt Disney's Snow White and the Seven Dwarfs*. New York: Harry Abrams Company, 1937.

Elliott, Harvey. "Britons Say No to Holidays at Home," *The Times,* 14 March 1996: 34.

Greenway, John. *Literature Among the Primitives*. Hatboro, Pennsylvania: Folklore Associates, 1964.

Grimm, Jacob and Wilhelm. *The Complete Grimms' Fairy Tales*. Tr. Margaret Hunt. New York: Pantheon, 1944.

Hamilton, Virginia. *Her Stories: African American Folktales, Fairy Tales, and True Tales*. Illus. Leo and Diane Dillon. New York: Scholastic, 1995.

———. *The Magical Adventures of Pretty Pearl*. New York: Harper, 1983.

———. *The People Could Fly*. Illus. Leo and Diane Dillon. New York: Knopf, 1985.

Heine, Helme. *Friends*. Köln, Germany: Gertraud Middelhauve Verlag; and London: J. M. Dent & Sons, 1982.

———. *L'exposition des trois amis*. Tr. from the German by Yves-Marie Maquet. Köln, Germany: Gertraud Middelhauve Verlag; and Paris: Gallimard, 1991.

Hurston, Zora Neale. [1935] *Mules and Men*. New York: Harper, 1990.

Jacobs, Joseph. *English Fairy Tales*. 3rd edition. New York: G. P. Putnam's Sons, 1911.

———. *More English Fairy Tales*. New York: G. P. Putnam's Sons, n.d.

Klapp, Orrin. "The Folk Hero," *Journal of American Folklore* 62 (1949): 17–25.

Lang, Andrew, (ed.). "The Shepherdess," in *Green Fairy Book*. New York: David McKay, 1948.

Leach, Maria, (ed.). *Dictionary of Folklore, Myth, and Legend, Volume Two: J–Z*. Chicago: Funk and Wagnall, 1950.

Lester, Julius. *Black Folktales*. Illus. Tom Feelings. New York: Grove Press, 1969. Evergreen Black Cat Edition, 1970.

Minard, Rosemary. *Womenfolk and Fairy Tales*. Boston: Houghton Mifflin, 1975.

Morrison, Toni. *Tar Baby*. New York: Knopf, 1981.

Perrault, Charles. "Cinderella or The Little Glass Slipper," in *The Classic Fairy Tales,* eds. Iona & Peter Opie. New York: Oxford University Press, 1974.

Puckett, Newbell Niles. *Folk Beliefs of the Southern Negro*. Chapel Hill: University of North Carolina Press, 1926.

Sanfield, Steve. *The Adventures of High John the Conqueror.* New York: Dell, 1989.

Thompson, Stith. *The Folktale.* New York: Dryden Press, 1946.

Torrence, Jackie. *More Jack Tales.* Columbia, Missouri: Nita Recordings, 1980.

Yolen, Jane. "America's Cinderella," *Children's Literature in Education* 8 (1977): 21–29.

Rides of Passage
Female Heroes in Pony Stories

ALISON HAYMONDS

Horses empower girls in pony books. A horse gives a girl a sense of her own identity, self-respect, control, and an almost mystical understanding of nature. Timid girls discover reserves of strength, diffident girls find self esteem, troubled girls attain peace with horses. Regarded as odd, even tedious, by family and some contemporaries because of their obsession with horses, girls in pony books are transformed by their association with ponies into physically adept, brave riders, tackling their own problems, and getting some measure of control of their own lives. In turn, neglected, wild or unmanageable ponies are transformed into sleek, shining horses leaping to success in the top jumping class, fitting mounts for heroes. As in all the best fairy stories, girls and ponies have been transformed by love. They have learned what G. K. Chesterton calls "the great lesson of *Beauty and the Beast,* that a thing must be loved *before* it is loveable."[1] Pony stories, like fairy tales, says Chesterton, are overtly moral and didactic, for the world of horses has an uncompromising code of ethics that descends directly from *Black Beauty.* They also are love stories in which the pony is rescued, tamed, and broken in by the love of a good woman, but he is *not* the animal groom of fairy tales. He remains safely within his animal skin. There can be no more satisfactory partner than the beautiful, well-schooled horse, strong yet dependent, on which a girl might practise her latent skills as wife and mother, homemaker, and working woman. The pony, a live object of desire that will not judge, assess, or complain, fulfils multiple needs for its young owner. Above all it enables her to become the hero of her own story.

In the post-war years, the female heroes of pony books created new social and psychological patterns for girls and bridged what feminist critic, Andrea Dworkin, calls the "Great Divide" between the heroes and heroines of the fairy stories:

> At some point the Great Divide took place: they (the boys) dreamed of mounting the Great Steed and buying Snow White from the dwarfs: we (the girls) aspired to become that object of every necrophiliac's lust—the innocent, victimised Sleeping Beauty. . . .[2]

In pony books, the girls were no longer passive, they mounted the Great Steed and took responsibility for their own destiny. It was a symbolic gesture when they bought their first pony with their hard-earned money, for they were the ones who owned and possessed after centuries of being the possessed.

When John Birks patronisingly dismissed girls in pony stories as "little self-conscious misses in jodhpurs" (Birks 1946, p. 166), he had little idea of the stampede of pony books heading his way, nor of the new type of female hero who was riding in with them. Far from being "little misses," girls in pony books were important role models for their readers in the post-war years. The heroism of these pony book girls was on a modest scale; they were the daughters of the Englishwomen who had kept the home fires burning during World War II and they shared their reticence and their stoicism, but not their thraldom to domestic life. Girls as diverse as Velvet Brown (*National Velvet*), Noel Kettering (*Six Ponies, et al.*), Rennie Jordan (*Rennie Goes Riding*), Janet Fraser (*Janet Must Ride*), Gill Caridia (*Dream of Fair Horses*), and Ruth Hollis (*Fly-by-Night, et al.*) wanted more to life than the office job and the kitchen sink but their chosen route to maturity was a hard one. Their "first love" came in the form of a pony, but it was a love that brought with it a great deal of responsibility. Girls had to solve problems normally associated with adulthood, with the provision and cost of feeding, kit (for themselves as well as the pony), stabling, and all the ills that horses are heir to. They had to learn skills unknown to their parents (whilst their readers also became armchair experts by absorbing page after page of undisguised instruction and information about horsemanship and stablecraft). The pony book girls had to learn to care for and nurture another creature; they had to display qualities of patience and self-discipline; and they had to be prepared to work long hours at hard, physical labour. Girls came of age with the help of their horses and their life with ponies was a trial run for

the sort of life post-war women had to learn to cope with, juggling relationships, responsibilities, work, and family.

Strange, then, that feminist critics seem to have ignored the pony
book while embracing other forms of popular fiction for girls, like the
school story. It could be that the genre is too narrow and specific for general application, and certainly it has long been ignored, or belittled, by
critics. Pony books owe less to literary models than to sociocultural influences, for Britain has traditionally been a nation of horse-lovers, and
sporting horsewomen have always been part of that tradition. In the late
1930s, 1940s, and 1950s, when the genre evolved and flourished, adolescent girls were becoming more independent, better educated, and had
higher expectations of choosing their own career and lifestyle. Many of
these girls were mad on ponies, and to a large extent they invented the
genre themselves. The earliest writers as well as the key names in the
genre—Moya Charlton, Primrose Cumming, Katharine Hull and Pamela
Whitlock, Josephine, Diana and Christine Pullein-Thompson, K. M. Peyton, Gillian Baxter—all started writing pony stories in their teens. They
wrote for themselves as much as for other girls and, because there was a
growing demand for children's books after the war, they had no trouble
in getting their stories published. Even the two adult pioneers of the
genre, Enid Bagnold and Joanna Cannan, wrote out of their own childhood love for horses and for their own pony-mad children. Many other
young riders also felt this compulsion to write as well as ride—it seemed
to be part of the pony-mad phase—and, paradoxically, the fictional pony
girls were avid readers of the genre. Jinny, one of the most popular contemporary female heroes of pony stories, in a time of crisis seeks comfort
in a favourite pony book:

> Sitting crouched over the Aga, reading, the security of the story wove a
> warm web round Jinny. No danger. No dreams. Only summer days
> filled with riding school ponies. (Leitch 1978, p. 107)

Pony stories, written by teenagers, are one form of children's literature that solve the ambiguity of children's books being written by adults.
The child, or adolescent, speaks directly to the child and is not filtered
through the vision of an adult. It is not hard to see why a teenager, who
was a keen rider and had read and enjoyed pony books, should not feel
confident about writing one herself. Publishers were quick to point out
the age of the writer on the fly leaf, so that the young writer's success and
the success of her female hero overlapped in a satisfying way. Readers

could identify with both author and female hero simultaneously. It was a strong and seductive message for the reader: "This was possible for me, so it is possible for you." The teenagers who wrote pony books were as much hero figures to their young readers as their fictional characters, and they acted like their own heroines—Primrose Cumming bought her first pony for £25, the money she earned from *Doney,* and Kathleen Peyton paid for riding lessons with the £75 she earned from her first book, *Sabre the Horse from the Sea.* Sometimes the line between fact and fiction becomes almost indistinguishable.

PIONEERS IN THE FIELD

Animals in children's literature act as surrogate heroes, a projection of what their readers would like to be, "brave, high-spirited, loyal, wily or mischievous" (Carlsen 1980, pp. 63–4). In a series of books, some of which were clearly autobiographical or semi-autobiographical, a horse or pony was the hero, even though it was often helpless at the hands of cruel humans. The earliest is *Memoirs of Dick, the little poney* (1800), the most famous, *Black Beauty* (1877), but there were dozens of others like *Moorland Mousie, Skewbald the New Forest Pony, Exmoor Lass, Doney, Kelpie, Wandy,* and *Bonny.* It was when ponies stopped being heroes of the stories and the focus of interest shifted to the young riders that the girl rider came into her own and the pony book, as we understand it, appeared. It can be defined as a story in a British setting, generally rural, with a young hero, nearly always female, whose relationship with her pony is central to the action. The formula seldom varied: girl acquires pony by luck, chance, as a reward, or by her own endeavours. It is often unrideable, badly treated, neglected, or has been written off, but its young owner, despite obstacles, transforms it by love, care and training, and rides it to success. The genre first appeared immediately before World War II, flourished in the 1940s, 1950s, and 1960s, but experienced a fairly steady decline since then (although it is still popular in continental Europe, particularly Scandinavia and Germany).

The two most influential books in the genre, which were the prototypes of the formula and set a standard that was rarely equalled, appeared within a year of each other: Enid Bagnold's *National Velvet* (1935) and Joanna Cannan's *A Pony for Jean* (1936). When Velvet Brown won the Grand National on a wild piebald only she could ride, and Jean Leslie was given a thin, neglected pony called "the Toastrack," romantically dubbed "Cavalier," and triumphed in the jumping class, a new kind of female hero was born. She had descended from a mixed heritage of real and fictional women: the dashing Memsahibs of the British Raj, the hard-riding women of the hunting field, and the self-effacing, socially awkward, but ultimately triumphant heroines of fiction, like Jane Eyre and the unnamed heroine of *Rebecca*. Velvet Brown and Jean Leslie were created by two well-established writers for adults and proved a lasting influence. Velvet was the fey daughter of a butcher, dreamy, thin, and plain, with steely courage, a passion for ponies and high expectations:

> "I want to be a famous rider, I should like to carry despatches, I should like to get a first at Olympia, I should like to ride in a great race, I should like to have so many horses that I could walk down between the two rows of loose boxes and ride what I chose." (Bagnold 1935, p. 71)

To Velvet, the horse meant liberation and power and her fervent wish was echoed by many pony-mad adolescents. Jean Leslie, whose father had lost his money, was several steps up the social ladder from Velvet Brown, but like Velvet she combined shyness and feelings of inadequacy with imagination and determination ("You're a persevering little bloke," her father says admiringly). Few of the subsequent writers matched these two early practitioners. Bagnold had not originally intended *National Velvet* as a children's book and made no concessions with her command of language and the subtlety of her depiction of relationships between her sometimes eccentric characters. Cannan was writing for children but her resolutely unsentimental tone and wide-ranging irony owed as much to Angela Thirkell as E Nesbit. Cannan dedicated *A Pony for Jean* to her three daughters, Josephine, Diana, and Christine Pullein-Thompson, and started a dynasty of pony book writers who are still producing books— even today the name Pullein-Thompson epitomises the pony story. In their early books, written when they were teenagers, Cannan's daughters faithfully followed her lead with variations on the gauche but gritty middle-class heroines, like the painfully self-conscious Noel Kettering (Josephine Pullein-Thompson *Six Ponies,* et al.), or spoilt, rich girls like Christina Carr (Diana Pullein-Thompson, *Three Ponies and Shannan,* et al.) who are transformed into female heroes by their ponies.

A combination of the two types of girl hero—dreamy and anxious on the one hand, hard-working and brave on the other—can be traced through scores of pony books by writers like Pamela MacGregor-Morris, Monica Edwards, Mary Treadgold, and Mary Gervaise. Ruby Ferguson's ever-popular Jill Crewe (1949 onwards), who was jollier and less angst-ridden than most, still embodied middle-class pluck. Even when the genre began to lose its momentum in the late 1960s and 1970s, and became notably less middle-class, three of its most memorable female heroes were cast in the same mould. Ruth Hollis (in K. M. Peyton's *Fly-by-Night,* etc.), Brenda Carter (in Vian Smith's *Come down the Mountain*), and Jinny Manders (in Patricia Leitch's *Jinny* series) were ordinary girls lifted into heroic status by their love for a difficult horse. Unlike the schoolgirl heroine who prospered in the protected, all-female world of girls' boarding-schools, pony book girls functioned within the family, the working world, and the sports field. They had a strong, almost fierce desire for freedom and individuality and resisted the conformity of school, the expectations of parents and peers, and the world of social gatherings and office jobs. It was taken for granted that these girl riders competed on equal terms in the show ring and hunting field against boys, and pony stories close with the gymkhana, the rosette, and the cup—the qualifications of horsemanship.

WILD HORSES

Women on horseback tend to be taken for granted in Britain, but less so in other societies. As recently as 1975, Elena Belotti in a discussion about female stereotypes in American and French children's literature, considered young riders there might feel self-conscious about their lack of "feminism." She argued that children's fiction had exerted a constant and subconscious pressure on girls to conform to stereotyped roles—the perfect, passive mother figure, or the pretty, helpless "heroine", and she criticised the lack of strong, positive female images in children's fiction:

> Many girls today are extremely good at skating or at riding ponies, but only those who cannot do these things are considered interesting . . . Girls who, in spite of being extremely good at sporting activities, see themselves presented by children's books as idealized models of fragility and ineptitude, cannot but feel the discomfort and unease of one who does not know to which model she should conform. (Belotti 1975, pp. 92–3)

This sounds odd to British ears, and in her introduction to Belotti's book, Margaret Drabble contends that these comments could hardly be applied to British fiction with its vast number of pony books for girls: "Perhaps outdoor, sporty, horsy women have always been more numerous in England than on the Continent and in the United States," she writes, and suggests that our tradition of dashing women riding to hounds may be the

reason for the popularity of the horses, even among girls who only occasionally visit riding stables and never hunt: Perhaps the popularity of
horse books supports Elena Belloti's point. Once an energetic, competitive outdoor sport is given the seal of approval, thousands of frustrated
indoor children, fed up with the nonglamorous inactivity of embroidery
and housekeeping, will rush to approve it, and to read about it even if
they are too poor or too urban to practise it (p.10).

It is significant that American horse stories that were popular during
much the same period as the British pony book have tended to be "rites
of passage" books for boys rather than girls. The coming of age of young
males is still one of the key themes of American literature, films, and
popular culture, and this also was true of the earlier and influential horse
stories. While the American genre is inextricably bound up with the story
of the Wild West, where the horse is part of a wider and wilder landscape,
and often the means of livelihood, the British pony story is placed firmly
in a rural, domestic setting and enclosed stableyard, with riding perceived
as a leisure or sporting pursuit. It is no coincidence that the American
stories so often have the word "wild" in the title (*Wild Horse Tamer, Wild
Spirit of the West, Wild Appaloosa*) or that the animals are so often stallions, strong virile creatures like Walter Farley's *Black Stallion,* "wildest
of all wild animals."

The first great classic American horse book, *Smoky,* the story of a
cow pony by Will James, an unsentimental, realistic story of a working
horse, was published in 1926 at the same time as the tales of native
ponies, "Exmoor," "Dartmoor," and "New Forest," were being produced
by Allen W. Seaby and Golden Gorse (Muriel Wace) in Britain. These
were no mustangs, but children's ponies, small, easily broken-in, pets
rather than workmates. British writers often quote the saying (attributed
to the Greeks), "The horse is a noble animal"; in America, however, the
horse is regarded more as a noble savage, and the feeling that exists between man and horse as a primeval one. John Steinbeck, in another classic of the genre, *The Red Pony,* captures that feeling:

> Out of a thousand centuries they drew the ancient admiration of the
> footman for a horseman. They knew instinctively that a man on a horse
> is spiritually as well as physically bigger than a man on foot. (Stein-
> beck 1933, p. 156)

Equine fiction has declined in America in recent years as in Britain,
and has been absorbed in the national obsession for series books, like

The Saddle Club series (1986 onwards), which combines instruction with teenage romance—a kind of "Sweet Valley High" with horses. The American horse books that endure are those preoccupied with the idea of the American West and the relationship between boy and horse, like *The Black Stallion* stories, successful for more than forty years, Rutherford Montgomery's *Golden Stallion* series, set in an idyllic American West, and Mary O'Hara's much-loved Flicka and Thunderhead books about life on a Wyoming ranch. Others, like Marguerite Henry's horse stories, are about particular native breeds and have a strong sense of American history. British horse and pony stories also link their young protagonists to the past but it is a past of myth, magic, and fiction in which girls, like Gill in *Dream of Fair Horses,* are transformed into heroic figures:

> I sat down in the saddle and touched Tessy into a canter and I was no longer a skinny, ugly girl on an old pony that didn't even belong to me: I was changed into Velvet on The Pie, Gandalf on Shadowfax, Bellerophon on Pegasus, Tom o'Bedlam astride his horse of air. The magic that had haunted my life for as long as I could remember was still as powerful as ever. (Leitch 1975, p. 42)

In myth and legend, the horse has always been endowed with speed, strength, beauty, and wisdom. It is no coincidence that Swift chose the Houyhnhnms, the horses endowed with reason, to reflect the highest virtues of simplicity and virtue, contrasted with the disgusting brutality of the Yahoos, beasts in human shape (*Gulliver's Travels* 1726).

GETTING THE WHIP HAND

Pony book girls followed a long British tradition of women riders. Powerful women like Queen Victoria and Florence Nightingale were passionate horsewomen, and many Victorian women learned to revel in the freedom of riding in India. Lady Violet Greville, in *Ladies in the Field* (1894), prescribed riding as a basic recipe for a sound mind and a sound body: "The sense of power conveyed by the easy gallop of a good horse, tends greatly to moral and physical well being and satisfaction."[3] The British community in India lived and talked horses and everyone was expected to ride and drive. The horse was a great liberating influence for the memsahib who followed English fashions and wore special riding breeches "because we were perpetually jumping on and off horses."[4] The military men and their wives, who came back from the Empire imbued with a passion for horses, passed on Indian words like "gymkhana" and "jodhpur" to thousands of pony-mad girls, and were influential in all aspects of the sport of riding, in particular the formation of the Pony Club in 1929, which played a key part in the popularity of riding. On the hunting field, women came into their own during World War I, when a number became Masters of Fox Hounds, and more and more became active followers. Girls in earlier pony books, like Alison, narrator of *I Wrote a Pony Book,* who said longingly: "I would dearly like to be the fastest woman to hounds on the Border" (Cannan 1950, p. 6), looked to these hunting women as their inspiration, but increasingly it was a new breed of British horsewomen, made accessible through television, who acted as role models. In 1947, the BBC televised the Royal International Horse Show at White City for the first time and soon Pat Smythe, Marion Mould, Anne Moore, and Liz Edgar were household names, beating male riders in international competitions, and becoming heroines for post-war girls. Some of the "horsey" élite (like Pat Smythe and Dorian Williams) joined the growing ranks of pony book authors and proved that good riders do not necessarily make good writers.

Josephine Pullein-Thompson says: "I think the reason horses appeal so much to girls is that when they are on horseback girls are absolutely equal, in fact in a lot of ways they are better."[5] A rider is only as good as his or her horse, and that is a great leveller—equestrian events are still the only ones in the Olympic Games in which men and women compete on equal terms. On horseback, men and women are virtually indistinguishable, they look at the world from the same angle, and they even wear the same clothes. Until World War I, women wore a riding habit that uneasily combined the masculine and feminine; thus, apart from her long skirt, Queen Victoria's costume—collar, tie, and top hat—was just like a man's. By the end of the war, women were starting to ride in breeches, jackets, collar, and tie, and soft felt hats, and girls were learning to ride astride their horse. Cross-dressing, with sexes identically dressed, became the norm, but it has its ambiguity. It can be sexually attractive,[6] yet it also disguises or denies femininity (Chernin 1985, p. 188). When fourteen-year-old Velvet Brown, still skinny and undeveloped, dreams of riding in the Grand National, she asks, "Who's to know I'm a girl?" In jockey silks she becomes "the little man." Velvet's attitude to her own femininity is equivocal. Lisa Tyler argues persuasively that Velvet is an anorexic who is rejecting her own femininity, while accepting her mother's "implicit warning about the incompatibility of femininity and achievement" (Tyler 1993–4, p. 154). Velvet's relationship with her mother, a hugely obese woman who once swam the Channel, is complex. Mrs Brown, as housebound as she is fat-bound, is a living example of what women can achieve and what they might decline to with motherhood and marriage. Velvet rejects this idea of maturity:

> ". . . it's awful to grow up," said Velvet. "All this changing and changing, an' got to be ready for something. I don't ever want children. Only horses." (Bagnold 1935, p. 33)[7]

Yet it is Mrs Brown, strong and "incredibly enduring," who tells her daughter, "Don't you dread nothing, Velvet," and enables her to ride in the National by paying the entrance fees. Velvet's androgynous looks and her "boy's face" are constantly stressed, and she has to cut her hair and dress as a boy to ride in the Grand National, but it is her "ascending spirit" that brings her victory, a spirit inherited from her mother.

The female heroes of pony books who followed Velvet Brown shared her contempt for girlish things and pretty clothes, living in Aertex shirts and baggy jodhpurs, but perversely they craved to conform by acquiring the uniform of riding. Lack of proper clothes clouded the lives of the female heroes and incorrect dress is despised by the richer riders. Gill, in *Dream of Fair Horses,* yearns to be inconspicuous:

> I'd spent ages doing my best to turn myself into a Pony Club type so that nobody would notice me. I was wearing a navy blue, polo-necked sweater . . . , blue jeans and black lacing shoes, and I'd tied back my hair with a bit of ribbon that Mummy had found for me. (Leitch 1975, p. 55)

In riding clothes, girls can pretend to be sexless, classless, and invisible. They are a magic cloak behind which girls can hide as they strive to find their place in a complex, adult world.

FORGING A CAREER

It is no coincidence that pony books flourished after the war. It was a period of change and transition, and women emerged into the sunlight of the 1950s with greater expectations. The changing status of women in the world of horses reflected the changing role of women generally. Two wars depleted the ranks of young men available to be grooms, and the new industries, with higher wages, lured many away. In 1946, Brigadier-General Marchant prophesied:

> The wages of grooms will probably not be less than £4 a week. This increase may not be sufficient to induce men to leave the factory for the stable, unless their love of horses is so great that they prefer to be with them at the expense of their pockets. (Marchant 1946, p.789)

What he prophesied came true. What he did not foresee was the emergence of girl grooms, prepared (as always) to accept the notoriously low wages for the love of looking after horses. As men took to machines, women took over in the stable. Even today, 80 percent of grooms are girls, but at last they are beginning to resent exploitation.[8] A full-time career with horses was far more desirable to girls in the 1950s, who were eagerly looking for new directions as they entered the job market. They still had conservative ideas of home, marriage, and family, but they questioned the stereotyped roles society expected of them. Their ambitions were in the male world of horses rather than in safe feminine occupations like nursing, teaching, and secretarial work, and this was reflected in pony books. More and more women were needed in the workplace, and the new careers novels for girls helped to open up the possibilities.[9]

Many of the pony books of this era were about girls starting or working in riding stables, like *Rennie Goes Riding* (1956) and *Susan's Riding School* (1956), which were published by Chatto & Windus in the Mary Dunn Career Novel series. Riding was not considered as desirable as "suitable" professions like social worker, beautician, cook, fashion buyer, and dancer, and there was still a great deal of resistance to women grooms even though the women of the Land Army had shown they were quite capable of doing physically demanding work. A relatively enlightened father like Mr Perriman, in *One More Pony* (1952), who expected his daughters to gain qualifications so they could pursue careers, was scathing about their ambitions to help on the farm. He considered farmwork too heavy for women: "That's why I'm in a way glad to see the Land Army go, for all they were a fine, ready lot of girls" (p 35). Mary and Josephine Chantry also faced opposition when they started *The Silver Eagle Riding School* (1938). Forced to work for their living when their father died, they were dismayed when their uncle suggested "suitable careers"—as secretary and domestic science teacher. Even their mother agreed: "I should love to have you at home, but I feel in these days, when girls are expected to have careers like boys, it would be wiser for you to learn some profession." Josephine's answer is significant: "But I don't want to be like other girls, and I don't want a career. I'd much rather stay at home with the horses" (Cumming 1938, p. 11). Girls in pony stories did not want to work in offices and despised girls who did. Their life was dedicated to horses and any desire to "stay at home" had nothing to do with domestic duties—or marriage.

Probably the reason so few of the pony books take the female heroes forward in time after the happy ending—the successful show or possession of the beloved pony—is because "what happened next?" is fraught with the potential difficulties of an adult world without ponies. *Susan's Riding School,* like other career books of the period, fudged the issue. Although there was an acknowledgement that marriage was still the desirable goal for most women, it was not allowed to interfere with good advice about getting qualifications and working hard. And at least marriage could be deferred beyond the end of the story. Susan Hunt, for example, gains her certificates, sets up her own riding school, and wins her class at the horse show, even though there is a man lurking respectfully in the background:

> Charles put a hand on her shoulder, "Jolly good show, Susan," he said quietly, "I'm proud of you. You've made a success of the school and now you've won the Riding School class. I warn you, I'm going to ask you to marry me one day, but it's no use just yet, I know. You're wedded to your horses."
>
> "No," said Susan. "It's no use yet. But don't forget your promise," she added, laughing. "'One day' may not be so very far off, you know." (Heath 1956, p. 138)

In pony stories, it is mainly parents who regard riding as an unsuitable career for girls. Janet Fraser's mother, in *A Horse for the Holidays* (1963), was particularly violent in her opposition:

> "Slavery, that's what it would mean. Day in, day out, toiling for someone else. Struggling to do a man's work because that's what would be expected of you—heavy, manual work, too." (Leitch 1963, p. 70)

The key word is "slavery," which her mother uses several times to describe working with horses. Women, born during the Depression, who had witnessed the new independence of women during the war, might well regard a badly paid job mucking out stables and grooming horses as a "come down." Mothers in these stories—like their real-life counterparts—wanted their daughters to make the most of the new opportunities for education, to better themselves, and get away from blue-collar manual work to "safe" white-collar office work. It was the women in Janet's family, her mother, aunt, and sister, who tried to browbeat her into going to commercial college, even though Janet said she would "rather die" than work as a shorthand typist, marry "a fat bank manager," and be shut indoors all day. "She wondered why she [her mother] hated horses so much and why she wanted to turn her daughter into a neat little office girl" (p. 36). The reason why parents were so opposed to the life, according to Mr Marshall, the riding school manager in *Susan's Riding School,* was because of their ignorance of horses. The parents of girls of the 1950s and 1960s grew up in a society where the horse had become obsolete in the working world and was regarded as a luxury, only for the leisured classes. They knew nothing about horses themselves and found it hard to understand their daughters' passions. The girls' growing expertise in an area of which they had little or no knowledge intensified the gap between them. This was a part of their children's lives they could not control and parents still took it for granted they had to be in control. Such tensions between parents and daughters were reflected in pony stories. As late as 1981, the warnings of Elaine's father in *Eventers' Dream* about a riding career are ignored:

> "He wasted no opportunity to remind me that in his opinion, the horse world had nothing to offer but low pay, bleak prospects, and broken promises." (Akrill 1981, p. 21)

By the 1960s, girls were becoming such a fixture in stables and the show ring that when David Smith, working-class hero of several of Christine Pullein-Thompson's books, told his mother he wanted to start a riding school, she objected: "I don't call it a real job. Not a man's job" (Pullein-Thompson 1957, p. 5). The hard work rather than the glamour of the job is stressed by modern writers, and there are even rumblings of discontent that the massive influx of women into the world of horses was downgrading the job, keeping wages low, and allowing owners to exploit the cheap labour. Nick Foster, in *Eventer's Dream* (1981), put the blame fairly and squarely on the girls themselves:

> "You girl grooms moan about being underpaid and overworked, but it's your own fault, you let yourselves be exploited all the way along.

> You're fools. . . . There is money in the horse world, but people have
> got used to having horse-mad girls on tap for cheap labour, it's going to
> take them a long time to learn that if they want a decent groom they
> have to pay a decent wage, even if it means they have to keep fewer
> horses." (pp. 104–5)

It is ironic that in winning their fight for independence, getting the
job they desired so passionately, female heroes of pony books found
themselves in a different kind of slavery, indentured by their love for
horses.

ANIMAL PASSIONS

Pony stories are, after all, love stories—girl meets pony, girl loses pony,
girl gets pony. But why ponies? There is no simple answer, rather a series
of suppositions. First, of course, ponies are animals and almost all children love stories about animals, particularly adolescents between the
ages of ten and fourteen. "Boys tend to prefer the animal story about the
wild and primitive beast in nature . . . while girls like the animal dependent upon human beings," wrote G. Robert Carlsen (Carlsen 1980, p.
24). Librarian, Bernard Poll suggests:

> The horse is a larger mammal with whom the child can identify, one
> with whom he can rest with utter security . . . Horses are better [than
> dogs] because they are larger, stronger and more powerful. They over-
> whelm with their strength and love, or are felt to do so by children.
> (Poll 1961, pp. 473–4)

The size, power, and physical beauty of the horse do seem to be key factors in their effect on adolescent girls. They are objects of desire for
young teenagers who can channel turbulent and often difficult emotions
safely into their passion for ponies. In the formula pony book, the girl is
central character with the pony filling an ambiguous role, one that is
closer to the traditional heroine who is often both victim and object of
desire. The desire is not gender-specific, for the ponies can be stallions,
mares, or geldings; their appeal is androgynous. They are not completely
personified but they are treated as three-dimensional characters and their
physical appearance and personality are described in great detail. The
more satisfying the book, the more powerful the equine character, and
the difficult ponies, like Enid Bagnold's "The Pie," K. M. Peyton's

"Darkling," and Patricia Leitch's "Shantih" are as memorable as the difficult heroes and heroines of fiction—Heathcliff, Maxim de Winter, Becky Sharp. Their beauty is described from the female perspective, reversing the classic tradition of romantic novels where women are seen through the male gaze. Sara, in *Prince Among Ponies,* says, on first seeing the "prince":

> "It's one of those heads that are so beautiful that it makes you feel queer to look at them."
> "It doesn't make me feel queer,"

says her brother Patrick sensibly (Pullein-Thompson 1952, p. 18).

Primrose Cumming, explaining to me why girls love ponies, put it succinctly: "Bossing big things." Controlling a large and powerful animal, the girl is learning to control the powerful emotions she is beginning to feel in her adolescence. Animal characters have commonly been used instead of humans to help children confront difficult questions of life and mortality, and it has become a cliché that the horse or pony replaces the male in books as sex object. The horse, mounted by a rider, has a closer physical relationship with a human than any other animal, a point not lost on George Eliot's ascetic heroine Dorothea Brooke, in *Middlemarch,* who regarded riding as an indulgence: "She felt that she enjoyed it in a pagan sensuous way, and always looked forward to renouncing it." Marghanita Laski is one of many writers to comment on the "obvious sexual symbolism" of pony stories. Tongue in cheek, she writes: "I am sure there is no conscious . . . wish to substitute for a passive sexual role an active one, for the human male, the horse that can be ridden and controlled" (Laski 1959, pp. 483–5). In Laski's interpretation, pony books, like other children's books, can help generalise experience. The adolescent girl can interpret her own new sensations and emotions: " 'It means,' she can thankfully reassure herself, 'that I want a horse' " (ibid.).

Other critics categorically assert that girls are quite unaware that they are transferring feelings of sexuality to the ponies. When Bernard Poll insists: "Those needs on the part of children which horse stories may tend to fulfill, are certainly not conscious," he is—unconsciously, perhaps—reinforcing the reluctance of adults to recognise a child has certain emotions and needs. Bruno Bettelheim is even more alarmist:

> Psychoanalytic investigation has revealed that over-involvement in and with horses can stand for many different emotional needs which the

girl is trying to satisfy. For example, by controlling this powerful animal she can come to feel that she is controlling the male, or sexually animalistic, within herself. Imagine what it would do to a girl's enjoyment of riding, to her self-respect, if she were made conscious of this desire which she is acting out in riding. She would be devastated—robbed of a harmless and enjoyable sublimation, and reduced in her own eyes to a bad person. (Bettelheim 1991, p. 56–7)

I would suggest that girls, as riders and readers, are made of stronger stuff than this. Rather than suppressing the male animal within herself, she is learning to assert herself as the equal of males. Astride a horse, a girl becomes powerful and gains self-esteem in the process. However strong and difficult the horse is to ride, the girl is the dominant partner in the relationship, mastering him by love and patience. She has chosen the horse, she has bought him, or rescued him. When the girl in the pony story sets her eyes on the pony for the first time, her reaction is immediate and possessive, "the pony must be mine." Even the titles of pony stories echo this new assertiveness—*I Wanted a Pony, I Had Two Ponies, A Pony of Our Own, Janet Must Ride.* At last, it is the girl who is saying what she wants, not what society wants for her.

Josephine Pullein-Thompson, too, rejects the notion that the horse is a sex object: "On the whole, the ordinary girl goes into riding and caring for horses simply to have a lovely living thing to nurture." G. Robert Carlsen points out: "In real life, what is more gratifying than having an animal dependent on one for food, care and affection? This feeling emanates vicariously in books" (Carlsen 1980, pp. 63–4). This maternal desire may be as strong as sexual desire. Horses, despite their strength, are vulnerable, prey to diseases, liable to be exploited and treated badly, and thus in need of protection. The sight of a neglected pony has driven numerous female heroes in pony stories to extraordinary lengths to rescue them, and restore them to health. Shy Georgie, in *A Pony of Your Own,* is happy to look after a sick pony and a neglected donkey even though she is terrified of horses; Brenda finds courage to outface her whole village community and rescue the starving racehorse in *Come Down the Mountain;* Ros, in *Poor Badger,* steals a badly treated pony in order to save it. Rescue and restoration are among the most potent themes of this genre. Monica Dickens's popular Follyfoot series, about a home for aged and neglected horses, is constantly in print, and one of the few new series of pony books, *Hollywell Stables,* has an identical story line.

The female hero, who is resolutely uninterested in traditionally fem-

inine tasks such as housework, fashion, and make-up, derives deep satisfaction from rising early to muck out and groom her pony, plan its diet
and clean its tack. This is an aspect of horses that girls enjoy more than
boys. In *The Team*, Jonathan tells Ruth he would not ride much if he had
to "do" the pony himself.

> "I like the doing part," Ruth said.
> "Jess [his sister] does too. Perhaps it's a female thing."
> "Could be. Like housework. Only girls aren't supposed to want to
> be like that any more, are they?" (Peyton 1975, p. 46)

But the girl is more than just the stereotyped "carer." When she rescues
the pony she is taking over the traditional role of the hero rescuing the
damsel in distress. She is also taking over responsibility for it. Sometimes this can become a burden. Jenny, in *Darkling*, is the only one who
can control a difficult colt, and she is weighed down by the responsibility
of his love for her. In the end she learns the lesson of all parents: "He will
have to learn to do without me" (Peyton 1991, p. 237). In the relationship
between girl and pony, the seeds of the adult relationships the girls will
have to cope with are sown. The ponies who are difficult, untrainable,
unlovable, neglected, sick, or old, test all the reserves of love and persistence these girls will need in later life.

Selina, in *Mr McFadden's Hallowe'en*, loves the cross-grained, bad-
mannered pony Haggis with fierce loyalty and, like many a girl in love,
transforms him into her own hero:

> Nobody knew what Haggis could become when he and Selina were
> alone: then she was Dick Turpin and he Black Bess, or he was the
> White Stallion, or a horse that danced in the circus, Selina his top-hat-
> ted rider, or he was the Queen's Charger and she the Queen at the
> Trooping the Colour; he was even the horse with wings that only a poet
> can ride . . . (Godden 1975, p. 20)

But Selina loves him for what he is, rather than what he could be, and she
does not try to change him, an extraordinarily mature attitude for an
eight-year-old.

The relationship between diffident female hero and difficult, fascinating horse is at the heart of most pony books and has obvious correla-
tions to human relationships in adult romances. Few pony books venture
into these dangerous areas. It is touched upon at the end of *Dream of Fair*

Horses. Obsessed with winning the Horse of the Year Show with the show pony Perdita, Gill learns the hard lesson that she must let the mare go to a better home. "We can possess nothing but ourselves," her father tells her. "Learn it now and you won't grow up thinking that other people can be possessed and owned" (Leitch 1975, p. 185). She does learn and at the end of the book is setting out for life in a Scottish community with her boyfriend, turning her back on "the desperate possession and the empty success."

K. M. Peyton is one of the very few writers who tackles real adolescent problems in pony books by following her characters' lives through subsequent books. Her young heroine, Ruth Hollis, naturally transfers her love of ponies to love for a man as she grows up and leaves her teenage obsessions behind. We first meet Ruth in *Fly-by-Night* (1968), as a pony-mad eleven-year-old, who typifies but transcends all pony book girls. She is a worrier, lacking in confidence but with a steely determination, looking at the horsey world from the sidelines—envying "children on ponies with parents in suede jackets" (p. 11). *Fly-by-Night,* and *The Team,* centre on her powerful love for two strong, temperamental ponies, Fly and the brilliant Toadhill Flax, to which her tentative relationships with boys take second place. In *The Beethoven Medal,* she is an intense sixteen-year-old, still yearning to work with horses when she leaves school but already falling in love with the difficult and brilliant Patrick Pennington (central character of several of K. M. Peyton's books) and this relationship leads to early motherhood and marriage in *Pennington's Heir.* In a moment of self-revelation, Ruth realises that she loves Pat because of his unpredictable and volatile personality:

> She had always been attracted by difficulties. Both her ponies had been difficult, not ready-schooled, well-mannered animals like Gordon Hargreaves, but prickly uncertain creatures with wild pasts. (Peyton 1971, p. 63)

Peyton shows Ruth moving naturally from ponies to boys, losing her interest in riding in a way inconceivable to the earlier pony book girls. Caroline Akrill can also handle relationships between girls, ponies, and boys, particularly in *Flying Changes* (1985) with its fascinating anti-hero Oliver. However, the problem of sex is still not confronted in the few contemporary pony stories being published now, because they tend to be aimed at younger readers, like Patricia Leitch's Kestrels series.

After a brief resurgence in the 1980s, the genre seems to have passed its peak, although interest in riding is probably greater now than it has ever been. There are about three million riders and more horses (about 750,000) than at the outbreak of World War I, but political correctness seems to have put a curb on the books that have always been perceived as middle class and élitist, despite the large number of working-class and impoverished families featured in the stories. Two of the key motifs of the genre also have lost their attraction: foxhunting faces fierce opposition, mainly from the young, and showjumping, made popular by television like other minority sports, became stale through over-coverage. Perhaps most significant of all, the adolescent girls who were entirely responsible for the popularity of the genre are reading less and the novelty of books written for young girls, about young girls, and often by young girls, which placed the female hero at the centre of the action, has worn off. Teenagers of the 1990s have less need for a female hero who excels on equal terms in a testing, physical sport and is responsible for the care, training, and transformation of a large, living being. Pony book girls, however, did have a considerable impact on a generation of adolescents growing up after the war, showing them that girls could—perhaps—be reborn in the saddle.

NOTES

1. G. K. Chesterton's *Orthodoxy,* quoted by Bruno Bettelheim in *The Uses of Enchantment,* [1976] Penguin 1991, p 64.

2. Andrea Dworkin's *Woman Hating,* quoted in Jack Zipes *Don't Bet on the Prince: Contemporary Feminist Fairy Tales in North America and England,* Aldershot: Gower 1986, p. 5.

3. Quoted in Joanna Trollope's *Britannia's Daughters: Women of the British Empire,* Hutchinson 1983.

4. Quoted in *Plain Tales from the Raj* (edited by Charles Allen, originally broadcast on BBC Radio 4 in 1974), published by Futura.

5. Interview with author, 6 June 1993.

6. For example: "Women in jodhpurs with boots and spurs and a little whip in their hand . . . it shows the outline of their bum and their legs. I think it's quite sexy." Michael Mac talking in a documentary on showjumping, "Jumpers," *Cutting Edge,* on Channel 4 Television, 20 February 1995.

7. This echoes a remark by Primrose Cumming in an interview with me (6 December 1994): "When I saw my first pony I said, 'I'm not going to get married

and have children. I'm going to have ponies. I knew my poor mother gave up her lovely horses for us and I wasn't going to do that.' "

8. "Why bosses have to do their own dirty work," *Daily Telegraph,* 19 April 1995, p. 15. The article reports a shortage of girl grooms who are actually prepared to muck out and do the dirty work, a backlash after the years of exploitation of horse-mad girls by many stable owners.

9. The first advertisement for the Bodley Head *Careers Books for Girls* appeared in the *Times Literary Supplement* in June 1953. Information from Deborah Philips and Ian Haywood.

BIBLIOGRAPHY

Fiction

Akrill, Caroline. *Eventer's Dream.* London: Arlington Books, 1981
———. *Flying Changes.* London: Arlington Books, 1985.
Alexander, Samantha. *Hollywell Stables* series. London: Macmillan Children's Books, 1995.
Bagnold, Enid. *National Velvet.* London: Heinemann, 1935.
Boden, Hilda. *One More Pony.* London: Adam & Charles Black, 1952.
Bryant, Bonnie *The Saddle Club* series. New York: Bantam Books, (1986 onwards).
Cannan, Joanna. *A Pony for Jean.* London: John Lane, The Bodley Head, 1936.
———. *I Wrote a Pony Book.* London: Collins, 1950.
Cumming, Primrose. *Doney.* London: Country Life, 1934.
———. *The Silver Eagle Riding School.* London: Adam & Charles Black, 1938.
Dickens, Monica. *Cobbler's Dream.* London: Michael Joseph, 1963.
Edwards, Monica. *Rennie Goes Riding.* London: The Bodley Head, 1956.
Farley, Walter. *The Black Stallion.* Random House, 1941.
Ferguson, Ruby. *Jill's Gymkhana.* London: Hodder & Stoughton, 1949.
Gervaise, Mary. *A Pony of Your Own.* London: Lutterworth Press, 1950.
Godden, Rumer. *Mr McFadden's Hallowe'en.* London: Macmillan, 1975.
Golden Gorse (Muriel Wace). *Moorland Mousie.* London: Country Life, 1929.
Heath, Veronica. *Susan's Riding School.* London: Chatto & Windus, 1956.
Hull, Katharine & Whitlock, Pamela. *The Far-Distant Oxus.* London: Cape, 1937.
James, Will. *Smoky the Cowhorse.* New York: Scribner, 1926.
Leitch, Patricia. *A Horse for the Holidays,* published as *Janet—Young Rider.* London: Constable, 1963.
———. *Dream of Fair Horses.* London: Collins, 1975.

————. *For Love of a Horse*. London: Armada, 1976.

————. *Night of the Red Horse*. London: Armada, 1978.

Memoirs of Dick, the little poney: supposed to be written by himself; and published for the instruction and amusement of little masters and mistresses. London: printed for J. Walker and sold by E Newbery, 1800.

Montgomery, Rutherford. *The Capture of the Golden Stallion*. Boston: Little Brown, 1951.

O'Hara, Mary. *My Friend Flicka*. London: Eyre & Spottiswoode, 1943.

Peyton, K. M. (as Kathleen Herald). *Sabre, the Horse from the Sea*. London: A. & C. Black, 1948.

————. *Fly-by-Night*. London: Oxford University Press, 1968.

————. *The Beethoven Medal*. London: Oxford University Press, 1971.

————. *Pennington's Heir*. London: Oxford University Press, 1973.

————. *The Team*. London: Oxford University Press, 1975.

————. *Darkling*. London: Doubleday, 1989.

————. *Poor Badger*. London: Doubleday, 1990.

Pullein-Thompson, Christine. *The Second Mount*. London: Burke, 1957.

Pullein-Thompson, Diana. *Three Ponies and Shannan*. London: Collins, 1947.

Pullein-Thompson, Josephine. *Six Ponies*. London: Collins, 1946.

————. *Prince of Ponies*. London: Collins, 1952.

Seaby, Allen W. *Skewbald the New Forest Pony*. London: A. & C. Black, 1923.

————. *Exmoor Lass, and other Pony Stories*. London: A. & C. Black, 1928.

Sewell, Anna. *Black Beauty*. Norfolk, 1877.

Smith, Vian. *Come Down the Mountain*. London: Constable Young Books, 1967.

Smythe, Pat. *Jacqueline Rides for a Fall*. London: Cassell, 1957.

Steinbeck, John. *The Red Pony*. London: Heinemann, 1933 (first appeared in the *North American Review*, 1949).

Literary criticism and non-fiction

Bagnold, Enid. *Autobiography*. London: Heinemann, 1969.

Belotti, Elena Gianini. *Little Girls: Social conditioning and its effects on the stereotypical role of women during infancy* (Intro. Margaret Drabble). London: Writers and Readers Publishing Cooperative, 1975.

Bettelheim, Bruno. *The Uses of Enchantment*. Thames & Hudson, Great Britain, 1976.

Carlsen, G. Robert. *Books and the Teenage Reader*. New York: Harper and Row, 1980.

Chernin, Kim. *The Hungry Self: Women, Eating and Identity*. New York: Times Books, 1985.

Kirkpatrick, D. L. (ed.) *Twentieth Century Children's Writers*. London: Macmillan, 1978.
Marwick, Arthur. *British Society since 1945*. London: Penguin, 1990.
Marchant, Brigadier-General T. H. S. "The Future of the Horse," in *The Book of the Horse,* ed. Brian Vesey-Fitzgerald. London: Nicholson and Watson, 1946.
Smith, Vian. *Parade of Horses*. London: Longman, 1970.
Tucker, Nicholas. *The Child and the Book.* Cambridge University Press, 1981.

Periodicals and Journalism

Birks, John. "Horses in Books," *The Junior Bookshelf,* December 1946, 10, No 4: 166–72.
Laski, Marghanita. "Horse, A Horse," *Twentieth Century,* CLXVI (1959): 483–85.
Lean, Geoffrey. "Horsiculture curbed to save countryside," *Independent on Sunday,* 3 July 1994: 8.
Poll, Bernard. "Why Children like Horse Stories," *Elementary English.* No 7: 38, November 1961: 473–4.
Strickland, Charlene. "Equine Fiction in the 1980s," *SLI School Library Journal,* 32: 10, August 1986: 36–7.
Treadgold, Mary. "For the Love of Horses," *Books for Your Children.* Spring 1982 17:1: 16–17.
Tyler, Lisa. "Food, Femininity, and Achievement: the mother-daughter relationship in *National Velvet,*" *Children's Literature Association Quarterly.* Winter 1993–4, 18:4: 154–8.

Seminar and Interviews

"Careers Stories for Girls in the 1950s." Deborah Philips and Ian Haywood, workshop at Children's Literature Conference, Roehampton, October 1993.
Interview with Josephine Pullein-Thompson, 6 June 1993.
Interview with editor in children's department of HarperCollins Publishers, May 1994.
Correspondence with Patricia Leitch, 3 October 1994.
Interview with K. M. Peyton, 20 November 1994.
Interview with Diana Pullein-Thompson, 29 November 1994.
Interview with Primrose Cumming, 6 December 1994.

Girls' Own Stories
Good Citizenship and Girls in British Postwar Popular Culture

DEBORAH PHILIPS

The popular image of the happy housewife "heroine" of the 1950s has become a fixed representation of femininity in the post-war period. But images of a woman thrilled with her fridge and family were constructed, it must be remembered, as advertising images.[1] That imagining of the 1950s woman should not be taken as representative of the aspirations of women and of girls in the post-war reconstruction. Images of heroines in fiction and in magazines can no more be taken as "authentic" representations of women's lives in the period, but the heroine in forms of popular culture produced by and for women suggest a language of female ambition that has been largely written out of accounts of the 1950s. Popular fictions often can be read as representations of aspirational fantasies and those written for young women and for girls in post-war Britain suggest that their ambitions extended a long way beyond hearth and home.

The "Woman Question" was very much on the agenda for the post-war reconstruction; it is a discourse that can be traced in official documents such as government reports on work, housing and health, and in education policy. The notion of woman as "citizen" also informs popular culture and impacts upon the heroines of fiction and magazines addressed to women and to girls. If, before the war, "education for citizenship" had been a concept almost exclusively addressed to men,[2] in the post-war reconstruction, it now had to include women, too. The incursion of women into the workforce during the war, and into forms of work that would have been previously denied them,[3] had reshaped the social and labour landscape of Britain after 1945:

73

In Britain, rates of female employment were higher in the post-war period than they had been for a century. Virtually all single women
worked in the 1950s and 1960s. Although the percentage of employed
married women declined immediately after the war, the figure rose
again during the 1950s. (Tilly & Scott 1978, p. 214)

In response to an economic survey of 1947, which demonstrated that
the labour force fell substantially short of that required for national production targets, the Ministry of Labour appealed to women who were in
a position to do so to enter the workforce, and recommended that em-
ployers should adjust conditions of employment to suit women workers.
This formal exhortation to women to work is expressed in government
documents on education and employment and it is also very much present in contemporary stories for young women and for girls.

One such official articulation of the shift in perspectives on gender is
to be found in a 1954 study entitled *The Education of Women for Citizenship,* written for the United Nations. The fact that the study was commissioned at all reflects contemporary concerns with the "proper" education
of young women within a post-war consensus:

As more and more women go out to work, it becomes essential to think
of the workplace as one of the learning-situations in a woman's life and
do our best to see that it teaches the right lessons. Teachers, welfare
and personnel officers, politicians and ordinary working women are all
concerned.[4]

It was not only these middle-class professionals who were "concerned"; popular fiction for young women was as committed as any other
form of culture to "teach the right lessons." The expectations and demands on femininity of the post-war "New Jerusalem" could often be
conflicting, requiring that women should simultaneously sustain the traditional values of femininity, and that they should articulate the "modernity" of the post-1945 welfare state. As Elizabeth Wilson has pointed out:

Women's traditional role as a stabilizing and civilizing force—the ideology of the Victorians—was made a lynchpin of consensus now that
women too were citizens. (Wilson 1980, p. 10)

Although women were expected to maintain "traditional" values,
their participation as citizens in the new democracy is celebrated in offi-

cial discourses and in popular culture as properly modern and progressive. The heroine of popular fiction for women, in adult romances and
in books and comics for girls, has to manage and to reconcile these conflicting ideologies of tradition and modernity. The recurrent heroine of
the Mills and Boon romance novel of the 1950s is the "Bachelor Girl,"
the young single woman poised on the edge of both a career and of romance; a young woman who simultaneously combines the qualities appropriate to both a responsible working woman and wife and mother.
The work ethic is not restricted to fictions for adult women: Forms of
popular narrative addressed to young girls, the next generation of the
"New Look" woman, also emphasise work and social responsibility as
necessary components in the proper journey into adulthood. The new
language of "citizenship" involved responsibility as well as opportunity,
and clearly demanded of women a willingness to contribute to the working world.

The working woman and citizen becomes a central concept in a contemporary ideal of British femininity, and therefore in the construction of
the heroine in popular fiction. The newly democratic and socially responsible heroine finds her way into romance novels for adults, and also
into a host of novels written for younger women, whose heroines are celebrations of female ambition.

Noel Streatfeild is the most familiar name among a great number of
women writers who wrote novels and stories that represented a new
genre of fiction for young women, and whose fictional heroines were engaged in exciting and glamorous pursuits: ballet, acting, journalism,
showjumping, and iceskating. Streatfeild did not confine herself to writing novels; she also edited a range of volumes directly concerned with
contemporary forms of femininity, such as *The Years of Grace* (1950)
and *Growing Up Gracefully* (1955), which were books of etiquette and
advice for the young girl of the 1950s. Of the five sections of *The Years of
Grace*, "You," "Your Home," "Leisure," "Sport," and "Careers," the most
substantial is the last one, which includes music, film making, teaching,
the civil service, nursing, and farming among the potential careers for its
readers. Even those sections dealing with personal rather than professional matters are not immune from the work ethic; the section "Your
Home," for example, includes an article on cookery that ends with a list
of suggestions of how to employ these skills professionally. There were
also profiles of (real) successful working women, like Mary Grieve, editor of *Woman*, then the largest selling magazine in the United Kingdom.
There is a clear assumption throughout *The Years of Grace* that the

young reader will grow up to enter the world of work, as Streatfeild's introductory poem indicates:

> *What are you going to do my girl,*
> *Now that the time is near*
> *When away on wings*
> *Flutter childish things*
> *And you have to choose a career? (p. 1)*

Although the 1955 *Growing Up Gracefully* is a manual largely concerned with manners and morality, and concludes with a chapter on marriage and weddings, there is also a section concerned with "Manners At Work," which not only assumes that readers will be working women, but ends with a ringing endorsement of female ambition: ". . . remember you won't always be at the bottom, we hope the day may come when you are the employer" (p. 286).

Ballet, which Streatfeild had written about in perhaps her most fondly remembered novel, *Ballet Shoes* (1936), features prominently in *The Years of Grace,* both as a potential career, and as a pleasurable hobby. Streatfeild continued to champion ballet as an appropriate form of activity for young girls throughout the 1950s, in volumes such as her 1959 *Noel Streatfeild's Ballet Annual.* The ballerina is the most frequently evoked heroine in fiction for young girls, in novels such as Lorna Hill's *Veronica at the Wells,* and in comic strips, as in the regular "Belle of the Ballet" storyline of *Girl* magazine. Ballet is perhaps the form of physical training that most successfully mediates the conflict between the old and new demands upon a contemporary femininity; it requires considerable professional dedication, demanding both physical skill and artistic ability, while the ballerina continues to uphold a traditionally "feminine" construct of grace and beauty.

Lalla and Harriet, the heroines of Streatfeild's 1951 novel *White Boots,* "grow up gracefully" both literally and figuratively through their dedication to an activity not dissimilar to ballet, ice skating. As heroines, they are dramatizations of the ideal of femininity recommended in manuals such as *The Years of Grace.* Ice skating is not, however, represented in the text as merely a childhood hobby, a pastime that will enhance their feminine attributes, but as a serious and demanding occupation; the two heroines are quite clearly poised at the end of the novel to take their sporting skills into an adult professionalism.

The decade of the 1950s saw the beginning of a new genre of fiction for young adults, and particularly for young women. The "career novel" launched a spate of novels whose narratives take a fictional heroine through the trials and tribulations of a range of careers. These are novels written by professional women for girls, and the career story can be understood as a site of the negotiation of a new social construction of femininity. The narratives are all about the initiation of young women into the world of work; although they centre around a fictional heroine progressing through a fictional company, they read as instruction manuals, including as they do the details of grants and application procedures for a range of career structures. Bodley Head launched its series of the *Bodley Head Career Novel for Girls* in 1953; each novel uses a heroine's progress through her chosen profession as a thinly disguised careers advice book on the structures of work in such professions as Floristry and Hairdressing. Chatto and Windus followed in 1954 with its series of *Mary Dunne Career Novels,* which included a much broader range of careers for women, among them broadcasting, social work, and librarianship.

The forms of work that the heroines pursue in these career novels are not restricted to the glamorous and "feminine" pursuits that tend to feature in other fictions for girls, such as the theatre, ice skating, and ballet. The *Batsford Career Books* series, launched in 1959, featured heroines embarking on lives in advertising, commerce, electronics, engineering, and hotel keeping. The volumes in such "career book" series are full-scale novels, but "career stories" featuring a working heroine also are regular features of short stories and magazine articles for girls. Mary Bolton's *Modern Careers for Girls,* and *Jeanne Heal's Book of Careers for Girls,* both published in 1957, are only two among many published compendiums of short stories and articles that use both forms to advise young women of their career opportunities and how to pursue them.

The story of ambition and achievement for girls was also a regular feature of comics for young women. The comic for girls (like popular romance fiction for adult women readers) has tended to be a despised and neglected form of culture, a set of lost narratives. However, the heroines of the comic strip for young girls offer a construction of a "femininity," which articulates the contradictions and expectations of a contemporary ideal of womanhood. The girl's comic also represents a form of culture that is almost exclusively read by girls and, to a very large extent, written by women.

Richard Hoggart, one of many contemporary critics who decried the influence of the American "comic" on young people, writes disparagingly of young readers experiencing "a passive visual taking-on of bad mass-art geared to a very low mental age" (Hoggart 1958, p.165). Hoggart describes the growth of the comic strip form in popular culture as an infection striking at the heart of an "authentic" British Youth culture:

> The "strips" spread like a rash, from the bottom corner of the back page through all the inner pages, take over a page of their own and still crop up here and there elsewhere. There has to be some verbal guidance to the action, but descriptive comment is kept to a minimum: the aim is to ensure that all necessary background information is contained in the dialogue which bubbles out of the characters' mouths. (p. 164)

If Hoggart had deigned to look at the equivalent form for young women, he would have found that, while magazines for girls were increasingly employing the comic strip format, the "dialogue which bubbles out of the characters' mouths" was not exclusively in the interests of furthering the narrative action. What Hoggart and other critics of the genre[5] failed to acknowledge was that the "bubbles" of the English comic strip were, in the ethos of the post-war reconstruction, being put to socially useful purposes.

The contents of girls' comics of the mid-1950s were hardly written for a passive readership; each title carried a number of regular articles full of injunctions to make things, to take up hobbies, and to become involved in the community. *School Friend* was first published in 1950, and produced a range of publications on Pets and Hobbies to supplement its weekly comic. *Girl* magazine followed in 1952, and led to a range of publications addressed to young women, including the *Girl Book of Modern Adventurers* (1952) and the *Girl Book of Hobbies* (1958). The 1955 *Girl Annual* includes along with its stories and "story strips" substantial sections on "Nature," "Hobbies," and "Interests," all of which were regular features in the weekly magazine.

In such magazines, the comic strips themselves were often employed to introduce girls to the new possibilities that the post-war reconstruction offered women. *Girl* magazine published a weekly career comic "strip," later collected in the 1957 *I Want To Be . . . A Girl Book of Careers*. As the introduction explains, the weekly comic strip had proved so popular that the strips were collected together in a permanent form. The language of the introductory essay, written by two careers "experts" with strings of qualifications after their names, clearly articulates a new awareness of citizenship for women, and exhorts girls to consider forms of work beyond the traditional expectations for femininity:

> The aim of many girls, when they leave school is to take up work
> which will be "useful" in one way or another when they get married.
> This is a good thing to do, but sometimes it leads to a great many possi-
> ble careers being overlooked . . . (Rodger and Cavanagh 1957, p. 8)

Girl comic clearly saw itself as a regular forum for careers advice: Readers of the *Girl Book of Careers* were encouraged by the (male) editor to
write to him for information about any career in which they were interested (p. 5).

The strip stories that followed, featured young heroines embarking
on a variety of careers, negotiating interviews, exploring training opportunities and grants and assessing the necessary qualifications. The speech
"bubbles" of both the compilation and the regular *Girl* career comic strip
contained practical and sensible advice about how girls could best pre-
pare themselves for their chosen profession. Some of these stories, but
by no means the majority, focussed on traditionally "feminine" occupations, in such fields as secretarial work, nursing, domestic science, sales,
beauty, and fashion. However, even those professions that might appear
to offer limited scope are presented as opportunities for the development
of female ambition: the secretary's story, for example, is introduced with
the rider:

> The secretary's career must not be regarded as a last resort for girls
> who cannot decide what to do . . . it may lead to a career in business,
> journalism and many other professions. Many successful business
> women started as secretaries, and from there seized all opportunities
> for promotion. (*A Girl Book of Careers*, p. 10)

If the *Girl Book of Careers* does feature many of the expected careers for
women, many more of the stories are concerned with those professions
that would have been considered as a male preserve before the war. The
strips also feature heroines embarking on careers as doctors, dentists,
farmers, bankers, radiographers, chemists, journalists, and managers. In
fact, the young adulthood of these heroines is more concerned with the
pursuit of personal ambition than with love and romance; men are present in the world of work, but peripheral to the heroine's professional
life. The heroine of the story, "I want to be a Fashion Artist," is typical in
her selection of priorities: The final frame shows a young man inviting
her out on a date, while her speech bubble reads: "I'm sorry, Simon, I'm
off to Paris in the morning" (*A Girl Book of Careers*, p. 51).

Such an emphasis on the world of work and on future careers for young women also informs other kinds of stories and articles in comics: The heroine of the 1951 *Girls' Crystal Annual*'s first story (which is illustrated, rather than in strip form) is "Julie—Girl Reporter." Julie not only beats her male rival to a journalistic scoop, but simultaneously rescues an internationally famous novelist from a kidnap attempt.[6]

The majority of stories, whether in comic strip form or illustrated, are structured around the achievement of a young heroine in the context of sporting or physical prowess, or some form of contribution to the community. The *Girls' Crystal Annual* also features heroines who have rescued animals from death or exploitation, or have retrieved lost and valuable objects. These are narratives that can be read as a form of *bildungsroman* for the girl on the edge of adulthood, in which a young woman is shown to devote herself to the acquisition of professional skills (healthy forms of physical activity, ballet, tennis, horse-riding, and sailing predominate) and through her dedication achieves greater wisdom. In the post-war context, the heroine's maturity is signalled through a recognition by the adult community of her qualities of responsible "citizenship."

The stories in comics and in their Annual compilations repeatedly stress that physical or creative abilities should not be limited to the achievement of personal glory, but should be directed to a common good. The heroine in "Belle of the Ballet," who demonstrates a talent for ballet, does not merely steal the end-of-term show, but uses her skills to find a home for an orphan.[7] The horse-riding heroine of "Susan's Ride" turns her abilities to fetching a doctor in a gale, and so saves the lives of her father and brother,[8] while the heroine of "Sally and the Tipper" uses her cycling speed to rescue a building site from fire and is thus granted an opportunity to become a civil engineer.[8]

Whatever the heroine's achievement in the narrative, the final frame is a recurrent trope, in which the heroine is awarded a prize for both her abilities and for her sense of social duty. She may be rewarded by a cup, a cheque, a place in a drama school, or ballet company; the precise nature of the reward is less significant than is the nature of its presentation. The stories recurrently end with a public acknowledgement of the heroine's achievement when she is commended by an official representative of the community (often, but importantly not always, a male figure): a mayor, head teacher, police officer, or doctor. She is thus welcomed into the wider adult world, her status as a new citizen civically acknowledged and rewarded.

The stories and articles in comics and in Annuals repeatedly feature working women, both contemporary and historical. There is a consistent celebration of female achievement, often in the guise of historical or geographical articles. The 1955 *Girl Annual* includes a section of five "real life stories" celebrating famous women of the past and present; among them is the (actually fictional) career story: "Passports to Stardom" about a young woman winning the gold medal at drama school.[10]

Comics such as *Schoolgirl, Girl's Crystal,* and *Girl* foreground the contemporary possibilities for young women, and celebrate female achievements. As in novels such as *White Boots* and *Ballet Shoes,* their heroines tend to inhabit an almost exclusively all-female world. The all-girl boarding school, which is a recurrent site of school adventure stories, offers a community free from male competition or distraction, but even those stories with a domestic setting feature men hardly at all. The achieving heroine of the mid-1950s is not positioned as sexual, masculinity is a concept relegated to the margins of experience; men are occasionally glimpsed, but as irritants rather than as a significant part of life, and usually in the form of fathers and brothers.

As the 1950s progressed, however, so too did the construction of the teenager. In the early and middle years of the decade, there is little recognition in fictions for young women of any division between the pre- and post-pubescent girl (although Noel Streatfeild's *The Years of Grace* does discreetly acknowledge "changes" in the body of a young girl). The young heroine of the comic strip is represented as adolescent, but her sexual characteristics are not emphasised in illustrations as they were to be in the latter years of the 1950s, and still more in the early 1960s. If the heroine of the mid-1950s comic is depicted leaping over hurdles, negotiating rapids, and riding and swimming her way to victory, the heroine of the late 1950s and early 1960s is physically constrained. She is drawn encased in wasp waists, her breasts emphasised, and "Boys" have become increasingly prominent in the illustrations and stories. The frontispiece of the 1961 *Collins Girls' Annual* (addressed to the same age group as *Girl* and *Girls' Crystal*) no longer features, as the cover illustrations of earlier Annuals do, groups of girls enjoying their physical prowess in sprinting or mountain climbing, but a prettily attired young girl waving at a male admirer. The front and inside covers depict smiling young women carrying piles of shopping.[11]

The post-war consumer culture capitalised on the "youth" market, and particularly, on young women as consumers. The consumer boom was, in fact, driven by the increased economic power of girls, newly empowered by salaries and expressing their independence through their purchase of commodities. As Hobsbawm has pointed out:

> The British "teen-age boom" which began at this time was based on the urban concentrations of relatively well-paid girls in the expanding offices and shops, often with more to spend than the boys, and in those days less committed to the traditional male patterns of expenditure on beer and cigarettes. The boom . . . first revealed its strength in fields where girls' purchases were pre-eminent, like blouses, skirts, cosmetics and pop records . . . (Hobsbawm 1994, p. 328)

From the publication of *Mirabelle* in 1956, a host of new titles addressed to young women were founded specifically on the market recognition of the female teenage consumer, and led to a new kind of magazine and a new type of heroine. 1957 was the year which saw the first publications of teenage girls' "magazines": *Romeo, Roxy,* and *Valentine,* titles that addressed their readers not as "girls" but as sexually aware young women. *Boyfriend* and *Marty* (titled after pop star Marty Wilde) followed in 1959—the year that also saw the publication of Mark Abrams' study *The Teenage Consumer* (Abrams 1959). As Hall and Whannel pointed out in *The Popular Arts,* Abrams' research recognised the cultural impact of the newly acquired spending power of young adults, and a new demand for particular kinds of consumer products, many of which feature prominently in young women's magazines of the period:

> In 1958 [Abrams] estimated that Britain's 5,000,000 unmarried teenagers were grossing about £1,480,000,000 annually. More significant was the proportion of uncommitted or 'discretionary' spending money they had available. . . . The significant point is the high concentration of spending in certain limited fields. Nearly a quarter of that sum went on clothing and footwear (£210,000,000), another 14 per cent on drink and tobacco (£125,000,000), 12 per cent on sweets, soft drinks and snacks (£105,000,000), £40,000,000 on records, record players, papers and magazines . . . (Hall and Whannel 1964, p. 277)

The readership of *Valentine* and *Mirabelle* was clearly not that different in age from that of *Girl* and *Girls' Crystal.* For example, the letters page of *Mirabelle* carries letters from readers aged from eleven to sixteen, but their sense of themselves as young women is much more marked. The new titles, the illustrations, the stories, and their heroines clearly signal that the primary concern is with "Romance," a phenome-non that is markedly absent from earlier comics. By 1961, the *School Friend,* with its emphasis on life outside the home, had changed its title to become *June.* The young women's magazine *Honey,* first published in 1960, was a forum specifically for the promotion of fashion and beauty products.

The heroine of stories in these new magazines for young women has changed from a socially responsible and active young woman into a self-conscious creature awaiting the attentions of a boy. Illustrations, adver-tisements, and articles now represent girls experiencing the pleasures of consumption and encourage the purchase of cosmetics, fashion, and music to help the reader in her quest for romance. *Valentine* was directly linked to record promotion, its stories titled with contemporary pop lyrics. Its comic strip narratives are organised around pin-ups of the male rock stars of the 1950s, and take the form of "Picture Romances"—"in-spired by song titles." *Marty,* like *Valentine,* "Brings You Love Stories in Pictures."

"Love" (as the titles imply) is clearly more important than work, with the majority of the heroines in these stories living at home with their parents, their sights set on marriage rather than a career. The expecta-tions of what is required in a wife are clearly signalled—as one hero tells his prospective fiancee: "The kind of girl I marry's got to be interested in Cooking, Sewing, Homemaking."[12] And the heroines of these stories are happy to concur. The heroine of "Forgotten Dreams," for example, does make some stab at independence and initially rejects her boyfriend's pro-posal, telling him: "I'm young—I want to see some life before I settle down."[13] The final frame, however, sees her clasped in his arms, agreeing to marriage with the words: "Whatever you say, Darling." The 1959 "I'm Confessin' " is an extreme example, but its priorities are implicit in all these stories; it features a heroine on her wedding day, and the final caption reads: "The girl who walked out of the church that morning would be different . . . no longer a carefree tomboy but a sober married woman."[14]

The heroines of the narratives in *Girl, Girls' Crystal,* and *School-friend* were hardly "carefree tomboys," but their sights were set on more than "sober married womanhood." Their ambitions were not only for themselves; their achievements were represented as a contribution to a post-war cultural consensus that women too should be "good citizens." The girls' comic and Annuals of the mid-1950s demonstrate that repre-sentations of independent achieving girls appealed to a wide reader-ship—an appeal testified to not only by the number of readers who still remember these texts with affection, but also by their continued circulation in second hand bookshops.[15] These are images of femininity that are at odds with a received wisdom that women in the 1950s were invariably represented as domesticated and husband bound. The "career girl" heroine of novels and short stories and the comic strip heroine offered a new and modern construction of young womanhood, whose concern was to contribute her skills and abilities to the post-war reconstruction. And the generation of girls who read these stories grew up to become the young women who championed the Women's Liberation Movement of the 1960s and 1970s.

NOTES

Some of the research for this article also provided data for an article "White Boots and Ballet Shoes—Girls Growing Up in the 1950s," in *Leisure Cultures: Values, Genders, Lifestyles,* ed. Graham McFee, Wilf Murphy, and Gary Whannel. Brighton: LSA Publications, 1995.

1. See, for example, the Chicpix postcard series.

2. For an account of the concept of "citizenship" in education for young people, see "Conservatism, citizenship and the 1944 settlement," in *Unpopular Education: Schooling and social democracy in England since 1944.* Education Group: Birmingham Centre for Cultural Studies, London: Hutchinson, 1981.

3. For a brief account of women's work during the war, see Philips and Tomlinson in "Homeward Bound," in *Come On Down: Post-war Popular Culture,* eds. Strinati and Wagg. London: Routledge, 1992.

4. Tait, Marjorie, *The Education of Women for Citizenship.* Problems in Education VIII, UNESCO 1954.

5. The 1950s had seen a general public concern with the impact of the comic book on young people in both Britain and America; in 1954 the Comics Code in America was set up in response to criticisms from government and public and prompted a group of American artists to organise a convention that monitored erotic or violent content in magazines for young readers.

6. "Julie's Most Amazing Scoop," in *Girls' Crystal Annual.* London: Fleetway House, 1951, pp. 3–24.

7. "Belle of the Ballet," in *Girl Annual.* London: Hulton Press, 1955, p. 81.

8. "Susan's Ride," in *Girl Annual.* 1955, p.76

9. "Sally and the Tipper" in *Girl Annual* 1955, p. 61.

10. "Passports to Stardom" in *Girl Annual* 1955, p.19.

11. *Collins Girls' Annual,* London: Collins, 1961.

12. "Love Is a Simple Thing," in *Valentine,* 10.9.60.

13. "Forgotten Dreams," in *Valentine,* 12.12.59.

14. "I'm Confessin'," in *Mirabelle,* 19.9.59.

15. Actual readership figures are impossible to establish because many of the publishers of girls' comics and Annuals have now ceased to exist, and of those that do, the research has long since vanished.

BIBLIOGRAPHY

Abrams, Mark. *The Teenage Consumer.* London: London Press Exchange, 1959.

Bolton, Mary. *Modern Careers for Girls.* London: W. Foulsham, 1957.

Girl Book of Modern Adventurers. London: Hulton Press, 1952.

Girl Book of Hobbies. London: Hulton Press, 1958.

Girl Annual. London: Hulton Press, 1955.

Hall, Stuart & Whannel, Paddy. *The Popular Arts.* London: Hutchinson, 1964.

Heal, Jeanne. *Jeanne Heal's Book of Careers for Girls.* London: Bodley Head, 1957.

Hobsbawm, Eric. *Age of Extremes: The Short Twentieth Century 1914–1991.* London: Michael Joseph, 1994.

Hoggart, Richard. *The Uses of Literacy: Aspects of working-class life with special reference to publications and entertainments.* Harmondsworth: Penguin Books, 1958.

"I want to be . . . A Secretary," in *A Girl Book of Careers.* London: Hulton Press, 1957.

"I want to be . . . A Fashion Artist," in *A Girl Book of Careers.* London: Hulton Press, 1957.

Morley, Louise. *Anne in Electronics,* London: Chatto & Windus, 1960

Rodger, A. & Cavanagh, P. "Choosing a Career," in *I Want to Be . . . A Girl Book of Careers.* London: Hulton Press, 1957.

Streatfeild, Noel. *The Years of Grace.* London: Evans Bros., 1950.

———. *Growing Up Gracefully.* London: Barker, 1955.

———. *Ballet Shoes.* London: J. M. Dent, 1936.

———. *Noel Streatfeild's Ballet Annual.* London and Glasgow: 1959.

———. *White Boots.* London: Collins, 1951.

Tilly, Louise A. & Scott, Joan W. *Women, Work and Family.* New York: Holt, Rinehart & Winston, 1978.

Wilson, Elizabeth. *Halfway to Paradise: Women in Post-war Britain between 1945 and 1968.* London: Tavistock Publications, 1980.

More Than Crime on Her Mind

Nancy Drew as Woman Hero

LINDA K. CHRISTIAN-SMITH

"Nancy [Drew] was a girl I wanted to be—smart and free as a bird." (Sarah Crane, fifty-nine-year-old former reader of Nancy Drew mysteries of European American and middle-class background)

"I had trouble identifying with Nancy. She was rich, had all these fine clothes and a servant to do the housework. However, the stories were interesting. . . . I also admired her independent spirit." (Corla Jefferson, fifty-year-old former reader of Nancy Drew fiction of African American and middle-class background)

Who can swim, sew, drive, dance, knit, karate chop, fly a plane, or fry an egg with the same skill as solving puzzling mysteries? The multitalented individual admired by Sarah and Corla above is an eighteen-year-old girl who has been going strong for sixty-five years in her fictional hometown of River Heights, USA. Nancy Drew is the larger-than-life character featured in the more than eighty million mystery novels sold to date and translated into twenty languages (Caprio 1992; Dyer & Romalov 1995). Since her debut in 1930, this "teen queen of detectives" has served as a constant companion and role model for millions of women readers across social classes, races, sexual orientations, generations, and national boundaries. Yet there are tensions surrounding this woman hero as indicated in the memories of Corla quoted above. How can a young woman hero appeal to readers across so many social differences? In this chapter, I consider this and other issues relating to Nancy Drew by reference to textual and reader studies of Nancy Drew fiction. I begin by discussing what may seem to some to be a contradiction in terms: a woman as hero and detective.

HEROIC JOURNEYS

In children's popular fiction series in the United States, the woman hero did not frequently appear until the advent of the Stratemeyer Syndicate in the early twentieth century. Fiction featuring male heroes such as Horatio Alger, Oliver Optic, and Nick Carter regularly paraded across the popular series fiction scene. In 1908, Edward Stratemeyer organized the Stratemeyer Syndicate, the modern equivalent of a book packaging company,[1] to capitalize on the increasing demand for his adventure-action books. Runaway best sellers featuring male heroes such as The Rover Boys, Tom Swift, and the Hardy Boys were accompanied by the woman hero series, The Bobbsey Twins, Ruth Fiedling, Betty Gordon, and, of course, Nancy Drew.

Betsey Caprio (1992) suggests that Nancy Drew herself demonstrates traditional heroic qualities in the mystery stories that are structured as heroic journeys. Throughout the novels, Nancy Drew represents the epitome of male heroic qualities. She is strong, resourceful, brave, daring, admired, and engages in risky undertakings. Whereas male heroes often combine extraordinary physical strength with a keen mind, Nancy's physical strength is sufficient to extricate herself and others from danger, but she also represents characteristics not usually found in male heroes: unbounded empathy and a sense of service to others, especially in the novels of the late 1950s.

Nancy Drew fiction—like other series novels—is written to a formula, that is, characters and plot follow a predetermined outline from novel to novel (Plunkett-Powell 1993).[2] Readers are immersed in fast-paced action from the very first page. In the middle of each chapter there is what Svenson calls "a dramatic point of excitement" (as discussed in Donelson 1978, p. 26) and a cliffhanger at the end of the chapter. The last paragraph of the novel "advertises" the next volume in the series. Caprio (1992) further suggests that Nancy Drew fiction represents a particular kind of formulaic writing: the heroic quest. Drawing on folklorist Vladimir Propp, Caprio (1992, pp. 137–40) identifies four key elements of Nancy Drew's heroic journey:

1. Departure from the Known
2. The Adventures

3. A Death-like Experience
4. New Life and the Return Home

In a typical Nancy Drew mystery, Nancy goes forth from her River Heights home to solve a mystery, usually involving a lost person or article. During her quest she is aided by friends, Helen Corning and the female cousins George Fayne and Bess Marvin, as well as her father Carson Drew, and, increasingly, the housekeeper, Hannah Gruen. Nancy's adventure tests her resourcefulness as she deals with dangerous individuals who often harm her and her friends. Despite being clubbed, knocked out, and imprisoned, Nancy rebounds unscathed, solves the mystery, and restores order. This pattern is repeated with numerous variations throughout the novels to date. The heroic quest is interwoven with the classical detective fiction form identified by Klein (1988, p. 224): "the hero distinguishes between good and evil, applies approved punishment, returns to the world the feeling of security it had before the outbreak of evil."

A HEROIC GOLD MINE

Nancy Drew's literary and social class antecedents may be found in American and British popular fiction of the nineteenth and early twentieth century: domestic and gothic fiction, "dime" and detective novels, and popular children's series fiction. From this tradition, romantic and domestic motifs combined with gothic and mysterious overtones and mystery to form the Nancy Drew mystery novels.

Domestic hardship and suffering were common themes in popular "domestic novels" for young women readers during the 1800s. The domestic space, far from being a haven, became a living hell as numerous dangers plagued women heroes within homes. The gothic novel of horror and suspense developed by Ann Radcliffe in *The Mysteries of Udolpho* kept nineteenth-century women readers on both sides of the Atlantic on the edge of their chairs. Young women heroes were often terrorized in sinister manor houses and castles by even more sinister men.

Predating the appearance of Arthur Conan Doyle's Sherlock Holmes, Anna Katharine Green's amateur detective Amelia Butterworth (*The Levenworth Case,* 1878) immediately garnered the attention of American readers. Green's introduction in 1915 of a second detective, the professional Violet Strange, made possible Butterworth's strong following through the 1930s. In turn-of-the-century America, adult women detectives also appeared in inexpensive paper books called "dime novels," which emphasized action (Klein 1988, p. 31). The more popular of these were Harlan P. Halsey's Kate Goelet *The Lady Detective* and Edward L. Wheeler's (pseudonym Deadwood Dick) Nell Niblo of *New York Nell, the boy-girl detective.* In early twentieth-century England, M. M. Bodkin introduced detective Dora Myrl, the daughter of an Oxford don; Dora was educated to be a scholar and lady. When her medical education fails to quickly provide her with a practice, Myrl turns to detective work after a succession of unsatisfactory jobs. Another possible influence is Agatha Christie's Miss Marple, who made her appearance in the same year as Nancy Drew in *Murder in the Vicarage* (1930). Like Miss Marple, Nancy's web of relationships, especially with women and her father, Carson Drew, are just as instrumental in solving mysteries as her keen logic, and like Dora Myrl and Miss Marple, Nancy is privileged by class and race. These connections greatly contribute to her mystery-solving abilities.

During the early twentieth century, young women detectives were popular both in the United States and abroad. Responsible for the bulk of children's series books in the United States from 1908–82, the Stratemeyer Syndicate's girls' series books of 1913–29 paralleled boys' fiction in terms of breakneck action.[3] In the 1920s, the Syndicate offered readers four girl detectives: Ruth Fielding, Billie Bradley, Betty Gordon, and Nan Sherwood. The Blythe Girls series, beginning in 1925, featured a romance narrative with mystery subplots. According to a former Stratemeyer Syndicate partner, Nancy Axelrad, Edward Stratemeyer's motivation for developing a new female detective series may have grown out of a desire "to find a mate for the Hardy Boys" and "wanting to give children something to think about other than problems at home" (Felder 1986, p. 30). Stratemeyer also was interested in furthering sales by developing a companion series to the best-selling Hardy Boys mystery series (Plunkett-Powell 1992). English girl detectives may have influenced the Nancy Drew series as well. As early as 1922 in Britain, John W. Bobin's female sleuth, Sylvia Silence, helped her investigator father in the story paper, *Schoolgirls' Weekly.* In 1933, Bobin invented another female detective, coincidentally called Valerie Drew (Billman 1986, p. 101).

The Nancy Drew mysteries stem from this rich popular literature tradition. As the first major full-time detective in American girls' series books, Nancy Drew has displayed an amazing lasting power.

FICTIONAL FATHER AND MOTHERS

I can recall my surprise and disappointment at discovering that Nancy Drew writer, Carolyn Keene, was a pseudonym. I had long cherished a desire to meet Carolyn Keene and this desire was partially fulfilled when I was introduced to Mildred Augustine Wirt Benson at a Nancy Drew Scholars Conference. Several writers, most prominently Harriet Stratemeyer Adams and Mildred Wirt Benson, were responsible for the series. However, Wirt Benson's authorship was never publicly acknowledged until well after she testified about her role during the 1980 trial pertaining to the lawsuit brought by the Syndicate's traditional publisher, Grosset & Dunlap, against Simon and Schuster (Gulf & Western), the new publisher contracted by Harriet S. Adams. In the past, Stratemeyer Syndicate writers had to sign away their rights to their books in order to be paid.

Adams's father, Edward Stratemeyer, developed the concept of Nancy Drew and constructed a detailed outline for the first three novels, as was his practice with other series. In New York, Stratemeyer met a young woman writer, Mildred Augustine Wirt Benson, from Iowa. He asked her to turn these outlines into three books. Benson was born into a European American middle-class Iowa family in 1905. As a college-trained journalist, she had written numerous children's stories and books under her own name and a variety of pseudonyms. However, according to Wirt Benson, Edward Stratemeyer did not care for her conception of the character of Nancy Drew:

> He said the character in particular was too—too flip, she was too vivacious—she was not the namby-pamby type of heroine that had been dominating series books for many, many years. He said I had missed it and he did not think that the publisher [Grosset & Dunlap] would probably either want it or care for it (*Grosset & Dunlap* versus *Gulf & Western*, p. 117, as cited in Johnson 1955, p. 36)

Nevertheless, Grosset & Dunlap were enthusiastic about Wirt Benson's work and ordered more Nancy Drew novels. Edward Stratemeyer did not live to witness the success of the series: He died in 1930, the year Nancy Drew made her public debut in *The Secret of the Old Clock*. Benson has now been credited with writing numbers 1–7 and 11–25 in the Nancy Drew mystery series (Caprio 1992; Dyer & Romalov 1995; Plunkett-Powell 1993).[4] Like the original Nancy Drew, Benson was herself a rarity in her day: a journalist, aviator, explorer, and early commentator on women's rights (Benson 1973). To this day, she continues her journalism career with her column in *The Toledo Blade.*

Harriet Stratemeyer was born in 1894 into a financially secure family. As a woman of European descent and member of the upper-middle class, her literary ambitions were confined to writing for newsletters of her various charitable organizations and proofreading manuscripts that her father, Edward Stratemeyer, would bring home from the office. Although a graduate of Wellesley College in Massachusetts, she was not a professionally trained writer. After Edward Stratemeyer's death, Harriet S. Adams fulfilled the literary ambitions that her father had deemed unsuitable for a "proper" woman of her social class (White 1980, p. B1). She became C.E.O. of the successful Stratemeyer Syndicate. Adams continued Edward Stratemeyer's practice of supplying detailed plot outlines to ghost writers who would write book-length manuscripts for around $150.00 and keep their identities secret. Adams took the syndicate to new heights while establishing herself as a strong force in popular children's fiction publishing.

Upon assuming leadership of the syndicate, Harriet Adams had other ideas about the character of Nancy Drew. Benson relates that this may have been the roots of the conflict between the two women, which culminated when Wirt Benson refused to write for the syndicate once the book fees dropped to $75.00:

> Mrs. Adams was an entirely different person; she was more cultured and more refined; I was probably a rough-and-tumble newspaper person who had to earn a living . . . my type of Nancy was making her way in life and trying to compete and have fun along the way. We just had different kinds of Nancys. . . . (*Grosset & Dunlap* versus *Gulf & Western,* p. 232, as cited in Johnson 1995, p. 37).

The character Nancy Drew emerges, then, from the traditional and independent sides of these two women and their struggles to transcend some of the confines of the traditional femininities of the mid-twentieth century America (Christian-Smith 1991).

THE MYSTERY OF NANCY DREW: RESEARCH PARTICIPANTS AND METHODOLOGIES

The discussion of Nancy Drew as woman hero is drawn primarily from a study of the Nancy Drew series, which spans seven years from 1988 to

1996. There are three major components: a study of the major writers of Nancy Drew, Mildred Wirt Benson and Harriet Stratemeyer Adams, Edward Stratemeyer and the Stratemeyer Syndicate; a textual analysis of over one hundred Nancy Drew mysteries written from 1930 to 1993; and a pilot and full-scale study of present and past readers of Nancy Drew. I was mainly interested in accounting for the lasting power of Nancy Drew and how social subjectivities (race, enthicity, class, gender, sexuality, and age) are constructed by the Nancy Drew novels and women readers. The reader study represents twenty-three female participants, aged nine to sixty-five, drawn from the responses to an advertisement placed in a metropolitan Midwestern United States newspaper. Ten participants, aged thirteen to sixty-five, were drawn from the responses to the advertisements for a pilot study in 1990–91. The pilot study revealed a pattern of women reading Nancy Drew novels in families across generations. The full-scale study ran from October 1994 through June 1995. The original ten participants and some of their female relatives joined the full-scale study to comprise the twenty-three participants who were mostly adult women who read Nancy Drew fiction at an earlier age, as well as current preadolescent female readers. The participants came from African American and European American middle-class and working-class backgrounds.

The theoretical framework and research design combined critical feminist poststructuralist perspectives (Weedon 1987), the researcher's autobiography (Benstock 1988), aspects of feminist critical ethnography (Clifford & Marcus 1986; Lather 1991; Opie 1992), and discourse analysis (Fairclough 1989). The data from the reader studies was collected through two reading interest surveys, one aimed at current Nancy Drew readers, and the other at adult women who had read the books at an earlier stage in their lives. I conducted structured and unstructured interviews of participants individually and in groups. The interviews of adult women used oral history methods as described in Casey (1993) and Yow (1994).[5] The researcher's autobiography, reader interviews, and the Nancy Drew fiction were regarded as social texts available for analysis. Discourse analysis provides a method for closely examining these texts to discern the patterns of meaning, contradictions, and inconsistencies in language and actions.[6] Lather (1986) suggests that ethnography should help participants to understand the perspectives and ideologies that legitimate the dominant order, and break their hold on participants. While some participants developed social critiques in the course of this study, the kinds of cultural transformation that Lather envisaged did not occur.

Autobiography provided information about my background, personal biases, and social and political factors that shaped the research and interpretations (Opie 1992).[7]

WHO I AM AS A WOMAN RESEARCHER AND READER

At the time of writing, I am a woman university teacher of curriculum
and instruction and a researcher, having formerly taught language arts
and reading in schools with diverse student populations for over a
decade. I occupy contradictory class positions[8]: middle class from the
standpoint of job and economic circumstances, and working class by
birth and political affiliation. I am a second generation European American. The reading of popular fiction has figured prominently throughout
much of my life, particularly as a young woman.

I received my first Nancy Drew novel, *The Secret of Red Gate Farm*,
as a birthday gift from my beloved grandmother. I found in Nancy Drew
one of the few younger women characters who led exciting lives free
from parents' constant surveillance. As a child in the 1940s and 1950s,
there were few books in my working-class home. I learned to read before
formal schooling through the efforts of Miss Dora Staley, a neighbor
who was an elementary teacher. Miss Dora always had a basket on her
back porch that was filled with books to borrow, particularly Nancy
Drew stories.

Nancy Drew mysteries were among several books I read as I marked
time from childhood until the day I left my small northern Minnesota
hometown. Speaking at the 1993 Nancy Drew Conference at the University of Iowa, I described my reading fantasies:

> When Nancy used to speed away from River Heights in her blue
> coupé, I sat in the passenger seat. Only I was speeding away from my
> small northern Minnesota town where women's destinies were to be
> good wives and mothers. I had other ideas. Nancy gave me a sense that
> a girl could do more than be a housewife and that her skills could be
> more than cooking and doing dishes. I wanted to be a teacher. (Sun-
> stein 1995, p. 111)

In my fantasies, I lived Nancy's life of comfort, independence, adventure, and accomplishment. Nancy Drew opened a new world of female
accomplishment outside of the home and taught me much about middle-
class culture. Later on, I realized that Nancy's life was far removed from

my realities as a second-generation American of Polish and working-class background. Nevertheless, I admired Nancy Drew.

As I grew older, I continued to divide my life between the world of Jane Austen, Charles Dickens, George Eliot, Jules Verne, my schooling, and my many domestic responsibilities. As a proficient reader with good grades in school, I was gaining more access to the middle class and its values. My mother used the family's improved economic circumstances to acquire middle-class material symbols such as a new home, car, furniture, and fashionable clothing. However, this class boundary crossing came with a high price: estrangement from my friends and family. In segments of the working class, being "bookish," especially if you are a woman, often results in being branded as "uppity," "selfish," and "strange," and labels you as preferring books to people, particularly boyfriends, and regarding yourself as better than others. Nor did I feel comfortable with my middle-class schoolmates. My father's militant unionism and my self-conscious speech and manner marked me as an outsider. I also was the object of the anti-Polish sentiments in my community.

I have found my background to be a strength and at times limiting in conducting literacy research pertaining to women. Because part of my background is similar to European American working-class participants, I have to keep in check my tendencies to regard literacy as emancipatory[9] and to romanticize the resistant practices of working class women, especially when these practices also reproduce dominant patterns of power. However, as a woman in the academy, I am aware of the power differences between myself and my participants and how those differences impact on research procedures and the interpretation of the data. As a European American woman conducting research with women of color, there are differences stemming from culture, power, and language, some of which I have experienced (and must continue to work through), and others that I have not experienced. Yet there is a sense of estrangement many women experience that runs across race, ethnicity, and social class.

A WOMAN HERO FOR ALL TIMES?

Who is Nancy Drew? In the twenty-odd novels written by Mildred Wirt Benson, Nancy Drew appears as bold, independent, resourceful, talented, capable, clean-cut, and attractive. She is also sharp-tongued and orders about her elderly housekeeper, Hannah Gruen. In the revisions of these novels begun in 1959, and subsequent titles associated with Harriet

S. Adams,[10] Nancy becomes more genteel and a professional helper. In the romance-novel-cum-mystery series, *The Nancy Drew Casefiles,* published by Simon and Schuster in 1986, Nancy combines her professional sleuthing with shopping, rock concerts, and several boyfriends. The appearance of a romanticized Nancy Drew set off massive protests among young women readers, resulting in the reinstatement of "good old Nancy." However, in the series as a whole, Nancy has two major loves in her life: her father, noted attorney Carson Drew, and solving mysteries.

Bumiller (1980) calls attention to the resemblance between the New Jersey home communities of Edward Stratemeyer and Harriet Adams, and Nancy's River Heights. These surroundings may have made their way into the plot outlines. Earlier in this century, Newark and Maplewood, New Jersey, had more than their share of mansions and places frequented by the rich and famous, but perhaps not the sky-rocketing crime rates of River Heights. Caprio (1992, pp. 77–86) suggests that Benson's midwestern roots in Iowa and Ohio shaped her creation of River Heights—a suggestion that has been confirmed by the author. Caprio further speculates that Holmes County, Ohio, may be the actual River Heights. Nancy herself lives in a single-parent household run by Hannah Gruen. Sixteen at the beginning of the series and later aged eighteen,[11] she enjoys a freedom uncommon for teenage girls for most of this century: she does not attend school, has her own car, charge accounts, a large disposable income and moves about with little restriction.

Analysis of several Nancy Drew novels reveals certain discourses that construct this fiction's version of the woman hero and structure the relations of race, ethnicity, class, gender, sexuality, and age. These are the discourses of "Ingenuity," "Super Girl," "Courage," "Domesticity," "Service," and "Danger." The content of each code can be summarized as follows:

1. "Ingenuity" involves a strong intellect and tenacity in overcoming obstacles and reaching a goal.
2. "Super Girl" shows exceptional cleverness and accomplishment in many aspects of life.
3. "Courage" involves initiative and persistence in the face of danger.
4. "Domesticity" refers to devotion to home, family, and the knowledge and skills associated with housekeeping.
5. "Service" means extending oneself to the care of others and placing their welfare above one's own.

As I discuss each discourse, I also will situate it within a larger social framework.

In the novels, Nancy Drew possesses much ingenuity and certainly has a mind of her own. No crime or mystery is too difficult for her agile mind. In the first volume, *The Secret of the Old Clock* (Keene 1930), Nancy's mind and stamina are tested as she must locate the missing will and restore the rightful heirs. Similarly, *The Secret of Red Gate Farm* (Keene 1931) requires Nancy to infiltrate a secret society to unlock the mystery of the farm and apprehend counterfeiters. In *The Bungalow Mystery* (Keene 1930), Nancy fixes a stalled outboard motor with a bobby pin. Nancy's investigations are considerably furthered through her relationship with her close female friends, Bess Marvin and George Fayne.

Like Miss Marple, Nancy Drew appears to be "down-to-earth" with "an inquiring mind" (Keene 1940, p. 10). However, that "inquiring mind" is not entirely natural, as Keene would have readers believe, but the result of the many material and social advantages of her background. As the daughter of famous attorney Carson Drew, Nancy has considerable authority. When it becomes known that Nancy is Carson's daughter, any doubts about her credibility are dispelled. As her detective reputation grows, Nancy achieves a status in her own right and she enjoys an independence few young women experience. Hannah Gruen, the housekeeper, frees Nancy from any domestic obligations other than those she voluntarily assumes. In addition, Nancy does not have to earn a living; she can spend all her time contemplating the twists and turns of her cases with assistance from (the equally privileged) Bess and George. Money, travel, cars, and social contacts provide the material basis for the larger-than-life qualities associated with being a hero.

Family relationships also are important in constituting Nancy Drew's heroism and helping her solve mysteries. Carson Drew and housekeeper Hannah Gruen constitute Nancy's only immediate family. Both are Nancy's confidants and soundingboards whenever she is investigating a case and her conversations with Carson become an exchange of ideas and a means of testing and critiquing ideas. In *The Clue of the Velvet Mask* (Keene 1953), Nancy tries to solve the mystery of break-ins at wealthy estates. Finding some numbers marked on the lining of an opera cloak, she is baffled until she discusses the robberies with Carson:

> She reported what she had been doing on the case, then told him of the numbers on the mask's lining.

"Read them to me," Mr. Drew suggested.

After Nancy did so, he said, "Very interesting. They sound like dates."

"You mean 621 is June twenty-first?"

"Yes. And the last one's the day after the Fourth of July." (p. 47–48)

Nancy and Hannah Gruen have a close mother-daughter relationship in several novels and Nancy looks to Hannah for support, occasional advice, and assistance in solving her mysteries. In *The Clue in the Camera* (Keene 1988), George and Nancy join Hannah in San Francisco for a visit with Hannah's journalist friend, Emily Foxworth. The vacation turns into a mystery when certain photographs from an exhibition of Emily's work disappear. When Hannah helps Nancy and George to find a pattern in an array of seemingly unconnected clues, the mystery is solved.

Jones (1973) suggests that Nancy Drew has many "supergirl" qualities, especially in the later novels. Readers encounter Nancy's exceptional capabilities in such 1930s novels as *The Secret of the Old Clock, The Hidden Staircase, The Bungalow Mystery, The Mystery at Lilac Inn, The Secret at Shadow Ranch,* and *The Secret of Red Gate Farm.* In these novels she is locked in closets, chained to a wall in an abandoned bungalow, tied up in a boat that is on fire and sinking, and repeatedly knocked out. Each time, she rebounds with no after-effects. Nancy is also an adept driver, swimmer, dancer, bridge player, gardener, and so forth. Despite her youth, Nancy speaks fluent French and has studied psychology on the side. She communicates easily and is well liked by her peers. In *Nancy's Mysterious Letter* (Keene 1932, p. 15), readers are told that Carson Drew, famous attorney, regards Nancy as "a more helpful partner . . . than any man [sic] he could pick from the legal talent of the country." Nancy has amazing resilience to the perils she endures in, for example, *The Mystery of the Black Keys* (Keene 1951) and *The Clue in the Camera* (Keene 1988). As a solver of mysteries, Nancy has no peer, including the police. Despite these larger-than-life qualities, she remains modest, uncomfortable with praise, and accepts no monetary reward for her endeavors. At this point she becomes the perfect woman hero.

Bravery is a dominant characteristic of traditional heroes and Nancy Drew is no exception. However, like so many heroes, she does have her vulnerable points: Her bravery is sometimes accompanied by a recklessness and a penchant for the dangerous (Caprio 1993), particularly in the later novels, when Nancy often places not just herself but also Bess and George in harm's way, despite admonitions from her father and Hannah Gruen. In *The Mystery of the Moss-Covered Mansion* (Keene 1971), the friends are attacked by lions and leopards, yet Nancy vows to continue with the case, despite Bess's fears.

In *The Secret of the Old Clock* (Keene 1930), the reader learns that her mother died when Nancy was nine years old. At that time, Nancy assumed women's traditional position as household manager. Her supervision of the hired help and creatively planned menus astound Carson Drew, as do her hostess skills. In *The Secret at Shadow Ranch* (Keene 1930), *The Password to Larkspur Lane* (Keene 1932), *The Secret in the Old Lace* (1980), and *Deadly Intent* (Keene 1986), Nancy manages to fit in shopping, gardening, preparing meals, and sewing, along with her sleuthing. The many descriptions of meals that Nancy and her friends enjoy helps to situate Nancy within a domestic context. Her ties to domesticity are reinforced through the setting of most of the novels: several are set in interior spaces[12] with her own home also providing the base for her detective activities. Most of the cases come to Nancy at home through her father and his clients and many are domestic in nature: restoring inheritances, keeping the family farm, ranch, or inn, and reuniting lost family members. Nancy maintains an amateur status through her father's financial support. Although a professional detective in *The Nancy Drew Case Files,* (1993) Nancy's source of outside income is not mentioned. Economically dependent and manager of the household, Nancy occupies the traditional position of a white middle-class woman of her time: the domestic discourse frames the gendered and economic dimensions of Nancy Drew as hero. Where traditional male heroes are free from domestic obligations, these novels are clear that domesticity is compatible with heroism, especially when women's domestic involvement is voluntary and managerial.

Nancy fights against all odds to right wrongs. After Harriet Adams began supervising the Nancy Drew series in 1931, the "professional helper" became central to Nancy's personality. Adams maintained that the Wellesley College motto, *Non Ministrari Sed Ministrare* (not to be ministered unto, but to minister) is the "philosophy" of the syndicate books, especially those that featured Nancy Drew (Adams 1977, p. 16). In *The Whispering Statue* (Keene 1937, p. 14), Nancy is described as "ever conscientious and sympathetic. Nancy enjoyed lending a helping hand to anyone in trouble." Nancy Drew's sleuthing constitutes a series of heroic acts which encapsulate a love of adventure and an ethic of altruism. In most of the novels, the major premise involves some wrong-doing against a kindly, morally upstanding individual or family: In *The Secret of the Old Clock* (Keene 1930), the relatives of Josiah Crowley are prevented from receiving their inheritance; *The Hidden Staircase* (Keene 1930) concerns the mysterious happenings in the old Hayes mansion which are terrorizing Helen Corning's aunt and cousin; and, in *The Triple Hoax* (Keene 1979), Nancy, Bess, and George help a family friend recover life savings from swindlers. It is worth noting that though Nancy's primary concern is with the welfare of others, it is primarily directed at members of her own social class who have fallen on difficult times.

RACE, CLASS, AND GENDER IN NANCY DREW FICTION

The discourses of Ingenuity, Super girl, Bravery, Domesticity, and Service shape, and are shaped by, the social relations of race, ethnicity, class, gender, sexuality, and age. Nancy Romalov (1993) and Betsy Caprio (1992) maintain that the lifestyle Nancy Drew embodies is highly problematic and out of reach for most readers. A study of Nancy Drew mysteries written from 1930 to 1993 reveals the relatively unchanging world of the European American upper-middle class and Nancy's position as symbol of that social world's power and authority. Yet I and many readers have aspired to this lifestyle. How can one explain this contradiction?

The mysteries until 1959 are overt tales of class and race supremacy where the poor and minorities are evil and to be feared. Forms of classism and racism can be found even in today's Nancy Drew mysteries. In the first seventeen Nancy Drew mysteries, seventeen African Americans are employed in domestic jobs and are shown to be untrustworthy. These novels' renditions of Black English Vernacular are characterized by "Yas mam's" and "sah's." White ethnics such as the Irish are invariably law enforcement officers who are not too intelligent. Italians are "dark and swarthy," a Chinese woman is "squint eyed," and gypsies are invariably sinister.[13] These groups were usually involved in robbery, kidnapping, arson, and assault. However, northern Europeans such as Germans, the English, and Scandinavians are more favorably portrayed. Similar racist stereotyping can be observed in Captain W. E. Johns' adventure hero for boys, Biggles, who is examined in Dennis Butts' article in this volume, as well as in the mystery and adventure fiction of another British writer for children, Enid Blyton.

It has been suggested that much of the blatant racism in Nancy Drew novels was edited out during the revisions of the 1960s and 1970s (Jones 1977). In the more recent novels, characters from culturally diverse backgrounds occupy service sector jobs as in *The Clue in the Camera* (1988), where the Chinese American Don Chin is a police lieutenant. However, these details are passing references without a discussion of any other aspect of the characters' backgrounds. In *The Case of the Artful Crime* (Keene 1992) and *The Mystery of the Masked Rider* (Keene 1993), the Hispanics, Diego San Marcos and Joseph Spaziente, are presented as suave, swaggering, dark, and surly—descriptions reminiscent of the early novels.

The Nancy Drew novels construct a strongly class-divided fictional world. A majority of the male villains are from the working class and are characterized by loud clothing, atrocious manners, and "bad grammar." However, in the older novels, the occasional hard-working farm girls of northern European background win Nancy's admiration. In the more recent novels, there are few characters from classes other than the upper-middle class. Nancy Drew's friends are not only from her own race, but social class as well, although she occasionally befriends individuals of the upper-middle class who are in difficult circumstances. Nancy's interactions with individuals and groups across race and class differences reinforce her social position as superior knower to the dangerous and mysterious other.

Nancy herself has changed very little since the early novels. She remains caring, nurturing, modest, and resourceful. Her "special friend," Ned Nickerson, has hovered on the margins of the novels since their inception, and they enjoy a chaste relationship free from sexual perils and pressures. Although other boys vie for Nancy's attentions in the current novels, romance is not Nancy's overriding interest. Nor is there anything but friendship between Nancy, Bess, and George. Chamberlin (1993) suggests that as the eternal girl, Nancy is a safe haven for some readers who can participate in the larger world from the safety of their fantasies.

NANCY DREW READERS THEN AND NOW

Commentators on the Nancy Drew mystery novels cite many instances of Nancy's heroic status in the reader's estimation, despite social differences between reader and character. My interviews with past and present readers of Nancy Drew confirm this. Their responses encapsulate the complexities when readers attempt to reconcile the discourses of the woman hero with women's centrality to relationships and to families. In the following discussion I summarize the preliminary findings through the words of key participants, Evelyn Jablonski[14] and Louise Jamison, and their female relatives, as well as other women readers in my study.

In the Nancy Drew mysteries, themes of young women's desire for independence in the wider world are combined with occasional romantic subplots involving Nancy and "special friend" Ned Nickerson. Twenty-two year-old European American middle-class Gib Greenwood, granddaughter of Evelyn Jablonski, was one of several readers who read Nancy Drew through the lens of romance. She recollected her "mad crush" on Ned Nickerson and how she imagined herself as Nancy, "melting into Ned's arms" upon being rescued. Gib also "felt bad for George who had no boyfriend." In several of the novels, Nancy Drew and her two female friends, George Fayne and Bess Marvin, debate the merits of romance. George scoffs at romantic attachments, preferring adventure and the company of close friends, Nancy and Bess. The new *Nancy Drew Files* feature a George who "likes boys as much as Bess" and is on the lookout for her true love (Keene 1986, pp. 4–5). However, this emphasis on romance did not find favor with all readers. Thirteen-year-old Karen Kanera commented:

> I read a few Nancy Drews that my mother had dumped in the basement. They were pretty good. Then in the grocery store I saw some new ones. I bought a couple. They were so stupid. Nancy acted weird. She was always thinking about boys. I found out that my mother's friend had a bunch of the old Nancy Drews. So I read tons of them. (European American and middle-class reader)

Karen added that the romantic motif was not "what Nancy is all about."

Several of the present and past readers of Nancy Drew comment that Nancy Drew and George Fayne taught them that a girl can be intelligent, brave, and resourceful: in other words, a hero. For past readers, Nancy opened up an entire world of women's accomplishment and daring outside of their immediate experiences. For ten-year-old Kim Beason (European American and middle class), "The books are cool. Nancy is very brave and popular, like she has all these friends and gets to go on exciting trips. She's quite intelligent and always solves the mystery." For the women of Evelyn Jablonski's family, Nancy Drew reading meshed with these readers' desires for "agentic femininities" characterized by women's achievement and control of their lives.[15] Here is Evelyn Jablonski's account of how she started reading Nancy Drew:

> My older sister Emma gave me this [*The Secret of the Old Clock*] for my eleventh birthday. Emma taught school over in Echo. I think she saw an ad. in a magazine and ordered some books. She was always trying to improve our minds. . . . I think I read this book in two days or so. I just loved it—how Nancy had her own room, money, car and stood up to everybody. And her adventures—I never dreamed a girl could do so many things . . . certainly not a farm girl like myself. (sixty-five-year-old European American middle-class woman)

Evelyn credits Nancy Drew with giving her the courage to seek a life beyond her family farm and "see more of the world." Evelyn's sister, Sarah Crane, is a fifty-nine-year-old white middle-class elementary teacher who has this to say about Nancy Drew: "Nancy was the girl I wanted to be—smart and free as a bird. She didn't have any curfews or parents constantly telling her that she couldn't do this or that." Dorothy Mason, Evelyn's youngest sister, "just loved the books, especially the ones where Nancy, Bess, and George visited far away places. I'd read them over and over. I guess they were kind of educational for me." Evelyn and her sisters were able to fit themselves into the affluent world of Nancy Drew with its large well-appointed homes, even when this world clashed with the austerity of farm life.

For African American Louise Jamison and her family, reading Nancy Drew posed many contradictions around race and class. Fifty-four-year-old Jamison, of a working-class background, seemed to fit herself into the universe of River Heights:

> Mama cleaned house for some families in Waycross. When I was eight or nine, I guess, she let me come along with her to help out. In one of the families they had a daughter about my age. Anyways, we used to play together and read books together. This girl had a collection of Nancy Drews. We read them over and over and made up plays about our adventures in mysterious houses and catching criminals. We dreamed we could become these famous detectives.

Nancy Drew was the vehicle for Louise to cross race and class boundaries in the imagination. However, in a later conversation, Louise commented that she "didn't like how black folks were described in the books—stupid, lazy and slow."[16] Yet the books' exciting stories and glimpses of the larger world maintained her interest. For Corla Jefferson, Louise's fifty-year-old sister, race and class differences figured prominently in her reading:

> I was put off at first by the pictures of Nancy—you know, blonde and light skin. I had trouble identifying with Nancy. She was rich, had all these fine clothes and a servant to do the housework. However, the stories were interesting. I especially enjoyed the stories set in foreign countries. I also admired her independent spirit. (African American and middle-class reader)[17]

Corla and Louise's reading produced a critique of the social world of Nancy Drew as well as reconstructing the text according to their interests and cultural values.

CONCLUSIONS

The textual analysis and reader study suggest that Nancy Drew fiction occupies a contradictory position in the lives of its readers. Nancy Drew is often read from ages eight to fifteen, when young women are exploring their subjectivities—who they want to be and what they want to do with their lives.[18] From the Nancy Drew novels, readers learn that women can be knowledgeable, competent, intelligent, and brave—characteristics that young women may not see in themselves, as many lose self-confidence during these years (Gilligan, Lyons, and Hanmer 1990). Nevertheless, Chamberlain (1993) suggests that Nancy Drew is too perfect to serve as a model for readers, despite the flaws that Caprio (1993) discusses. My study of readers indicates they take up certain aspects of Nancy's characters while refusing others. That the conservative, social world of Nancy Drew fiction was not unilaterally accepted by readers is apparent in the criticisms of African American readers and younger readers. Despite this, readers find in Nancy Drew a woman of heroic stature who is worthy of emulation.

The Nancy Drew mysteries were developed at a time in the United States of competing femininities when many women were straining against the social boundaries that limited their horizons. Many longed for worlds beyond home and family. However, as Alice Kessler-Harris (1982) notes, European and African American women from the working class have always had to juggle the incredible load of wage work, home, and family. Romalov (1993) suggests that the dual constructions of Nancy's freedom and domesticity perform the cultural work of assurance that the "liberated" woman does not necessarily have to upset the social order.

Nancy's character may be a fictional response to the forces that kept women in their places and the many new ideas about women's places in the world. Harriet S. Adams attributed the original impulses behind Nancy's character to Edward Stratemeyer "who understood but did not admire weepy women, 'fraidy' cats, and overfeminine girls." Because of this, Nancy became "a level headed, logical-thinking teenage detective" (Keene 1978, p. 81). Edward Stratemeyer also was very attuned to balancing the iconoclastic and conservative aspects of his fictional characters to retain sales (Praeger 1971). Mildred W. Benson once remarked:

> I sort of liked the character from the beginning. Now, that kind of woman is common, but then it was a new concept, though not to me. I just naturally thought that girls could do the things boys did. (Brown 1993, p. 6)

The words of Harriet S. Adams are equally revealing:

> I think women are just as bright as men, though I don't think they are physically as strong. I'm all for women so long as they are old-fashioned in their family lives, which means having children and bringing them up strictly. . . . I think many of the feminists overdo it, though I do think women have a place in this world and that mentally, they are equal to men. (Foreman 1980, p. 10)

NOTES

1. Book packaging companies are quite common today. They employ writers and often hold the copyright on books, which are then printed by other publishers.

2. For more information, see Plunkett-Powell (1993) and Caprio (1992).

3. In the United States, Head-Boy Scoutmaster K. Franklin Matthews attacked Stratemeyer Syndicate books for their violence and breakneck action. Because sales somewhat dipped, Stratemeyer slowed the pace of series books.

4. Mildred Wirt Benson, Walter Karig, and several other "ghost writers" claim authorship for the Nancy Drew mysteries.

5. For a more thorough treatment of oral history methods, see Yow (1994).

6. For an extended discussion of discourse theory and discourse analysis see Fairclough (1989), Foucault (1980), and Potter and Wetherell (1987).

7. The autobiographical framework used in the Nancy Drew study stems from Brodzki and Schneck (1988), who question the traditional masculine view of autobiography as a mirror reflecting one's ability to represent an untroubled reflection of identity. Rather, Brodzki and Schneck regard one's selves as mediated by language and culture. These plural selves are contradictory, inconsistent, and in progress. Understood in this way, autobiography can be an important means for tracing the development of self-reflexivity.

8. Wright (1982) claims that the middle class and women simultaneously occupy several class positions depending upon the criteria used. In my case, these criteria involve political affiliation, income, culture, education, and birth family background.

9. For a critique of the notion of literacy as emancipatory, see Baker and Luke (1991), Cherland (1994), Christian-Smith (1990, 1993), and Lankshear and Lawler (1987).

10. Beginning in 1959, all the Nancy Drew mysteries were revised because of charges of race and class biases. The revisions begun in 1959 also involved editing several older novels for appeal to current audiences. Sometimes these were released under a new title. Other novels were totally rewritten or combined into a single "new release." See Caprio (1992) for more details.

11. Adams changed Nancy Drew's age to eighteen to conform to changed ages for issuing a driver's license.

12. Caprio (1992) suggests that these locations represent the maternal aspects of Nancy's character, while Mason (1975) interprets this as a stereotypically feminine and conservative aspect of the Nancy Drew series.

13. Romalov (1993) provides an excellent discussion of these and other points.

14. (Note: All names are pseudonyms.) I first met Evelyn Jablonski when she sold me her Nancy Drew books because her granddaughters and grandnieces had moved on to the Nancy Drew paperbacks. Evelyn's old, dark, blueback novels had circulated among several female members of her family since Evelyn's childhood. Like Evelyn, Louise Jamison sold me the books her granddaughters had outgrown.

15. See Cherland (1994) and Christian-Smith (1990, 1993) for a discussion of reading to construct agentic femininities among young women.

16. Louise's perceptions are similar to those discussed in Jones (1973).

17. See Sunstein (1995) for more examples of Nancy Drew as role model.

18. The original Nancy Drews were advertised for ten- to fifteen-year-olds; by the 1970s, the series was aimed at readers aged eight to twelve. The Nancy

Drew novels from the 1930s–1960s are still read by preadolescent readers and are steadily growing in popularity.

BIBLIOGRAPHY

Baker, C. D. & Luke, A. *Towards a critical sociology of reading pedagogy.* Amsterdam: John Benjams, 1991.

Benstock, S. *The private self: Theory and practice of women's autobiography.* Chapel Hill, NC: The University of North Carolina Press, 1988.

Benson, M. W. *The ghost of Ladora.* Books at Iowa, 19, 24–29, 1973.

Billman, C. *The secret of the Stratemeyer syndicate.* New York: Ungar Press, 1986.

Brown, P. L. "Nancy Drew writer finally gets honors." *The Stevens Point Journal,* p. 6. (May 12, 1993)

Brodzki, B., & Schenck, C. *Lifelines: Theorizing women's autobiography.* Ithaca, NY: Cornell University Press, 1988.

Bumiller, E. (1980, April 25). "After 50 years: Nancy Drew still poised, proper." *Albany Times-Union,* n.p. (April 25, 1980)

Caprio, B. *Girl sleuth on the couch.* Culver City, CA: The Center for Sacred Psychology, 1992.

Casey, K. *I answer with my life.* New York: Routledge, 1993.

Chamberlain, K. "Nancy Drew in the 1990s: A Feminist Update." Paper presented at The Nancy Drew Scholars Conference, The University of Iowa, Iowa City, IA. (April, 1993)

Cherland, M. *Girls reading gender.* London: The Falmer Press, 1994.

Christian-Smith, L. K. *Becoming a woman through romance.* New York: Routledge, Chapman and Hall, 1990.

Christian-Smith., L. K. "Sweet dreams: Gender and desire in teen romance novels." *Texts of desire: Essays on fiction, femininity and schooling* (pp. 45–68). London: The Falmer Press, 1993.

Christian-Smith, L. K. "Changed and unchanged melodies: Constructing gender, class, race and sexuality in Nancy Drew mystery books." Paper presented at the University of Wisconsin's Women's Studies Conference at the University of Wisconsin-Milwaukee, October 18, 1991.

Clifford, J., & Marcus, G. E. *Writing culture: The politics of ethnography.* Berkeley: University of California Press, 1986.

Donelson, K. "Nancy, Tom and assorted friends in the Stratemeyer Syndicate then and now." *Children's Literature: Annual of the Modern Language Association Group on Children's Literature and the Children's Literature Association.* 7 (1978): 16–44.

Dyer, C. S., & Romalov, N. T. *Rediscovering Nancy Drew*. Iowa City: The University of Iowa Press, 1995.

Fairclough, N. *Language and power*. London: Longman, 1989.

Felder, D. "Nancy Drew: Then and now." *Publishers Weekly* (1986, May 30): 30–34.

Foreman, J. "The saga of the mysterious writer." *The Boston Globe*. (1980, July 3): 9–10.

Foucault, M. *Power/knowledge: Selected interviews and other writings 1972–1977*. Brighton: Harvester, 1980.

Gavey, N. (1989). "Feminist poststructuralism and discourse analysis: Contributions to feminist psychology." *Psychology of Women Quarterly,* 13 (1989): 459–475.

Gilligan, C., Lyons, N. P. & Hanmer, T. J. *Making connections: The relational worlds of adolescent girls at Emma Willard School*. Cambridge, MA: Harvard University Press, 1990.

Glover, C. D. "The stuff that dreams are made of: Masculinity, femininity and the thrill." In *Gender, genre and narrative pleasure,* ed. D. Longhurst. London: Unwin Hyman, 1989: 67–83.

Johnson, D. "From paragraphs to pages: The writing and development of Stratemeyer Syndicate series." In *Rediscovering Nancy Drew,* eds. C. S. Dyer & N. T. Romalov. Iowa City: The University of Iowa Press, 1995: 29–40.

Jones, J. P. "Nancy Drew, WASP super girl of the 1930s." *Journal of Popular Culture,* 6 (1973): 707–716.

Keene, C. "Nancy Drew." In *The great detectives,* ed. O. Penzler. Boston: Little, Brown and Company, 1978: 81–86.

Kessler-Harris, A. *Out to work*. Oxford: Oxford University Press, 1982.

Klein, K. G. *The woman detective: Gender and genre*. Urbana and Chicago: The University of Illinois Press, 1988.

Lankshear, C., & Lawler, M. *Literacy, schooling and revolution*. London: The Falmer Press, 1987.

Lather, P. *Getting smart: Feminist research and pedagogy with/in the postmodern*. New York: Routledge, 1991.

Mason, B. A. *The girl sleuth*. Old Westbury, CT: The Feminist Press, 1975.

Opie, A. "Qualitative research: Appropriation of the 'other' and empowerment." *Feminist Review,* 40 (1992): 52–69.

Potter, J., & Wetherell, M. *Discourse and social psychology*. London: Sage Publications, 1987.

Peshkin, A. "In search of subjectivity—one's own." *Educational Researcher,* 17 (1988): 17–21.

Plunkett-Powell, K. *The Nancy Drew scrapbook.* New York: St. Martin's Press, 1993.

Praeger, A. "Edward Stratemeyer and his book machine." *The Saturday Review,* (July 10, 1971): 15–53.

Romalov, N. "Lady and the tramps: The cultural work of Gypsies in Nancy Drew and her foremothers." Paper presented at The Nancy Drew Scholars Conference, The University of Iowa, Iowa City, IA., April, 1993.

Sunstein, B. S. " 'Reading' the stories of reading: Nancy Drew testimonials." In *Rediscovering Nancy Drew,* eds. C. S. Dyer & N. T. Romalov. 1995: 95–112. Iowa City: The University of Iowa Press.

White, J. S. "Nancy Drew's success is still a mystery." *Virginia Pilot.* (Feb. 20, 1980): B1–B2.

Weedon, C. *Feminist practice and post-structuralist theory.* Oxford: Basil Blackwell, 1987.

Wright, E. O. "The status of the political in the concept of class structure." *Politics and Society,* 11 (1982): 321–341.

Yow, V. R. *Recording oral history.* Thousand Oaks, CA: Sage Publications, 1994.

Nancy Drew books by Carolyn Keene cited in this chapter

Published by Grosset & Dunlap

1930
The secret of the old clock
The hidden staircase
The bungalow mystery
The mystery at Lilac Inn

1931
The secret at Shadow Ranch
The secret of Red Gate Farm

1932
Nancy's mysterious letter
The password to Larkspur Lane

1937
The whispering statue

1951
The mystery of the black keys

1953
The clue of the velvet mask

1971
The mystery of the moss-covered mansion

Published by Simon & Schuster

1979
The triple hoax

1980
The secret in the old lace

1986
Deadly Intent

1988
The clue in the camera

1992
The case of the artful crime

1993
The mystery of the masked rider
The Nancy Drew Casefiles

Reconstructing Robin Hood
Ideology, Popular Film, and Television

DUDLEY JONES

I had a Robin Hood period in childhood. Like most childhoods, mine is patchily remembered, misty. Through a mist—one of these delightful early summer morning mists, unfrightening, full of promise—I perceive the green figures of Robin Hood and his men slipping, sliding, wavering. Over how long a time? I don't know. Perhaps one summer? Surely several?

Certainly the season was summer, or spring: not winter. I remember standing with string tied around the middle of my cotton dress, on a corner of our lawn . . . I also remember strolling slowly across the meadow opposite . . . very probably in a similar dress, similarly belted. I wasn't doing anything particular that anyone could observe: not speaking, not gesticulating. But on both occasions, *I was Robin Hood.* (Philippa Pearce 1985, p. 159)

Robin Hood is a part of my inner society and has never stopped being in my thoughts, but it's only recently that I've become fully aware of how far the theme of that child's book has gone beyond childhood. . . . Legends, myth and fantasy both ask and tell us how life is, and there seems to be a strong need in us to think about the theme that is in *Robin Hood:* the absorption into law and order of that mysterious, chthonic, demiurgic power that we vitally need but cannot socially tolerate. We regret the loss of it and we rationalise the necessity of that loss. We say to it, 'Yes, be there. But lose yourself in us at the proper time. Grow up.' But I wonder what the proper time is, and I wonder if the loss is necessary. (Russell Hoban 1976, pp. 7, 9,12)

Philippa Pearce and Russell Hoban are the authors respectively of *Tom's Midnight Garden* and *A Mouse and his Child*, acknowledged classics of modern children's literature, and their tributes provide eloquent testimony to the enduring appeal of Robin Hood. An appeal, Pearce and Hoban emphasise, which is not simply felt by children but lingers to exert a seductive power and influence upon the adult.

If further evidence of the potency of the legend were needed, one could cite the different forms in which tales of Robin Hood have circulated, including ballads, plays, operas, pantomimes, musicals, novels, television series, films, and most recently, theme parks. In trying to account for the continuing popularity of Robin Hood, this chapter traces the development of the legend and examines the ideological significance of specific re-workings of the Robin Hood story. Concentrating mainly on twentieth-century mediations through film and television, it looks at the way constructions of Robin Hood as heroic figure reflect contemporary historical events and changing cultural values.

The earliest extant source materials for the legend—a handful of surviving medieval ballads and a fragment of a play—provided a sketchy framework of a story that was added to by succeeding generations. In the sixteenth century, for example, Robin became associated with the May games, and new characters like Friar Tuck and Maid Marian (who as the May Queen would partner Robin, the May King or Summer Lord) were introduced. There were three comic operas about the legendary outlaw in the eighteenth century and several plays in the nineteenth, including Tennyson's *The Foresters,* as well as less serious incarnations on stage in pantomime (where Robin often appears in *Babes in the Wood*) and, two ill-fated musicals—Lionel Bart's *Twang* in 1965 and *Robin, Prince of Sherwood* in 1993. Robin Hood (and Maid Marian) also appeared in many nineteenth century poems and novels: In Sir Walter Scott's, *Ivanhoe,* for example, Robin became the champion of oppressed Saxons fighting the injustices of Norman overlords—a development to the story eagerly adopted by later writers. In the field of children's literature there have been scores of re-tellings for children, ranging from Henry Gilbert's *Robin Hood and his Merry Men* (1912), remembered with particular affection by Philippa Pearce, to versions by Enid Blyton,[1] Geoffrey Trease,[2] Rosemary Sutcliff,[3] Roger Lancelyn Green,[4] as well as a Ladybird series of the tales for younger children.

On television there was the long-running *Adventures of Robin Hood* in the 1950s starring Richard Greene, *Robin of Sherwood* with Michael

Praed and later Jason Connery in the title role (1984–86), and Tony Robinson's jokey role-reversal series in the late 1980s, *Maid Marian and Her Merry Men.* On the larger screen, over thirty feature films have been produced, including animated versions from the Disney, Appia, and Sovfilm studios, and the illustrious hero's offspring have featured in "son and daughter of Robin Hood" films. Finally, there is the theme park, "Tales of Robin Hood," located in the heart of the city of Nottingham—proof that "Robin Hood" is a polysemous, cross-cultural text embracing different forms, and connecting with the heritage and tourist industries.

A case can therefore be made for Robin Hood as the most popular and enduring legendary figure in Britain and America. But what are the reasons for his continuing appeal and why should the myth continually be reinterpreted and reconstructed? Most commentators agree that the appeal of the myth has much to do with the egalitarian, populist associations of Robin Hood—an outlaw who robbed the rich to give to the poor, who fought injustice and corruption in church and state, who was anti-clerical yet deeply devoted to the Virgin Mary, and who opposed all forms of authority but was steadfastly loyal to, and ready to lay down his life for, the king. In short, a ludic, subversive figure, a charismatic leader of a band of "merry men" who—because he incorporated contradictory elements and because his status veered between yeoman and (displaced) aristocrat—could attract support from across the social spectrum, appealing to both radical and conservative elements.

Yet, important though these factors clearly are, they still do not quite explain the longevity and fascination of the Robin Hood myth. To account for this, one has to go deeper and explore Robin's association with the regenerative myth of the Green Man. Robin's myth, like the Green Man's, activates a set of oppositions between nature and industry or commerce, fertility and decay, countryside (or forest) and town, and freedom and constraint. William Anderson, in *The Green Man,* discusses the links between the two myths, pointing out they are both linked to May Day festivities and that Robin Hood's "connection with the Green Man is strong not simply because of the green he and his merry men wore but because so many inns called 'The Green Man' portrayed him on their signs" (Anderson 1990, p. 29). Interestingly, in the well-received film version, starring Patrick Bergin (*Robin Hood* 1991), Robin and his men gain entrance to Nottingham Castle by joining the May Day festivities disguised as clowns and revellers in the Lord-of-Misrule carnival procession. In the wedding that concludes the film, Robin and Marian are framed in a wreath of flowers and leaves under the beneficent gaze of a figure dressed as the Green Man.

The cinematic resurgence of Robin Hood in the 1990s (with three Hollywood productions in the first half of the decade focussing on the outlaw hero) is perhaps not surprising in view of increasing concern on both sides of the Atlantic about urban sprawl and environmental pollution. However, there is nothing new about the nostalgic desire to return to a pre-industrial period. This romantic view of the past as a Golden Age when man lived in harmony with nature, is itself a myth and one that has been drawn upon by writers in different periods over the past four centuries. In *As You Like It,* for example, Shakespeare used Robin Hood to symbolise this idealised view of the past. In the Forest of Arden, we are told, Duke Senior and his "merry men . . . live like the old Robin Hood of England" and "young gentlemen flock to him every day, and fleet the time carelessly, as they did in the Golden World" (*As You Like It* Act 1, I 105–109).

Of course, the term "green" often serves as an eponym for the environmental movement, and I suspect Philippa Pearce had this in mind when she described Robin Hood as "a good, green authority . . . a law unto himself, in a green kingdom." (Pearce 1985, p. 161).

Two other important attributes Pearce refers to, which might help to account for the continuing appeal of the outlaw hero, are his "almost superhuman" woodcraft and bowmanship and—in Henry Gilbert's retelling—an interweaving of magic and mystery with the realism of the stories. The mystery (and power) Pearce says, "express themselves again and again in disguisings" as Robin adopts a variety of disguises (thus demonstrating his kinship also with trickster figures of legend) to outwit or embarrass his enemies, rescue his friends or simply engage in high-spirited pranks.

Finally, there is the way the myth constantly tantalises us with the prospect of discovering a real historical model for Robin. Numerous contenders for the role of the "original" Robin, have been suggested and a variety of locations nominated as the setting for his exploits, with Nottingham and Barnsdale in Yorkshire emerging as the front runners, and historians lining up to validate their own candidate's claim to authenticity. After all, there is a Royal Forest of Sherwood—and of Barnsdale; there was a sheriff of Nottingham, and a King Richard the Lionheart. Who knows, around the corner, may lie the piece of historical evidence that establishes, beyond all possible doubt, the legitimacy of this or that candidate's claim to be the *true* Robin Hood.

CONSTRUCTING A HEROIC MYTH: ROBIN HOOD, IDEOLOGY, NATIONAL HERITAGE, AND EDUCATION

Situated on the interface between legend and history, the Robin Hood story has for centuries been a source of inspiration to writers and, more recently, film makers. While the search for a definitive historical model for Robin Hood has proved elusive, the basic narrative has provided a very "open" text, generating diverse, sometimes conflicting, interpretations and accommodating changes to Robin's background and circumstances. This "open-ness" and the powerful sociocultural resonances inherent in the story were instrumental in creating a text that has acted as a vehicle for different ideological views. Thus the threat to the social order posed by the early sixteenth-century Robin Hood—an anti-authority outlaw figure associated with May games and festivities, and the "Lords of Misrule"—was defused by Tudor dramatists who removed his plebeian origins, converting him from a yeoman into the Earl of Huntingdon, a displaced aristocrat (Wiles 1981, p. 49). This change of status, part of a process described by Stephen Knight as the "gentrification" of Robin Hood, is reproduced in most subsequent re-workings of the legend. Furthermore, Robin—a subject of King Edward the Second in the *Gest* ballad—is later transferred to the reign of Richard the Lionheart. When Robin Hood becomes a subject of Richard, the absentee invader, he is, claims David Wiles, "instantaneously and conveniently transformed into a national patriot" (ibid.).

Stephen Knight has examined the way notions of English national identity and heritage were promoted through a flourishing Robin Hood literature for children in the late nineteenth and twentieth centuries. The concept of childhood as a separate and distinctive phase was really a product of the Romantic movement; it is not until about the middle of the nineteenth century that a sub-genre of children's literature starts to develop, and only in the latter part of the century that a large number of Robin Hood anthologies begin to appear. In America, there were almost as many children's re-tellings as in Britain, and one anthology, first published in 1883, which enjoyed huge success in both countries, was by a young American illustrator, Howard Pyle, who was "the first to make Robin Hood a part of the 'English heritage' mainstream" (Knight 1994, p. 204).

Heritage, Knight demonstrates, could be used to project a "newly strident nationalism" and the setting of the Robin Hood anthologies provided "a sense that the country had once been great and powerful in simpler and more admirable ways than the modern world permitted" (ibid.). In the first part of the twentieth century, there was a flood of educational texts representing Robin as a right wing liberal patriot, and one of the key figures in promoting the Robin Hood stories in schools was the jingoistic poet Sir Henry Newbolt, who not only chaired a committee that produced a report on *The Teaching of English in England* in 1921, but also edited a Nelson's "Teaching of English" series that included a Robin Hood play and several patriotic essays in its list.

It is interesting to compare the way values associated with Robin Hood, heritage and nationalism, were mediated though the English curriculum for schools in the early part of this century, with the recent emphasis in the National Curriculum in England and Wales on making available to children "our" (national) literary heritage. In both cases the ideological intention seems clear. Critics of the National Curriculum have observed, for example, that the emphasis on "our" literary heritage in the National Curriculum encourages the transmission of a traditional literary canon that takes little account of ethnic and cultural diversity.

The Nottingham theme park, "Tales of Robin Hood," provides evidence of the continuing link between the outlaw hero and the heritage and education industries. Billed as "The World's Greatest Medieval Adventure," it invites the visitor to "Live the Legend" by engaging in such activities as riding through the magical forest, shooting the Sheriff ("Your chance to try archery—with real bows and arrows") and "Feasting under the Greenwood Tree." From "the definitive exhibition" (created by a team led by the "distinguished Robin Hood scholar" Sir James Holt), one can purchase an education pack that includes history projects specifically related to the Key Stages of the National Curriculum in England and Wales as well as TVEI (Technical and Vocational Initiative) projects on the tourist industry in Nottingham. This illustrates the city's major financial investment in Robin Hood; there is a symbiotic relationship between the heritage, tourist, and education industries, with heritage and tourism forming an enterprise culture nourished and legitimated by the involvement of academia and a clear educational function.

REPRESENTATIONS OF ROBIN HOOD
IN POPULAR FILM AND TELEVISION

The film industry—in particular, because of its financial gearing, the Hollywood film industry—was uniquely equipped to exploit the transcultural appeal of the legendary hero. Robin Hood might have flourished in nineteenth-century theatres, but with film there was no need to enjoin the audience to piece out its imperfections with their thoughts, for the cinema could transport the viewer to sylvan setting or castle walls, stage a forest ambush, and present, with breathtaking verisimilitude, spectacular sword fights, forest ambushes, and amazing feats of archery. With the arrival of colour, moreover, the cinema's ability to offer visual pleasure was immeasurably enhanced.

Knight argues that the potency of the Robin Hood story in the cinema is demonstrated by the simple yet dramatic statistic that five Robin Hood films were made before 1914. He also suggests the special significance of the outlaw hero is not simply related to the number of film productions, for the same kind of popularity is found in ballad or popular theatre in some periods. In the filmic medium, however, the myth:

> has considerably higher status and wider dissemination than in prose, verse or drama. It is still a "popular" topic, in the evaluative sense, as art houses have rarely shown the films, though critical analysis has been known to deal with them and the myth is structurally important within the genre of film as several classic productions have come from the tradition. But that quality is added to remarkable quantity, and it would seem this century has achieved a well recorded parallel to the lively and variable patterns of performance that previously were in play-game, harlequinade and, becoming better recorded last century, comedy and pantomime. (Knight, p. 18)

Part of the attraction of the swashbuckling and western genres to the film industry was their cross-generational popularity. Unlike genres such as romance and film noir, they appealed to both children and adults, and successful family films often meant larger profits. The sense of a dual audience also enabled directors and scriptwriters to address social and political issues, secure in the knowledge that so long as these were embedded in an action-packed scenario with heroic characters and strong dramatic oppositions, box-office returns would be enhanced rather than diminished.

In focusing on particular Robin Hood films, I want to analyse the ideologies inscribed within them, concentrating not only on the heroic figure, the nature of heroism, and what constitutes heroic action, but also on the interaction between the hero and contemporary society—on how the films engage with, and respond to, contemporary historical events and changing attitudes and values. Whilst all of the film's ideological sub-text may not have been accessible to younger members of the audience, it seems likely they would have been aware of the way general issues about heroism were being raised and, in later films, problematised.

In examining the representation of Robin Hood in Hollywood film, I have chosen films from three different periods: *The Adventures of Robin Hood* (1938), directed by Michael Curtiz, starring Errol Flynn; *Robin and Marian* (1976), directed by Dick Lester, starring Sean Connery; and *Robin Hood—Prince of Thieves* (1991), directed by Kevin Reynolds, starring Kevin Costner. I also will be considering the contribution of three television series to the Robin Hood canon.

HEROIC RESISTANCE: MICHAEL CURTIZ'S *THE ADVENTURES OF ROBIN HOOD*

There is general agreement among critics that Curtiz's film represents the definitive Robin Hood, setting the standard by which previous and subsequent Robin Hood films would be measured. The former claimant to that title, the 1922 Douglas Fairbanks Sr.'s *Robin Hood,* suffered in comparison not so much because it lacked sound as because it lacked colour—the gorgeous, lustrous Technicolor that is such a visual pleasure in the Curtiz film.

No expense was spared on *The Adventures of Robin Hood.* It cost nearly two million dollars to make and won Academy Awards for Erich Korngold's sweeping, majestic score, Ralph Dawson's editing, and Carl Jules Weyl's art direction. Warner Brothers had assembled a superb cast: Errol Flynn at the height of his powers—dashing, athletic, and graceful; Olivia de Havilland, radiantly beautiful; and two memorable villains— Claude Rains, a silky smooth Prince John, almost relishing the impudence of Robin, and Basil Rathbone's Guy Gisbourne, ruthless and disdainful, a worthy swordfighting adversary of Robin in the splendid duel that provides a spectacular climax. The result, comments Jeffrey

Richards, "is a film that ravishes the senses, tantalises the taste buds and stirs up the blood" (Richards 1977, p. 197).

In *The Adventures of Robin Hood,* the audience is presented with a series of oppositions that relate both to what one might describe as the timeless elements of the legend and to the specific political situation in 1938. These oppositions are conveyed through camera angles, lighting, the *mise-en-scène,* and through the diegesis. The opposition between Norman and Saxon is symbolised in the visual contrast of the sombre, claustrophobic interiors of Nottingham Castle and the light, airy, natural setting of Sherwood Forest. The Norman stronghold is associated with deceit and intrigue, the forest with freedom, comradeship, and loyalty to King Richard. Michael Curtiz's film reproduces the Tudor view of Sherwood Forest as a kind of Arcadia: Robin's encampment—consistently shot in bright sunlight—is characterised by gastronomic plenty, singing, and dancing, and provides an Edenic refuge from Norman oppression. Even Marian finds it difficult to resist the carnival atmosphere when she is taken there by Robin.

Significantly, it is in the forest that Robin gets his men to kneel and swear to fight for a free England and to protect her from oppressors until the return of King Richard. Robin, the charismatic leader, is positioned above his men to deliver a presidential-style address. Ina Rae Hark[5] sees the film in the context of New Deal policies, arguing that the heroes Robin and Richard, in large part, stand in for Franklin Roosevelt. She suggests Robin's relationship with his band, and with the Saxon peasantry, symbolises the FDR-type democracy that Richard will supposedly reinstate.

Certainly a note of New Deal rhetoric can be detected in the vision of social inclusiveness that the film projects. There are several references to Normans and Saxons living together peacefully and sharing the same rights: "It's injustice I hate, not the Normans," says Robin—and Marion acknowledges that he has taught her that England is bigger than just Normans and Saxons hating each other, that in fact it belongs to all of them, to live together in harmony.

Characters like Prince John and Guy of Gisbourne should not be viewed, therefore, as representative of all, or even a majority, of the Normans. The position of these characters seems analogous to that of the Nazis in Germany—a feeling reinforced by the evocation of Nazi atrocities through a montage of scenes depicting the torture, rape, and murder of Saxon peasants by Norman soldiers. In an interview years later, Olivia de Havilland, the actress who played Marian, commented: "In a way, I suppose, unconsciously, we were preparing for another terrible conflict, because there really were the good guys and there really *was* a bad guy and that was Hitler . . . and anyone who fought him became a kind of Errol Flynn."[6]

Contemporary European politics are one important reason why issues of good and evil, right and wrong, are presented here in a simple, clear-cut way and why heroism is constituted as unproblematic. Errol Flynn is a romantic, swashbuckling hero; there is never any doubt about who the enemy is or the kind of action the hero should undertake. Warner Brothers, the producers of the film, had good cause for attacking Nazis because their agent in Berlin, a Jew, had been beaten to death by a Nazi mob in 1935. It would be misleading, however, simply to interpret *The Adventures of Robin Hood* as a call for heroic action in defence of the victims of fascist regimes in Europe, for there is within the narrative, a contradictory impulse towards neutrality and non-involvement by America in European affairs. Support for an isolationist policy was still strong in America and was represented in a number of films during this period. Even in *The Adventures of Robin Hood,* any European involvement by Britain (and thus—by extension—America) appears to be discouraged in the final part of the film. Following the *Gest* tradition, King Richard returns to England disguised as an abbot. He talks about the fear he has seen on thousands of faces since his return and acknowledges he ought never to have left England. The message is reinforced in his encounter with Robin who, unaware that he is speaking to the king, justifies his lawbreaking, saying: "I blame Richard. His task was here at home defending his own people instead of deserting them to fight in foreign lands." The coded message to Roosevelt (whose sympathy towards Britain and the victims of Nazi aggression was evident despite his ostensible impartiality) seems clear. Many Americans still recalled the horrific experiences of World War I and were resolutely opposed to any involvement in European problems; Roosevelt could not afford to ignore this strength of feeling.

The isolationist stance is even more apparent in Curtiz's *The Private Lives of Elizabeth and Essex,* which appeared the following year and starred Flynn as Essex alongside Bette Davis as Queen Elizabeth. Essex, returning home victorious after a skirmish with the Spanish, is rebuked by Elizabeth who tells him that to follow his example would "endanger the very peace and stability of England" and boasts that she has kept the peace and given her people happiness, relieved the poor, and restored their coinage. As John Davis points out this could almost be a Roosevelt campaign speech (Davis 1972, p. 27). The isolationist message of the film is summed up in Elizabeth's declaration that, "it takes more courage not to fight when one is surrounded by foolish hotheads urging wars in all directions."

ROBIN HOOD ON THE SMALL SCREEN

If the enemy in the late 1930s and 1940s was Nazi Germany, by the 1950s it had become the threat of Communist infiltration and subversion by America's erstwhile ally, Russia. However, while the atrocities carried out by the Sheriff's soldiers in the 1938 film seem designed to conjure up images of the jackboot menace of Nazi Germany, in the 1950s an extraordinary twist in the use of the Robin Hood story meant that it became a vehicle, in the popular British television series, *The Adventures of Robin Hood* (later sold to American TV networks), for attacking the injustices experienced by writers and directors blacklisted in Hollywood for their alleged communist sympathies. Norman persecution was therefore to be seen not as representing Russian tyranny in the Cold War period but as a cancer in the body politic of America that had given rise to the McCarthyite witch hunts, the hearings of the House Committee for Un-American Activities (H.U.A.C.), and the betrayal of former comrades and colleagues by figures who, in order to appease the Committee and protect their own livelihood, "named names."

Faced by financial ruin and destitution, some of those who had been blacklisted after their appearance before the House Committee sought employment in Britain. Ring Lardner Jr., for example, a successful young writer in the 1940s, was one of the Hollywood Ten imprisoned for a year for contempt of Congress after the H.U.A.C. hearings. Blacklisted on his release, he was unable to get work in America and, with another blacklisted writer, Ian McClellan Hunter, wrote the first episode (and many others) for the British television series, *The Adventures of Robin Hood,* starring Richard Greene, which ran from 1955 until 1958. The credits for the first episode identify the writers as Ian Larkin and Eric Heath but, as Lardner explained in a television programme in 1989,[7] he and Hunter employed a variety of pseudonyms, because if a particular name recurred too often on the credits of a series, the network might want to contact that writer to commission other work. Unable to visit Britain to work on the series because they could not obtain passports, Lardner and Hunter's scripts had to be smuggled out of the country. Other blacklisted writers who were able to get to Britain sometimes found themselves involved in the tawdry business of paying an existing, usually unsuccessful, writer a percentage of their fee for the "privilege" of using that writer's name. This process is dramatised in Michael Eaton's screenplay for the film, *Fellow Traveller* (1990), where the hero resents the way he is being exploited but relishes the task of writing episodes of *The Adventures of Robin Hood* for the newly formed independent television channel because the Robin Hood story provides the ideal allegorical model for attacking the McCarthy witch-hunts in America that have led to his own exile.

Not surprisingly, one of the recurrent motifs of the series, for which Ring Lardner Jr. wrote over forty episodes, were scenes where Saxon peasants were threatened with torture and death by Norman soldiers or the sheriff's men if they refused to disclose information about Robin's whereabouts. While betrayal often features in films and stories about Robin Hood, it rarely assumes the thematic prominence accorded it in the television series of the 1950s, which obviously reflects the bitterness of those "named" in the H.U.A.C. meetings.

The series was originally directed towards children, but clearly appealed to a large adult audience as well, and the popularity of the Robin Hood story is evident from the viewing figures in England, and also in Australia where the programme was still running on some channels until the advent of colour in 1974.

Stephen Knight argues that not only was the series inherently populist in mode but that it also came "in a time and place where the restrained radicalism that had pervaded the myth from time to time was widely acceptable" (Knight, p. 235). Though the Labour government had been defeated in 1951, there was still a political consensus in favour of the welfare state and people on both sides of the political divide "assumed that combination of the people was inherently a good thing, and also—where left-wing labour parted company—that it was natural for a leader of a higher class to supervise social improvement" (ibid.).

Apart from its relatively "leftist" politics, says Knight, the other striking element of the series was how well it fitted a televisual mode:

> There was little intercutting between different strands as is now the mode in soap opera; each episode was a playlet, rather like an extended ballad or indeed like the two-scene drama that actually survives from the fifteenth century. If the television medium took the form back to quite antique fashions, so did the relative poverty of production. The series was pruned down, like the spare narrative of the early ballads,

and there was almost no plot decoration or elaboration; the feel of the early black and white drama had just the spare, impersonal character of the early ballads. (Knight, p. 236)

Richard Greene, a straightforward, clean-cut, no-nonsense type of hero, commanded his men like a military officer. In a delightful scene in *Fellow Traveller,* the American scriptwriter, Asa Kaufman, outlines his concept of Robin Hood to the prospective English producer who, slightly alarmed by the American's emphasis on Robin as "a man of the people," counters with "but he was an aristocrat." Kaufman strives earnestly to second-guess and satisfy the producer's expectations: "a man of action—but serious," he assures him. "Quite," rejoins the producer, "we don't want to make it look as if he's enjoying himself with all those merry men," and he is finally won round when Kaufman says, "I see him more as a Battle of Britain pilot type." Although Eaton has his own dramatic agenda and is using the actual television series for his own fictional ends, there seems to be a clear (and intended) correspondence between Robin's characterisation in the 1950s series and Kaufman's concept of Robin.

In 1975, the BBC produced *The Legend of Robin Hood,* a series of six hour-long episodes starring Martin Potter as Robin and Diane Keen as Marion. This provoked a good deal of criticism from the regular "television watchdog" committees who were concerned that since the series was transmitted in the five o'clock slot for children's television, the violence contained in some episodes might be upsetting to younger viewers.[8]

The BBC series, however, lacked the innovative flair of the next incarnation of Robin Hood on television screens, which enjoyed both critical and commercial success. *Robin of Sherwood* (1984–86), made for HTV by Goldcrest, offered a skilful meld of realism and the supernatural. Its positioning within the TV schedules suggested a target audience of children but the dark, matinée-idol looks of its youthful star, Michael Praed, ensured a wider following. Richard Carpenter's screenplay incorporated the links made by scholars like William Anderson and John Matthews, of Robin Hood with paganism, the Green Man, and Celtic mythology. Robin, the son of serfs murdered by Normans when he is a child, is chosen by Herne the Hunter (a giant figure wearing stag's antlers on his head and living deep within the forest on an island in a lake) as "The Hooded Man" who will lead resistance to the Normans. According to Knight, Herne "goes back to Cernunnos, the Celtic 'horned one' who is (in so far as the Celts had anything so inflexible) the lord of animals in their informal pantheon" (Knight, p. 239). With a haunting, ethereal soundtrack by Clannad, a folk group with Celtic associations, this was a Robin Hood perfectly in tune with the ecological "Green" movement and the New Age philosophy of the mid-1980s. Michael Eaton described the series as "a much more mystical vision which drew on Celtic mythology to present Robin Hood as a sort of anthropomorphic embodiment of the forest itself, a green hero for a green age."[9]

It would be a mistake, however, to suggest that this emphasis on the supernatural was at the expense of realism or that it inhibited the articulation of social and political concerns: There was an authentic feel to the costumes and the medieval setting and the themes of class exploitation and legitimate rebellion were explored realistically in ways that gave them both an historical relevance and a contemporary relevance to the political agendas of Britain in the 1980s.

Richard Carpenter, who wrote the screenplays for *Robin of Sherwood,* also neatly solved the problem of how to accommodate a successor to Michael Praed when he decided to leave the series. Since Robin was as much a mythological as a human character (the "hooded man" chosen by Herne), the mantle could be passed on after his death to Robert (Jason Connery), son of the Earl of Huntingdon. Jason Connery, "a scion of film aristocracy, seemed like a natural inheritor to the role his father had previously held" (Knight, p. 240) in the film *Robin and Marian.* However, the conversion from a serf's son to earl's could be seen as a sign of gentrification in a decade that, as it progressed, produced a hardening of right-wing political attitudes in Britain.

Robin of Sherwood undoubtedly represented a major re-working of the Robin Hood story and reflected the time in which it was made. Similar claims also could be made for the irreverent *Maid Marian and her Merry Men* (1988–89). This series, written by Tony Robinson (who played Baldrick in the BBC's highly successful TV comedy series, *Blackadder*) adopted a pantomime, comic-book style to debunk male heroism and gleefully poke fun at almost all the traditional associations of the myth. The focus switches from Robin to Marian; it is she who assembles the Merry Men and she is the only one to display courage, resourcefulness, and intelligence. The rest of the outlaw "goodies" (as they are described in the credits) vie with the "baddies" for incompetence and stupidity. Robin is transformed into a cowardly, inept, and somewhat effete yuppie (from Kensington), Little John becomes Little Ron (a ferocious dwarf), Rabies is a half-wit with a speech impediment, and a

Rastafarian called Barrington, whose rap lyrics introduce each episode and provide narrative links, assumes Allan-a-Dale's minstrel role. The chief "baddie," the Sheriff of Nottingham, (played with a villainous exuberance by writer Tony Robinson) is clearly never intended to be taken seriously and fails to strike terror into either his own soldiers or the Merry Men.

Although Marian is given a very positive role as the active, independent heroine and Robin's heroic pretensions are continually mocked (he attends the World Archery Championship disguised appropriately as a chicken) the farcical, knockabout humour and the scatter-gun approach to the satirical targets mean that the feminist claims sometimes made for the series need be treated with caution.

Each of these television series had a transmission time that suggests a target audience of children (*Maid Marian* was shown at 5.10 pm on Wednesday afternoon and repeated on Sunday afternoon), yet the viewing figures indicate a significant proportion of the audience must have been adults and the probability is that the programme makers—like their counterparts in the film industry—always had their sights firmly set on a dual audience. Since, apart from *The Legend of Robin Hood,* these series were sold to U.S. TV networks and proved popular with American audiences, it is surprising that American television companies allowed British companies to exploit the continued interest in the Robin Hood myth unchallenged, especially in the light of the influence of *Robin of Sherwood* and *Maid Marian and Her Merry Men* on recent Hollywood productions: The success of Goldcrest's *Robin of Sherwood* was no doubt a significant factor in the appearance of two Hollywood Robin Hood films in 1991, whilst the influence of *Maid Marian* is apparent from Mel Brooks borrowing not just the comic-book style of Tony Robinson's series but also the Rastafarian minstrel figure for his *Robin Hood: Men in Tights* (1993).

INTERROGATING THE HEROIC FIGURE: DICK LESTER'S *ROBIN AND MARIAN*

The success of Curtiz's *The Adventures of Robin Hood* encouraged Hollywood studios in the post-war period to produce Robin Hood films at regular intervals, and in Britain, in the period between 1958 and 1973, four were made by Hammer Studios. These were all fairly routine movies, however, adopting a traditional, orthodox approach to the subject. *Robin and Marian* in 1976 was the first film since the war to offer a distinctly original and innovative treatment of the myth and is the only Robin Hood film to portray the hero's death.

Scriptwriter James Goldman kept faithfully to the depiction of Robin's death in the *Gest*—where it is only briefly mentioned—and to the fuller account found in versions of a later eighteenth century ballad entitled "The Death of Robin Hood." Both ballads attribute Robin's death to poisoning by his kinswoman, the Abbess of Kirklees Priory, but the later one has the familiar motif of Robin shooting an arrow and telling Little John to bury him where it falls. Goldman's script reproduces this ending but changes the reason for Robin visiting the Priory (in the ballad, growing old and ill, he goes to the Abbess, a famed healer, for bloodletting) as well as the motivation for the murder. In the film, Marian, tired of waiting for Robin's return from the crusades, has become the Abbess. Robin has been seriously injured in a climactic duel with the sheriff, many of his followers have been killed and Marian, unable to face the prospect of him being tracked down like a wounded animal, decides to give him poison in a drink that she then consumes herself: Her administering poison is thus an act of love rather than betrayal. The film concludes with a moving re-affirmation of their love for each other.

As Knight points out, *Robin and Marian* can be regarded as a radical re-working of the tradition in that it "breaks the mould by admitting time and reality, and indicates that these figures are in fact locked within the passing of human time" (Knight, p. 238). But the differences between this and other screen representations of Robin Hood go much deeper; compared with Curtiz's film, for example, the portrayal of the heroic figure (Robin *and* King Richard) is far more ambivalent.

Lester's *Robin and Marian* begins in France with the Crusades and a middle-aged Robin, played by Sean Connery, refusing to carry out Richard the Lionheart's order to slaughter the women and children of a castle at Chaluz. Having spent the last twenty years loyally serving King Richard (Richard Harris), he has become sickened by the atrocities perpetrated in the Holy Land. An air of futility pervades the opening sequence of the film: We see huge stones being catapulted against the walls of an undefended castle. Eventually, the supposed "treasure" that has inspired the siege is revealed to be nothing more than a rock.

And Richard is not the noble and wise monarch of legend; he is a capricious psychopath motivated by greed rather than religious belief. After the king's death from a wound received at Chaluz, Robin, accompanied by his faithful friend, Little John, returns to England. When they encounter Will Scarlett and Friar Tuck in Sherwood Forest, the film's de-mythologisation of the heroic figure continues. Robin is astonished to find that he and the outlaws have become the subject of heroic ballads—Will says he doesn't know where the songs come from but everyone wants to hear about the things they did. He laughs when Robin protests that they never performed half the deeds they have been credited with: "I know that," he replies. What we are shown, in fact, is a group of elderly men trying to rekindle memories of a glorious past, which, by their own admission, is largely fabricated. Even the cynical, level-headed Will has become seduced by the myth: "If ever there was a time for us it's now," he declares. "They'd come to you, Robin, the people, they'd come to you if you called them."

Goldman demonstrates the dangerous potential of the legend. The ordinary people of Nottingham do indeed come to Robin. The ballads have persuaded them he possesses the strength and invincibility of a super-hero—ultimately, however, the decision to join Robin proves dis-astrous. For the new recruits are old men and boys, farmers not soldiers: presumably the Crusades took all the young men of the region. And Robin and Little John, though clearly the wrong side of forty and suffer-ing from arthritis ("the geriatric guerrillas" as one critic dubs them[10]), are basically schoolboys who have never grown up ("those were good days, fighting the sheriff," says Robin wistfully).

When it comes to a showdown, faced by overwhelming odds, they will obviously be no match for the sheriff and his highly trained soldiers. Robin tries to protect his motley band of followers by persuading the sheriff to agree that the two of them, as champions of their respective sides, will settle matters by single combat. If Robin loses, his men, lack-ing a leader, will disperse and return to their homes; if the sheriff loses, he promises that Robin and his followers will be allowed to live in peace in the forest. The sheriff, though shrewd and determined, is far from being the traditional, stereotypical villain: he is a man of honour who re-spects Robin and adheres to the same chivalric code, but both men are portrayed as anachronistic figures. When the sheriff is slain after a bloody, protracted duel (entirely lacking the athletic grace and artistry of Flynn's duels—here the combatants are weighed down by heavy chain mail and broadswords), Sir Ranulf, King John's representative, reneges on the agreement made by the sheriff and orders his soldiers to attack. Robin's men, armed with little more than pitchforks, are overwhelmed and, although we are not shown the final outcome, their slaughter seems inevitable. The gladiatorial contest of Robin and the sheriff is shown to be a chivalric remnant of a bygone age, replaced by the modern, cynical *realpolitik* of Sir Ranulph.

Essentially Robin is trapped by the imperatives of the heroic myth. On the one hand he is sickened by the butchery of the Crusades; he tells Marian that Richard's one great victory in the Crusades—achieved when the king was sick in bed—led to the massacre of thousands of women and children. On the other hand, back in the greenwood, the legend beckons, promising both a revival of the chivalric ideal (hence his challenge to the sheriff) and the restoration of his youthful strength and potency. The grizzled warrior's attempt to re-assert his heroic image is both touching and disturbing. Having decided to abandon the protection of the forest, to carry the fight to the sheriff and his army on the plain, he tries to justify his decision to Marian: "You think I'm old and grey, well I'm not . . . I'm all I ever was." Thus heroism becomes bound up in notions of masculinity and, unlike Curtiz's film, heroic action is represented in morally ambiguous terms. In *Robin and Marian*, Robin's heroic action condemns his men to death. Furthermore, values associated with heroism—such as patriotism and loyalty to one's king—are systematically undermined. Asked by Marian why he didn't desert Richard after the massacre and return home, Robin simply replies: "He was my king."

One can see in all this a reflection of the cynicism and disillusionment that existed in America in the aftermath of the Vietnam War. The film was released in 1976, two years after the end of the war, and many would have been aware of the parallels with the Vietnam experience: the same scepticism about the underlying motives for a war fought thousands of miles away on foreign soil; Richard's massacre in the Holy Land and Lieutenant Calley's at My Lai. In 1938 with a war looming, where the distinction between right and wrong seemed clear, one could celebrate Errol Flynn's heroic exploits; in 1976 heroic action was regarded as outmoded or morally suspect.

A "POLITICALLY CORRECT" ROBIN? ROBIN HOOD IN THE NINETIES

Influenced no doubt by the success of *Robin of Sherwood* on American television, major Hollywood studios displayed a renewed interest in the Robin Hood story with Warner Brothers and Twentieth Century Fox competing with each other to be the first to release a new film. In fact, both appeared in 1991, with the race being narrowly won by Kevin

Reynolds' *Robin Hood: Prince of Thieves* made for Warner Bros. by Morgan Creek and starring Kevin Costner, with Working Titles' *Robin of Sherwood* for Twentieth Century Fox appearing a few months later.

Reynolds reverts to the traditional representation of Robin as a dashing young nobleman. The film begins with Robin's escape from a prison in Jerusalem. Accompanied by the Moor, Azeem (Morgan Freeman), whose life he has saved and who has assisted him in the escape, he returns to England to find that his father, Lord Locksley, has been killed by the Sheriff of Nottingham for refusing to join a conspiracy to usurp Richard's throne. Subsequent action focuses on Robin's efforts to avenge his father's death, thwart the sheriff's plot, and atone for his past mistakes—we learn that he was a spoilt, arrogant lordling who rejected a father who had found comfort in the arms of a peasant woman after the death of Robin's mother.

In many ways, Robin is the conventional hero. Although the threatened amputation of his hand in the extremely violent opening sequence could be interpreted as a fear of castration, elsewhere the film displays a confidence in the masculine power and virility of the heroic figure. He is brave and resolute and Marian's initial resistance to him (she remembers his petulant ways before he left for the Crusades) is soon overcome. Nevertheless, there are moments when Robin is forced to review the consequences of heroic action and question the motives that inspired it. In slashing open the sheriff's cheek with a dagger and stealing his horse, Robin involves Little John's outlaw band in a war not of their own choosing. He usurps Little John's position as leader, and brushes aside objections to his proposed campaign of open rebellion, but it is not clear whether he is acting in the interests of the outlaws or simply wants to pursue his own vendetta against the Sheriff. Azeem warns him: "Christian, these are simple people . . . not warriors. Be careful you do not do this for your own purposes." Robin's uncharacteristically harsh dismissal of Azeem suggests the Moor's comments have touched a raw nerve.

The fears of those, like Will Scarlett, who argue the outlaws do not possess the resources to challenge well-armed soldiers, seem confirmed by the sheriff's retribution, which is swift and cruel. Local peasants, seeing their homes burnt to the ground, flee to the forest and, when they come across the outlaw band, blame Robin for their injuries and the loss of their homes. Although Robin is visibly shaken by their criticism, the threat to his leadership is only fleeting. After a momentary hesitation, his authority is restored—he recovers his confidence, rallies his men, and his judgment is vindicated by a successful attack on Nottingham Castle.

The problems, therefore, surrounding the hero's responsibility to the community and the legitimacy of heroic action, which jeopardises the lives of his followers, are not central to the film as they are in *Robin and Marian;* they are raised but too easily resolved. This would matter less if it didn't apply to other issues like the representation of women, racial tolerance, and class conflict—issues negotiated in a way that seems intended to establish the film's "politically correct" credentials. Marian, for example, is a feisty, strong-willed and independent woman quite capable of ousting a man in single combat, but Kevin Costner's Robin has little difficulty in accommodating her feminist tendencies, and her initial hostility to him quickly evaporates.

Similarly Robin feels no racial or religious prejudice towards the Moor, Azeem. The Crusades have obviously transformed him into a thoroughgoing liberal; he endorses his father's rejection of the Crusades as a foolish quest ("he said it was vanity to force other men to our religion") and he is quick to condemn any slight to Azeem after they join Little John's outlaws. Later Azeem gains full acceptance when he performs a breach birth on Little John's wife, thus saving the baby. This is an interesting scene signifying Azeem's integration with the outlaws, the promotion of inter-racial harmony, and religious understanding (Friar Tuck, who has previously been suspicious of the Moor, acknowledges he has been taught a fine lesson).

Robin assists Azeem with the baby's delivery and we see his tears when Duncan, his loyal servant, dies so he is not simply defined by the conventionally "macho" traits of the heroic figure; he is also endowed with a sensitivity and an emotional vulnerability that presumably are intended to mark him out as the new, caring man of the nineties.

Will Scarlett, eventually revealed as Robin's half brother (a kinship Robin remains unaware of until late in the film), addresses him as "rich boy" and repeatedly accuses Robin of serving his own class interests rather than those of the peasantry. This charge perhaps represents the greatest challenge to Robin's principles. Although Will's hostility to him has already been evident in the scene examined earlier (where Robin confronts the villagers driven from their homes through his precipitate action), one senses that his distrust of Robin's motives is, in fact, fuelled by more personal reasons. This is confirmed when we learn Robin has forced his father to abandon Will's mother, presumably because he felt a liaison with a peasant woman brought dishonour on the family and betrayed his mother's memory (thus the political is displaced onto the personal). In robbing the rich to give to the poor, Robin may seek to atone for his former rejection of the peasantry, but in championing their rights, he imposes an autocratic style of leadership on Little John's band of outlaws.

Robin Hood: Prince of Thieves is obviously trying to engage with discourses of gender, ethnicity, and class, and its concern for other cultures and oppressed groups of people may reflect the influence of Kevin Costner, whose *Dances with Wolves* articulated similar concerns. The film clearly wants to adopt a progressive stance in relation to important and controversial issues in contemporary society. However, since these issues are not really developed and worked through the text, they begin to look like fashionable accessories tacked on to what is fundamentally an entertaining action movie.

In the traditional epic romance, the hero is engaged in a quest—Robin's quest here is largely one of personal redemption, of overcoming the worst in himself. But as Richard Combs commented in his *Sight and Sound* review,[11] there was a fatal blandness about a hero so fundamentally decent that he had little to overcome. There also was a problem in achieving a balance of acting styles with a curiously flat performance by Costner overshadowed by a gloriously uninhibited, "hammy" performance by Alan Rickman as the Sheriff of Nottingham. Nevertheless, having a former Robin, Sean Connery, appear in the final scene to give his blessing to Robin and Marian's marriage, is a nice touch. As Combs points out, symbolically it represents Robin's reconciliation with the father denied him on his return from the Crusades and also echoes the development of the father/son theme between these two actors in *The Untouchables*.

There are significant differences in the way these films represent the heroic figure and evaluate heroic action, and each needs to be viewed in its socio-historical context. *The Adventures of Robin Hood* (1938) offers the traditional, romantic portrait of the outlaw as dispossessed aristocrat. His courageous fight against foreign tyrants is celebrated and the growing menace of fascist dictatorships in Europe means that the hero is untroubled by questions of conscience and motivation. *Robin and Marian* (1976) reverts to the ballad tradition, portraying Robin as a man of the people, a yeoman, but also as a hero lacking Flynn's youthful athleticism, a hero in mid-life crisis; and this crisis seems linked to a profound unease about the rhetoric of heroism, and about American involvement in Vietnam. In *Robin Hood: Prince of Thieves* (1991), the hero is once again the dispossessed aristocrat, Robin of Locksley—a politically correct hero whose liberal views are never really tested by the film's vague gesturing towards more radical political positions.

What each of these films offers is a view of the quintessentially English outlaw and his merry men, of "Merrie England," which incorporates a distinctively American sub-text. As Ina Rae Hark has perceptively demonstrated,[12] the visual strategies of *The Adventures of Robin Hood* and Flynn's heroic status need to be seen in the context of Roosevelt's New Deal policies and concerns about the implications for American foreign policy posed by the threat of fascist dictatorships in Europe. In the period 1937 to 1941, Warner Brothers made a number of films on historical subjects that contained veiled (or sometimes quite explicit) allusions to contemporary European politics. These films tended to vacillate between supporting either an isolationist or an interventionist policy in relation to European affairs—with the balance tilting in the latter part of this period towards a more explicit commitment to intervention[13] In 1938, however, despite Jack Warner's friendship with the president and the murder of Warner Brother's Jewish agent in Germany, the interventionist tendencies of the narrative of *The Adventures of Robin Hood* (the montage of scenes, for example, where Norman soldiers carry out Nazi-style atrocities on Saxon peasants) are balanced by the isolationist tendencies identified earlier in this chapter. Curtiz combines these specific contemporary references with a mythicised construction of rural England/Sherwood Forest that emphasises its timeless and Arcadian qualities. Like most other versions, Robin—the legendary hero whose natural habitat is the forest—is subject neither to time nor mutability.

This is where *Robin and Marion* represents a radical re-working of the traditional story in "cutting across the timelessness of the myth" (Knight, p. 237), by portraying Robin as a battle-scarred, weary, and middle-aged figure, clearly disillusioned with his king and the Crusades. Knight, while clearly admiring the film, argues that "it makes a deep-seated breach in the mythic conventions of timeless and symbolic activity; the myth is imprisoned by Lester within a cage of credibility" (Knight, p. 238). Although Knight attributes this breach to Richard Lester, the film's British director, it might more justly be credited to its American scriptwriter, James Goldman, whose introduction to the published film-script documents his long-standing fascination with the Robin Hood story and his extended search over a period of several years to interest a Hollywood studio and a director in his script (Goldman 1976, pp. 38–42). There are no allusions or oblique references to the Vietnam war in Goldman's lengthy introduction, but it seems to me legitimate to ascribe his ambivalent portrayal of the heroic figure and the disillusionment provoked by massacres carried out in the prosecution of a "just war," to the traumatic impact of the Vietnam War on the American public psyche.

The third film considered here, *Robin Hood: Prince of Thieves,* had the black actor Morgan Freeman co-starring as Azeem, Robin's Arab ally. Knight points out, that though the British television series, *Robin of Sherwood,* also had an Arab ally for Robin, Azeem is "much more attuned to a U.S. audience: Freeman is an American black in person and his character is firmly Islamic, so a black Moslem hero is validated along with a white liberal one" (Knight, p. 243). This is a view endorsed by Michael Eaton, who argues the depiction of a friendship between a black and a white man was the film's most original contribution to the Robin Hood story and that it underlined the American-ness of the production, linking it with an American literary tradition focusing on friendship between people of different races, which stretches back to Fennimore Cooper's Hawkeye and Chinganook.[14]

* * *

The Robin Hood story as portrayed in film and television (and, usually, in literary and theatrical forms) has always appealed to a dual audience. The degree of identification with Robin by young, and sometimes older, members of this audience has often been extraordinary. Philippa Pearce, in describing the Robin Hood games she played, repeats the phrase, *"I was Robin Hood"* (her emphasis) three times within two paragraphs, suggesting the outlaw hero's appeal is not confined to the male sex. However, she does not recall joining in the "opulently equipped play of Robin Hood" one of her brothers devised because she would only have been allowed to play Little John—or "might even have been condemned to Maid Marian" (Pearce 1985, p. 160).

Pearce's distaste for the supporting role of Marian may be understandable, but is still surprising given the active nature of this role: Marian willingly exchanges a life of privilege and luxury in the town for an outlaw camp in the forest having already, in many versions, warned Robin—at no little cost to her own safety—of impending betrayal and attack by the sheriff's men. Once in the forest, she also, traditionally, adopts the unisex garb of Lincoln green, a type of cross-dressing that perhaps reminds us more of the principal boy in pantomime (which, of course, includes *Robin Hood* in its repertoire) than of Rosalind and Celia in the forest of Arden.

Interest in the Robin Hood story, in its historical and mythological associations, continues undiminished. For almost eight centuries, audiences, both young and old, primitive and sophisticated, have responded to the myth's enactment of the struggle between rich and poor, freedom and tyranny, justice and injustice, respect for authority (in the person of the rightful king) and defiance of it (in the person of the Sheriff), reverence towards the Virgin Mary, and hostility towards corrupt clerics. And as people grow ever more concerned in the late twentieth century about environmental pollution and the encroachment of town upon countryside, they find that the Robin Hood myth speaks eloquently of the liberating power of nature and the greenwood, whilst the popularity of New Age philosophies, and an increasing readiness to examine paranormal phenomena, has prompted renewed interest in the links between Robin Hood, Celtic folklore, and archetypal figures such as the Green Man. Two of the most popular forms of entertainment—television and the cinema—have re-worked and re-interpreted the myth in ways that reflect changing attitudes and values, and the appearance of Kevin Costner's and Patrick Bergin's Robin Hood in the same year (1991), as well as Mel Brooks' farcical romp, *Men in Tights* (1993), indicates that, even into the twenty-first century, the legend has lost none of its appeal to a mass audience.

NOTES

1. Blyton, Enid. *Tales of Robin Hood.*
2. Trease, Geoffrey. *Bows Against the Barons.*
3. Sutcliff, Rosemary. *The Chronicles of Robin Hood.*
4. Green, Roger Lancelyn. *The Adventures of Robin Hood.*
5. Hark, Ina Rae. "The Visual Politics of *The Adventures of Robin Hood,*" *Journal of Popular Film,* Vol. 5, No. 1, 1976, pp. 3–17.
6. Quoted in Hark, Ina Rae. *The Journal of Popular Film.* 1976, p. 4.
7. Ring Lardner Jr., in *Moving Pictures,* BBC2 TV, 3 November 1990.
8. See David Turner's *Robin of the Movies,* 1989.
9. Michael Eaton, in *Moving Pictures,* BBC 2 TV, 3 November 1990.
10. Richards, Jeffrey. *Swordsmen of the Screen.* 1977, p209.
11. Combs, Richard. *Sight and Sound.* August 1991 pp. 52–53.
12. Hark, Ina Rae. "The Visual Politics of *The Adventures of Robin Hood.*" 1976, p. 4.
13. For a more extended discussion of these tendencies in Hollywood film, see John Davis's "Notes on Warner Brothers Foreign Policy 1914–1948," in *The*

Velvet Light Trap 4, 1972, and Colin Shindler's *Hollywood Goes to War: Film and American Society 1939–1952*, 1979, pp. 2–9.

14. Michael Eaton, in *Robin Hood: Man, Myth, or . . . ?* BBC Radio 2, 3 May 1996.

BIBLIOGRAPHY

Anderson, William. *The Green Man: The Archetype of Oneness with the Earth.* London; San Francisco: Harper Collins, 1990.

Blyton, Enid. *Tales of Robin Hood.* London: Newnes, 1930.

Combs, Richard. "*Robin Hood: Prince of Thieves.*" (review article) *Sight and Sound* Aug. 1991: 52–53.

Davis, John. "Notes on Warner Brothers Foreign Policy 1918–1948." *The Velvet Light Trap* 4 (1972): 23–33.

Goldman, James. *Robin and Marian.* New York: Bantam, 1976.

Green, Roger Lancelyn. *The Adventures of Robin Hood.* London: Puffin, 1956.

Hark, Ina Rae. "The Visual Politics of *The Adventures of Robin Hood,*" *Journal of Popular Film,* 5 (1976): 3–17.

Hoban, Russell. "Thoughts on a shirtless cyclist, Robin Hood, Johann Sebastian Bach and one or two other things." *Children's Literature in Education* 4 (1971): 3–24.

Knight, Stephen. *Robin Hood: A Complete Study of the English Outlaw.* Oxford, U.K. & Cambridge, Mass.: Blackwell, 1994.

Pearce, Philippa. "*Robin Hood and His Merry Men:* A Re-reading," in *Children's Literature in Education,* Vol. 16, No. 3 (1985): 159–164.

Pyle, Howard. *The Merry Adventures of Robin Hood of Great Renown in Nottinghamshire.* New York: Scribners, 1883.

Richards, Jeffrey. *Swordsmen of the Screen: From Douglas Fairbanks to Michael York.* London: Routledge, 1977.

Scott, Sir Walter. *Ivanhoe.* Edinburgh: Edinburgh University Press, 1989.

Sutcliff, Rosemary. *The Chronicles of Robin Hood.* Oxford, U.K.: Oxford University Press, 1950.

Tennyson, Lord Alfred. *The Foresters in Poems and Plays.* London: Oxford University Press, 1965 (1891).

Trease, Geoffrey. *Bows Against the Barons.* London: Martin Lawrence, 1934.

Turner, David. *Robin of the Movies (A Cinematic History of the Outlaw of Sherwood Forest).* Kingswinford, U.K.: Yeoman Publishing, 1989.

Wiles, David. *The Early Plays of Robin Hood.* Cambridge, U.K.: D. S. Brewer, 1981

Biggles—Hero of the Air

DENNIS BUTTS

It is only natural that the boy of today should look upward for his ideal hero. Blackbeard and his pirates, Dick Turpin, Robin Hood, and Buffalo Bill—these may still stir his imagination, but in his heart he knows that they belong to the past. Galleons, quarterstaffs, and tomahawks have been relegated to the museums. But the aeroplane is a thing of the present, it offers to the modern adventurer his greatest opportunity; and Biggles, with his courage, his audacity, his resourcefulness, symbolizes the spirit of the new age.[1]

What would someone who knew nothing of life on this planet learn about it from these stories? He would deduce that nearly all the world's surface was jungle and desert, inhabited only by bestial savages; that civilisation was only to be found in a place called variously "Home" or "England," whence men came by private aeroplanes to solve the problems of the dark places of the world; that these problems consisted always of evil men plotting the world's destruction for their own not-very-clearly-defined purposes; that these evil men could easily be recognized—big, black Negroes, harsh Prussian officers, fat, suave Eurasians; and that the only cure for their problems was to fight these evil men with their own weapons. (Barnes 1963, p. 116)

Heroes come in all sorts of shapes and sizes from the valorous and sulking Achilles to the diminutive, stone-slinging boy David, but there is one particularly English type of hero, the gentlemanly amateur, like Sir Percy Blakeney or Lord Peter Wimsey, who combines the aristocratic and even effete air of the dilettante with an ice-cold professionalism underneath. James Bond, with his philandering and his deadly licence to kill, is a contemporary example, and Biggles, the intrepid air-fighter, with his boyish slang and aerial supremacy, has some of the same characteristics.

Although flying stories had begun to appear before 1914, it was the onset of World War I that really established the genre. While the conflict on the ground seemed to be bogged down (often literally) in the deployment of massive armies in what came close to inert trench warfare, the war in the air, with its opportunities for speed and individual combat, rapidly acquired a romantic glamour. The invention of the synchronised machine-gun fitted to fighter-planes made aerial duels between single combatants possible. A new word, the "ace," was coined for such men as Billy Bishop and the German pilot, von Richtofen, known as the "Red Baron," and stories about them resembled the knightly tales in Malory's *Le Morte D'Arthur.* The British Prime Minister Lloyd George actually described these aviators as "the Cavalry of the clouds . . . the knighthood of the war, without fear and without reproach. They recall the old legends of chivalry, not merely the daring of their exploits, but by the nobility of their spirit, and, amongst the multitude of heroes, let us think of the chivalry of the air" (Goldstein 1986, p. 87).

Percy F. Westerman (1876–1959) became the first popular writer of flying stories for boys, with such books as *Winning his Wings: a Story of the R.A.F.,* published in 1919, but during the 1930s flying stories by W. E. Johns (1893–1968) began to appear, which were eventually to completely eclipse Westerman's popularity. Originally a soldier who had experienced trench warfare at Gallipoli, Johns successfully transferred to the newly established Royal Flying Corps in 1917, and as a member of the 55th Squadron, was involved in bombing raids on Germany. Shot down in 1918, he finished the war in a prison camp, but remained in the Royal Air Force until 1927, obtaining further experience in India and Iraq, and even claiming to have interviewed T. E. Lawrence (of Arabia) when he applied to join the R.A.F. under a pseudonym.

In 1932 he published "The White Fokker," his first story about Biggles, the pilot who would become his most famous creation, in the magazine *Popular Flying.* "Biggles" is the nickname of James Bigglesworth, at this time a teenager but already a Flight Commander on active service in France during World War I, and the first tale narrates an episode of the war in which members of Biggles' squadron are regularly being ambushed and killed by a German Fokker aircraft until Biggles manages to trap and shoot down the German pilot.

Such magazine stories, with their fresh and authentic accounts of flying adventures, soon proved popular with young readers as well as the adults for whom they were originally intended, and were collected and published in such books as *The Camels Are Coming* (1932), *Biggles of the Camel Squadron* (1934), and *Biggles Learns to Fly* (1935). Biggles was on his way as a popular hero. To begin with he is no stereotyped, tight-lipped figure, but a patriotic, skilful and highly strung young man who several times comes close to tears, even hysteria, when comrades are lost:

> Bigglesworth, commonly called Biggles, a fair-haired good-looking lad still in his 'teens', but an acting Flight-Commander, was talking; not of wine or women, as novelists would have us believe, but of a new fusee *(sic)* spring for a Vickers gun which would speed it up another hundred rounds a minute. His deep-set hazel eyes were never still and held a glint of yellow fire that somehow seemed out of place in a pale face upon which the strain of war, and sight of sudden death, had already graven little lines. His hands, small and delicate as a girl's, fidgeted continually with the tunic fastening at his throat. He had killed a man not six hours before. He had killed six men during the past month—or was it a year?—he had forgotten. Time had become extremely telescoped lately. What did it matter anyway? He knew he had to die sometime and had long ago ceased to worry about it. His careless attitude told one story, but the irritating little falsetto laugh which continually punctuated his tale told another. (Johns 1932, p. 14)

Biggles is a slim, boyish, fair-haired young hero at the beginning of his adventures, clearly feeling the strain of war, but apparently concealing it beneath a certain degree of insouciance. There is more than a touch of public school humour about Biggles at this stage, not only in his persistently addressing colleagues as "laddie" or "old boy," and his use of such phrases as "Great Scott!" and "Holy Mackerel!", but in his playing so many practical jokes. In *Biggles of 266,* for example, the 1955 collection of stories first printed in the 1930s, Biggles demonstrates his high spirits by flying over enemy lines to hunt a turkey for Christmas, but he also plays a practical joke on a colleague who has let him down, by dropping his clothes over the German lines, and later disguises himself as a colonel in order to fool an arrogant commanding officer.

It is this brand of humour, slang, and irony mixed with practical joking, combined with aerial skill and courage, which proved such an irresistible concoction of youthful heroism. Here is Biggles in a spot of bother in *The Camels Are Coming* as his Camel plane is attacked by German Albatrosses who also are involved in an battle with an American Spad Squadron:

> A green Albatross came at him head-on, and, as he charged it, another with a white-and-blue checked fuselage sent a tracer through his top plane. The green machine swerved and he flung the Camel round behind it; but the checked machine had followed him and he had to pull up in a wild zoom to escape the hail of lead it spat at him. "Strewth!" grunted Biggles, as his wind-screen flew to pieces. "This is getting too hot! My gosh! What a mess!" A Spad and an Albatross, locked together, careered earthwards in a flat spin. A Camel, spinning viciously, whirled past him, and another Albatross, wrapped in a sheet of flame, flashed past his nose, the doomed pilot leaping into space even as it passed.
>
> Biggles snatched a quick glance upwards. A swarm of Albatrosses were dropping like vultures out of the sky into the fight; he had a fleeting glimpse of other machines far above and then he turned again to the work on hand. Where were the Spads? Ah, there was one, on the tail of an Albatross. He tore after it, but the Spad pilot saw him and waved him away. Biggles grinned. "Go to it, laddie," he yelled exultantly, but a frown swept the grin from his face as a jagged machine darted in behind the Spad and poured in a murderous stream of lead. Biggles shot down on the tail of the Hun. The Spad pilot saw his danger and twisted sideways to escape, but an invisible cord seemed to hold the Albatross to the tail of the American machine. Biggles took the jagged machine in his sights and raked it from end to end in a long deadly burst. There was no question of missing at that range; the enemy pilot slumped forward in his seat and the machine went to pieces in the air. (Johns [1932] 1983, pp. 32–33)

The sources of the inspiration for the creation of Biggles, who continued to enjoy new flying adventures until 1970, have naturally aroused considerable interest. According to people who knew W. E. Johns well, there are grounds for believing that "Biggles" was based upon Air Commodore C. G. Wigglesworth or Air Commodore A. W. Bigsworth, both of whom had long and distinguished careers in the Royal Air Force. More recently, Professor Jeffrey Richards has suggested that Biggles was based upon the character of Lawrence of Arabia, whom Johns met in the 1920s. But Johns himself always claimed that Biggles was a representative figure, based upon the character and exploits of a number of individuals who fought in World War I:

> "Captain James Bigglesworth is a fictitious character," he said, "yet he could have been found in any R.F.C. [Royal Flying Corps] mess during those great days of 1917 and 1918 when air combat had become the order of the day and air duelling was a fine art." In an interview he gave in 1938, he even said, "In a way he is myself." (Berresford Ellis & Schofield 1993, pp. 184–185, 262–264)

But Biggles was not on his own, and part of the appeal of the Biggles' stories lies in their being about a group of adventurers, though Biggles is always the leader. His immediate superior and boss, variously ranked as Colonel, Wing Commander, or Air Commodore Raymond, according to the changing background of Biggles' career, remains a shadowy figure, rarely more than the messenger who brings Biggles some momentous task and congratulates him when it has been successfully accomplished. Biggles' cousin, the Honourable Algernon (but always known as Algy) Lacey, joins him in World War I, and though Biggles resents him for his inexperience at first, soon becomes his trusted lieutenant. Flight-Sergeant Smyth is the skilful and reliable mechanic through many adventures, and other members of No. 266 Squadron also recur in the stories with a World War I setting.

The problem for W. E. Johns was where to go once he had exhausted his writing about his war experiences. *The Cruise of the Condor* (1933) pointed the way in a tale about the post-war adventures of Biggles, Algy, and Flight-Sergeant Smyth in a treasure-hunt in the wilds of Brazil. Similar stories with equally exotic settings were to follow: *Biggles Flies West* (1937), about a search for treasure in the Caribbean; *Biggles Flies South* (1938), about the search for a Lost Oasis; and *Biggles Flies North* (1939), about the gold-fields of North-West Canada.

Although some of these stories suggest that Johns was cleverly reworking some classic children's books for the air age, and Professor Richards has pointed to the influence of Stevenson's *Treasure Island* upon *Biggles Flies West,* and of Rider Haggard upon *Biggles Flies South,* Johns was, in fact, introducing other changes into his novels.[2] Biggles himself was no longer the courageous but slightly hysterical young hero of World War I, whose boyish high spirits often found an outlet in practical jokes. As Johns himself said, Biggles had "developed under the stress of war into the sort of man most men would like to be; fearless but modest, efficient and resolute in what he undertook."[3] By the late 1930s, Biggles has become a confident, almost imperturbable leader, and he gradually hardens into an increasingly masterful hero, impervious to almost all dangers.

But Johns realised that Biggles was also getting older. Born about 1900, he was beginning to approach middle-age by the nineteen-thirties, perhaps a shade too old for his juvenile readers to identify with. So in *The Black Peril* of 1935, Johns introduced a new, more youthful hero, Ginger Hebblethwaite (originally Habblethwaite): "a lad of fifteen or sixteen years of age. He was in rags, dirty beyond description, but above a collarless shirt rose a frank, alert, freckled face, surmounted by a mop of tousled red hair."[4] The son of a coal-miner, Ginger is mad on flying, and with the reward he gets for helping Biggles defeat a Russian plot, goes to flying school and subsequently accompanies him on many later adventures.

With the addition of Ginger, Johns' team of post-war adventurers was complete, and he was able to use them to develop more complicated plots, spread over a whole novel, rather than the books about World War I, which tended to be made up of separate episodes. When a group is involved in solving a mystery or fighting unknown antagonists, it is possible for members of the group to take on different tasks, or to pursue their activities independently. W. E. Johns, in fact, tended to develop very formulaic plots along these lines when he moved away from stories about World War I, in which Biggles was often the sole hero, to later books, such as *Biggles—Air Commodore* (1937), for example, in which Biggles, Algy, and Ginger set out together to investigate why some merchant ships have been sunk under mysterious circumstances in the Indian Ocean. When they separate to begin their search, Ginger and Algy crash in the jungle, and Biggles has to rescue them, but later, when Biggles and Ginger are lost on an island, Algy has to come to their rescue. Although this device was obviously used to create suspense, the formula did become too predictable at times.

Most enduring heroes need a recurring villain—one thinks of Robin Hood and the Sheriff of Nottingham, or Sherlock Holmes and Professor Moriarty—and in 1935 we hear of Biggles' arch-enemy, Erich von Stalheim.

Von Stalheim first appears in *Biggles Flies East* (1935), a story about experiences in World War I, which Biggles has felt such distaste for that he has always kept quiet about them. The tale reveals how, by a case of mistaken identity, Biggles is recruited as a German spy, and goes along with the error in order to discover enemy secrets. Posted to the Middle East, Biggles finds himself working for a formidable German officer:

> In appearance he was tall, slim, and good-looking in a rather foppish way, but he had been a soldier for many years and there was a grim re-lentlessness about his manner that quickly told Biggles that he was a man to be feared. He had been wounded early in the war, and walked with a permanent limp with the aid of two sticks, and this physical defect added something to his sinister bearing. Unlike most of his countrymen, he was dark, with cold brooding eyes that were hard to meet and held a steel-like quality that the monocle he habitually wore could not dispel. Such was Hauptmann Erich von Stalheim. (Johns 1942, p. 25)

Despite von Stalheim's suspicions about him, Biggles manages to outwit him and defeat the German plot, and the story ends with Biggles believing that von Stalheim is dead, shot down by anti-aircraft guns. Such a villain was not to be got rid of so easily, however, and a year later in a story about adventures after the war, *Biggles & Co* (1936), when Biggles, Algy, Ginger, and Flight-Sergeant Smyth are trying to protect gold-shipments from being robbed, Algy finds himself captured by a fa-miliar German figure:

> "Good heavens!" he breathed, through lips that had turned dry. "It's von Stalheim." The other nodded affably. "Yes," he said quietly. "No less. And here, after all these years, is the Honourable Algernon Lacey still scouting for trouble."
> Algy ignored the thrust. "But I thought you were dead," he blurted, with an astonishment he made no attempt to conceal. "I hoped you would," answered von Stalheim simply. "But we of the German Secret Service do not die so easily." (Johns 1946, pp. 119–20)

In fact, Von Stalheim was to engage in many more adventures with Big-gies, and to survive for another thirty years.

The outbreak of World War II in 1939 presented W. E. Johns with se-rious problems, however. The difficulty lay in the fact that Johns himself was a veteran of World War I and the Royal Flying Corps, relying on his earlier experiences and still using outdated flying slang such as "archie" for "flak." But Johns' readers now expected Biggles to fly the kinds of planes in the kinds of dogfights they were to learn about from the Battle of Britain. In *Spitfire Parade* (1941), Johns made a particularly unsuccessful attempt to update his material, revising old Royal Flying Corps stories that had already appeared in Biggles in France in 1935. In later stories, such as *Biggles in the Orient* (1944), Johns not only achieved more realism with new flying terms ("bandit," "Wimpey," "gone for a Burton"), but also successfully invented another group of flyers. As well as introducing a new major character Lord "Bertie" Lissie, a "silly-ass" type hero with a monocle, Johns seemed to use his new No. 666 (Fighter) Squadron to suggest something of the new democratic spirit which Angus Calder[5] saw as a characteristic of World War II:

> There was "Ginger" Hebblethwaite, a waif who had attached himself to Biggles and Algy before the war, and who had almost forgotten the slum in which he had been born; "Tex" O'Hara, a product of the wide open spaces of Texas, U.S.A.; "Taffy" Hughes, whose paternal ancestors may have been one of those Welsh knifemen that helped the Black Prince to make a name for valour; "Tug" Carrington, a Cockney and proud of it, handy with his "dukes," hating all aggressors (and Nazis in particular) with a passion that sometimes startled the others; Henry Harcourt, a thin, pale, thoughtful-eyed Oxford undergraduate, who really loathed war yet had learned how to fight; and "Ferocity" Ferris, who, born in a back street in Liverpool, had got his commission, not by accident (as he sometimes said) but by sheer flying ability. (Johns [1945] 1983, p. 291)

After this declaration of social equality, it is a little disturbing to learn that Biggles has moulded the group into an efficient team that is characterised not by patriotism or love of freedom but loyalty—"loyalty to the service, to the team, and above all to the leader" (ibid.). It is not the only incongruous note in a tale of genuine mystery as Biggles and his squadron fly to India to investigate the reason so many transport planes have disappeared en route for China without any obvious explanation.

With the end of World War II, Johns had to re-invent his hero's career for a third time, and this he did by transferring Biggles' old boss, Air Commodore Raymond, back to Criminal Investigation Department (C.I.D.) and Scotland Yard, and by Raymond's then inviting Biggles, Algy, Ginger, and Bertie to join him in the formation of a squad of flying detectives. In *Sergeant Bigglesworth of the C.I.D.* (1946), Biggles and his colleagues are soon in pursuit of a gang of jewel-thieves, and there are plenty of opportunities for flying adventures as the trail leads them to Libya and Abyssinia, before the criminals are finally brought to justice. This new formula was an effective one, and in such books as *Biggles Breaks the Silence* (1949) and *Biggles in Australia* (1955), Johns was able to depict baffling crimes, to introduce enemies from the other side the Iron Curtain, and to continue the running feud between Biggles and von Stalheim. The rivalry between Biggles and von Stalheim only ended in fact in *Biggles Buries the Hatchet* in 1958, when Biggles rescues von Stalheim from a Russian prison camp, and a later book, *Biggles Looks Back* (1965), actually sees them working together in a rare story about Biggles' relations with women.

For many readers Biggies always seemed a permanent bachelor, loyal to his friends and needing only male company. But an early World War I story, "Affaire de Coeur" (in *The Camels Are Coming,* 1932) had depicted the young Biggles falling passionately in love with a French-woman, Marie Janis, whom he met when he made a forced landing. She is described as "a vision of blonde loveliness, wrapped up in blue silk," and when Biggles greets her, he says "I've been looking for you all my life. I didn't think I'd ever find you" (Johns [1932] 1983, p. 116). Al-though Marie subsequently turns out to have been a German spy, she genuinely loved Biggles, and tried to redeem her attempted betrayal, but tragic circumstances intervened and Biggles came to believe that she had been killed in the war. Now in the 1960s he learns from von Stalheim that Marie is still alive, but virtually imprisoned in communist Czechoslova-kia. "Did you ever wonder what became of Marie Janis?" von Stalheim asks, and Biggles answers "I've never stopped wondering. War threw us together. War tore us apart" (Johns 1965, p. 11).

Moved by the news of Marie's plight, Biggles plots to rescue her from her castle in communist-ruled eastern Europe. When he has done so, he continues to support her in "a cottage in the Hampshire village where she now lives, Biggles and von Stalheim often running down for the weekend to talk of their many adventures" (Johns 1965, p. 190). It could be argued, therefore, that Biggles is neither asexual nor a repressed homosexual, but a romantic hero, like Sydney Carton in *A Tale of Two Cities,* tragically loyal to the only woman he ever really loved.

In the years after World War II, Johns' books became extremely pop-ular, and were translated into numerous European languages, including Danish, Dutch, Finnish, Flemish, German, Hungarian, Icelandic, Italian, Norwegian, Portuguese, Spanish, and Swedish. He also was translated into Bahasi Malaysian, and no fewer than thirty-seven of his books appeared in Braille editions for the blind. In the 1950s he became the fourth best-selling author in France, and also enjoyed great popularity in Australia and New Zealand; in the 1970s, Biggles books were selling half a million copies annually.

The B.B.C. frequently broadcast dramatised versions of Johns' stories, from *Biggles Flies West* in 1948 to *Biggles Presses On* in 1959, and in Australia Biggles almost became a radio institution with over two hundred programmes about him that also were distributed in New Zealand and South Africa. Granada Television in Britain also produced a popular series of forty-four programmes featuring Biggles in 1960. With all this it is not too surprising to learn that by 1964 the UNESCO Statistical Yearbook reported that Biggles books had been placed twenty-ninth on the list of the most translated books in the world, and that Biggles was the most popular juvenile hero in the world.[6]

Though Johns had created in Biggles a hero who had almost become a synonym for the bold and fearless flyer, adverse criticism of his books began to appear as his work achieved its greatest popularity. Geoffrey Trease had voiced some concerns about Johns' nationalistic bias, his attitude to foreigners, and the question of violence in *Tales Out of School* (first published in 1949), and by the 1960s such criticism was widespread. Some librarians even began to take Johns' books from the shelves, and the Biggles' books were particularly attacked for their sexism, their violence, and their racism.[7]

The accusation of sexism seems the least appropriate. Johns was writing adventure stories about a masculine culture in which girls and young women inevitably played a minor part at the time. And he would probably have agreed with Frank Richards's reply to George Orwell's accusation that the Greyfriars school stories were sexless: "Sex certainly does enter uncomfortably into the experience of the adolescent, but surely the less he thinks about it at an early age the better" (Richards 1940, p. 348). Yet Johns does portray Biggles' unhappy relationship with Marie Jenis in *The Camels Are Coming* and *Biggles Looks Back* and gives an account of Ginger's love-affair in *Biggles Fails to Return* (1943). The most telling reason for questioning accusations of Johns being sexist, however, is found in the sequence of eleven novels beginning with *Worrals of the WAAF* (1941), in which he depicts the exploits of a brave female pilot, Joan Worralson. On the evidence of these stories, there is even a case for suggesting that Johns was a pioneering feminist!

The accusation of war-mongering and excessive violence is more complicated. No one who has read the early books with the picture of an at times strained young Biggles or Johns' moving accounts of fatalities in *Biggles Pioneer Air Fighter,* for example, could doubt that he was seriously concerned to depict the horrors of war. Adventure stories about wars also contain frequent scenes of fights and battles as a characteristic of their genre, so readers should not be surprised by fist-fights or by shooting. The question is, therefore, one of treatment, and here there are problems that challenge the view that "Biggles knocked a man down on several occasions but only when he had to" (Berresford Ellis & Schofield 1993, p. 235). There is, for example, a disturbing episode from *Biggles in the Orient,* a World War II story, where Biggles watches two Japanese soldiers approach a dead British flyer:

> They broke into an excited jabber as they walked on to the fuselage. When one of them pointed at the dead pilot and burst out laughing, after a momentary look of wonder Biggles frowned: friend or foe, to European eyes the sight was anything but funny. When one of them kicked the body every vestige of colour drained from his face. His lips came together in a hard line; his nostrils quivered. Still he did not move. But when one of the men, with what was evidently a remark intended to be jocular, bent down and inserted his cigarette between the dead pilot's lips, and then, shouting with laughter, stepped back to observe the effort, Biggles' pent-up anger could no longer be restrained. "'You scum," he grated. The words were low but distinct.
>
> The two Japanese spun round as if a shot had been fired. They stared in goggle-eyed amazement, no longer laughing, but fearful, as though confronted by a ghost—the ghost of the body they had violated. Superstitious by nature, they may have believed that. Biggles spoke again. "You utter swine," he breathed.
>
> This spurred the Japanese to movement. With a curious cry one of them threw up his rifle. Biggles fired. The man twitched convulsively. Again Biggles' automatic roared. The men's legs crumpled under him; the rifle fell from his hands and he slumped choking. The second man started to run. Quite dispassionately, Biggles took deliberate aim and fired. The Jap pitched forward on his face, but crying loudly started to get up. Biggles walked forward and with calculated precision fired two more shots at point-blank range. His lips were drawn back, showing the teeth, "You unutterable thug!" he rasped. The man lay still. (Johns 1945, pp. 60–61)

Such things happen in war, we say, and Johns has captured the incident with power and feeling. But what exactly is his attitude? Is there not something, even when we recognize the strength of our feelings about Japanese atrocities, too cold-blooded, racist, and vindictive mixed up in Johns' approval of Biggles' behaviour? What are we, or Johns' school-boy readers, meant to feel about the first man's convulsive twitching, or when Biggles shoots the wounded second man? How does this action match that convention of the adventure code (as in western films) where the hero never strikes first? How does it square with Johns' own state-ment of 1947 that "Biggles . . . has only once struck a man, and that was a matter of life and death" (Trease 1965, p. 80)?

The question of Johns' racism has to be viewed historically. Johns was not a deliberate racist. He had an honourable record of opposing the appeasement of Nazi Germany before World War II, and would undoubt-edly have agreed with the words he puts into Biggles mouth in his story *Biggles Delivers the Goods* in 1946:

> "While men are decent to me I've tried to be decent to them, regardless of race, colour, politics, creed or anything else," asserted Biggles curtly. "I've travelled a lot, and taking the world by and large, it's my experience that with a few exceptions there's nothing wrong with the people on it, if only they were left alone to live as they want to live." (Berresford Ellis & Schofield 1993, p. 243)

Nevertheless, with the exception of the early books about World War I, where there is a recognition of the existence of good Germans as well as bad ones, most of Johns' stories about Biggles reflect what Jeffrey Richards has called "casual racism."[8] This does not necessarily mean that the villains are always black, Asian, or half-caste, but that Johns' characters frequently demean such people by the way they refer to them. Indeed, Johns seems particularly upset by any signs of miscegenation, commenting, for example, on a Turko-Greek in *Biggles Flies South,* as "a type common in the Middle East, where east and west are all too often blended with unfortunate results" (Johns 1938, p. 52). As early as 1934 in *Biggles Flies Again,* Algy talks of offering "Joy Rides for Niggers, Flip-Flops for Cannibals." In *Biggles—Air Commodore* (1937), Biggles talks about "wogs," and as late as 1955 calls an Australian aborigine a "wop" in *Biggles in Australia.*[9]

The fact is that Captain W. E. Johns, as he called himself, was a product of his age, born in the heyday of British imperialism, and his work, consciously or unconsciously, reflects the racist ideology of impe-rialism. When Geoffrey Trease asked him why he wrote for children, Johns' answer, while claiming the primacy of entertainment, concluded:

I teach at the same time, under a camouflage. Juveniles are keen to learn, but the educational aspect must not be too obvious as they become suspicious of its intention. I teach a boy to be a man, for without that essential qualification he will never be anything. I teach sportsmanship according to the British idea. One doesn't need blood and thunder to do that. In more than forty novels about my hero Biggles he has only once struck a man and that was a matter of life and death. I teach that decent behaviour wins in the end as a natural order of things. I teach the spirit of team-work, loyalty to the Crown, the Empire, and to rightful authority. (Trease 1965, p. 80)

So great was the appeal of Johns' books, however, so thrilling were the adventures of his hero Biggles, that even the great Kenyan novelist Ngugi wa Thiong'o found them compulsive reading, despite considerable ambivalence about their values. Ngugi's older brother ran away to join the Mau Mau army, which was formed to oust the British from Kenya, and was the subject of intense bombing by the Royal Air Force. "So," Ngugi says, "in reading Biggles in the years 1955 and 1956 I was involved in a drama of contradictions. Biggles could have been dropping bombs on my own brother in the forests of Mount Kenya. Or he could have been sent by Raymond to ferret out those who were plotting against the British Empire in Kenya. Either way he would have been pitted against my own brother . . ."

Yet Ngugi devoured these stories about Biggles:

It was also a stage in my life when what was most important in literature was the story and the element of what happens next. And this the Biggles books had in plenty. The Biggles series were full of actions, intrigues, thrills, twists, surprises and a very simple morality of right against wrong, angels against devils, with the good always triumphant. It was adventure all the way, on land and in the sky. And what is more you did not have to read more than fifty pages before you were in the thick of the action. They were the kind of books that told a young man: once you start reading me, you will not put me down. It was the strong action which made one forget, or swallow, all the racist epithets of the narratives. The books did not invite meditation; just the involvement of the hero and his band of faithfuls.[10]

That helps to explain very well the enduring appeal of the Biggles books, despite all their faults. The legendary hero continues to survive. In 1993 the centenary of Johns' birth was celebrated on radio, in the press, and at numerous exhibitions and gatherings, including a W. E. Johns Centenary Luncheon at the Royal Air Force Club. An International Biggles Association has been formed in the Netherlands, and, most significant of all perhaps, Red Fox, who began reprinting Biggles books in 1992, were able by April 1993 to report sales of one hundred thousand copies. (Berresford Ellis & Schofield 1993, p. 261)

It is impossible to know exactly how powerful the impact of Johns' flying hero Biggles has been upon the public. In James Thurber's "Secret Life of Walter Mitty," was Walter's aerial fantasy ("It takes two men to handle that bomber and the Archies are pounding hell out of the air") influenced by Biggles (Thurber 1962, p. 41)? Did the pilots of the Battle of Britain learn some of their apparent insouciance from the same source? The legend still lives on. One can see it behind Steven Spielberg's film *Raiders of the Lost Ark,* an adventure story about a journey to retrieve the Lost Ark of the Covenant from headhunters, snakepits, and Nazi villains, in a chase involving the plane "Flying Wing," that takes the hero right round the world in a manner deliberately based on the serials of the 1930s and 1940s.[11] One sees it even more explicitly in the following exchange in *Biggles,* the bold and not entirely unsuccessful film attempt to capture the spirit of Johns' early books, which was made in 1986:

> "Jim, won't you please tell me what's going on?"
> "O.K. Debbie, but I'm telling you no one ever believes it... I keep falling through this hole in time, going back to 1917."
> "Go on!"
> "Do you believe me?"
> "Well, if you say so, Jim, I guess I believe you."
> "Debbie, I keep going back to World War I where I'm helping this guy Biggles find and destroy a German secret weapon . . ."[12]

NOTES

1. Publicity advertisement for W. E. Johns, *Biggles Defies the Swastika,* 1941.

2. Professor Jeffrey Richards, "Biggles of the British Empire" (an unpublished paper), Oxford, 1994.

3. Quoted from the *TV Times,* 27 March 1960 by Peter Berresford Ellis & Jennifer Schofield in *Biggles! The Life Story of Capt. W. E. Johns, Creator of Biggles, Worrals, Gimlet, & Steeley,* 1993.

4. *Biggles and the Black Peril* [*The Black Peril*] n.d., p. 34.

5. Angus Calder, *The People's War: Britain 1939–45*, 1969, p. 17.

6. See Peter Berresford Ellis and Jennifer Schofield, op. cit., pp. 207–08, 211, 311–12.

7. See, for example, Geoffrey Trease, *Tales Out of School*, 1965; D. R. Barnes, "Captain Johns and the Adult World" in *Young Writers, Young Readers*, 1965; Bob Dixon, *Catching Them Young: Political Ideas in Children's Fiction*, 1977.

8. Professor Jeffrey Richards, op. cit. p. 20.

9. *Biggles Flies Again.* n.d., p. 16; *Biggles—AirCommodore*, 1937, p. 198; *Biggles in Australia*, 1955, p. 97.

10. Nugugi Wa Thiong'o, "Ambivalent feelings about Biggles," *The Guardian*, 13 August 1992.

11. *Raiders of the Lost Ark*, dir. Steven Spielberg, Paramount, U.S.A., 1981.

12. *Biggles*, dir. John Hough, Great Britain, 1986.

BIBLIOGRAPHY

Barnes, D. R. "Captain Johns and the Adult World," in *Young Writers, Young Readers*, ed. Boris Ford. London: Hutchinson, 1963: 115–122..

Berresford Ellis, P. & Schofield, J. *Biggles! The Life Story of Capt. W. E. Johns, Creator of Biggles, Worrals, Gimlet & Steeley.* Dorset: Veloce, 1993

Calder, Angus. *The People's War.* London: Cape, 1965

Dixon, Bob. *Catching Them Young: Political Ideas in Children's Fiction.* London: Pluto Press, 1977

Goldstein, Laurence. *The Flying Machine and Modern Literature.* London: Macmillan, 1986.

Johns, W. E. "The White Fokker," in *Popular Flying*. Vol. 1, No. 1 London, 1932.

———. *The Camels Are Coming.* [orig. 1932] reprinted in *The Bumper Biggles Book*. 1983: 287–437.

———. *Biggles and the Black Peril* [orig. published as *The Black Peril*, 1925] London: Dean & Son, n.d.

———. *Biggles Flies Again.* London: Thames, n.d.

———. *Biggles—AirCommodore.* London: Oxford University Press, 1937.

———. *Biggles Flies South.* London: Oxford University Press, 1938.

———. *Biggles Flies East* [orig. 1935] London: Hodder & Stoughton, 1942.

———. *Biggles in the Orient.* London: Hodder & Stoughton, 1945.

———. *Biggles & Co.* London: Oxford University Press, 1946.

———. *Biggles in Australia.* London: Hodder & Stoughton, 1955.

———. *Biggles Looks Back.* London: Hodder & Stoughton, 1965.

————. *The Bumper Biggles Book* (*Biggles, Pioneer Air Fighter; Biggles Flies South; Biggles in the Orient; Biggles Defies the Swastika; Biggles in the Jungle*) London: Chancellor Press, 1983.

Richards, Frank. "A Reply to George Orwell," *Horizon,* May 1940: 346–355.

Thurber, James. "The Secret Life of Walter Mitty," *The Thurber Carnival.* Harmondsworth: Penguin, 1962.

Trease, Geoffrey. *Tales Out of School.* 2nd ed. London: Heinemann, 1965.

Piloting the Nation
Dan Dare and the 1950s

TONY WATKINS

> The time was ripe for a space hero of the technological post-war era and Dan Dare was the right hero in the right comic at the right time. (Wright & Higgs 1990, p. 4)

> Dan Dare was a hero created for a time, and do people want a hero any more? I don't know . . . I just don't know. (Frank Hampson, creator of *Dan Dare,* interviewed in 1974)

These statements underlie much of this chapter, which will explore the senses in which the comic-book character, Dan Dare, was constructed as a national hero to be a "pilot" for a specific period, namely, the 1950s. The strip cartoon, which first appeared in the *Eagle* comic in April 1950, makes an interesting case-study of a deliberate intervention to provide children at a specific moment in history with a narrative that carried clear moral and ideological ways of seeing the present, the past and the future—ways of seeing that grew out of a combination of nationalism, idealism, and a mythology shaped by Britain's experience of World War II. Those values, of course, can only be read through a consideration of the male adventure *genre* to which "Dan Dare Pilot of the Future" belongs and a consideration of the *form* of the comic strip in which they were presented. It is the argument of this chapter, then, that to understand the significance of Dan Dare as a heroic figure in children's popular culture, we need to regard him as "a pilot for the nation," constructed at a particular moment in British history through the re-articulation of the conventions of the male adventure story and of the strip cartoon. Furthermore, the article will discuss how contemporary discourses around heroes may now shape our view of such a national fictional hero as Dan Dare. Certainly, to make any adequate reading of a historical text, we must recognise our own historicity as readers.

It is now clear to most analysts that comics use their visual narratives to embody ideological and moral structures (Sillars 1995, p. 133). An analysis of the Dan Dare strip soon reveals that it is characterised by moral and ideological discourses around heroism and, to a lesser extent, around gender and ethnicity. In addition, it re-works the Romantic debate about technology and human values and, politically, it displays a liberal form of nationalism and imperialism, tempered by faith in the United Nations. Historically, these values and ideologies are worked through the mythic discourses "born of the experience of Britain at war, when Britain stood alone against Hitler . . . backs to the wall . . . our gallant airmen . . . blood, sweat and tears" (James 1987, p. 43). These, in turn, link the strip to the values of the liberal-minded utopian planners of British post-war reconstruction. Dan Dare is a British hero, in particular a very *English* hero, re-presenting myths of national identity through the fantasy mode of a history of the future.

However, the problem for post-war utopian thinking was the fact that the Brave New World had to be built on what has been described as the " 'Cruel Real World' of a bankrupt Britain with a ruined export trade and vanished overseas investments." Some historians, therefore, dismiss the idealism of a Labour party that wanted "an end to unemployment, homelessness, want, hunger, ignorance, disease and social privilege" (James 1987, p. 44) as a failure to grasp the economic realities of the post-war situation: "British total strategy between 1945 and 1950 was shaped less by the realities of Britain's post-war plight than by the nation's dreams and illusions" (Barnett 1995, pp. xix, xiii). But such arguments obviously resurrect the debate about the value or otherwise of utopian visions. Certainly, the immediate post-war period out of which Dan Dare was constructed as a national hero *was* marked nationally by an economic crisis in the balance of payments, homelessness, physical privations, and food shortages: bread rationing was introduced on 21 July 1946 and, by the end of that year, some fifty thousand squatters were living, illegally, in disused army camps and "pre-fabs" (pre-fabricated houses). The bitter-cold winter of 1946–47 was the prelude to further hardship in the form of the floods of March 1947 and, by the summer of that year, water shortages (James 1987, p. 44). As one historian puts it: "there was no brave new world, *no land fit for heroes* [my emphasis], no tangible victory. Britain had not emerged into the light. . . . The bomb sites gaped like great open wounds on the city faces" (Montgomery 1965, p. 38).

However, just prior to the publication of *Eagle* in 1950, there was a gradual change towards a more hopeful national situation:

> By 1948 or 1949, the end of the privations of 1946 and 1947 was in sight, and some of the these hopes for a future utopia returned. Bread rationing ended in July 1948; sweet rationing ended (temporarily) in April 1949; clothes rationing ended in November 1949; a host of other restrictions came to an end in 1950. For those who were to buy the first copy of the *Eagle*, all this was an introduction to a world they had never known (James 1987 p. 44).

But, by the beginning of the 1950s, the *international* situation still seemed grim to most people: The Chinese communists had controlled the mainland for two years; the Russians were regarded as a more dangerous enemy than the Germans had been; the Korean War, declared on 25 June 1950, threatened to start World War III. The United Nations acted swiftly over Korea, but when calls for a cease-fire were ignored, American troops moved in—the official American view being "that communism must be halted by force in Korea" (Montgomery 1965, p. 65). However, one result of the Korean War was to increase anxiety about the future: The American and British governments considerably increased expenditure on armaments, while in Britain, the number of U.S. bomber bases grew and National Service was extended from eighteen months to two years. Above all, there was the fear of nuclear weapons. As one commentator of the time put it: "People everywhere are deeply troubled by what seems like a fated and predetermined march towards even greater disaster. The hydrogen bomb must be considered not as an engine of victory but solely as a an engine of destruction" (quoted in Montgomery 1965, p. 96).

It is out of this complex social and political history that "Dan Dare—Pilot of the Future" was published in the first issue of the comic, *Eagle*, on 14 April 1950. *Eagle* had its origins in the late 1940s when the Rev. Marcus Morris formed the "Society for Christian Publicity" as a forum for Christian discussion. Because he felt the church was not communicating as it should, he started a magazine called *The Anvil* "to hammer out important issues of the day" (Crompton 1985, p. 26). There were many important issues to discuss: the war had recently ended and, in a landslide election, the Labour government had been brought to power "intent on building a brave new world" based on the welfare state (ibid.). The Rev. Marcus Morris' prime concern, however, was with morality and the young and the focus of his anxiety was the horror comics being imported from America. In an article for the *Sunday Dispatch,* he wrote: "Horror has crept into the British nursery. Morals of little girls in plaits and boys with marbles bulging their pockets are being corrupted by a torrent of indecent coloured magazines that are flooding bookstalls and newsagents . . . Not mere 'thrillers' as we used to know them, nor the once-familiar 'school stories'. These are evil and dangerous—graphic coloured illustrations of modern city and crime" (Morris 1949, p. 4).

Morris claimed that these comics influenced children to commit crimes of violence and he ended his article with a clear moral programme of reform, including a call to construct national heroes of a particular kind for children—heroic adventurers who displayed Christian zeal:

> I shall not feel I have done my duty as a parson and a father of children until I have seen on the market a genuinely popular children's comic where adventure is once more the clean and exciting business I remember in my own schooldays . . . Surely, there is adventure enough for any boy or girl in the lives of men like Grenville of Labrador? And some of the daily dangers St. Paul met would make even Dick Barton look a cissy. There is a healthy humour that does not involve a bang on the head with a blunt instrument. Children are born hero worshippers, not born ghouls. They will admire what they are given to admire. It is up to us—whether or not we go to Church each Sunday—to see they get a glimpse of what really brave men have done in this world, and share laughter that comes from the heart, not from the gutter (quoted in Crompton 1985, p. 33).

Morris' arguments were the beginning of what was to become a concerted campaign against horror comics leading, eventually, to their ban in Britain in the Children and Young Persons (Harmful Publications) Act, 1955.[1] Martin Barker, in his study of the horror comics campaign, contextualises it historically, arguing that the campaign displayed a "powerful sense of beleaguered hope. On the one hand, the Cold War, the Korean War, rearmament: all these were part of a strong sense of Britain in an international setting that was getting very dark. On the other hand, [the positive feeling] was a peculiar combination of nationalism and idealism" (Barker 1984, p. 181). It is this "peculiar combination of nationalism and idealism" that is displayed so clearly in the construction of Dan Dare as a hero for the nation.

Although strongly opposed to horror-comics, Marcus Morris was not against the comic-strip as a form; indeed, he stated in his introduction to his edited selection, *Best of Eagle,* that it was clear to him in the late 1940s that

> the strip cartoon was capable of development in a way not yet seen in England except in one or two of the daily and Sunday newspapers—and that it was a new and important medium of communication with its own laws and limitations. Here, surely, was a form which could be used to convey to the child the right kind of standards, values and attitudes, combined with the necessary amount of excitement and adventure. (Morris 1977, p. 3)

In 1948, Morris had met Frank Hampson. Although Hampson had hoped to fly in the RAF, he had served in the army during the war, and had experienced the bombing of Antwerp by the rocketbombs called "Rheinbote" ("Rhine Messenger").[2] Demobbed from the army in 1946, Hampson had enrolled on a course at Southport School of Arts and Craft. He was not religious in the same way as Morris, but he admired Morris and was "infected by his desire to . . . 'publish morality' " (Vince 1994, p. 13), and, from the beginning of 1949, the two of them planned what Morris later called "an entirely new, original children's paper of our own" (Morris 1977, p. 4). The comic was originally called *Dragon,* but Hampson's wife suggested the title *Eagle* from the eagle-shaped lectern used in many churches. The model for the eagle on the cover of the comic was the top of a large brass inkwell and the lettering came from Bernard Wolpe of Faber & Faber (Morris 1977, p. 5).

But the *full* title of the new comic was, significantly, *Eagle—The New National Strip Cartoon Weekly.* As Stuart Sillars has pointed out, " 'weekly' stressed its orderly regular appearance and its superiority over 'fly-by-night horror comics' while 'National' suggested the embodiment of British values, as well as rebutting the overseas elements implicit within the transatlantically influenced comic books" (Sillars 1995, p. 134). As for the emblematic Eagle masthead, Sillars comments that the typeface was "a specially designed italic capital which has small serifs and is still quite formal, but which continues the energetic diagonal of the eagle's wings," while the eagle flying from left to right led the reader across to the first frame: "Taken together, these elements reveal the masthead as a masterful piece of design and ideology, establishing a symbolic significance which has a clear moral thrust with a typeface that is authoritative but not old-fashioned, stating a clear 'product identity' while dynamically involving the reader and leading him or her to the action of the comic's first strip" (Sillars 1995, p. 135).

Morris and Hampson were determined to produce an important long-lasting character for the front page of *Eagle* and after wrestling with the idea of a woman detective called Dorothy Dare and a fighting parson from the East End of London who later developed into "a flying padre" with the name Lex Christian, they settled on the science fiction Space Fleet commander, Dan Dare, Pilot of the Future. The careful construction of the name, the genre, and the role of the character in guiding the young and giving them a hope for the future, were quite deliberate. As Hampson explained in an interview in 1974:

> when Dan was finalised it was as a *Pilot* of the Future, which had an apt double meaning. . . . I was *determined* to produce a real character and a consistent character, for the front page. Something people would notice—sugar on the pill, if you like. Science fiction, being such a flexible medium, was ideal for this. I also felt that young people were getting a rough deal in those years so soon after the end of the war. Everything was so pessimistic, what with the Bomb and all . . . I wanted to give them something that made the future more hopeful in human terms. (Vince 1994, p. 13)

On another occasion, Hampson explained how his hopeful vision of the future for children was combined with a belief in the potentiality of science and technology to open up "new worlds"—a belief he shared with Arthur C. Clarke, who acted as adviser for the "Dan Dare" comic strip for its first six months: "I felt the prognostications about technology were too gloomy. Attitudes were so pessimistic, with The Bomb, the Cold War and rationing in the forefront of everyone's mind. I wanted to give hope for the future, to show that rockets and science in general could reveal new worlds, new opportunities. I was sure that space travel would be a reality" (quoted in Crompton 1985, p. 50).[3] But, in his foreword to *Dan Dare's Spacebook* (1953), Hampson reiterates rhetorically how his dreams for *the future* were shaped by his experiences of *the past:*

Most of Dan Dare's adventures take place in 2000 A.D. But they all began, really, in Belgium in 1944 . . . 'Rocketbombs' pounded the city that was pumping the lifeblood of supplies into the arteries of the Western Allied Armies.

On the quays of Antwerp you could watch the birth of Space Travel . . . in those neat cottonwool lines reaching up into the clear blue winter sky. The lines were, alas, the first realisation of the dreams of scientist and inventors who had been working for years . . . Hitler warped their dreams into ends that were foul and repulsive. But dreamers have a habit of not giving up . . . (quoted in Wright & Higgs 1990, p. 5)

Dan Dare, Pilot of *the Future,* was a character constructed out of *the past* (especially the mythic and heroic discourses surrounding the experience of World War II) and *the present* in 1950 (in particular, the contradictory discourses of despair and hope that surrounded technology, food supplies, and the possibility of World War III) but presented as a character living in *the future,* of the 1990s.

In 1949, Morris and Hampson gathered a team of artists around them and created dummies of issues of *Eagle.* Hulton Press agreed to publish it and the launch was carefully planned: there were loudspeakers on cars, free comic tokens for children, and copies were supplied on a sale or return basis to newsagents. Nearly one million copies of the first issue of *Eagle* went on sale on 14 April 1950 (Wright & Higgs 1990). Morris and Hampson had decided to produce "an entirely new, original children's paper of [their] own." Part of that originality was the choice of format: British comics such as *Dandy, Beano, Film Fun,* and *Radio Fun* were printed on cheap newsprint; Hampson chose a large format (14.5 inches deep by 10.5 inches across) and full colour. The visual technique of the comics of the time was limited: They treated "each frame as a 'stage' on which all the characters had to appear, and they simply changed positions from box to box—the boxes being generally all the same size, with the same perspective and without close-ups, cut-outs" (Crompton 1985, p. 29).

But Hampson had formed his ideas about strip-cartoons as a direct result of an interest in American comics and he tried to make "Dan Dare," and the other *Eagle* strips he drew, more dynamic than anything that had appeared previously in a *British* comic. In particular, Hampson admired the work of Hal Foster and Milton Caniff (Vince 1994, p. 8). Foster was the creator of the "Prince Valiant" strips (1937) and from them Hampson took some of Dan Dare's spirit of chivalry and the characteristics central to the genre of the male adventure hero in general: "Son of a dethroned king who had come to seek refuge at King Arthur's court, Valiant was good looking, fearless and resourceful and Frank admired these characteristics and was later to build them into Dare" (Crompton 1985, p. 18). However, it will become clear that Hampson also was drawing upon the tradition of the nineteenth-century boys' adventure story. From Milton Caniff (creator of "Terry and the Pirates" in 1934), Hampson learned the techniques of the cinema translated into the comic-strip form: "it is to Caniff in particular that credit belongs for bringing the techniques of the cinema, long shots, close-ups and panoramic effects to the comic strip. Caniff became a master of the skilful use of light, elaborate chiaroscuro effects and dramatic contrasts in black and white" (ibid.).

Like a third cartoonist, Alex Raymond (who drew Rip Kirby), Hampson's pictures "were precise, clear and incisive, he developed a harmony between his pictures and the plot and became brilliant at leaving his readers on a cliff hanger every three frames" (Crompton 1985, p. 18). Hampson is credited with the fine quality of the artwork in the Dan Dare strip, because of his relentless insistence on "perfection." Much of the artwork was produced on the "studio system" somewhat akin to a film animation studio, with every member of team making a contribution. However, Hampson took the lead, and retained control of standards and editorial direction (Vince 1994, p. 34). For example, he displayed meticulous concern for accuracy by constructing "dozens of models . . . These included rockets, weapons, buildings and even plaster busts of the main characters. Space suits were made, and members of the team would pose in them for photographic sessions."[4] In addition, Hampson made "a comprehensive record of everything connected with the Dan Dare strip [including] hundreds of photographs, plan and reference sheets detailing the minutiae of the characters, backgrounds, aliens, etc.; in fact of every aspect of the strip," to ensure that any of the studio's artists "could accurately depict any of the uniforms or items of hardware" that he had created. Finally, Hampson "would inspect, correct and often reject the work, insisting always on perfection in each frame" (Wright & Higgs 1990, pp. 10–11).

The *Eagle,* and, in particular, the Dan Dare strip, was an immediate success, and Hulton Press capitalised on it by raising advertising rates and the cover price of the comic just over a year after the first issue was published. In addition, Hulton developed the relatively new process of character merchandising and granted hundreds of licences for a whole range of products linked to Dan Dare and to *Eagle.*[5] As Wright and Higgs argue, "if a character's popularity can be assessed by the amount of merchandising they attract then there can be no doubt that during the 1950s Dan Dare was far and away the most popular character going" (Wright & Higgs 1990, p. 46).

At this point, it is important to remember what kind of text we are discussing. Dan Dare is the male hero of an adventure story, a type of text that can be described, in J. G. Cawelti's terms, as a formula: "Formulas are ways in which specific cultural themes and stereotypes become embodied in more universal story archetypes . . . A formula is a combination or synthesis of a number of specific cultural conventions with a more universal story form or archetype. It is also similar in many ways to the traditional literary conception of a genre" (Cawelti 1976, p. 6). A formal approach to the adventure story, such as that by Northrop Frye and specifically related to children's literature by Dennis Butts (Frye 1957; Butts 1992), reveals structural elements and conventions that link the adventure story to patterns of traditional hero-myths (what Cawelti, who also owes much to Frye, would classify as "a universal story form or archetype"). Frye sees the adventure story as a form of romance: "the adventure hero himself is an idealized figure whose actions render him superior to other characters and to the environment in which he moves" (Dawson 1994, p. 55). But Butts argues that the "classic" adventure story (especially the late nineteenth-century boys' adventure story) blends the "probable with the extraordinary"; and that the sense of the probable is usually achieved "by establishing the hero as a very normal and identifiable kind of person . . . from a respectable, but never wealthy home." The adventure begins when the protagonist leaves home, often acquiring a faithful companion, and encounters dangers and difficulties in settings that are often strange and exotic. The narrative of the adventure story "rises by a series of minor crises to the great climax, which is often a ferocious battle against powerful adversaries"; and the hero is usually rewarded with substantial wealth and honours (Butts 1992). The pleasurable characteristics of the adventure story include entering "an imaginary world in which the audience can encounter a maximum of excitement without being confronted with an overpowering sense of insecurity and danger that accompanies such forms of excitement in reality" (Cawelti 1976, p. 16). Pleasure is also derived from the presence of the formula, and from the way writers "vary the expected pattern or use it to embody values or a personal vision" (Butts 1992).

Such an approach is useful for understanding the structure of many of Dan Dare's adventures (for example, the first adventure which is usually referred to as "The Voyage to Venus"[6]), but the problem with Frye and with formalist approaches generally is that they tend to be ahistorical. As Graham Dawson argues, in order to account for the power of the adventure story at particular historical moments, we need to see the genre itself historically:

> Developments in the generic tradition occur when its inherited forms are activated within new social conditions and draw on the imaginaries currently investing them, to produce new kinds of quest. Any adventure text involves an encounter between the historically formed motifs and sedimented structure of the genre and new developments in the cultural imaginaries resonant at the moment of its production. (Dawson 1994, pp. 57–58)

I want to argue that "Dan Dare-Pilot of the Future" represents just such an encounter: the strip draws upon historically developed conventions of the late nineteenth-century boys' adventure story, but it also is shaped by the "cultural imaginaries" of post-war Britain. To illustrate the argument, the focus will be on the complex discourses around gender, class, and imperialism.

Dawson argues that by the late nineteenth century, there were two distinct gendered romance narratives: "'Masculine romance', from *Boys Own Paper* to James Bond, now became exclusively concerned with adventure scenarios of 'male camaraderie, rivalry and contest', in an imagined world quite distinct from that of 'domestic femininity' constituted by 'feminine romance' which was now exclusively preoccupied with the search for fulfilment through heterosexual love" (Dawson 1994, pp. 63–64). Dan Dare carries on much of this tradition of "masculine romance": There is male camaraderie among Dare's friends who are *types* (but not all *stereotypes*) of the male adventure story. On the one hand, there are the unproblematic figures such as Sir Hubert Gascoigne Guest, ex-RAF, who is Controller of the Interplanet Space Fleet and father-figure to the group; and the representative "ally figures": Pierre and Hank (Hampson describes Pierre as "Hank's 'copain' or pal" and Hank as "Pierre's particular buddy"). Hampson had wanted to have a Russian in his space fleet, but "the cold war was bitter in 1950 and he was dissuaded from introducing Boris" (Crompton 1985, p. 187). Then there is Digby, the joker in the group, who is described by Hampson as "Dan's batman and faithful companion" and by Sillars as "a working-class northerner, the kind of supporting figure familiar from Ealing films of the war years"

(Sillars 1995, p. 136). Nevertheless, Digby is intelligent and "quite capable of piloting a spaceship" (Vince 1994, p. 27).

But it is not a all-male club: In the first adventure, a Professor Peabody joins the crew of the spaceship bound for Venus. They are expecting "some old greybeard" but Professor Peabody turns out to be a woman—Professor Jocelyn Peabody—whose first words are: "I don't see what all the fuss is about . . . I'm a first class geologist, botanist, agriculturalist and the cabinet agree I'm the best person to reconnoitre Venus as a source of food—I'm a qualified space pilot as well" (*Eagle*, No. 5, 12 May 1950).[7] In the 1974 interview, Hampson said of Peabody:

> I didn't want to produce a strip without a female. In a way I struck a blow for Women's Lib! She was shown as a very clever, attractive young lady. It also paved the way for a few arguments between her and Sir Hubert in the first story—a nice *human* touch . . . she was just a very normal, efficient, competent girl (Vince 1994, p. 27).

But Hampson's feminist attitude in this statement is to some extent undercut by his use of the conventions of the male romance adventure genre, and he adds in the same interview: "[Peabody] was there to be rescued" (Vince 1994, p. 27). Nevertheless, it is worth noting that Hampson's original idea for the Dan Dare strip was a strip featuring a *female* protagonist—a detective called Dorothy Dare (Vince 1994, p. 13).

As for Dan Dare himself, he seems to embody many of the qualities associated with the male hero of nineteenth-century boys' adventure stories, while displaying others that arise from the ideological discourses of post-war Britain in which the strip was constructed. The *Dan Dare Dossier* reveals that Dare was born in 1967 in Manchester from a family of "warriors": one of his ancestors fought on Cromwell's side, another fought at Waterloo. Dare's father was an explorer and climber but disappeared when employed as a test pilot; Dare's mother's ancestor was Scottish and fought under Prince Charles in the 1745 rebellion. Dan Dare's hobbies (which were obviously similar to those of many of his readers) included cricket, fencing, riding, painting, and model making (Wright & Higgs 1990, p. 16). In many respects, Dan Dare also incorporates and continues the code of the nineteenth-century chivalrous gentleman who was expected to be

> brave, straightforward and honourable, loyal to his monarch, country and friends, unfailingly true to his word, ready to take issue with any-

one he saw ill-treating a woman, a child or an animal. He was a natural leader of men, and others unhesitatingly followed his lead. He was fearless in war and on the hunting field and excelled at all manly sports; but, however tough with the tough, he was invariably gentle to the weak; above all he was always tender, respectful and courteous to women, regardless of their rank. . . . He was an honourable opponent and a good loser; he played games for the pleasure of playing, not to win (Girouard 1981, p. 260).

The *Dan Dare Dossier* echoes much of this language when it describes Dare as "a natural leader and a man who inspires those around him to give of their best. His word is his bond no matter how treacherous his adversaries are" (Wright & Higgs 1990, p. 16). The code of behaviour, described by Girouard above, operated in the classrooms and on the playing fields of the Public Schools in late nineteenth-century Britain. As on the playing field, so on the battlefield. The code of chivalry reinforced male comradeship, especially in fighting: "bands of brothers," "fellowship knights," "happy warriors" loyal to their own group or to a leader, fought honourably, side by side. World War I was to shatter such fictional images, but they continued to exercise some of their power in twentieth-century popular fiction (Watkins 1994, p. xii). However, although Dan Dare is often involved in war situations (for example, against the Treens), he is not the conventional superhuman male soldier hero who defeats his enemies through violence and killing: Hampson said that he planned that Dan Dare should act, not as a superman, but "prevail by intelligence, common-sense, and determination" (Vince 1994, p. 21).[8] At the same time, Hampson did create an idealised figure: Dare, he said, "was the man I always wanted to be; Digby, his batman, was the man I saw myself as" (Crompton 1985, p. 51).

The late nineteenth-century boys' adventure story was bound up with the ideology of imperialism.[9] As Butts says of such stories: "their authors did try to guide their young readers towards upholding such secular virtues as loyalty, pluck and resourcefulness, usually stressing the ideological assumption that the British possession of such qualities is unequalled, and that the British Empire was an unrivalled instrument for universal harmony and justice. Some writers, indeed, articulated the values of late nineteenth-century British imperialism quite emphatically, as G. A. Henty did . . ." (Butts 1992, pp. 72–73). However, Dan Dare was a hero constructed out of the *decline* of Britain's imperial position in the world: During the late 1940s and early 1950s, the colonial empire almost vanished. Churchill said that he had no intention of "presiding over the dissolution of the British Empire," but, by 1951, "the process had pro- gressed so far that it was impossible to return to the old Imperialist order" (Montgomery 1965, p. 96). Frank Hampson tried, somewhat nostalgi- cally, to recuperate the appeal of the male imperial adventure hero and to re-articulate it within the genre of science fiction adventure: "I wanted to hold up in science an example of adventuring, like the empire-building sagas of G. A. Henty I had read as a boy. It was Marco Polo discovering China simply brought up to date" (quoted in Crompton 1985, p. 51).

Indeed, *Eagle* comic as a whole, as Tulloch and Alvarado have pointed out, combined adventure with its historical "Great Men" series that "juxtaposed the themes of Christian heroes (like St. Paul and St. Patrick) with heroes of British imperialism (like Winston Churchill) while others, like David Livingstone, quite overtly combined the two" (Tulloch & Alvarado 1983, p. 43). But the context of the strip's construc- tion gives a more complex post-imperial quality to Dan Dare as adven- ture hero. In the first adventure, the Treens are eventually defeated at the Battle of Mekonta by an international *United Nations* force consisting of cavalry made up of Texan cowboys, British Lifeguards, South West African police, Sikhs, Canadian mounties, and archery club members led by U.N. Police Commandant Bunche who is African or Afro-Caribbean. Digby later hails the success of the attack with words that sound uneasy to late twentieth-century sensibilities: "He's done it sir! The black boy's done it" (*Eagle* Vol. 2 No. 22, 7 September 1951). But the imperialism in the strip is apparently the imperialism of the United Nations, rather than of Britain. In Dan Dare's second adventure, "The Red Moon Mystery," Hampson devotes a full page frame to a utopian vision of the faces of people from all over the world staring at the asteroid Red Moon, with the caption: "These self-governing people have been engaged in a mighty drive to end poverty and squalor. Individual liberty and equality is se- cure, regardless of race, colour or creed, under the elected World Federal Government and the protection of the incorruptible U.N. Police" (*Eagle* Vol. 3 No. 2, 18 April 1952).

However, in true imperialist (or perhaps evangelical) fashion, such liberal democratic ideology had to be spread to all corners of the uni- verse. In the fifth adventure, "Prisoners of Space," Dan Dare reminds Digby that, "The whole purpose of our peaceful penetration into outer space has been to show dwellers on other planets that earth's code is the finest way of life . . . We've got to set an example of truth and honour to the rest of the universe *at whatever cost*" (*Eagle* Vol. 5 No. 31, 30 July

1954). The reason for this outburst is because Digby has caused Dan to break his "word of honour to the Mekon!" Change the wording of Dan's speech slightly, substitute "England's" for "earth's," and we are close to the sentiments of imperialists like Cecil Rhodes and the code of honour of the nineteenth-century chivalrous gentleman as mediated by, say, Robert Baden-Powell's *Scouting for Boys*. It is the imperial ideal given a new moral direction; Tulloch and Alvarado describe it as combining "a 'United Nations' inflection of the British imperial ideal with Protestant evangelism" (Tulloch & Alvarado 1983, p. 48).

Examination of other aspects of the strip reinforces the idea that Dan Dare was constructed as a national hero to chart a clear moral and ideological course through the troubled waters of post-war Britain—to act, in fact, as a pilot to children in Britain in the 1950s. As this chapter has tried to show, the moral and ideological discourses of the strip derive in part from the conventions of the nineteenth-century boys' adventure story, but it is important to demonstrate further how they are combined with nineteenth-century cultural debates around mechanism and technology and mythological discourses of national identity.

The contemporary nature of what purports to be the future is shown in the very first frame of Dan Dare (*Eagle* No. 1, 14 April 1950), which depicts "the Headquarters of the Interplanet Space Fleet" over which flies a jet-propelled vehicle resembling a helicopter. As Stuart Sillars comments, in this "filmic establishing shot, buildings recognisable from recent British originals like Tecton's Finsbury Health Centre make the scene credible, and above it flies a jet capsule which looks remarkably like the cockpit of a Westland Dragonfly, then the latest British military helicopter" (Sillars 1995, p. 137). The Cabinet, which controls Space Fleet, appears to operate from near Space Fleet Headquarters in London and Space Fleet itself is staffed largely by "Englishmen wearing cast-off British army uniforms dyed green" (James 1987, p. 49). At the beginning of the first Dan Dare adventure, the Cabinet is in session because of the threat of world-wide food shortages: The world government has ended wars, there is no poverty, nearly all diseases have been conquered, but there is no food. In a clear extrapolation from the late 1940s, Sir Hubert Guest explains that world population has doubled since 1950 and food supplies have grown less because "vast areas of the earth have been exhausted by bad farming in the past" (*Eagle* No. 4, 5 May 1950), while headlines declare food riots all over the world. As James puts it, "The world inhabited by Dan Dare, Sir Hubert Guest and their colleagues was in one sense not far removed from the austerities of Britain of 1950. Indeed, rationing was even worse in 1996 [the year in which the story is set] than in 1950" (James 1987, p. 48).[10] Spaceships are dispatched to find food supplies on Venus but Dan and his companions encounter the enemy Treens led by the Mekon. When Sir Hubert asks of the Treens, "Who or what are they Dan?" Dan replies, using a 1950s colloquialism for scientists, "Boffins run wild, sir—and quite inhuman—they seem to have no emotions at all" (*Eagle* No. 21, 1 September 1950).

The Treens and their leader, the Mekon, represent the worst aspects of "the mechanistic rationalism of science" as Tulloch and Alvarado put it, comparing the Treens to the later Daleks of *Dr. Who* (Tulloch & Alvarado 1983, p. 45). The Mekon (born, interestingly, around 1750, roughly at the beginning of the Industrial Revolution), Hampson explained, "was meant to show the depths that a scientifically-based society could sink to. A specially bred superbrain with no emotions at all. All that mattered was the advance of Mekon-science and universal domination by the Treens." The Mekon's name was "arrived at by thinking about something mechanical . . . mech-an, Mek-on . . ." (Vince 1994, p. 22). Hampson adds that the Treens were made "slightly reptilian to add to [the] cold, ruthless, scientific image" but then adds, revealingly, "basically we were fighting the Second World War again . . . the Treens were the Nazis" (Vince 1994, p. 21).

The fight between the liberal democratic allies and the forces of fascism is re-played in "Dan Dare," but this time it is a conflict between, on the one hand, the imperialism of a liberal humanism, which must be spread to all parts of the universe under the control of the United Nations World Government, and, on the other hand, the fascistic imperialism of the Mekon and Treens, who use their "scientific rationality" to try to enslave earth's inhabitants and make them obedient automata.

The strip is full of the rhetoric, the language and the mythologies of World War II, mixed with the Christian and humanist moralistic discourse of the nineteenth-century public schoolboys' adventure story. At one level, there is the use of contemporary military slang and parodies of military language: This is particularly true of the first adventure (which ran until 28 September 1951), but is also partly true for the later adventures as well. For example, a spaceship is referred to as a "kite" (*Eagle* 26 No. 7, May 1950); as Dan approaches a brightly-lit Atlantine village, he comments: "They don't have a blackout any way" (*Eagle* No. 45, 16 February 1951); and, as the Theron space ships come to rescue the threatened spacefleet, Dan rejoices in their victory with phrases reminiscent of a Battle of Britain dogfight: "Oh, Tally Ho!," "Wizard!," "Bang

On!," and "Yippee!" (*Eagle* Vol. 2 No. 13, 6 July 1951). Even in the later "Prisoners of Space" adventure, there are World War II phrases such as "blighters," "hush-hush job," "boffins" (*Eagle* Vol. 5. No. 22, 28 May, 1954) and "Treen flak" (*Eagle,* 8 October 1954). The mythological "lessons" of Britain's resistance against fascism in World War II, combined with the debate about humanism versus scientific rationality, appear in such declarations as the following: "Your Mekon should have studied the history of the world more carefully, Sondar, if they had they'd realise that, despite all logic and reason, you can never quite kill the last spark of spirit and hope in a human being" (*Eagle* Vol. 2, No. 16, 27 July 1951). But Dan is here commenting to the Treen, Sondar, on the fact that the Atlantine, Dapon, has sacrificed himself to save Dan and his companions from destruction by Treen fighters, and in a phrase reminiscent of that applied to Captain Oates from Scott's ill-fated Antarctic expedition, Dan speaks of the end of "a very gallant gentleman" (Vol. 2 No. 16, 27 July 1951). This gentlemanly heroic ideal of self-sacrificial honour occurs frequently in the strip, as, for example, in the "Prisoners of Space" adventure, where Dan heroically offers to sacrifice himself for the lives of Flamer Spry, Steve Valiant, and Groupie. When Peabody protests that: "Honour means less than nothing to the Mekon. Why observe it when dealing with the beast?" Dan replies: "We've fought the good fight to save honour and to spread our ideals wherever spacefleet penetrates. To sacrifice them—*even once*—is the first step towards the Mekon's way of life" (*Eagle* Vol. 5 No. 29, 16 July, 1954).

In this case, the moral position seems clear-cut. But there are many instances where "Dan Dare—Pilot of the Future" tries to hold together contradictory positions within moral and ideological discourses. For instance, as James points out, Dan Dare (born 1967) was apparently brought up on the lessons of World War II. The Mercurians "are simple and friendly and peace-loving. They hate bloodshed and war more than anything in life" (*Eagle* Vol. 3 No. 43, 30 January 1953). But Dan needs to enlist their help in his fight against the dictator, Mekon. He warns the Mercurians that, if the Mekon succeeds, "freedom will vanish forever from the inner planets. Believe me, my friends, appeasement never pays...the best form of defence is attack! . . . Strike now before it is too late!" (*Eagle* Vol. 3, No. 44, 6 February 1953). However, the preferred ideological position obviously changes with a change in circumstances: In an earlier adventure, Dan, in his victory speech set against the background of a United Nations flag and the head of one of the British lifeguards (complete with plumed helmet), tells the conquered Treens that the victors are neither conquerors nor looters: "We of the earth have learned our peacemaking in a hard, bitter school. Now we have a one-word policy for both victor and vanquished—DISARMAMENT!" (*Eagle* Vol. 2 No. 25, 28 September 1951).

In a continuation of the nineteenth-century conflict of "human values and aspirations against the mechanistic rationalism of science" (Tulloch & Alvarado 1983, p. 45), the strip displays an ambivalent and almost contradictory stance towards the development of science and technology. The apparently benevolent imperialism inherent in taking the values of liberal humanism to other planets depends upon the development of space technology, and the strip featured an increasing amount of such "hardware" from the helicar to the jepeet (or gyroscopic jeep), and the "Anastasia" (a spaceship-cum-aeroplane). Yet, when the members of the Cabinet of the United Nations complain that the inhabitants of Earth are, scientifically, "centuries behind" the conflicting races on Venus, the Treens and Therons, Dan Dare defends the "unscientific" illogicality of human impulse and desire:

> It is true that the Treens have gone ahead of us scientifically but on the way they've lost a lot of qualities we value . . . Our illogical human love of things for their own sake and not their practical value—the impulse that makes a man sail a yacht in a world of diesel engines or ride a horse in a world of motor cars—the love of silent, soaring flight that makes a pilot fly a glider when he could have a jet . . . Our "waste of time"—indulging in sports for the sheer fun of it . . . (*Eagle* Vol. 2 No. 20, 24 August 1951)[11]

It was the strip's science fiction genre that enabled it to present, often within a single frame, seemingly contradictory ideological positions. The complexity of such "fantasy" is nowhere better illustrated than in the preparation for the battle of Mekonta. A rocket ship flown by Dan Dare with Professor Peabody on board has just landed, with the aid of parachutes, at the edge of the special force training area. The language used has been that associated with hot air balloons: "Trim Ship! Let Go Ballast!" In the next frame, we see Dare and Peabody looking out towards us over the gate in a stone wall in what looks like the Cotswolds region of England: Behind them, with parachutes draped over the tops of the trees, lies the spaceship. In front of them, a parade on black horses, of Royal Lifeguards, complete with shining breastplates and plumed helmets. Peabody exclaims: "Gosh, it—it's fantastic! Stepping out of a rocket ship into the middle of an old fashioned print!" In an extraordinary way, possible in the fantasy mode, the frame holds together the contradictory elements of old and new military technology, tradition and novelty, history and the future, combined with an acute sense of the English countryside under threat. Dan Dare is a very *British* hero, with ancestors from England and Scotland. But it is *English* national identity, embodied in the English landscape, that is under threat from the Treens who want to make everyone into unthinking slaves. What is at stake is shown in the leading frame to *Eagle*, Vol. 2 No. 18, 10 August 1951. It shows a peaceful village green on a sunny afternoon and, in the background, a thatched cottage and a church flying the cross of St. George on its spire. On the village green the 94th Annual Cricket match between Nether Wallop and Picrust Parva is taking place; a boy looks up and sees the Treen spaceships coming in to land, but he refers to them as "Flying Saucers."[12] Englishness is defined in terms of rural simplicity, political stability,[13] continuity and loveable eccentricity and, as Edward James argues, "Hampson was proud of the Englishness of *Dan Dare, Pilot of the Future;* the *Eagle* had, after all, been started in the atmosphere of public disquiet at the violence and horror of imported American comics" (James 1987, p. 49).

That very British hero, Dan Dare, is part of the "powerful sense of beleaguered hope" that characterised not only the campaign against horror comics but other aspects of British post-war culture. Because "a country's culture is the means both of expressing national identity and maintaining . . . political consensus," the greatness of post-war, post-imperial Britain had to be asserted not "through Empire, but through carrying our culture to the world," and one of the main ways of carrying British culture to the world was the Festival of Britain in 1951 (Hewison 1995, pp. xvii–xviii; Barker 1984). The Festival, "suitably backward-looking as well as forward-looking," was a "celebration of past and present" held to commemorate the Great Exhibition of 1851 (James 1987, p. 44). Not only did it express the values of the radical middle classes and the utopian idealism of the planners of post-war reconstruction, it was also a way of "propagandising modern styles" (Addison 1995, pp. 208–9).[14] Much of the utopian idealism and many of these "modern styles" had already appeared in the pages of "Dan Dare" (see, for example, the comments at the beginning of this chapter on the first frame of the first issue) and James suggests that, to many readers of *Eagle* who "by this time were familiar with the symmetries of Treen city architecture, and the lush Utopian architecture of the Therons, much of [the Festival of Britain] must have seemed rather dull" (James 1987, p. 45).

What significance does Dan Dare, the pilot of the 1950s have at the end of the twentieth century? To undertake that task properly is beyond the scope of this chapter. It would involve analysis not only of the history from which "Dan Dare" was produced, but analysis of the "history of the future" that the comic strip presents and analysis of ourselves as historically and culturally situated readers. In other words, it would involve our becoming "dialectically historicist." As Jeremy Hawthorn argues, "such an investigation must also focus upon the interaction between our own historically situated selves and the art of the past" (Hawthorn 1996, p. 84). That historicism would need to include analysis of the way contemporary discourses around heroism are articulated, analysis of developments in the heroic adventure story, in the science fiction genre, in the art of the strip cartoon, and so on.

The figure Dan Dare has survived as an iconographic hero for a half-century, in spite of the comments of people such as Chris Lowder of IPC who justified stopping publication of *Eagle* in 1969 by arguing that, "Looked at with a cold unprejudiced eye, *Eagle* was merely a symbol of its time, and no more" (quoted in Crompton 1985, p. 190). For others such as Wolf Mankovitz, Frank Hampson was "the creator of a new twenty-first century mythology and a great artist in his extraordinary powerful medium" (quoted in Crompton 1985, p. 211), and the authors of the *Dan Dare Dossier* in 1990 claim that despite "the technological advances of the last forty years, Dan Dare still remains Britain's number one space hero" (Wright & Higgs 1990, p. 33). But what *kind* of hero is Dan Dare at the end of one millennium and the beginning of another? The problem is that, as Fred Inglis points out, "in a state of unbelief, in which no system of values is shared, . . . it is hard to know what heroism can look like" (Inglis 1981, p. 148). We can get some idea by looking at Dan Dare's brief re-appearance in 1996, in the ill-fated newspaper, *The Planet on Sunday,* which survived for just one issue. The paper had been published because of the publisher's belief that "the declining environment is now the greatest threat to Britain's future growth and to our hopes for rising living standards and improving quality of life" (Hards 1996, p. 4), but it seemed equally concerned to ensure that Britain's economic progress took place "in a free society unburdened by oppressive government and excessive regulation" (ibid.). Dan Dare appeared in a strip by Sydney Jordan and Theyen Rich. Jordan recalled the original

Dan Dare as being "just like a cross between Biggles in space and a boy scout," but the 1990s Dan Dare would "have to shape up to the stark realities of the world" because "he's going to be faced with grimmer alternatives such as the depletion of the ozone layer."[15]

Heroes, such as Dan Dare, pilot of the 1950s and, for some, pilot of later decades, are constructed, as Raphael Samuel argues, "as a by-product of grand narratives. New movements bring new measures of significance" (Samuel 1995, p. 27). Although Samuel's focus here is on historical heroes, his words are equally appropriate to Dan Dare: "If heroes and heroines are myth, a projection of our longings, . . . they are nevertheless a necessary fantasy" (ibid.).

NOTES

1. For a useful account of the campaign, see Martin Barker, *The Haunt of Fears: The Strange History of the British Horror Comics Campaign,* London: Pluto Press 1984.

2. See also Hans K. Kaiser, *Rockets and Spaceflight* (trans. Alex Helm), London: Scientific Book Club/Faber & Faber, 1961, p. 35.

3. For Clarke's role in acting as adviser, see Clute & Nicholls 1993, p. 297. Edward James points out the similarity between Hampson's ideas and those of Arthur C. Clarke: "Clarke's own attitude towards the future has hardly changed since the 1950s . . . but that does not mean that it is a simple one . . . He believes in the power of technology to better the human condition, yet realises the possibility that humanity might misuse it. He deplores religious fanaticism and extols scientific rationality, yet seems himself to have a strong religious streak. He is optimistic about the future of humanity, yet seems to have doubts that it can reach its goals without outside help. He affirms humanity's strengths, yet remains awestruck at the immensity and mystery of the universe which it confronts" (James 1987: Editorial).

4. For details of the increasing amount of "space hardware" displayed in the strip, see Wright & Higgs, 1990, pp. 18–25.

5. For example, Wright and Higgs state that:

> Young enthusiasts could buy everything from the 'Dan Dare military hair brush' to Dan Dare slippers, with Dan Dare garments to clothe every part of the body in between. They could use their Dan Dare Spaceship Fountain Pen . . . taken from their nine inch long Dan Dare Spaceship Pencil Box . . . to write their *Eagle* birthday cards . . . The Dan Dare Stationery . . . could be used to

write 'thank you' letters to all those relatives who had deluged them with Dan Dare gifts for birthday or Christmas.

> For the more energetic boy there were Dan Dare Football Boots and Dan Dare Roller Skates . . . Those boys with less interest in sport might well have asked for the 3D Dan Dare Painting Plaque or one of the Dan Dare Spaceship Builder Kits. Stamp enthusiasts could hinge their collection into their Dan Dare Stamp Album . . . The most popular ranges of Dan Dare merchandising were those featuring the weapons such as the Dan Dare Rocket Gun, the Dan Dare Cosmic Ray Gun; and the Dan Dare Aqua Jet Gun. (Wright & Higgs 1990, p. 45).

6. It ran from *Eagle* Vol. 1, No. 1, April 1950 to Vol. 2, No. 25, September 1951.

7. The *Dan Dare Dossier* states that Professor Peabody held the degrees of BSc and PhD; she was appointed Professor of Plant Biochemistry at a young age (and was the youngest lecturer in Oxford); she had a specialised knowledge of food science and was awarded the World Government Star for services to humanity. She was also a linguistic expert (Wright & Higgs 1990, p. 16).

8. The pacifist side to Dan Dare's character is obviously related to Hampson's experience in World War II and his humanist admiration for Christ. For example, he said of his strip on the life of Christ entitled, *The Road of Courage:*

> I tried to get away from the woolly Never-Never Land of the Sunday School stories of my youth and show the harsh political realities of the turbulent, rebellious Palestine, when the Jews were seething with revolt against Rome, much as Europe was against the Nazis in our day. To me this makes the steadfast refusal of Christ to condone any resort to violence all the more remarkable, as it took place in circumstances when most political and religious leaders of our day would consider it fully justified to resort to violence. (Vince 1994, p. 43)

9. See, for example, Dawson 1994, p. 58: "The historical importance to British national development of the acquisition of an empire can be seen . . . to have become deeply embedded in the English language, giving the cultural significance of 'adventure' in Britain explicitly militarist, capitalist and colonialist connotations that run right through to the present." Dawson goes on to refer to Martin Green, *Dreams of Adventure, Deeds of Empire* (1980), and argues that "the very form of the modern adventure tale is imbued with the imaginative reso-

nance of colonial power relations underpinned by science and technology" (Dawson 1994, p. 59).

10. In *Eagle* No. 25 (29 September 1950), a newspaper item declares that "a whole unblemished peanut was handed to the Minister of Food by a delegation representing equally the native tribes in the groundnut area and the survivors of the Strachey scheme"—a reference to the infamous post-war "groundnut scheme" in Central Africa, which was sponsored by the British government and which lost £36 million.

11. Later, Dare says "[The Treens] have little speedy physical co-ordination because they despise sports—they have a highly centralised mass mentality—accustomed to orders from the top like bees in a hive—with the breakdown of communications, they'll find it hard to improvise!" (*Eagle* Vol. 2 No. 20, 24 August 1951).

12. "Between 1947 and 1952 some 3,000 flying saucers were reported to have been seen in various parts of the world, and towards the end of 1952 there was an increase in the number of reports of flying saucers seen over Europe" (Montgomery 1965, pp. 78,79).

13. Tulloch and Alvarado comment: "Here the generic theme of 'human' emotional wholeness, and brotherhood against 'alien' rationalism and exploitation is inflected in terms of the 'natural' bond between comical Hampshire villagers and their gentry" (Tulloch & Alvarado 1983, p. 48).

14. Sir Hugh Casson is quoted by Addison as saying: "We all had, I suppose in a way, rather naive views that England could be better and was going to be better—that the arts and architecture and music and healthy air and Jaeger underwear and all these things, which the garden movement stood for, were in fact the keys to some sort of vague Utopia" (quoted in Addison 1995, pp. 208–9).

15. "Daring to be different," *The Planet on Sunday,* 16 June 1996, No. 1, p. 37.

BIBLIOGRAPHY

Addison, Paul. *Now the War is Over: A Social History of Britain 1945–51.* London: Pimlico 1995 (originally published 1985).

Barker, Martin. *The Haunt of Fears: The Strange History of the British Horror Comics Campaign.* London: Pluto Press 1984.

Barnett, Corelli. *The Lost Victory: British Dreams, British Realities 1945–1950.* London: Macmillan 1995.

Butts, Dennis. "The Adventure Story," in *Stories and Society: Children's Literature in Its Social Context,* ed. Dennis Butts. London: Macmillan 1992: 65–83.

Cawelti, J. G. *Adventure, Mystery and Romance: Formula Stories as Art and Popular Culture.* Chicago: University of Chicago Press 1976.

Clute, John and Nicholls, Peter. *The Encyclopaedia of Science-Fiction.* London: Orbit 1993.

Crompton, Alastair. *The Man Who Drew Tomorrow.* Bournemouth: Who Dares Publishing 1985.

Dawson, Graham. *Soldier Heroes: British Adventure, Empire and the Imagining of Masculinities.* London & New York: Routledge 1994.

Kaiser, Hans K. *Rockets and Spaceflight* (trans. Alex Helm). London: Scientific Book Club/Faber & Faber 1961.

Frye, Northrop. *The Anatomy of Criticism.* Princeton, N.J.: Princeton University Press 1957.

Girouard, Mark. *The Return to Camelot: Chivalry and the British Gentleman.* New Haven & London: Yale University Press 1981.

Hards, Cliff. "A Letter from the Publisher: We must stay free and independent," *The Planet on Sunday,* 16 June 1996, No. 1.

Hawthorne, Jeremy. *Cunning Passages: New Historicism, Cultural Materialism and Marxism in the Contemporary Literary Debate.* London: Arnold 1996.

Hewison, Robert. *Culture and Consensus: England, Art and Politics Since 1940.* London: Methuen 1995.

Inglis, Fred. *The Promise of Happiness: Value and Meaning in Children's Fiction.* Cambridge, U.K.: Cambridge University Press 1981.

James, Edward. "The Future Viewed from Mid-Century Britain: Clarke, Hampson and the Festival of Britain," *Foundation: The Review of Science Fiction* Number 41, Winter 1987: 42–51.

Montgomery, John. *The Fifties.* London: Allen & Unwin 1965.

Morris, the Rev. Marcus. " 'Comics' That Take Horror into the Nursery," *Sunday Dispatch,* 13 February 1949: 4.

Morris, the Revd. Marcus (ed.). *The Best of Eagle.* London: Michael Joseph 1977.

Samuels, Raphael. "The People with Stars in Their Eyes." *The Guardian,* 23 September 1995, p. 27.

Sillars, Stuart. *Visualisation in Popular Fiction 1860–1960: Graphic narratives, fictional images.* London & New York: Routledge 1995.

Tulloch, John & Alvarado, Manuel. *Doctor Who: The Unfolding Text.* London: Macmillan 1983.

Vince, Alan. *The Frank Hampson Interview.* Cambridge, U.K.: Astral Publications in association with the Eagle Society 1994.

Watkins, Tony. "Introduction" to Anthony Hope, *The Prisoner of Zenda.* (World's Classics) Oxford: Oxford University Press 1994: vii–xxii.

Wright, Norman & Higgs, Mike. *The Dan Dare Dossier.* London: Hawk Books 1990.

Golden Boys and Golden Memories
Fiction, Ideology, and Reality in *Roy of the Rovers* and the Death of the Hero

ALAN TOMLINSON AND CHRISTOPHER YOUNG

Roy of the Rovers started life as a weekly comic in September 1976, devoted to soccer adventure tales.[1] "Roy" (Roy Race, a star soccer player with Melchester Rovers), had appeared as a comic strip hero in the first issue of the comic *Tiger,* on 11 September 1954; and as the lead feature in other comic outlets, before the launch of the eponymous title. Almost forty years on, toward the mid-1990s, Roy was still prominent in popular cultural narratives, going strong as team manager. If not able personally to score heroic goals, he contributed by example and inspiration to overall team moves and scores. Throughout this period, Roy Race, like all popular cultural heroes in fictional forms, had performed miracles of chronology as well as of sports performance. In the mid-1980s, for instance, he was still characterized by an eternal youthfulness, a sporting Peter Pan never needing to grow up. His face had become a little fuller, and he may have become burdened by the pressures and obligations of club management and marriage respectively, but he weathered all this well to survive as the blond-haired legendary hero of a big-selling weekly. Indeed, notwithstanding changes in image and style from the mid-1950s to the mid-1980s, the later Roy had a more youthful and streetwise look about him than the original (Brown 1984, p. 5).

Many things happened to Roy in this thirty-year spell at the top. First, ironically, as he aged, he played more active football. In the early years he was as much an adventure hero off-pitch, as on; later, his heroism was mostly on-field. He also had "married, separated, [been] shot, fathered three children, fallen into a coma and starred with Sharon Davies and Suzanne Dando in a Christmas panto" (Brown 1984, p. 5).

Sharon Davies and Suzanne Dando were Britain's sexy sportswomen of the time, from the worlds of swimming and gymnastics respectively. For thirteen years, Roy's team went almost unbeaten, but in 1967 a more realistic emphasis introduced the notion of defeat and, consequently, the element of restoration, into the Melchester narrative. In a more modern world, Roy came to be given his fair share of problems: family, age, defeat. But his main rivals remained the unsportsmanlike "hard men" of the football world, often from foreign lands.

Roy of the Rovers in its mid-1980s form was made up of nine stories, a "Roy Race Talk-In," a quiz, soccer jokes, and a team chart through which readers could "keep tabs" on their favorite real-life team. The comic was produced by IPC Magazines as one of a number of "boys' adventure titles," categorized not as a sports magazine but as an adventure comic, along with titles on war and science fiction. Around the height of its popularity, during the period January–June 1983, weekly sales were almost 102,000. At the same time, the sports magazine *Shoot,* a feature and documentary weekly on soccer, was selling over 176,000 weekly copies. Soccer and sports stories also featured in several other of IPC's weekly comics. Although *Roy of the Rovers* was not one of IPC's highest selling weeklies, for a one-sport comic its sales were high and, without doubt, its readership was far higher than its sales, as siblings (mainly brothers) and fathers throughout a recipient household kept pace with the saga of Race and his boys.[2]

IPC Magazines also produced a *Roy of the Rovers Annual* for the Christmas present market. This ran for many years, from before Roy actually had his own comic. Earlier editions included prose and photo-features on a variety of sports but, by the mid-1980s, the annuals were almost totally made up of extra-long comic-strip soccer stories—a bumper edition, in effect, of the weekly comic. The increasing popularity of the feature or magazine format (in titles such as *Shoot*) polarized the forms, the comic-strip publication making few concessions to the nonvisual, or the exploration of the "real world," in features.

The demise of the *Roy of the Rovers* comic coincided with the increasing popularity of computer games, portable television sets, and an explosion of football coverage in the media (the emergence of glossier magazine titles on sport and football in particular), and more fashionable enthusiasms such as "fantasy football."[3] In March 1993, the separate comic was no longer financially viable, and in the final issue, Roy Race was feared dead in a helicopter crash. He soon resurfaced, however, in time for the new football season, in Fleetwood Editions' *Roy of the Rovers Monthly* in September 1993. This made front-page news in one of

Britain's daily broadsheets, *The Guardian*. The writer of the new comic, Stuart Green, commented: "It seemed that the nation was grieving for Roy and wanted him to return. We were inundated with calls asking for Roy to come back" (Chaudhary 1993, p. 1). Alas, this comeback, focused upon Roy's sixteen-year-old son Rocky, as Roy Race himself limped one-footed but alive out of the helicopter crash and into Italian football management, lasted for only nineteen issues, and the magazine *Shoot,* which had continued to feature Roy, also dropped him. In his last *Roy of the Rovers* Monthly editorial, The Gaffer wrote that "nothing could disguise the fact that we have been failing to pull in sufficient supporters to keep the magazine going" (final issue, March 1995, p. 3).

Roy of the Rovers ceased publication in March 1993, a matter of days after the death of Bobby Moore, golden-haired captain of England's World Cup winning football team of 1966. Despite the demise of the Roy Race publishing profile, the connotations of his career and the echo of the manner and style of his heroic accomplishments have continued to resonate in male sporting discourse, consonant with a nostalgic celebration of a simpler age of sporting prowess. The fictional hero and the real-life superstar may have seemed worlds apart, but in the popular memory of what Roy Race stood for, and the appreciation of what Bobby Moore symbolized, there is a fascinating consonance of meanings and values. In this chapter, therefore, we consider how fiction and reality have blended and overlapped in the recognition and perpetuation of heroic qualities in football. In order to do this, we concentrate upon the peak years of Roy Race's popularity, as the fictional figure negotiated the changes of the 1950s to the 1980s: "Roy emerged into a post-war sporting society which thrived on the exploits of real goal-scoring heroes such as Jackie Milburn and Nat Lofthouse. His career began at about the same time as Manchester United's Bobby Charlton and down the years a host of forwards have been tagged 'real-life Roys' " (Express Reporter, 1994, p. 25). The complexity of popular cultural hermeneutics can be seen in the ways in which the representational fiction of Race and Melchester Rovers, and the outpouring of appreciation for Moore's achievements, speak to the same set of acclaimed heroic values.

ROY OF THE ROVERS, THE SPORTS HERO, AND THE CONSTRUCTION OF "ROY RACE"

To have run for over forty years, *Roy of the Rovers* certainly had a winning formula, and this lay in part in the structure of its story-lines. In narrative theory, "formula" has "a [. . .] specialized meaning [which] invites us to look for rules of construction that underlie the form of the story, governing the interactions between characters, and inviting a kind of interest as the story unfolds. In this sense, to look for a formula, is to look for common elements within the stories which govern more than the pace at which stories unfold" (Barker 1989, p. 36). The formula of *Roy of the Rovers* can profitably be divided into three key elements: plot, technique, and master narrative.

In their analysis of imperialist ideology in the Disney comic, Dorfman and Mattelart noted that the emphases in comic strip storytelling are often made at the expense of other possible emphases. Disney's stories are told in terms of avoidances just as much as in terms of issues that are actually dealt with. Thus, the Disney comic strips avoid the realities of sex and children, producing parent-less, sex-less narratives—Disney's characters are "eunuchs" who "live in an eternal foreplay with their impossible virgins" (Dorfman and Mattelart 1975, p. 39). In *Roy of the Rovers,* it is the work involved in sustaining life as a professional sportsman that is given this particular elliptical treatment. Roy and his Melchester squad are rarely depicted hard at work. When they are, it is usually to highlight some personal drama. A training session, for instance, may be where a recalcitrant member of the squad—whose refractoriness is usually based in entrenched jealousy of Roy Race's talents and skills—attempts to undermine Roy's authority. Systematic and sustained physical work, though, is not presented as the prerequisite for glories in the public arena. This gives the top-level action—the main focus of the Roy narratives—a quality of effortlessness. New generations of readers receive the impression that success comes relatively easily. In training sessions it is only clashes of personality that prevent the smooth flow of preparation: pain, resentment, tedium, boredom, physical exploitation—these are rarely featured. Interestingly, in popularity charts of stories in *Roy of the Rovers* (based on readers' own votes), the two least popular stories/items (in late 1983) were "The Apprentices" and "The Best of *Roy of the Rovers.*" The latter (old stories of Roy in the past) may have been confusing for a young, contemporary readership; but in "The Apprentices," the theme of young professionals working hard in the hope of making the grade, the very centrality of work, threatens the glamour and romance that is at the heart of the *Roy of the Rovers* stories. The *Roy of the Rovers* myth works around a romance of physicality in which physical decay does not set in, and injuries are easily overcome. Physicality as labor—sport as work—is significant by its very absence.

It has been suggested that the *Roy of the Rovers* adventure or romance is a version of the giant-killing myth, in which a team of Davids humbles one of "the tournament's Goliaths" (Wren-Lewis and Clarke 1983, p. 130). Although there is a giant-killer motif in some of the stories in the comic, the *Roy of the Rovers* romance is really the romance of the *immortality of the overdog,* rather than the momentary and fleeting triumph of the underdog. The David/Goliath theme is just one minor variation of the *Roy of the Rovers* romance, and it is the manner of the Rovers' victory that invokes the comparison. In the most important matches, victory is almost inevitably snatched from the jaws of defeat in the most spectacular fashion. In League Championship deciders, and the finals of the F.A. Cup (known in British soccer discourse as "the best club competition in the world") and various European championships, Rovers fall behind, perhaps after taking an early lead, or having been impeded by an injury to, or the kidnapping of, a key player. In such circumstances, a comeback of Herculean proportions is needed to save the Rovers' dreams, and avert a nightmarish conclusion. The last phase of the match invariably sees a resurgent Rovers—spurred on either through a change of tactics, the reappearance of their absent star, or a change in hitherto impossible climatic conditions—rampage to victory in the dying seconds of the game. This form of dramatic last-gasp conquest is a defining feature of the *Roy of the Rovers* formula.

Another element of the formula—the artistic technique used to depict the recurrent action—is inextricably linked with the plot. The repetition of themes is underpinned by a variation on certain key frames. Roy's own decisive part in the action is captured by the single frame that portrays the gargantuan effort needed to produce "Racey's Rocket," a long-range shot that shoots "like a pile-driver" into the top corner of the net, leaving the goalkeeper helpless in its wake. Often it simultaneously depicts the amazement of overjoyed fans, the carpet of flailing limbs through which the maestro has woven his magical path, or the adulation of relieved Rovers team-mates: "The City men packed their goalmouth. Then, with barely seconds left, Pierre shot hard and low for the corner of the net—only for a sprawling defender to get his boot to it" (Caption 1); "The ball bounced clear of the goal. Players scrambled frantically to get to it—then Roy leapt into the air, caught the ball on the volley, and crashed it into the net" (Caption 2); "Full-time came before the game could restart, and the victorious Rovers trotted delightedly off the field" (Caption 3).[4] Equally familiar frames are those that portray a whole intricate movement of play, involving the breathtakingly accurate weaving of passes that play the Rovers into a winning position, or a diving action that sees the player's head avoid the brutal dangers of incoming studs and the upright post of the goal in a moment of daring in which the ball is squeezed through an impossibly tight space into the net. Such frames tap into the fantasy of the readers: There are no scrappy or unadventurous goals. From the 1950s through to the 1980s, it was common for boys to play football not just within the framework of properly arranged matches on regulation grass pitches, but in the street or alley way, using coats and school-bags as goal posts. In this latter environment, which accounted for the greater part of the everyday football experience of the comic's readers, fantasy played a major role: boys took on the persona of their favorite players (some, no doubt, taken from the world of the comic), mimicked the roar of the crowd through hoarse tones issuing from the back of the throat as they played, and scored goals (to their minds) of consummate skill, ease, and finesse. The youthful mind relied heavily on the fantasy of its own ability to perform the finest deeds of its hero, and it is precisely this fantasy of the self that the pictorial formulae of *Roy of the Rovers* both fed and fed off.

The master narrative of the Rovers' life and exploits is constructed around the notion of circularity and restoration. "Because an average of only three pages of Roy strip were published each week, the comic itself illustrated the season in broad brush strokes—one year concentrating on a cup run, the next on a league campaign" (Acton and Jarman 1994, p. 7). The strip-writers often used this practical difficulty to their advantage, exploiting it to increase the drama of a further match. For instance, Rovers might have won a European competition, but once the perspective has a chance to switch to the end of the domestic season, we find them struggling against relegation to a lower division. After scenes of triumph, tension is thus regained instantly. Moreover, after an excellent season, something befalls the Rovers at the commencement of the following one that makes them struggle unaccountably, thus producing tension and the need for restoration over a longer span of the narrative. For instance, at the beginning of the season 1973–74, Rovers line up for a team photograph, displaying the European Cup, a new coach, and a striking new kit. The sole comment is a voice from the crowd that announces: "What an outfit! Let's hope they *play* as good as they *look!*"[5] By November, the team's league form has been so consistently poor that the players begin to believe the new football kit is jinxed. Only Roy's research into the Melchester archives, which shows that the club had won the F.A. Cup in 1907 wearing a similar strip, manages to break the jinx. Fittingly, then, while it is too late for Rovers to regain the league title they are defending, they proceed to win the one trophy that had eluded them in the previous season, the F.A. Cup. The cyclical, ever-recurring nature of the sports calendar, therefore, offers a master narrative built on the sense that if you don't triumph this time, then there's always the next match, tournament or season. The physical demands and constraints of the comic's format converge with the natural rhythms of the football season to produce a framework within which the Rover's modulating fortunes can be exploited to the full. This is typified by the comments of manager Ben Galloway on the open-top bus tour to celebrate the Rovers' victory in the World Club Championship of 1969: "Things aren't as good as they look. A lot of things about that match worried me. There'll have to be big changes."[6]

Against this backdrop of success, challenge, and restoration, one feature remains constant: the character of Roy himself. His skills and energies are unquestionably superior to those around him, but this does not stop him leading from the front. In that sense he functions like a hero from Greek legend who is superior yet still in touch with, and loved by, his men. Witness the reaction when he is first appointed captain in 1958: "With whoops of delight, the Rovers shot up their hands"; "Roy—Skipper! Yippee!"; "There's no-one against, guv'nor! Roy's the lad to lead us"; "What a tonic! Watch us start winning from now on!"[7] However, it is not only through his deeds, but also his almost obsessive concern for his teammates that Roy leads the Rovers. In his debut for the England international team in 1963, Roy is pictured lying forlornly on the pitch: "I'm making a real mess of my first game for England. But if only I knew what was happening at Melchester."[8] News screamed from the touch-line, informing the striker that his club side are in fact leading, breaks the spell and Racey's Rocket saves the day for England. Roy is the tactical maestro behind the team's successes, often taking daring decisions against the odds that only *he* understands: in the 1975 European Cup-Winners Final, Roy controversially substitutes his best defender, Lofty Peak, much to the consternation of longtime companion, Blackie Gray: "Roy, I . . . I guess you know what you're doing."[9] Inevitably the shape of the game changes, allowing the Rovers to slip their markers and set up the ball for a Racey Rocket. Throughout these tempestuous matches, Roy remains the embodiment of calm and composure. Only under extreme circumstances is the veneer broken: In the 1973–74 season, the club directors have offered the players a financial reward for each individual goal scored, causing the team to disintegrate into a group of bounty-hunters. "Roy's anger spilled over onto the pitch, where a series of rash tackles almost saw his name in the book—only Roy's exemplary past playing record persuaded the referee to defer a booking and issue a stern verbal caution . . . chastened, Roy went back to doing what he does best. . . ." Roy's brush with unthinkable moral punishment is enough to bring the Rovers out of their selfish state and return them to their normal winning ways. The master narrative of the protagonist's career portrays him as a man of deeds, a tactical genius, and the personification of the English gentleman.

CONSTRUCTION OF ROY'S IDEOLOGICAL WORLD

The construction of Roy just outlined does not take place in a vacuum, rather it evolves within a context of conventions. "Conventions in comic strips condense social relationships; they help to determine the kind of reader we become. They make reading a social activity between us and the text" (Barker 1989, p. 11). This social activity is underpinned in *Roy of the Rovers* by the appeal to the reader's own footballing experience, knowledge, and fantasy. The conventions that are punctuated by resonances of a real discourse of football converge to form an ideological world. For ease of analysis, the construction of this ideological sphere will be divided into two distinct units, gender and nationality, each of which will be examined within the parameters of the same theory. The theoretical approach on which the following is based stems from Kristeva's writings on gender, which permit a broad ideological sweep rather than a narrow focus on a single aspect. Kristeva's theory rests on her notions of marginality, subversion, and patriarchy. "In so far as women are defined as marginal by patriarchy, their struggle can be theorized in the same way as any other struggle against a centralized power structure" (Moi 1985, p. 164). Kristeva deliberately avoids a clear articulation of the female or femininity, setting up instead a relational definition such as "that which is marginalized by the patriarchal symbolic order." This same definition served her purposes in describing intellectuals, authors, and the working class, as it will serve here also to explore the notion of nationality.

One important feature of marginality which needs to be emphasized is summarized aptly by Moi (1985, p. 167):

> If patriarchy sees women as occupying a marginal position within the symbolic order, then it can construe them as the limit or borderline of that order. From a phallocentric point of view, women will then come to represent the necessary frontier between man and chaos; but be-

cause of their very marginality they will also always seem to recede into and merge with the chaos outside. Women seen as the limit of the symbolic order will in other words share in the disconcerting properties of all frontiers: they will be neither inside nor outside, neither known or unknown. It is this position which has enabled male culture sometimes to vilify women as representing darkness and chaos, to view them as Lilith or the Whore of Babylon, and sometimes to elevate them as the representatives of a higher and purer nature, to venerate them as Virgins and Mothers of God.

The first image is seen as the outer edge of the borderline, bounded by, touching and forming a part of the chaotic outside, whereas the second is seen as the inner edge, protecting the center from that which lies beyond. From this picture of ideological processes, one might expect genders and nations to be subject to both positive and negative portrayals.

A fine example of this duality in the realm of gender portrayal comes in the season 1962–63, when Rovers reach the final of the European Cup against Italian side Nettruno in Paris. Jealousy over Suzanne Cerise, a French film star, causes a feud between Rovers star Blackie Gray and stuntman Ed Garrard. The potential *ménage-à-trois* causes Blackie to arrive at the stadium at the last minute, but not before rendering the Rovers tense and disconcerted at the thought of his absence. By half-time, the team trails by one goal, leaving Roy in need of "something to boost their morale." Minutes later he enters the dressing room on the arm of the French star, who, complete with Brigitte Bardot bob and pout, whimpers at the team: "Mes heros! You win for me, yes? I have a surprise for you eef you do."[10] In the second half, the Rovers duly play "like men inspired," Blackie securing the winning goal "a split second before the final whistle." At the celebration party, however, Cerise asks the last-minute hero: "You weel be our best man, yes? I love the Rovers—mais alors, I can only marry one man, Ed Garrard." In the course of the story, Suzanne Cerise is viewed both positively and negatively: she causes Rovers' first-half deficit, but inspires them to win in the end. However, the message is clear: A woman's word is ambivalent. Cerise's promise of a surprise turns out to be a grave disappointment, in view of which there can be only one solution. This comes from the mouth of Roy at the end of the episode: "Phew, now Blackie won't have Suzanne on his mind anymore. He can concentrate on football."[11] After an exploration of women in their role as inspiration and disappointment, they are firmly relocated at the margins of the male environment.

To this end, women are normally absent, or function unobtrusively in the background as servicing or enabling agents. The Melchester secretary is a woman, and players' wives and mothers are often depicted providing the domestic services that are an important basis from which the protagonists can launch themselves on their adventures. In the portrayal of important matches, however, we are also shown the situation of the fan watching at home on the television. Recreating the reader in the text, such shots are laden with significance for the construction of a symbolic order. These scenes tap into the traditions and folklore familiar to those who watched the F.A. Cup final: the long side-by-side march of both finalists onto the pitch, the playing of the national anthem, the introduction of the teams to a member of the royal family. Against this background of realism, the positioning and make-up of the group gathered around the set itself becomes significant. In 1966, for instance, we are given the view of a young boy kneeling down between two adult men (father and uncle?) indulging in prematch drinks and sandwiches.[12] At the side of the frame, standing, therefore transitory, is a female teenager (an older sister?), wearing a look of slight disdain. In this domestic setting she is as marginalized and insignificant to the male order as Suzanne Cerise in the romantic milieu of Paris. During the same final, the closing moments of the game are transmitted through the T.V. set of another sitting room.[13] At the decisive point of the match, three men sit in suspense with hands on head, as a mother figure, clad in floral pinafore and head scarf, intrudes on the side of the frame bearing a tray of steaming tea. Here, even the servicing role of women is undermined: What use is tea when the Rovers are on the brink of going a goal down? The fact that women do not even comprehend the male order is echoed in another story within the *Roy of the Rovers* magazine, "Billy's Boots." Schoolboy Billy Dane is the owner of a pair of football boots that belong to a dead star named Dead Shot Keen. The boots help Billy emulate the feats of the deceased, but are frequently replaced at Christmas and on birthdays by Billy's grandmother and guardian who throws "those tatty old things" away. Weeks of dreadful form on the pitch ensue, until Billy recovers his lost treasures: The smooth reproduction of male success in sport is threatened by women abandoning their appropriate and "natural" position in the social order, interfering in areas beyond their comprehension.

The disturbing effect of women's attempt to move in from the margins can be seen most dramatically in its repercussions on the field of play. The season 1975–76 is the worst since the comic's inception, Rovers failing to pick up a single honor: They are sensationally knocked out of the League Cup in the semifinal by Hansfield, a team from a lower division, lose the League Championship by one point, and are overcome by rivals Oldfield in the final of the F.A. Cup. It can be no coincidence that this last failure, in the worst season ever, comes on the eve of Roy's wedding to club secretary Penny Laine. As the opponents collect the trophy, Roy tries to cheer up his team with an old male cliché: "So . . . heads up, Rovers! I don't want to see any cup-final blues on my final day of freedom."[14] At the wedding reception Roy assures his wife that their honeymoon destination will offer a "complete break," "nothing to do with football." Weeks later, however, the trip is cut short for Roy to compete for a Europe Select XI in Brazil where he is named Man of the Tournament. The female forces that threatened the male order have therefore been held at bay: By pushing his matrimonial bliss to the margins, Roy effectively becomes the best player in the world. In the 1980–81 season, however, the unthinkable happens: Against the background of arguments between Roy and Penny at home, Rovers are relegated to the second division. Again, in his brief spell with Walford, Penny is convinced that Roy is having an affair with his new club's secretary, Sandy Lewis, causing the star to underperform in the most humiliating fashion on the pitch. Throughout this argument, the readers are constantly assured that Roy is only performing his duty by accompanying Sandy to the supporters' club dance. The movement of women away from the margins therefore disrupts the very symbolic centre of male performance and identity.

Boys constituted 88 percent of the readership of *Roy of the Rovers* in 1982, and many continued to read the comic *through* their mid-adolescent years. IPC's figures showed this clearly: of the overall readership, 9 percent were aged seven to eight, 18 percent aged nine to ten; 57 percent of the readership was within the age-band eleven to fourteen; fifteen- to sixteen-year-olds made up only 6 percent, but 10 percent of the readership was made up of seventeen- to nineteen-year-olds. There was clearly a drop-out rate as readers got older, but comics also circulated among brothers, sisters, school friends; and one in six of these male readers was of, or beyond, school-leaving age. It is doubtful that any comic for girls would have followed this pattern. *Bunty* was a long-established comic for prepubescent girls; *Jackie* targeted mid-adolescent girls (McRobbie 1977; Dunne 1982). Work on these two comics has shown how an assertive physicality in prepubescence is superseded by an emphasis on girls' main work—the construction of themselves as objects of potential consumption by men. A new comic in the British market in early 1985, *Nikki*, combined elements of both *Bunty* and *Jackie*, as the ideology of adolescent femininity was targeted at even younger markets. The girls' comic market looked as if it had been cunningly plotted by a team of developmental psychologists, subtly sensitive to the crises of femininity and sexuality of the adolescent female. *Roy of the Rovers,* read fervently by boys from seven to nineteen years of age, embodied no such dilemma of gender identity. Being male, surviving with an unquestioned maleness, accomplishing heroic male feats—the message was that this was normal enough for the boy-soon-to-be-man.[15]

Marginality plays an important role in the emergence of a national identity within the master narrative of the comic, as the team both travels outside its national boundaries and has its own space invaded by opponents from without. In 1960, for instance, the Rovers travel to play San Angino in South America, but after a plane crash, the players are kidnapped amidst the Beltiguan civil war. This tale of disaster had a happy ending for the team, which managed to be delivered only bruised and bewildered, but will have had great resonance for all readers in light of the tragedy that had killed eight members of the Manchester United team just two years before, on their return journey from Belgrade when, after a refuelling stop in the snow and ice of Munich, the plane crashed on its third attempt to take off.[16] The message is clear: Venturing out of home territory can prove very dangerous indeed. In 1964, Rovers are once again subjected to a kidnapping ordeal in South America. Released only minutes before the kick-off, they commence the game having had no sleep for forty-eight hours. At half time, however, their former captors appear in the changing rooms and provide the Rovers with magical "Carioca Juice," which fuels an astonishing recovery. Rovers lift the World Club Cup, and are hoisted on the shoulders of their captors as Roy intones: "This is the first time I've gone for a ride on a brigand."[17] Here the distant Continent is portrayed in a dual light: It is a dangerous domain of possible peril, and the realm where victory is made possible. However, the manner of this victory strikes a warning note: It is only by means of a magic potion, given by untrustworthy characters, that the Rovers can succeed. The far-off continent is therefore portrayed as one where the real and the fantastic merge in a dangerous concoction. It is highly likely that this corresponds in some measure to a Eurocentric view of South American soccer at the time: Brazil, helped by the wizardry of Pelé, had dominated football by winning two consecutive World Cups, in Sweden (1958) and Chile (1962). It is only by borrowing some of their dangerous magic that Rovers are able to assert their own dominance of the world.

Within Europe, Rovers' success in interclub competitions projects a range of British perceptions across a spectrum of countries. This can be illustrated by reference to the team's victorious run in the 1966-67 European Cup-Winners Cup. In the preliminary round, Rovers trail to Villa Florina, but as the minutes pass, the Italians run out of puff, allowing the superior fitness of the English side to secure progress into the next stage with three late goals. In the next round, the Greek champions Paniakos take an early lead and try to achieve victory by dull, defensive play. Undeterred, the Rovers move into the next phase where they are almost defeated by the dazzling intensity of the sun in Turkey. In the semifinal against Real Corbao, Rovers eventually win out by making the Spanish defender, Hernandez, crack under pressure. Through to the final, Melchester then face the physical challenge of defeating a Portuguese side whose center forward is a giant. The opening frame of the sequence shows Roy dwarfed by the foreign striker, but at the end it is English skill and tenacity that wins through again. The portrayal of Rovers' successive victories mirrors British postwar views on other nations: They are unfit, tactically unaware, lacking in nerve, and only approach victory by playing under blazing sunshine, or fielding physical mutants.

Analysis of the Rovers' European opponents in the 1960s and 1970s is revealing in terms of absences. In view of the situation in contemporaneous football, one might have expected high profile matches against teams from two countries in particular: Spain and Germany. The Spanish side Real Madrid had won the European Cup five times in succession (a record never likely to be equalled), from its inauguration in 1956 to 1960, dominating European football with their brilliance. Germany had been England's opponents in the 1966 World Cup final at Wembley Stadium, which the home nation won in a close encounter in extra time; but had avenged this defeat with a masterful 3–1 victory in a European Nations Championship qualifier at Wembley in 1972, and gone on to win the tournament later that year, and the World Cup two years later. While teams from these two countries do feature in the Rovers' campaigns, they rarely feature in the games of most importance. In the late 1950s and early 1960s, Rovers' great rivals are Schonved, the champions of Hungary, while in the 1960s and early 1970s they are replaced by teams from Italy and Portugal. In this, the Rovers' exploits and rivalries are in some way meant to capture and reflect moments of importance for the real English national team. The matches against Schonved would have tapped into the deep shock that resonated for decades within English football: the first defeat of the national side at Wembley stadium, by six goals to three at the hands of a dazzling Hungarian side in November

1953, and the subsequent humiliation (by seven goals to one) in the return match in Budapest the following summer. This was the moment when English football, which had retained pretensions of elitism as founders of the game, was forced to realize that world football had progressed beyond recognition. By avoiding major clashes with German sides, the comic was probably intent on avoiding the anti-German feeling of other children's publications of the time, which featured "over-the-top" heroes such as Captain Hurricane of *Valiant,* who every week lost his temper with the "Huns," and went barefisted to teach them a "jolly good lesson" (Barker 1989, p. 18). Italy struck a chord in the national football consciousness by taking away the nation's best players (e.g., John Charles, Jimmy Greaves, Denis Law) through the "lure of the lire." After Germany, Portugal proved to be England's closest rivals in the mid-1960s, pushing England hard in the semifinal of the World Cup in 1966, and possessing Europe's top player, Eusebio.

This reflection of a real discourse of football occurs again in 1978, when the national game was at its lowest ebb. For the second time in succession, England had failed to qualify for the final stages of the World Cup. In the comic, this national trauma is beyond the scope of Rovers' restorative powers, and Roy is made temporary manager of the England side. With a team made up of Rovers, players from other comic strips, and a few real-life players, Roy's England put on a dazzling display against Holland (runners-up in the 1974 World Cup, and favorites for the forthcoming finals in Argentina), thrashing what was considered to be the world's best team by five goals to one. During the match, Roy praises his own tactical genius: "That's been the trouble with England managers in the past. They were frightened to take a gamble."[18] After the final whistle, as Roy accepts the congratulations of the Dutch captain, Johann (is this a reference to the world's best player Johann Cruyff?), a joyous family gathering is pictured around a T.V. set from which a commentary is emanating: "Just listen to that crowd! With his untried team Roy Race has combined courage, fitness and flair to give English football its greatest night in years."[19] Narratologically speaking, the Rovers' role as an embodiment of national fantasy has been temporarily displaced by Roy himself: it is striking that after the national side's momentous victory in the comic, the Rovers are permitted to lose their first European final, against the Dutch club side Alkhoven. That the Rovers continue to mediate the fantastic fulfilment of the national football discourse is evident from the choice of caretaker manager to guide the Rovers in 1982 when Roy is lying in a coma after being shot. The appointment of Sir Alf Ramsay, manager of England's World Cup winning side of 1966 but dismissed by the English Football Association in 1973 after England failed to qualify for the following year's World Cup Finals, is an outdated and unfashionable choice for the 1980s, only comprehensible if the Rovers' exploits are indeed understood in the manner just outlined: While Rovers take on the role of fulfilling the expectations and mending the wounds of a nation's footballing discourse, it is only fitting that the representative of its finest hour comes to the rescue of the Rovers in their time of need.[20] He leads them in an unbeaten run ending in a record-breaking 14–0 victory.

One further important national boundary needs to be explored: the comic's stance toward Scotland. For while the Rovers are an English team through and through, the comic was popular throughout the Celtic fringes. The "Sign Please!" feature of the comic, in the early 1980s based on reader requests for autographed pin-ups of their favorite players, gave Scottish readers a chance to place their Scottish stars in the center pages of the comic; Scottish club champions, Rangers, figured prominently on the back-page of a 1989 issue; and a hardy favorite in the comic's stories was, for many years, Hot-Shot Hamish Balfour, a gentle Celtic giant whose Sylvester Stallone-like physique and cannon-ball shot (known as Hamish's Hammer) could neutralize the most ruthless of football hard men and thugs. As described above, Roy plays for, captains, and sometimes manages the England team, but the matches that feature the national side are restricted in number. Certainly, although Roy is regularly picked to represent his country in World Cup finals, the comic never portrays Roy or his Rovers teammates representing England in other contexts. Scottish readers are therefore not alienated by overexposure of the England team. In 1967, Rovers' match against Sporting Alcero in the final of the European Cup-Winners Cup is staged at Hampden Park, home of the Scottish national side. This venue has deep resonances within the discourse of British football: It is held to be the scene of the best European final ever witnessed (Real Madrid's 7–3 victory over Eintracht Frankfurt in 1960), as well as having staged the unique match, in 1947, in which a Great Britain XI defeated a Rest of Europe side by six goals to one in front of one hundred thirty-five thousand spectators. The significance of the venue, however, extends beyond such folkloric resonances. The artist has taken as much care to capture the essential features of the stadium as when he draws Wembley, the home of English soccer, and scene of Rovers' many F.A. Cup victories: The open-back terraces, the high stands, and even the distinct shape of the goals of Glasgow are as much in evidence as the famous twin towers of London. The trouble taken with the venue is obviously an inclusive gesture to Scottish readers, but this is surpassed by the inclusion of a Scottish "reader within the text" itself, "young Jock." He saves the Rovers by catching a banner, dropped by reckless Alcero fans climbing on the floodlights, which would have injured Roy himself, while several whole frames portray his reaction at various stages of the match: "Roy's done it! I knew he would! Rovers are in the lead!"; "I canna' bear to look."[21] The final two frames at the end of the sequence are most telling. In the first, Roy, shaking Jock by the hand, thanks his young friend for his assistance, prompting the reply: "Will my picture be in the papers? I want all my mates to see it—or they'll never believe this!"[22] The second focuses in further on Jock's reaction as he returns to his companions, one of whom states: "What a day this has been! We've seen the Rovers win the cup—and we helped them do it!"[23] Similarly, in the 1975 European Cup-Winners' Cup final against the Greek side Niarkos, also held at Hampden Park, the Rovers are struggling until a "shattering, crashing roar began to thunder around the mighty stadium."[24] As a full frame depicts the terraces full of men in Tartan hats, ringing out to the cheers of "Rovers! Rovers!," Roy thinks to himself: "The Hampden Roar . . . and it's unnerving the Greek players. I guess they've never heard anything like it."[25] Given the more than healthy sales figures in the subsequent years north of the border, such techniques must well have helped Scottish readers come to terms with Roy's nonobtrusive Englishness. This was one margin the publishers could not afford to create.

THE SYMBIOTIC RELATIONSHIP TO REALITY: CELEBRITIES IN FICTION, FICTION AS EVERYDAY TROPE, AND THE DEATH OF THE HERO

The inclusion of real-life characters within the fiction, and the use of the *Roy of the Rovers* metaphor in sports writing and in forms of talk in everyday life, demonstrate an interdependency of reality and fiction in the ideological impact and cultural currency of the fictional hero. It is these forms of interdependency that contribute to the framing of the perception and memory of heroic sporting figures, so that the great achievements of past footballing heroes (such as Bobby Moore) can be recalled, at their death, in terms, and around themes, common to the fictional Melchester dramas of Roy Race.

Real-life characters featured in the comic included Liverpool footballer Emlyn Hughes, Newcastle center-forward Malcolm MacDonald, and celebrities from other sports. The reality of change and progress in the football world also was mirrored in the comic, with the recognition of modernizing influences such as sponsorship. And the latest renaissance of Roy Race, in 1997, was in BBC Television's *Match of the Day* magazine, in its "Football Focus" subsection. The first caption of the two-page comic strip, in its third *Match of the Day* appearance (September 1997, pp. 18–19), informed readers that Melchester Rovers had been "saved from relegation to Division Two by a late penalty in last season's final game." Manager Roy Race was able to report that in "a lively close season for new signings", the club's "first 'capture' was a new shirt-sponsorship deal with McDonald's."

But ordinary life is a complex multilayered process: We strike bargains with our idealized conceptions of what-life-should-be-like. We often read the world and ourselves in terms of the textual representations with which we are familiar: It is not possible simply to separate ordinary life from myth. *Roy of the Rovers* tells boys and youths that life is a game and that male dominance in that game might sometimes be problematic, but can be taken-for-granted. Young people's own dilemmas of self-identity and sexuality might carry a different message. But such lived-through difficulties do not necessarily displace the myth. They might, in fact, be smoothed over by the constantly reiterated potency of the myth itself.

Roy of the Rovers offered a smoother than smooth path to male glory. In a move toward the participatory, readers were sometimes asked into the text, to evaluate stories and so produce ratings and charts of popularity. In similar adventure comics, this constitution of the reader's own potentially heroic subjectivity has been taken to its limit. The bubbles of dialogue in the picture strips leave the name of the protagonist unwritten—simply write in your own name! Also, in the way in which real-life sport stars came to be invited into the text, Roy was presented as a form of pseudoreality. Roy became more real, as the reader-protagonist became more fictional. With swimmer Sharron Davies in the 24 December 1983 issue, and cricketer Geoffrey Boycott (Melchester's new chairman) in the 18 August 1984 issue, Roy Race mixed with the real-life stars of the time. For the young reader, intimate with Race and such associates, life away from the comic might be lived as a comparatively dull and routine existence, an existence that only really *came to life* in the glory-seeking pages of the weekly fantasy.

The metaphor of the Roy Race narrative has echoed within the everyday discourse of generations of football followers and sports commentators. Exceptional goal-scoring in everyday football culture is referred to widely, by sports players, commentators and fans, as "real *Roy of the*

Rovers stuff." The meaning of the term now resonates far beyond the comic's text. What it implies, generally, is the reaffirmation of a supraordinary male heroism—the continuing triumph of the dominant, whatever odds or challenges have to be faced, and a traditional sense of fair play within the competitive sports ethos. The everyday resonance of the *Roy of the Rovers* myth, as a recurrent metaphor within football discourse, has transcended the currency of the popular cultural publishing profile. Examples from the popular and specialist media show how, beyond the publishing apogee of his fictional profile, Roy Race's ideological world has sustained an expressive currency within football commentary. Public references to "Roy of the Rovers" connote images of nostalgic reflection upon a lost age, the celebration of clean-cut contemporary sport stars, and the magic moments of memorable sports dramas. Rugby and cricket stars also have been depicted within the same discourse.[26]

The celebration of a past and lost age of core values draws powerfully upon the Roy Race trope. This prioritizes the clean-cut, wholesome side of the Roy image, rather than the flashier side of spectacular performance. Peter Beardsley could use the term to refer to an adventurous but incautious style of play: "We're not going to try to win in *Roy of the Rovers* style, but we'll attack sensibly" (Hodgson 1994, p. 42). One of Beardsley's earlier coaches also recalled that, as a younger player, "he was *Roy of the Rovers*. He was always trying to do fantastic things when a simple one would do" (Mott 1993, section 2 p. 5). This is a negative connotation of the metaphor, implying a self-glorification that does not fit with pragmatic reality, implying that the "*Roy of the Rover's* stuff" of heroic accomplishments is not in itself sufficient for the well-rounded star and hero: It needs to be matched by an adherence to the core values of a bygone age. In this, the rise to superstar status of English striker, Alan Shearer, proved irresistible to football feature-writers, especially so when Shearer was on the verge of blasting the fallen giant and unfashionable club, Blackburn **Rovers** (our emphasis), to the English Premiership football title in 1995. He went on to captain the English national side in the following year. Dave Hill (1995, p. 6), introduces Shearer as the new Player of the Year, a clean-cut level-headed goal king:

> The leading scorer of Blackburn Rovers, the cotton town team on the verge of becoming English champions, resembles the very model of the classic working-class sporting hero and suits the language to match: still only 24, Shearer is "upright," "clean-limbed," "well-made," everything legend demands an English centre-forward should be. And the

qualities of his play are receptive to old-fashioned metaphors. There's an urge to compare his courage to a lion's and an impulse to liken his long shots at goal to the flight of cannon balls.

Clean of mind and body was the old athletic ideal, and impressions of Shearer conform to it; here, you feel, is a fellow who washes behind *everything;* who, amid the muck and brass neck of modern football, might be shocked to learn that coke can be something other than a fizzy drink or a derivative of coal, and who has only ever thought of a bung as just a different kind of stopper.

As a striker, he comes closer to fitting the *Roy Of the Rovers* fantasy than anyone else lately admired by English crowds. He is a thoughtful player as well as instinctive, but what he communicates most directly to the average supporter are the power, strength and sweat of the vintage number nine rather than something rational, calm and quick like Gary Lineker, or mysterious and dark, like Eric Cantona.

Many of these images are, of course, illusions but their persuasiveness is still revealing.

When the captaincy of his country came Shearer's way, Glenn Moore (1996, p. 26) revived the trope—"After all those years when we thought *Roy of the Rovers* was a fictional character it turns out he really does exist . . . Truly a Boy's Own Story."

Shearer is a striker, as was Roy Race, but these core values can be embodied by players whose all-round image and ideological values are more important than spectacular performances. Ivan Ponting's (1994, p. 10) obituary on Billy Wright, II a former Wolverhampton Wanderers stalwart and England captain of the 1950s is a tribute to such all-roundedness:

> If Billy Wright had been trotted out as a comic-strip hero, he would
> have been ridiculed as being too good to be true. Blond and handsome,
> personable and clean-living, he was England's football captain and the
> first man from any country to win a century of international caps . . .
>
> Wright was a paragon of sporting and family virtue. He exuded
> wholesome, uncomplicated enthusiasm, was a slave to the work ethic,
> and modest to a fault. In fact, though they could hardly be described as
> blots on his escutcheon, there were certain differences between the ge-
> nial Salopian and *Roy of the Rovers* . . . he was a defender, and not a
> spectacular match-winner; and not that skilled, or blessed with natural
> talent, being most of all a thinker and a reader . . . it is as England's

golden-haired captain, he of the Boy Scout image on and off the pitch, that Billy Wright claims a special place in the annals of British sporting history.

This mourning for a lost age of dedication, honesty, and commitment was also expressed in 1993, in response to the death of Bobby Moore, another golden-haired English defender and captain. Moore was a very different figure to Wright, as a hugely and nationally profiled captain of the World Cup-winning England side of 1966 who exploited the commercial opportunities of the victory: "The cream of English footballers suddenly became the most highly visible examples of that still novel phenomenon, the working-class boy made good, and *Roy of the Rovers* would never again be the lad who lives next door" (Hill 1996, p. 4). Yet despite this difference, consideration of the popular media response to Moore's death confirms the homologous relation of the fictional discourse and the media reportage of an historical reality, as they contribute, in turn, to the perpetuation of the male fantasy of the football romance. Bobby Moore became remembered as the heroic depiction of the man of deeds from a classic era, understood by generations of sports fans, players and commentators in post-World War II Britain in the same terms as they recalled the heyday of Roy Race and his men of Melchester.

Like Roy Race, Moore was for most of his playing career a loyal one-club man, playing for the London club, West Ham United, but his greatest accomplishment is seen to be his role as captain in the only English national side to win the World Cup. This victory over West Germany in the summer of 1966 was achieved in an encounter memorable for the closeness of the contest (achieved only in extra time), and for the intense rivalry between the two nations which a mere twenty-one years previously had been locked in much more serious forms of combat. In February 1993, Moore died at the age of fifty-two, and as such the first one of the fêted 1966 World Cup winning team to die. His death provoked a literature of tribute (Powell 1993), and a phenomenal response in the press. Both the broadsheet and tabloid press gave extensive coverage to his memory and to the symbolic import of his death, and the meaning of England's world cup triumph in 1966. Hugh McIlvanney of *The Observer* (28 February 1993, p. 23) referred to that victory as having "a lasting resonance . . . something of a golden age . . . and the blond, upright, regally composed figure who orchestrated the defeat of West Germany at Wembley on a July afternoon nearly 27 years ago was naturally freeze-framed in the mind's eye as its golden symbol . . .". Moore's bearing was recalled by McIlvanney as "majestic," having "an aura of imperious authority . . .". The tabloid *Daily Mirror* recalled Moore as "a great footballer and a true gentleman . . . as much an ambassador for his country off the pitch as he was a supreme artist on it . . . he was the ultimate symbol of an age where there was true pride in pulling on an England shirt." In the *Daily Telegraph*, journalist and broadcaster Michael Parkinson contrasted the mercenary rewards of the future with the core values of a less commercially tarnished age:

> The captain of the next England team to win the World Cup will drive home in a platinum Rolls Royce, over a silver drawbridge across a moat of liquid gold. But I doubt he'll be a hero like Bobby Moore.
>
> I am glad I saw him when I did, when the England shirt was pristine and not daubed with commercial graffiti, when there was still honor in the game, style and, most of all, humor. The lasting image of that time, will always be Moore, slim as a reed, holding aloft the trophy at Wembley. It was the moment when the boy from Barking became the golden icon of the Sixties. (Parkinson, *Daily Telegraph*, 1 March 1993, in Parkinson [1995, p. 208])

In such outlets, across the press and the popular media, tributes and commentaries transmitted and reflected a certain common sentiment, in which several themes prevailed. Bobby Moore's playing career spanned the twenty years from the late 1950s to the late 1970s, and, on his death, his place in the national and sporting culture was evoked around themes remarkably similar to those at the center of the Roy Race fiction and ideology. First, aligned with the unusual outpouring of grief at the loss of a mere individual, was a clear sense of mourning for the loss of an age. This age was perceived as the lost golden age, a time of English football dominance depicted also in the character and achievements of Melchester Rovers and Roy Race. Since 1970, the national side's achievements had been nonexistent, negligible, or short-lived; for several years from the mid-1980s, English club sides had been exiled from European competition as a result of the Heysel disaster.[27] Both factors contributed to a sense of national sporting decline in an age of growing commercial exploitation. The commentaries on Moore's death celebrated and mourned the 1960s as a lost age of stability and desirable values now in need of restoration.

Secondly, explicit in the presentation of his core qualities, is an emphasis upon an extraordinary capacity to accomplish the task to hand. The more challenging this task, the greater the ease with which the goal is reached. His vision of the game is said to have enabled him to stroll effortlessly toward the peaks of performance—as confirmed by Moore's first England manager, Walter Winterbottom, who recalls the fashion in which his authority was exerted by action and example, not by shouted commands or loud gestures (interview with authors, Cranleigh, Surrey, 24 November 1996). The recollection of Moore by his West Ham and England teammate, Geoff Hurst, depicts the accomplishments of the man of deeds as almost supernatural: "He made himself a great player, and the bigger the stage, the better he performed. If the world had played Mars, he would have been man of the match" (Hutchinson 1995, p. 210). This view is also implicitly captured in visual form by the two most popular images chosen to commemorate Moore's achievements both in the national press and in various international media. One depicts Moore hoisted triumphantly upon the shoulders of his team mates, holding aloft the World Cup trophy. It is held comfortably, rather than shaken wildly; his demeanor is relaxed, his smile assuredly contented, the golden locks are perfectly groomed as if he had played for a few minutes in a Sunday morning practice match rather than for two hours on a hot summer's day for the biggest prize of all. It is an image that has transcended national cultures. In its commemoration of World Cup winning nations in its publication, *100 ans de football en France,* the French Football Federation singles out England (for once, the nation to have won the trophy the least number of times), for the final image and commentary: "Consécration pour l'Angleterre, organisateur et vainqueur de la Coup du Monde 1966. Porté en triomphe par ses coéquipiers, Bobby Moore brandit la légendaire 'Victoire aux ailes d'or' " (Fédération Française de Football, undated).[28] In this quasireligious cum military language of dedication and warrior's display of victory, this moment is immortalized. In further photographs from the same sequence of events, Moore can be seen standing in the center of the other players, trophy still nonchalantly held in display, his cool authority in marked contrast to the Charlton brothers: Bobby in tears, Jack with gargoyle snarl of victory. In this sequence there is transmitted a vision of Moore as the conquering hero, loved and adored by his men, yet at the same time superior. He could be straight out of Homer or the Germanic Epic.[29] The other popular image dates from 1970, after England's 1–0 defeat at the hands of Brazil in a preliminary round of the World Cup finals and also features on the back dust-cover of Moore's authorized biography. This match was recognized as one of the greatest international encounters in football history. Moore stands a few inches above Brazil's Pelé (widely perceived as the greatest player of the modern era); the players have exchanged shirts that they each hold in one hand. With the other, they embrace, Pelé's arm and hand straddling Moore's shoulder and the nape of his neck; Moore's hand caressing the cheek of the great black player. Their eyes are locked in intense yet relaxed gazes of mutual respect, mouths drawn into uncannily identical smiles of deep contentedness. This is a meeting of champions, in which the result mattered less than the magnificent meeting of equals. It is like when Germanic warriors swap shields, or two boxers, such as Ali and Fraser collapse into each others arms after a struggle of titanic proportions.[30] It is a contentedness borne of the recognition of equal supremacy, and in the accomplishment of deeds, to fulfill oneself at the highest possible level. In both these visual moments, it is the effortless, tranquil, and apparently natural *state* of achievement rather than the *act* of achievement which is "freeze-framed," to use MacIlvenney's term, and thus generates the model of the heroic for posterity.

The third of the prevailing themes centers around "the element of nationalism." Critcher notes how, in the accounts of Moore's death, the past is looked to for guidance, but cannot be reproduced, for "nationalism is rooted in past glories which we should like to emulate but cannot" (1994, p. 85). Moore is depicted as the perfect ambassador for his country, one who is proud to wear the colors of the nation. However, what becomes clear in the tributes is a sense that more is to be mourned than the loss of the representative of the nation, namely, the loss of that for which the representative stood: the nation and its former glories. Aligned with this is the perceived loss of the manner of the achievement on behalf of the nation: the demise of the gentleman and sportsman, quintessentially established in the nineteenth-century public schools' athleticist ideology (Mangan 1986), and reaffirmed and diffused in a wide range of institutional practices and cultural formations. In this context, the evocation of the socially mobile working-class boy's qualities as essentially gentlemanly and sportsmanlike was a nostalgic plea for the return of the lost values of an earlier age, in which such forms of conduct were integral to the depiction of the national image.

Fourthly, Moore is remembered for his pure football accomplishments within the lost age, rather than for any wider sense of celebrity. His connection with any cultural revolution and a break from traditional mores and values (Marwick 1986), in the form of his celebrity pin-up status and his desirability to women (Emery 1993, p. 133), is marginalized.

The themes discussed with reference to both Roy Race and Bobby Moore—the loss of an age, the extraordinary qualities of an individual (its image captured in freeze-frame), nationalism and the values of the English gentleman, and the marginal status of women—hold true for both how the reality of Bobby Moore, and the interpretive and ideological impact of fictional football hero Roy Race, are understood. In popular cultural hermeneutics, Wilson (1993, p. 6) argues, the sense-making viewer of television, responding to and identifying with a text, "moves within and between roles," including the role of distanciated reader, which "resists" any "easy endorsement of a hierarchy of meaning, familiarity and apparent truth centred on a subject" (Wilson 1993, p. 196). In an interesting way, young readers of the Roy Race narrative have sought such an easy endorsement, but with a combination of playfulness and fantasy; and in their later years, as an ironic and nostalgic distanciation, applied interpretively to the nonfictional realities of sporting cultures and discourse. In such a case, fiction and reality coalesce in a patriarchal, nationalist ideology of male heroism in sport, rooted in a nostalgia for childhood memories of both fictional and lived forms of the football culture.

Reading *Roy of the Rovers,* and reflecting upon the response to the death of sporting heroes such as Bobby Moore, demonstrates how children's popular cultural experiences, and the recollections of them in later life, traverse the boundaries of, and fuse, the fictional and the real. Heroic figures from the fantasy pages of the comic strip provide an interpretive framework that need not fade away with age, experience, or the intrusion of the world of everyday reality. The world of representation in the comic strip is mobilized as an everyday trope, tapping into modes of thinking within the reality of football discourse; and in turn, football discourse draws upon the narratives, conventions, and myths of football fictions. In such a fashion, fantasy feeds reality in the perpetuation of the master narrative of untarnished male heroism in the ever-recurring drama and romance of sports culture. As in the reader's response to any media text, reading *Roy of the Rovers* as child, adult, or critic, is to "do three actions almost simultaneously. We read, we comprehend and we interpret" (Real 1996, p. 103). Understanding the widespread and persistent influence of the Roy Race trope reminds us of the capacity that our interpretation of fictional media texts has to inform our memories and understandings of everyday realities. The discourse of sports writing, in both the children's comic fiction and the culture of sports reportage, is shown to be in symbiotic, dialectical relation with readers' memories and experiences of the sports culture.

NOTES

1. The Roy Race story is covered in part in an earlier analysis (Tomlinson 1997) upon which parts of this article draw.

2. This readership data was kindly provided by Hilary Cross, Consumer Research Manager, Marketing Research, Youth & Practical G, IPC Magazines on 15 September 1983.

3. Fantasy Football began life in the early 1990s in Britain, as a form of pastiche of the game. It began on late-night television, allowing fans to play out their fantasies, pick their own teams from real-life players, deal in transfer markets, and play the role of the manager of the team. It consolidated its popularity in the print media, spanning the popular tabloids and the quality broadsheets.

4. The following quotations are from Acton and Jarmon (1994). Any wider sample of citations from the comic would corroborate the typicality of Acton and Jarman's selection. The three captions referred to here are on p. 21.

5. Ibid. p. 92

6. Ibid. p. 73

7. Ibid. p. 25

8. Ibid. p. 43

9. Ibid. p. 99

10. Ibid. p. 45

11. Ibid. p. 46

12. Ibid. p. 52

13. Ibid. p. 55

14. Ibid. p. 106

15. This pattern of readership is exclusive to *Roy of the Rovers*. IPC's rival "boy's" adventure comic, *Victor,* had a readership that faded at the ages of thirteen/fourteen and that, astonishingly, rose again at the ages of seventeen to nineteen. It is as if boys of thirteen to sixteen think that they have grown up or become adult, before recognizing that the essence of masculinity is not growing up at all. The magazine/feature soccer publication *Shoot* lost its readership dramatically at the ages of seventeen to nineteen with pseudo-realism displaced, perhaps, by fantasy and idealised fictional heroes. Similarly, the specialist science-fiction comic *2000 AD* was taken up again by seventeen- to nineteen-year-olds, after a mid-adolescent fall in readership. Sport and space seem to offer similar sets of

possibilities in the masculinist imagination, a recurring sense of masculinity as adventure and glory.

16. For an evocative account of the tragedy, see Dunphy 1991, pp. 219–236.

17. Acton and Jarman, p. 48.

18. Ibid. p. 114

19. Ibid. p. 117

20. Such extraordinary measures are adopted in real-life situations. Uruguay, host and winner of the inaugural World Cup in 1930, and desperate to recapture its former glories after failing to qualify for the World Cup finals in 1998, in 1997 appointed as national coach an aged star of its historic World Cup triumph of 1950. It was as if the aura of an ancient champion was expected to transmit itself directly to the national side.

21. Acton and Jarman, p. 59.

22. Ibid. p. 60

23. Ibid. p. 60

24. Ibid. p. 100

25. Ibid. p. 100

26. We have found dozens of examples of the use of the metaphor in broadcasting sports commentary, and tabloid and broadsheet journalism—most revealingly, months and years after the cessation of the publication of the comic. The examples cited here are those in which the metaphor is contextualized most fully, for the assumptions, shared interpretations, and common childhood memories to which they refer.

27. At the Heysel Stadium in Brussels, Belgium, in the May 1985 final of the European Cup, many Italians, fans of the Juventus club, died when crushed in a terrace tragedy that was at least in part provoked by the conduct of the fans of the English club Liverpool.

28. In English: "Consecration for England, host and winner of the 1966 World Cup. Carried triumphantly by his team mates, Bobby Moore brandishes the legendary 'Golden-Winged Victory' " (our translation). Although in the list of references, this source is undated, it is likely to date from the early 1990s, possibly 1992, the centenary of the formation, in 1892, of the football section of Le Havre Athletic Club (see Oliver 1995, p. 303).

29. Spoof, pastiche or not, the associated image of Moore's moment of triumph on receiving the trophy from the Queen of England is evocatively covered in the reminiscences of David Lodge's character, Tubby Passmore. For Tubby, the death of Moore and the recollection of his deeds is the basis for an encomium to the memory of the man: ". . . the way he would bring the ball out of defense and into attack, head up, back straight, like a captain leading a cavalry charge. He

looked like a Greek god, with his clean-cut limbs and short golden curls. They don't make them like that any more" (Lodge 1996, p. 90).

30. Cf. Gehrman (1996) and Rauch (1996) for accounts of the heroic style of losing boxers such as Schmeling and Carpentier.

BIBLIOGRAPHY

Acton, P. & C. M. Jarman. *"Roy of the Rovers": The Playing Years.* Harpenden: Queen Anne Press, 1994.

Barker, M. *Comics: Ideology, Power and the Critics.* Manchester: Manchester University Press, 1989.

Brown, M. "Wallop! Goal! Roy's still over the moon at 30," *The Sunday Times,* 9 September 1984, p. 5.

Chaudhary, V. "Melchester hero answers soccer fans' pleas to return," *The Guardian,* 12 August 1993, p. 1.

Critcher, C. "England and the World Cup: World Cup willies, English football and the myth of 1966," In *Hosts and Champions: Soccer Cultures, National Identities and the USA World Cup,* eds. J. Sugden & A. Tomlinson. Aldershot: Arena/Ashgate Publishing Ltd., 1994: 77–92.

Dorfman, A. & A. Mattelart. *How to Read "Donald Duck": Imperialist Ideology in the Disney Comics.* New York: International General, 1975.

Dunne, Mary. "An introduction to some of the images of sport in girls' comics," In *Sporting Fictions.* Birmingham: Centre for Contemporary Cultural Studies/University of Birmingham, 1982: 36–59.

Dunphy, E. *A Strange Kind of Glory: Sir Matt Busby & Manchester United.* London: Heinemann, 1991.

Emery, D., ed. *Bobby Moore—The Illustrated Biography of a Footballing Legend.* London: Headline, 1993.

Express reporter. "Roy's own story of soccer giant," *Daily Express,* 27 October 1994, p. 25.

Fédération Française de Football. *100 ans de football en France.* Paris: Fédération Française de Football, n.d.

Gehrmann, S. "Symbol of national resurrection: Max Schmeling, German sports idol," in *European Heroes: Myth, Identity, Sport,* R. Holt, J. A. Mangan, and P. Lanfrichi, eds., pp. 101–113.

Hill, D. "The real *Roy of the Rovers,*" *The Guardian 2,* 10 April 1995, pp. 6–7 [on front page, byline: *"Roy of the Rovers*—Does Blackburn's Alan Shearer, model footballer and Boy's Own hero, represent a revival of lost virtues? Profile 6/7"].

Hill, D. "The kicks en route to '96," *The Observer Review,* Sunday 2 June 1996, p. 4.

Hodgson, G. "Beardsley boosts Newcastle with surprise return," *The Independent,* Tuesday 13 September, 1994, p. 42.

Holt, R., J. A. Mangan, and P. Lanfrachi, eds. *European heroes: Myth, Identity, Sport* (Special Issue of *The International Journal of the History of Sport,* Vol. 13 No.1) London: Frank Cass, 1996.

Hutchinson, R. . . . *It Is Now! The Real Story of England's 1966 World Cup Triumph.* Edinburgh and London: Mainstream Publishing, 1995.

Lodge, D. *Therapy—A Novel.* Harmondsworth: Penguin, 1996.

Mangan, J. A. "'Muscular, militaristic and manly': The British middle-class hero as moral messenger," *European Heroes: Myth, Identity, Sport,* in R. Holt, J. A. Mangan and P. Lanfrichi, eds. pp. 28–47.

Marwick, A. "A social history of Britain 1945–1983," in D. Punter, ed., *Introduction to contemporary cultural studies.* London: Longman, 1986: 19–46.

McRobbie, A. *Jackie: an ideology of adolescent femininity.* Stencilled Occasional Paper, Women Series SP N. 53, Birmingham Centre for Contemporary Cultural Studies/University of Birmingham, 1977.

Moi, T. *Sexual/textual politics: Feminist literary theory.* London: Routledge, 1985.

Moore, G. "Captain Shearer answers Hoddle's call," *The Independent,* 31 August 1996, p. 26.

Mott, S. "King Beardsley's fatal attraction" (The Sue Mott Profile), *The Sunday Times,* 19 December 1993, Section 2 p. 5 (Sport).

Oliver, G. *The Guiness Book of World Soccer (2nd edition): The History of the Game in over 150 Countries.* London: Guiness Publishing, 1995.

Parkinson, M. *Sporting Profiles—Sixty Heroes of Sport.* London: Pavilion, 1995.

Ponting, I. "Billy Wright," *The Independent [Obituaries],* Monday 5 September, p. 10. 1994.

Powell, J. *Bobby Moore: The Life and Times of a Sporting Hero.* London: Robson Books.

Real, M. R. *Exploring Media Culture: A Guide.* London: Sage, 1996.

Rauch, A. "Courage against cupidity: Carpentier and Dempsey—Symbols of cultural confrontation," in *European Heroes: Myth, Identity, Sport,* R. Holt, J. A. Mangan, P. Lanfranchi, eds., pp. 101–13.

Sugden, J. & A. Tomlinson, eds., *Hosts and Champions. Soccer Cultures, National Identities and the USA World Cup.* Aldershot: Arena/Ashgate Publishing Ltd., 1994.

Tomlinson, A. "Ideologies of physicality, masculinity and femininity: Comments on *Roy of the Rovers* and the women's fitness boom," in *Gender, Sport and*

Leisure: Continuities and Challenges. [CSRC Edition Volume 3], ed. A. Tomlinson. Aachen: Meyer and Meyer, 1997: 135–71 [1st pub. by University of Brighton, CSRC Topic Report 4, 1995].

Wilson, T. *Watching Television: Hermeneutics, Reception and Popular Culture.* Cambridge, U.K.: Polity Press, 1993.

Wren-Lewis, J. & A. Clarke. "The World Cup—a political football," *Theory, Culture and Society—Explorations in Critical Social Science.* Vol. 1 No. 3, 1983: 123–32.

Heroines of Empire
British Imperialism and the Reproduction of Femininity in Girls' Fiction, 1900–1930

J. S. BRATTON

The ideology of British imperialism is commonly defined in terms also culturally associated with masculinity. The dispensing of justice and reason, racial superiority, loyalty to peer groups and to the nation, heroism, enterprise, patriotic aggression, militarism, all seem inappropriate or positively counter to the values promulgated as the late Victorian and Edwardian ideal of womanhood. John MacKenzie, outlining the impact of imperial feeling upon popular culture,[1] uses masculine examples and the male pronoun almost exclusively, and the evidence he offers of its attraction for working-class children is related to its consonance with cultural traditions such as "the assertion of masculinity."[2] The British Empire, however, had some use for girls. In their discussion of the English-woman,[3] Jane Mackay and Pat Thorne begin with the proposition that "nationality . . . played a more significant role in the redefinition of masculinity as it emerged in the later nineteenth century than in that of femininity," but add:

> this is not to say that women were not expected to be patriotic . . .
> rather that they were identified not with nation but with race. The role
> of females . . . was to contribute to the preservation, perpetuation and
> enhancement of the race both physically and spiritually; the male role
> was to defend and preserve the nation . . . The essential distinction was
> between a female role which was biological and spiritually dedicated
> to the production and rearing of healthy children, the support of men
> and the guardianship of the spiritual and moral values of the English,
> and a male role which was virile and intellectual, dedicated to the

protection and perpetuation of the nation and its institutions through
activity at all levels in politics, administration, the armed services business and finance ... Domestic harmony, created and sustained by
women was presented as desirable, even essential, for the defence of
Britain against her rivals overseas, indeed for the defence of the whole
British Empire.[4]

The middle-class girl, in particular, had to learn to be wife and mother to
the pioneer and the soldier, and therefore the depository of the "home
values" and the guarantor of "higher" feelings and motives for the men's
conquests. The ladies at home were both the motive for fighting and
striving, in themselves—in their need for protection, and their ability to
offer rewards to the victor—and the guardians and transmitters of a more
abstract justification, of ideals, a sense of purpose and rectitude. They
were both the warriors' prize and the embodied ideal.

The two aspects of this female function, the spiritual and the biological, were, in practical terms, somewhat contradictory. Women in a
proper state of iconic passivity are liable to ill-health, and that weakness
had been institutionalised in the mid-Victorian vision of the home, where
the delicate young mother reigned in the hearts of her brood from a pros-
trate position amidst the sofa cushions. This was not suggestive of good
breeding stock, and moreover was a vision difficult to transfer to log
cabin or military station. Colonial writers since the 1830s, especially female writers, repeatedly warned that ladies (and indeed gentlemen) were
going out to the Colonies fatally unfit in mind and body to meet the demands of a settler's life.[5] But these writers still stressed the prime importance of refinement, of home-centred feminine culture. The rising tide of
demand from women themselves for greater activity and independence
and participation in some masculine activities was feared as being,
amongst other things, the beginning of the disintegration of the value
system which justified the imposition of British culture on the rest of the
world. Feminism was anti-imperialist.

Thus we find, by the turn of the nineteenth century, educational and
scientific theorists inventing a whole new science, eugenics, and performing extraordinary argumentative contortions in its name, largely
in order to prop up the vision of women which combined notions of
motherhood, homemaking, spirituality and nationalistic idealism. Troubled by the numbers of middle-class women who looked outside the
family sphere for their life's work, a tendency on which they blamed the
fall in the middle-class birth rate, they attempted to argue against female

education, including physical education, as leading to this reprehensible independence, while still insisting upon the glorification of healthy minds in healthy bodies.[6]

The writers of fiction for girls were thus presented with a very difficult task, if they were to transmit such a blend of aspirations and restraints to their readers. In practical terms, new narrative and character models, which would maintain the old values but offer a more modern standard of activity for girls, were not easy to set up. A century of writing for girls had established the norm of the domestic tale, in which the trials of the heroine were involved with the learning of discipline, the internalisation of the feminine values of self-abnegation, obedience and subordination. This pattern could easily accommodate the sacrificial and inspiring aspect of the imperial lady. But no model which could be utilised for the representation of the sterner face of pioneering and imperialist motherhood had yet been established. Since at least the 1860s the passive model of female perfection had been under criticism, and writers such as Charlotte Yonge, who resisted all modification of acceptable activities and attitudes for girls, rejecting schools, for example, and insisting upon home discipline, were very old-fashioned by the 1880s. But encouraging independence and self-reliance and the cultivation of physical and mental strength might easily prove subversive, fuelling rebelliousness against the other restrictions of the doctrine of separate spheres. It was difficult to find a balance in narrative romance between such opposite ideological constructs as spiritualised, disembodied femininity and vigorous pioneering motherhood. Complex ideological manoeuvres, visible in a series of convoluted narrative strategies, were required if the story-tellers were to capture the aspirations of girls for the furtherance of the "imperial race."

Periodicals for the young are often the site of the sharpest conflicts over socialisation, and the Edwardian magazines display this particular ideological battle very clearly. Mackay and Thorne have explored the clash between domestic ideology and the new aspirations of women in *The Girl's Own Paper,*[7] and shown there a persistent advocacy of the domestic ideal, "often explicitly associated with the imperial role of the Englishwoman." In less deliberately designed and skilfully managed periodicals than those of the Religious Tract Society, the gaps in the ideological pattern can show up sharply. *The Girls' Empire; An Annual for English Speaking Girls All Over the World,* published by Andrew Melrose in London, is a cheaply printed, short-lived periodical of which the British Library holds three years, 1902–1904. The non-fictional content appears to be quite close to the everyday concerns of a lower-middle-class girl readership, and combines domestic and "modern" girlish interests unselfconsciously. Volume I includes cookery, pigeon-keeping, literary notes, articles advocating fitness, and two describing jobs, typing and nursing. By contrast, the soft news content of the papers is determinedly connected with the Empire. The 1902 issue has a frontispiece of King Edward and Queen Alexandra, and a eulogistic article (pp. 89–90) on "A Maori Princess: Te Rangi Pai," which urges upon readers the duty of reading about the Empire, since "Thoughtful girls cannot fail to feel an interest in the possible development of those races which constitute Greater Britain." The princess is the daughter of Col. Porter, of Gisbourne, New Zealand, and his Maori wife Herewaka, and thus "a chieftainess of the first rank, who is also an English lady." "As the daughter of two empire-builders, we find in her one who forges a golden link of sympathy and interest between ourselves and a distant possession." More earnest and traditional in its cultural imperialism is the flat, pseudo-scientific description (p. 441) of the unconverted "Children of the Congo" by a missionary's wife. There are few other factual articles; the periodical is dominated by fiction or fictionalised history.

The space devoted to fiction is so extensive that most current kinds of tales are represented, but an effort has clearly been made to find or commission suitable fiction, and several stories either present the people and places of the (white) Colonies, or have a strong current of militarism. The Australian writer Louise Mack, who had recently left her native Sydney for Europe on the proceeds of her first two stories for girls,[8] provided two serials. The first, *Girls Together* (Vol. II, 1903) was previously published in Australia in 1898. It concerns the homecoming of Mabel James, with her "boyish curls and the frank, firm mouth that showed square white teeth" (p. 27) who returns from studying art in Paris, with refined manners and grown-up possessions. A ritual exchange of vigour from the Colonies with culture from Europe is embodied in a domestic tale.

Perhaps the publishers asked the prolific Evelyn Everett Green to add an imperial dimension to her second serial for them, or perhaps she was simply responding, like any popular writer, to the contemporary atmosphere of defensive militarism when she produced *The Three Graces* (Vol. II, 1903). It is set in England, but concerns the Anglo-Boer war. It is the story of Kitty, who "thought very little of the Boers—great ugly, frowsty men—dirty in their habits and tricky in their policy" (p. 225) and shared the expectation of her genteel friends that there would be "a speedy settlement" of the war by "a little wholesome bloodletting" (p. 225). The import of the tale is that these superior attitudes, though ultimately justifiable, have led to complacency, and the honour of England has to be retrieved by her less polished sons, like Jim. Jim is a rough diamond, of unspecified class status, who has not been to Sandhurst, and refuses to be seen dressed up in his khaki, but has remarkable foresight about the requirements of guerrilla warfare. He trains his horses to stand fire, and going out to Ladysmith, becomes a scout, fends for himself when his men are cut up, and is "received as a countryman, his accent and vocabulary passing muster with the Colonials" (p. 438). When he returns to Kitty, however, this same experience, far from confirming his rough impatience with gentility, has magically transformed him into a gentleman: "everything that was coarse or common seemed to have been carved away, and the square brow and the square jaw had a power which she had never fully realized before." Even his dress sense is improved: his "strong personality" remains, while his "impossible checks" have given way to "quiet tweed" (p. 437–438), since "the rough and tumble and hard discipline of campaigning had knocked him into shape" (p. 468). Her part in his military career has been to give him a bible, a talisman by which his life is literally preserved when it is recognised as he lies worn out and dying amongst the Colonials. On his return, transformed into a polite and considerate suitor, he gets Kitty's Cambridge sister to teach him maths, and in return teaches her about gunnery. This exchange of knowledge is presumably symbolic of the assimilation of his warlike capacities with a modern but still civilised world of ladies, though it seems to be stretching things a little for that to include an active interest in ballistics.

A story by Grace Toplis, *How Barbara Led a Forlorn Hope* (Vol. III, 1904, pp. 145–148), goes further by transferring the values of militarism to the female sphere, instead of merely endorsing their manifestation in men. Her heroine is a student teacher who, filling in a year between "a great school" and Girton, finds herself in a hopelessly run-down school where the head's husband has absconded with the fees, the servants are leaving, and the pupils are unsupervised. She summons up her English blood:

> It was not for nothing that she came of a good old stock: soldiers who had served their country for generations before the Indian Mutiny brought out their highest gifts; explorers and travellers who recognised no such thing as hardship for themselves if they could but do their duty and bring advantage or glory to old England; brave women who had trained heroes in happy homes. Barbara could fight too. (p. 145)

Her first, indeed her only move is to inspire with the same fighting spirit the only other mistress, who is apparently unpromising—a "frivolous faded 'made-up' old Frenchwoman"—but responds to her exhortation that surely "it is worth fighting for, to save honour and reputation." Madame rises with dignity to this bait: " 'Come with me to Miss Smith,' she said. 'Little one, you have touched the right chord. My grandfather was an officer in Napoleon's Old Guard' " (p. 147). The securing of this powerful ally wins Barbara the whole battle, saves the school, and brings her a chance to learn perfect French and secure a Girton scholarship: one must conclude that she has officer quality. It is rather difficult to imagine the response of the intended reader, for the story appears perfectly ludicrous in its implausibility to the modern eye; but as a fantasy of triumph for the young idealist, who conquers both hostile inferiors (the schoolgirls) and inadequate superiors (the two older mistresses) it may have touched powerful springs in the aspiring young woman. By its militaristic imagery, it might also have created or reinforced a particular cast in those aspirations.

Two stories in *The Girls' Empire* push beyond this point, and attempt to combine an endorsement of ladylike values with an appeal to the modern girl's aspirations to freedom of personal action, and they both set the fantasy fulfilment of these aims in the context of the Empire. They display very clearly the difficulties of making this combination work, and the writers' uneasy consciousness of the problem.

Interestingly, both seem to be written by men. "A Ride for Life: a Girl's Adventure During the Great Mutiny" by H. Hervey {Vol. III, Oct. 1903–Sept. 1904, pp. 231–234 and 275–276) concerns Fanny Barklay, aged eighteen, who keeps house for her brother Captain Ted and one other white man, in charge of two squadrons of Bengal Cavalry, thirty miles from Sanghur. She has all the accomplishments of a young lady, improbably inflected for Indian use—she sings and plays and dances, and speaks fluent Hindi. The story attempts to combine old and new femininity: Fanny plays Lady Bountiful to the (Muslim) soldiers by giving them laudanum and surreptitious glasses of old port for medicinal purposes. She provokes the special gratitude of one trooper, and when the outbreak occurs he warns her, and they both ride to safety, recapturing between them thirty horses with which to mount English troops to rescue her brother. She returns riding at the head of the rescuers herself, adored by them all. Any girl's fantasy of power over men and horses could hardly be better gratified—but Fanny's triumph depends, as we are supposed to remember, on her previous womanly instincts as a nurse, and her ministering services to her brother's men.

In *The Raid on Cedar Creek* by Ernest Richards (Vol. III, pp. 363–365 and 403–406), feminine feeling is invoked at the climax of the tale itself, in direct opposition to the action required, producing a clash in the narrative which is then resolved by an appeal to biological femaleness, the mothering instinct. Mary is left alone with her baby and a French servant, in a log cabin in Ontario, in "the fall of '61." She enlists a noble savage helper, by feeding a passing Iraquois chieftain; he returns to warn her that the servants and some half-breeds (as in boys' tales, the racial decadence is significant) are about to attack and rob her; barring her doors, he speeds away to fetch her husband. They attack and she fires back, wounding two of them with one shot.

> The excitement of the fray caused the perspiration to stand in beads on her forehead, and she might have fainted at the hateful thought of having shot, though under compulsion, a human being, but just then, in the midst of the tragedy, the plaintive noise of little Jackie's cry broke on her ear. That cry steadied her nerve and rallied her to action once more. (p. 404)

The working-out of the tale after this point is a precipitate retreat into conventional values—she is rescued by the Indians "under their white leader" her husband, the men she shot survive to be hung, so that she does not have "to blame herself for the death of a fellow-creature" (p. 406), and her husband eventually becomes pastor to a settlement where White Bear (humanised by the acquisition of a name) comes to worship in the congregation.

Allowing the heroine active participation in imperial adventures inevitably leads, at some point, to a clash of ideological designs, in which masculine behaviour will be demanded of her. Participation in violence is the most common flashpoint. In story after story there comes the moment where the girl pulls the trigger, or strikes the blow and instantly faints away, overcome by the conflicting imperatives of Englishness and femininity. Very few writers managed to find a narrative formula that could cope; the only outstanding example is Bessie Marchant.

Marchant's 150-plus adventure stories had a huge readership amongst young women in the first quarter of the twentieth century. It is not difficult to see why. In beautiful distant lands, wonderful girls undergo thrilling adventures and win health and happiness. They are gifted, and beautiful; they are also frequently in positions of autonomous power which is unruffled by their acquisition, on the last page, of husbands "to take care of them." The traditional pattern of the heroine's progress, from ignorance, self-importance and disobedience, via trials and punishment to a right self-estimate and a permanent place of subordination in marriage, is but faintly reflected in these novels. Three of them can illustrate Marchant's steady departure from the pattern.

In *A Heroine of the Sea*, 1904, we are introduced to Maudie, one of a parentless family of Canadian fishers and trappers, and immediately informed of the path marked out for her education. She spends her time trapping otters and fishing, and laughs at domesticity,

> declaring that any stupid person could run a house and cook food, but that it took a person with brains to . . . secure a good haul of halibut and herring. So the care of the domestic *ménage* was left to Hooee, . . . under . . . little Paul. There was no denying the fact that she worked as hard as either of her brothers, or that she was perfectly happy and contented in her toil, never even wishing for luxuries or prettiness, such as the hearts of most girls yearn after. One reason for this content most probably lay in the fact that she had never known any other kind of life . . . being a healthy girl, with a happy, good-natured temperament. (pp. 9–10)

The elements which are to be fostered—health, good nature, industry—and those which are to be corrected—a sense of her own cleverness, lack of domesticity (compounded by its transference to a boy, little Paul, who is consequently effeminate and sickly)—are very clear. More equivocal is the author's attitude to the appeal of "luxuries and prettinesses" to a girl, seen to some extent as a weakness from which Maude is laudably free, but also, and this is borne out by the role they play in her conversion to womanliness, seen as a "natural" part of girlhood, and an element in the woman's duty to brighten the home for men. A competent housekeeper and surrogate mother is introduced into the story, contriving miracles of comfort—she welcomes Maudie in from a day's fishing with a blazing fire, roast goose, and a ready-poured hot bath. Maudie goes away to the city to learn more of women's work. The resolution comes through a fantastic combination of domesticity and adventuring: brother Jim falls ill, and "the urgent need there was of the girl's immediate presence in the home" (p. 203) justifies her setting out, utilising her great strength and skill in the backwoods, to tow a doctor to his bedside, on a sledge. This feat partly affects Jim's cure, but it also requires her recognition of a more abstract transgression: he is dying because she has caused him anxiety. Brother Basil is in danger of arrest for murder, and Maudie has made an independent judgement that he is guilty, instead of taking the proper womanly course of believing in family, right or wrong. Jim has feared she might betray Basil's whereabouts to the police. Her "bitter self-reproach" (p. 206) for this threat to the patriarchal order of the household is necessary to his recovery.

The hold of convention over the heroine's progress in *No Ordinary Girl,* 1908, is considerably less. There are two girls. The first is Daisy, gold-medallist graduate of a Canadian teacher training college, whose quest for the story of her family constitutes the plot. Personally she has nothing left to learn, having suffered and worked to arrive at the state of independence in which she starts the book. The second, Juanita, seen normally through Daisy's eyes, is the equivalent of Maudie both in her need to learn and her remoteness from the readers' world; but in this case the exotic is also glamorous, and her need for socialisation is presented as an element of that glamour, rather than as a moral lack. She is the possessor of a remote South American feudal territory, and when first seen is "robed in white . . . a tall, slight figure, a diamond necklace gleaming on her white throat, whilst a tiara set with the same flashing gems glittered among the coils of her soft dark hair" (p. 81). She nevertheless proceeds to make a hearty meal of seven or eight courses, since she had been "shooting paro since dawn this morning, and yesterday . . . up in the mountains stalking wild sheep" (p. 84). She clings to Daisy for affection, and also receives formal education, since by a whim of her Spanish mother she has been brought up illiterate. She has numerous outdoor skills, more exotic than Maudie's—she goes prospecting for gold with a crew of female attendants at one point—but her agricultural and administrative genius does not impair her femininity. When Daisy remarks upon this,

> Juanita sprang to her feet, and swept Daisy a gay, graceful, little curtsy. "Thanks many, you could not have paid me a more delightful compliment than to call me essentially feminine. I have always maintained that no girl need drift into a mere imitation of a man unless she chooses, no matter how hard or masculine the nature of her daily work." (p. 141)

All she lacks is emotional fulfilment, which the plot brings to her, turning Daisy into a sister and supplying a young man for a husband in the last few pages.

In *The Gold-marked Charm* (1919) the ordinary and extraordinary heroines are combined in one: Audrey Felsham, who is also Lady of the Sun, ruler of a desert tribe, whom we meet on the first page giving imperious orders to her Baggara horsemen, as she hunts quails for her father's supper. She is mistress of an exotic world, like Juanita, but the reader is close to her consciousness as she makes her mistakes, and is placed in situations of danger, humiliation, and consequently learning. In *No Ordinary Girl,* Daisy's adventures and sufferings were the focus, but here we are brought closer to the exotic and powerful young woman. Her process of maturation is by no means the normal subordination and disciplining. Her errors are those of inexperience and bad advice, her judgements early in the tale are sometimes hasty, but always directed by right feeling, and as she learns from them she handles crisis situations with strength and diplomacy. These heroines are women of unlimited potential, and indeed of present power.

Most of that power is exercised in the domination of their environment. The settings are exotic in order to provide the ground for physical adventures, but they are more than that; they are one of the most important elements in the ideological pattern. In each of these three novels, a girl owns a sizeable chunk of the world—in two out of three she is sole possessor, in her own right and name. Juanita's stepfather, and Audrey's father, are both elderly and incapacitated, and possession of the estates, both legally and in terms of work done and management undertaken, is in the hands of the girls themselves. Maudie is an equal working partner in the family business, and does even more of the outdoor work, in person, than the later examples. The houses in which Juanita and Audrey live, furnished with fabulous wealth in minerals, ebony and ivory, are but the centres of a widespread domain of varied cultivation and pasture, hunting and prospecting grounds, mines and industries, peopled and worked by whole tribes of loyal retainers and servants. Both girls have devoted personal households, who provide constant physical back-up to their domination of the people, herds and lands. Their chosen activities consist in tending and overseeing the estates:

> As (Juanita) rode past banana patches and plantations of plantains and other fruits, her quick eyes took keen note of the quality and quantity of the crop. . . . There was little that escaped her eye, trained to the

minute observation necessary to good husbandry. (*No Ordinary Girl,* p.152)

Anything could be grown at El Draan if only water was given to it. There were acres of *dhurra,* great patches of maize, and yams . . . Avenues of date-palms led outward from the river. Under these . . . a small army of waterers toiled . . . So many industries, most of them carried on in very primitive fashion, demanded constant oversight. Audrey felt she ought to have been out-of-doors, directing things, from morning until night, and she sorely begrudged the time she spent in writing out her father's notes. (*The Gold -Marked Charm,* pp. 88–89)[9]

Their rule is feudal, and based on complex blood entitlements which exclude their guardians; by themselves they more than fulfil the lord's role in the romantic vision of that system, tending and standing for their people at home and abroad. The central importance of the domain, the girl's own kingdom, appears in many more of Marchant's books; it is embodied in titles like *Greta's Domain: a Tale of Chiloe.*

It seems possible to regard this as Marchant's solution of the narrative problem posed by the bringing-together of domestic and imperialistic values. The girl's proper sphere is the home; when she becomes the heroine of an adventure story, home duties become the paradigm of her conquest of the wider world. Thrift and forethought are scaled up from the kitchen to the gold-mine and the camel-farm; motherly rule through personal devotion is transferred from the brood of children to the tribe of retainers. The sacred ties of the hearth become, by an extension which had after all been made before, those of the feudal domain, but without the displacement which that had previously entailed on to a male head of the house. The old men are not the superiors; Juanita's father is very ill, and not in his right mind for much of the story, and Mr Felsham is an absent-minded scholar, in serious dereliction of his duty as an Englishman, in that he winks at the slave trade—with the result that he is himself enslaved, and Audrey eventually rescues him single-handed. So by a manoeuvre which removes the male head from power in these households, the girl's domain becomes unbounded: the nest becomes an empire.

Of course, it cannot be supposed that Marchant conceived of her manipulation of plot in these terms, and intended to enlist her readers' deeply-conditioned domestic aspirations, alongside their yearning for a wider sphere, in the service of an imperialist vision. The adventures are fantasies of power, no doubt very acceptable as such to consumers in a powerless position. But the configuration of that power in feudal-colonial images must be relevant to the aligning of the girl readers' view of the world with contemporary conceptions of British worldwide rule. The racial assumptions of the stories are an obvious sign of this. Juanita and Audrey both have immensely complicated ancestry, which is designed to bring them two benefits of blood: their inherited right to rule the primitive tribes under their domain, and their equally strongly stressed inheritance of Englishness, and consequent ability to go about that dominion humanely and effectively:

> the third Maestrante—Juanita's mother—seemed to have absorbed all the prejudices and ideas of her Spanish father, and to be utterly lacking in the fine qualities of her English mother. Under her rule the servants might speedily have become slaves again, but . . . happy fortune . . . gave her Captain Lander for a second husband. He spent much time and thought for the welfare of the little people who were so faithful . . . old feudal conditions . . . were swept away to be replaced by a sort of limited liability company, with Juanita for manager and director. (pp. 152–153)

These "little people" need to be ruled; they are upright and simple, and hard-working, but refuse to be educated. In *The Gold-marked Charm,* Audrey's dealings with the desert tribes are based on the knowledge that they will do no work if unsupervised, that they are boastful and vengeful, and that beyond her own estate, they are avaricious liars. There are faithful retainers in all three books, indispensable aides, but incorrigibly primitive, in some cases stupid, and in all given to emotional extravagance which is represented alternately as touching and comical. They all need their mistresses, and they need them to be English.

Marchant has been called "the girls' Henty," but while Henty was the best known of innumerable purveyors of historical and colonial adventure stories for boys, Marchant is unique among the major writers for girls. Her affiliations are with the writers of adult romances, Ouida, Ethel M. Dell, Elinor Glyn and the like, whose works belong to a division of popular literature which most writers for girls deliberate eschewed as idle, fantastical, and ultimately immoral. While Henty's work was regarded as educational, and his books became part of the avowed as well as the hidden curriculum of the British Empire, the respected girls' writers were those who deliberately set out to provide usefully instructive books which could be read instead of the "cheap romances" to which Marchant's books approached. They therefore forfeited the opportunity to use settings and plots which are directly imperialistic. This is not to say, however, that the powerful ideological influence of imperialism was excluded from respectable fiction for girls. The *Girls' Empire* stories demonstrate some of its clumsier manifestations; these did not on the whole outlive the charged atmosphere of the first years of the century. But it is also present in the making of a more extensive body of story-telling which sprang directly from the endeavours of didactic writers to influence the modern girl through their tales. This is the fiction associated with the Girl Guide Movement.

How imperialistic the early Guide Movement actually was has been discussed elsewhere. Several commentators have seen it as particularly reactionary in its inception, motivated by Tory imperialism and invented to impose the dominant ideology in its conservative and repressive forms.[10] Allen Warren[11] contests these absolute views, but shows that at the outset Guiding was certainly more deliberately oriented than Scouting towards a mystical ideal of empire. This was partly due to the influence of Agnes Baden-Powell, into whose hands her brother entrusted the girls who attempted to join the fledgling Scout Movement. Together they produced *The Handbook for Girl Guides, or How girls can help build the Empire,* in 1912. Like other theorists before them, they invoked the imperial ideal for the purposes of containing an unexpected and potentially threatening manifestation by girls of a desire to participate in the public display and physical freedoms offered to boys. As Warren remarks, "ideas of a healthy population with all their eugenic undertones inform much of Baden-Powell's writing for girls and their future responsibilities as wives and mothers."[12] He goes on to argue that Baden-Powell's own attitudes changed, and that Guiding was transformed by his deliberate decision to move Agnes aside and put the younger Olave, his wife, in charge; he contends that both Scout and Guide organisations became internationalist rather than imperialist after the First World War, and under Baden-Powell's deliberate guidance moved away from a militaristic ethos towards an emphasis on woodcraft and camping, consonant with the wider enthusiasm for the outdoor life in the 1920s and 1930s.

Baden-Powell re-wrote the Guide handbook in this light, offering girls more access to "masculine" activities involving physical fitness and the outdoor life. An imperialistic framework remains, however, to sanction these changes and to control them. The outdoor life of partnership with men is presented in terms of pioneering, the frontier life; and in this as in all aspects of the Guide's activities, the racial importance of motherhood is invoked as the highest claim, to which all else must be subordinated. Warren asserts that "In fact, the Scout and Guide movements were in many ways at their most 'imperial' between 1920 and 1955"[13] and suggests that their "ideological underpinnings" were complex. The function of imperialism in the cultural reproduction of femininity, reconciling greater freedom and fitness for girls with their continued subordination to the patriarchal order, is one of these underpinnings.

The manifestation of these protracted hegemonic negotiations in fiction, and the part played by that fiction in the negotiations is important in two ways. Firstly, stories about Guiding, like stories about boarding-schools, had at least two ideological functions in relation to what they were supposed to describe. They took over the real experience and imposed upon it, through a highly conventionalised narrative, an interpretation which, via the reading of the books, became part of the experience itself and conditioned its meaning for participants. They also extended the ideological construct to many readers who had no chance of direct participation in the experience. Secondly, in a voluntary and decentralised organisation likely to be resistant to central policy-making, the experience of those who staffed and joined the Movement may not be well represented by the pronouncements of Headquarters. The fiction, often produced by women actively working in the movement, and read by Guides and would-be Guides, is an image (not necessarily a realistic picture, often a highly formalised and idealised vision) of what the people at the grass roots thought Guiding was about.

The character of Guide literature under Agnes Baden-Powell's superintendance is very clear. The early issues of *The Girl Guides' Gazette* (started in January 1914) are as taken up with imperialism as *The Girls' Empire*. Britannia pictured on the cover dominates not only one Guide saluting and one who is knitting, but also a large globe, with India and Australia visible in outline, and the motto "For God our King and Empire." There is a letter from Agnes Baden-Powell in the first issue, urging Guides to be useful "by making others happy, and, secondly, by making ourselves into something better than we are" (p. 2), with a parable about worms digesting leaves they have pulled down into their holes—"busy little workers...doing good out of sight" (p. 3). This extreme vision of female self-effacement is not echoed in the first story, *Won by Deeds: How a Company of Guides Proved Their Worth* by Jesse Cameron (p. 10), where the girls, suitably employed upon the charitable cleaning-out of a poor woman's sixth-floor tenement flat, find themselves involved in dashing heroics, rescuing small children from a fire by a rope of sheets, before a cheering crowd. By this feat—not the scrubbing—they convince the doubting Sir Thomas of their right to exist. The suspicious patriarch is a significant figure in very many subsequent tales.

The representative of reactionary views on girls is sometimes female, as in *Miss Priscilla's Conversion*, by Alice and Claude Askew, which begins in Issue 4, April 1914. She thinks Girl Guides "rough tomboys—hoydens" (p. 2). She is opposed by Mrs Marchant, "wife of an officer serving his country on the Indian frontier" (p. 2) who wishes to start a company for local girls "to help them form their characters and learn to be useful members of society—good daughters, loyal friends, loving wives, splendid mothers" and "above all things, womanly." (p. 2) Her daughter enthuses about taking Miss Priscilla by storm, and Mrs Marchant recognises in her "the spirit that has set England in the fore ranks of the nations—the great invincible spirit of patriotism and high endeavour" (p. 4). In Part Three (June 1914), at the first Guide meeting, Mrs Marchant is brought the news that her husband is mortally wounded. She is convulsed, then

> raised the Union Jack again. "Girls—Girl Guides, this is the flag under which our soldiers fight, and die. I - I salute it." . . . She still held the flag up. "Preserving peace on our borders . . . that was his work, stamping out revolt, keeping India for England, doing his duty." The tears were lashing madly down her face. (p. 6)

The young Marchants give a practical demonstration of Guiding skills, rescuing Miss Priscilla's niece Lillian from gypsies by their tracking (carried out at quick marching pace) and ambulance drill; the rescue sequence, found in both these tales, becomes another almost obligatory trope in the Guiding story, and of course converts Miss Priscilla (in the final part, September 1914), in a climactic scene over which once again the Union flag is flying: "Our country's flag. The flag that women work under and men fight and die for . . . the old lady gazed at the flag [and] suddenly understood what patriotism really means . . ." she declares Lillian shall be a Guide, and ". . .'help to keep the British flag flying' " (p. 8). In excuse for such jingoistic excess one might point out that the war broke out during the run of this serial. It is not usual in Guiding stories, which tend more often to adopt Kipling's attitude in *Stalky and Co.*, where silent self-dedication and the stiff upper lip are truer expressions of patriotism than flag-wagging, and anything other than jokey reference to one's dearest beliefs is bad form. Some pre-war Guiding stories

clearly aim to admit girls to participation in masculine codes of public
school life which underpin the ethic of British imperialism as popularly
represented.[14]

The only story-book obtainable in 1914 direct from Guide HQ was
A.M. Irvine's *Nora the Girl Guide* (1913), which offers an illustration of
this. The story explores the concept of honour. The boarders at Ab-
botswell Hall School, led by Nora, have a code of mutual loyalty and
support, and resistance to outsiders; by holding together, they are subversive of the aims of the teachers, and oppressive of an inferior class, the
day girls. They are represented much as Hughes depicted Rugby before
Arnold, in *Tom Brown's Schooldays*. A Guide, Brenda, introduces a different code of honour: the first Guide Law is "A Guide's honour is to be
trusted." The staff seize upon this. They offer the girls the freedoms for
which they are fighting—freedom to learn about things outside the regular curriculum, to select their own leaders, to make their own decisions
and to take responsibility for themselves—if they will accept them
within the honour system, as applied in masculine organisations (such as
Arnoldian public schools) made over to girls via Guiding. The two kinds
of loyalty are made to clash dramatically in the conflict of Nora and
Brenda; Brenda triumphs and converts Nora, by adhering to both codes
in a situation which leads her to be suspected and punished by the au-
thorities. The testing of the Guide code is the climax of the book, in a
tracking expedition which leads to an accident. Obedience to orders,
cheerfulness under difficulties, elementary skills in first aid and observation, and finally officerly self-sacrifice, preserve the girls from death
and bring them Guiding honours—a Bronze Cross and even a Silver
Fish. (The ending of the book in a shower of "crosses and fishes" was
to become an ironic allusion in later stories.) The moral is finally pointed
by the headmistress, in a passage which is quoted in the *Girl Guide
Gazette:*

> instead of dishonesty and evasion, we have now unflinching honour
> and unswerving truth. In the place of the old slackness in our studies,
> we have a keen enthusiasm and desire to learn which makes teaching
> the most inspiring of all professions. . . . For secret disobedience we
> have open loyalty. . . . Where we mistresses distrusted and suspected,
> we now rely with confidence upon your honour. . . . If we issue an
> order, we know that it will be faithfully fulfilled. . . . The spirit of com-
> radeship and love has penetrated to the core of the school . . . and in
> conclusion I think I may say that if the day should ever dawn when all

English schoolgirls become Girl Guides—it will be a happy day for England! (pp. 323–324)

Well may she congratulate herself; containment within Guiding, perceived as a strongly internalised code of obedience and discipline, has turned the girls' urge to freedom and self-determination into subjection to a quasi-masculine reinforcement of their female conditioning.

Post-war Guiding fiction elaborates the narratives that carry out this three-sided negotiation between femininity, "masculine" outdoor/militaristic pursuits, and the girls' desire for freedom and self-determination. During the 1920s and 1930s there is a perceptible change from a defensive to a more self-assured presentation of the Movement, as the need to stave off the post-war suspicions about "preparing girls for the next war" faded away. There are also differences of emphasis between writers who picked up Guiding as an idea, to embellish or illustrate a larger didactic argument, and those who wrote from personal experience as Guiders, who were more often projecting an ideal vision of their own aims and satisfactions in the movement. E. M. Channon's *The Honour of a Guide*, 1926, offers an example of the outsider's use of the notion of Guiding. The title seems a mere catchpenny, since it has nothing to do with the story, which is a parable of enlightened imperialism told in terms of the training of girls. Innocent savagery, in the person of Ethne O'Hea, brought up in the depths of ignorance and Ireland by an artistic father, is subjugated by her English great aunt, who calls her Ethel, and sets out to force her into the outdated mould of the Victorian girl. She is rescued by the vicar, whose hard-working though blue-blooded wife and three schoolgirl Guide daughters provide models for modern femininity. The girls have measles for most of the book, and contribute little to the action; the contribution of Guiding itself is emblematic, an idea of freedom which Ethne gleans from seeing a company at their weekly drill. Along with the sensitive vicar, it represents the enlightened way of turning the Irish girl into an Englishwoman.

Equally concerned with ideological levels of the action, but more interested in their specific manifestation in the practice of Guiding, is Nancy M. Hayes's *The Plucky Patrol*, 1924. The author does not seem to have had any official involvement in Guiding,[15] but she produced five story-books on the subject between 1924 and 1926. She is certainly knowledgeable about its avowed aims, and begins and ends this story by invoking the call of the outdoor life, in line with Baden-Powell's new emphasis. There is much lovingly detailed description of the camp, of the comic experiences of unfit and inexperienced Guides, and of their swimming lessons and their Company log, which is a compendium of the Guiding virtues, being orderly and methodical as well as embellished with "small neat drawings" and with Georgian poetical effusions about the call of the river and the open road. The plot, and the ideological design, concern the challenging of their ethic by another "young savage," the daughter of the local suspicious patriarch Sir Howard. She puzzles the Patrol Leader sorely by being already more capable in outdoor pursuits than they, and yet not regenerated by her privileged contact with nature; she is scoffing and selfish. "The other girls had *wanted* to make the patrol a success, had *wanted* to hang together and to play the game . . . Of course, it was no use...to force a girl to obey as though this were a school or an army. Yet how on earth could she manage to make Phil *want* to play the game?" (pp. 48–49). Phil cuts their tent ropes and drops the log in the mud, and her father sets the village against them, so that they cannot get provisions. The climax of the story is the usual sequence in which Guiding pluck, discipline and skills—boating, life-saving, signalling, knots, first aid, cheerfulness and childcare—are brought into play, this time in rescuing not only Phil but the whole village (which has been left temporarily without its able-bodied men) from a flash flood. The exploit converts all disbelievers, including Philippa and Sir Howard; but instead of ending there, the story goes on, clearly to complete the ideological design. A misunderstanding over her conduct in the emergency causes Phil to run away, so that the patrol chase after her, and deluge her with their love and concern. It is this that conquers:

> "Oh, girls," she cried, "I *am* a beast! . . . You've come all this way to tell me—and I—oh, what a little pig I am." And to the Curlew's consternation, she threw herself down upon the grass in a passion of tears. "Oh, Phil, *dear!*" cried the Curlews, dropping beside her. And so Phil came home. (p. 211)

Hayes is obviously very concerned with the moral and psychological power of the Movement in the lives of the girls, their transformation into capable and responsible citizens through mutual self-help, and ultimately through love. This is in fact the direction in which most Guiders who tell tales move the ideological centre. They do not dispute the patriotic/imperialistic matrix, the paramount importance of service, and they continue to employ and refine its combination of ideas about femininity, national well-being and the incorporation of the girls' own

desires and interests; but they take its macrocosmic application as needing no comment. They develop a style and tone in which such things are
too large or too sacred to be mentioned, and the reader is engaged instead
upon a personal, often a comic level, where the obvious values at stake
are those of the microcosm, expressed as love, personal fulfilment, concern and mutuality.

Frances Nash, for example, became a Guider in 1920 and worked in
the Movement until 1936. Her Guiding stories begin in 1922 with *How
Audrey Became a Guide,*[16] and are very unusual in that they make Audrey the first-person narrator. The result is a very assured control of tone:
Nash has only to establish a distance between the point of view of the
narrator and that shared by author and reader to give herself a finely-
tuned tonal scale, from idealism to debunking, with which to handle each
eventuality. Thus Audrey's childish enthusiasm, the subtle bathos of her
style, is used to disarm scepticism when she states the analogy—one
often invoked more clumsily by other writers—between the Guide Law
and Arthurian chivalry:

> I shall never forget how romantic it made ordinary, everyday life seem
> when one suddenly looked at it from the Guide point of view! At first
> the Guide Laws seemed an awful lot to learn, but when I knew that
> they were taken from King Arthur's ten Laws of Chivalry, and imag-
> ined myself an honourable knight riding about and helping other peo-
> ple at all times; always courteous and loyal and a friend to animals, and
> everything weak and defenceless; it made it seem much easier. (p. 12)

The usual excitements of Guide stories are quietly mocked: Audrey casts
a well-disposed but shy Mr Griggs as suspicious patriarch, and they
spend a lot of time avoiding each other. Nothing is made, except by judi-
cious placing, of such bits of information as that Audrey failed her Domestic and Cook's badges disastrously, and that, while her stepmother is
a Commissioner, her patrol leader is a shop servant. The alert reader will
smile, all will get the messages.

Dorothy Osborn Hann shared Nash's desire to play down sensation-
alism, and attempted to use humour to do so, but she had not the same literary gifts. A vicar's wife who started as a Captain in his working-class
parishes in 1921, she became a District Commissioner in 1935, and remained active until 1944; she wrote a series of fictionalised accounts
of her own Guides, beginning with *Peg's Patrol* in 1924. Deliberately
eschewing rhetoric, avoiding opportunities to include speeches about

Guiding, she acknowledges her Christian allegiance within the stories, but makes it very clear that it was to be lived, not preached. Her real message is the worth of working-class girls, when they are given an opportunity to serve the greater good. She seems to feel obliged to include exciting elements of the Guiding plot, such as the rescuing of others by Guiding skills, but clearly does not believe in them, and huddles them into odd chapters unconnected with any larger design. Despite the photographs of real Guides on whom her characters are based, her characterisation is deeply conventional and one-dimensional: "Spud," whom Commissioner Roch rightly calls "the comic man" in the Preface to *Peg's Patrol*, is the most obvious example; her comic rhymes and quaint exploits are hopelessly stagey.

There are very many more Guide stories, and the conventional incidents and figures are used with more or less panache by writers of varying talent. It is by no means the moribund genre implied by Cadogan and Craig, whose misunderstanding, born of ideological prejudice, is clear in their condemnation of the fantasist Dorothea Moore and preference for Dorothy Hann's well-meant ineptitudes.[17] The vigour of the genre is evident in its manipulation of its own conventions, its taste for irony and parody. A good instance is the mixture of humour and excitement in Margaret Middleton's *The Guide Camp at Heron's Bay,* 1927. Middleton started as a Lieutenant to the 8th Ealing Company in 1921, and by 1935 was Division Commissioner for Twickenham. She wrote only three books, of which this was the first, dedicated to the 6th Ealing Guides as a "most untruthful story." It has a rattling good hidden treasure plot—as the Guides remark appreciatively on several occasions—and it employs the Guiding skills, just as the archetype requires. "Morse! Guides always did morse at an emergency in stories. She smiled to herself a trifle grimly" (p. 128) while tapping out the necessary dots and dashes. The narrative makes affectionate allusions to such things as the emotional satisfactions of adoring one's leaders, which loom very large in many stories: the Lieutenant has a picture of "one of the exalted personages of the Guide Movement" for whom she has "a weakness that still lingered from her school days"—"Leff's pash," about which the whole Company tease her (p. 91). The pleasures and discomforts of camping are celebrated, but with considerable *sprezzatura*. Discipline and routine are fervently cultivated, but steadily mocked. As the leaders dig rubbish pits they complain that "clay was the foundation of the British Empire" (p.155); patrols race to erect tents, "triumphantly taut and trim . . . with . . . walls rolled up and complete to the last brailing peg" in four-and-a-half minutes; but after this feat, as the winning Patrol Leader salutes smartly, Captain says, " 'Very nicely done, my child,' . . . patting her on the head as if she were six. 'Carry on, luv' " (p.37). She dissolves in giggles, and militarism is put in its place. The Company gives a display, to convert the village—a realistic variant upon the heroic rescue sequence—at which they do the "well-worn ambulance stunt, improvised stretcher and all. It always impresses grown-ups immensely" because they do not know "how jolly easy it is" (p. 76).

The main flavour of the book comes from its four chief characters, Pamela the Captain, her lieutenant, Leff, and two senior patrol leaders, all within a few years of each other in age, and given to expressing their enjoyment of each other's company in a stream of wisecracks. The leaders, especially, have a cross-talk act that tempers all their most serious moments. The service ethic is made explicit, in personal terms, through their jokes: they act for the sake of the younger Guides, even, one might say, for the love of them. The moments they find worthwhile are when they discover two girls have beaten them to the washing-up after the display, or when, worried about the threats that hang over the camp, they overhear another pair admiring the canvas roof that Leff has sewn with much grumbling and erected over the washing tent. " 'When you were very young . . . [says Leff] . . . did you ever give rapturous thanks for the bathroom ceiling?' " and Pamela replies " 'I shalln't and won't strike this camp' " (p. 104–105).

But the macrocosmic dimension of service also remains. Amidst the jokes and sending-up of all the pieties of the Movement and the conventions of the stories, the central ideal is glimpsed: at the end of the display, Pam is cooking sausages with smoke in her eyes while all the villagers play "Donkey's Tail":

> "Oh, this fire! The sboke chases you rowd ad rowd—look out—take theb off—" "Colours, Madam," said a quiet voice from behind. The five pans were snatched away and dumped on the grass, and the flames of the fire burned unchecked. Perhaps in all Pamela's carefully planned afternoon nothing left such a deep impression on the parents as that sudden glimpse of what, to the camp, was everyday routine. They saw the most wildly hilarious Guides, who had been racing about the field a moment before, spin suddenly round to face the flagstaff, spring to attention, and stand silent and rigid as statues. The flag was struck and sank down the mast on to the shoulder of the colour-bearer, where it rested, draping her from head to foot while she unknotted the halliards.

The little ceremony was over in two or three minutes, and work and play went on as before, but the knowledge of it remained in the hearts of the older onlookers. (pp. 115–116)

The Empire's flag still flies at the heart of the book's ideology. As the final justification for the concept of service, of devotion to the cause and obedience to the code, it remains the over-arching framework which sanctions girls' admittance to the freedoms of camp, to adventures, to the mysteries of "masculine" codes of honour and physical skills. Incorporating the modern girl's demand for self-determination, for a wider field in which to develop and to excel, it maintains the essential feminine value of instrumentality and subordination.

NOTES

1. John M MacKenzie. (ed.). *Imperialism and Popular Culture.* Manchester, 1986, pp. 116.

2. Ibid., p. 6.

3. Jane Mackay and Pat Thorne, "The Englishwoman," in Robert Colls and Philip Dodd (eds.) *Englishness, Politics and Culture 1880–1920,* London, 1986, pp. 191–229.

4. Ibid., pp. 192, 193.

5. See the various pamphlets published by W. H. G. Kingston, as secretary for the Colonization Society and through the SPCK series of Emigrant Tracts; and for the lady colonists' view, C. P. Strickland (Mrs Traill), *The Backwoods of Canada, being letters from the wife of an emigrant officer illustrative of the domestic economy of British America,* London, 1836.

6. See Anna Davin, "Imperialism and motherhood" *History Workshop Journal,* 5, 1978, pp. 9–65, esp. pp. 9–12, 20–21.

7. Mackay and Thorne, "The Englishwoman," pp. 193–197.

8. For a discussion of Mack in her Australian context, see Brenda Niall, *Australia Through the Looking Glass,* Melbourne, 1984, pp. 170–76.

9. Quoted from The Bessie Marchant Omnibus Book, London, n.d.

10. See John Springhall, *Youth, Empire and Society: British Youth Movements 1883–1940,* London, 1977; Samuel Hynes, *The Edwardian Turn of Mind,* London, 1968; and Carol Dyhouse, *Girls Growing up in Late Victorian and Edwardian England,* London, 1981.

11. Allen Warren, "Citizens of the Empire: Baden-Powell, scouts and guides and an imperial ideal, 1900–1940," in John MacKenzie (ed.), *Imperialism and Popular Culture,* Manchester, 1986, pp. 232–256.

12. Warren, "Citizens of the Empire," p. 238.

13. Ibid., p. 236.

14. For a demonstration of this connection, see Jeffrey Richards, *Visions of Yesterday,* London, 1973, pp. 44–63.

15. Information about membership of the Guide Movement is all taken from the archives at GGA headquarters; my thanks are due to Sue Stott for her help in making these available to me.

16. Quoted from an omnibus edition, *The Audrey Books,* London, n.d. (1933).

17. See *You're a Brick, Angela!* London, 1976, pp. 140–158.

"Get Ready for Action!"
Reading Action Man Toys

JONATHAN BIGNELL

Action Man is the name of a large range of interrelated children's products predominantly used by boys between the ages of five and eleven. Action Man denotes a series of twelve-inch tall toy figures, all dressed in different costumes and equipped with accessories. Accompanying Action Man figures, and conforming to the same scale, are several vehicles and accessory packs. There are also toys sold under the Action Man brand, such as toy guns, which are of an appropriate size to be used in play independently of the miniature Action Man world. In addition to the toys, there is an *Action Man* comic, a comic-book annual, and in 1995 a new animated television series. So Action Man is not just the name of an imaginary heroic individual embodied in a toy figure. He is also a commercial brand name, a range of interrelated children's products and texts, and the title of a coherent mythical world. This article discusses Action Man as a heroic figure by analysing a few key components of the Action Man myth. Because Action Man is a brand, the first section considers his commercial context and history; the second section deals with the versions of masculine heroism which the various incarnations of Action Man might construct; and the third section shows how Action Man's heroic meanings depend on the narratives, produced by the manufacturer and by children themselves, into which the toys and the mythic figure are inserted. The final section contrasts Action Man's meanings for adults with his meanings for children.

THE ACTION MAN BRAND

The Action Man toy figure was introduced into the British toy market at London's Earls Court Toy Fair in January 1966.[1] Initially there were only three costumed figures in the range: soldier, sailor and pilot. Since then the number of different incarnations of Action Man has exceeded 350. The majority of these have been military figures, and all of them have represented heroic masculine identities, like polar explorer, footballer, space ranger, or lifeguard. Action Man's body shape has remained basically the same during the thirty-year life of the toy, though refinements in construction have occurred. In 1973 gripping hands were introduced, directable Eagle Eyes in 1979, and other physical functions have periodically been incorporated into the figure including kicking legs and a cord-operated voicebox producing several phrases. The period of highest sales of Action Man toys was the late 1960s and early 1970s, when costume designs were changed in a regular three-year cycle, and between three and four million Action Man figures were sold per year. It was estimated that, on average, each male child in Britain had 1.3 Action Man figures. To satisfy this level of demand, GI Joe figures (the American equivalent of Action Man) were shipped to Britain for repackaging to be sold as Action Man.

A more recent peak in sales occured in 1982, when Action Man in Special Air Service (SAS) uniform again became one of Britain's ten best-selling toys. It was in 1982 that the film *Who Dares Wins,* an action-adventure depicting SAS troops, was released, and in 1982 that Britain went to war with Argentina over the Falklands/Malvinas islands. Previously, in 1980, SAS troops had been shown live on television bursting into the Iranian Embassy in London to shoot terrorists who were holding hostages there. Conflicts involving the British military appear to have stimulated sales of Action Man in British uniforms, and this is a feature of soldier toy consumption. The first mass-marketed soldier figures were made by the aptly-named Britains Ltd, whose three-inch tall painted lead figures representing British imperial troops were launched in 1893 and remained successful for decades. While Action Man is an individual heroic soldier-adventurer, the way he and other soldier toys are represented depends on the wider social and historical circumstances in which he exists.[2]

After 1945, plastic Second World War and Wild West figures rose to market domination in Britain. The cheaper injection moulding techniques for plastic soldiers, the production of war films, representations of the wild west in film and television, export of toy production to the Far East, and multinational toy marketing under the control of American corporations, were some of the determining factors in this process. Action Man's appearance in 1966 occurred in a specific historical and commercial context, in which representations of soldiers in toys were becoming less specifically British and more generally Western, just as the toy industry (like other industries) became less national and more global. The heroic figure of the soldier retains some links with national representations, as the sales peak in Britain in 1982 shows. But the New World Order of NATO and the UN, with its American hegemony, is represented in the forms of toy figure which are now produced by the international toy industry.[3] Today's Action Man figures are almost all either American in costume, or international by virtue of representing UN troops or non-nationally-specific explorer-adventurers, for instance.

The Action Man toy range was relaunched by its manufacturer Hasbro-Bradley in 1994, with additional figures and accessories and new-look packaging. The toys are divided mainly into four product groupings: Military (including Special Forces and Rapid Fire figures); Urban (including the Street Combat figure and Missile Bike); Adventure (including the Mission Extreme figure and Survival Base Camp playset); and Aviation (including the Operation P.I.L.O.T. figure and Stealth Surveillance equipment pack). Each grouping includes figures, packs of equipment sold separately from the figures, and vehicles or other large accessories. In addition, Action Man has an opponent, a supervillain called Dr X, who is also sold as a costumed figure. The various equipment packs, figures, vehicles and accessories currently range in price from about £5 to about £40.

The presence of relatively cheap and relatively expensive products in the toy range allows for different patterns of ownership and toy-buying. Cheaper equipment packs might be purchased by children themselves several times in a year, while expensive vehicles could be reserved for Christmas or birthday presents bought by adults. More fortunate or affluent children may be able to possess most or all of the range of toys, but even economically disadvantaged children or families can buy into the Action Man brand for a few pounds. The availability of a large number of Action Man products, and the introduction of new products at regular intervals, allows for collectability and the reinforcement of brand loyalty to Action Man rather than his numerous competitor soldier figures. As a long-lived and widely-recognised brand, Action Man can also be attached to other children's consumer products by other manufacturers using the

Action Man logo or image under licence, thus stimulating sales of Action Man products as well as those featuring his likeness or logo.

Hasbro-Bradley is one of the largest of the world's toy manufacturers, and is linked into a network of subsidiary companies, affiliated producers of children's consumer products, and licencees with rights to use Hasbro brands to market further products. In the field of action figures marketed to boys, for instance, the Action Man figure is made by Hasbro-Bradley but was originally designed by the Research and Development staff of Palitoy, while Hasbro-Bradley not only produces GI Joe as well as Action Man but also distributes VR Troopers and Mighty Morphin' Power Rangers, which are owned by Saban Entertainment. Hasbro-Bradley toy packages sometimes include the names of affiliates or subsidiaries like Milton-Bradley or Sunbow, for instance, while Hasbro-Bradley toy figures like Transformers are represented in videos made by DIC in association with Tempo. Action Man has also appeared in a new television series made by DIC, which is affiliated with Turner Broadcasting, which controls First Independent Films. The *Action Man* comic is published by Tower Magazines, while, for example, the *Action Man Bumper 1996 Annual* was published by Pedigree books, part of Pedigree Toys.

This discussion of Action Man as a representation of heroism goes on to focus on Action Man toys, and on the weave of texts which set the terms for children's and parents' understanding of Action Man's cultural meanings. But it is crucial to point out that Action Man is not simply a material object, or a series of texts, or a set of uses of these objects and texts by actual individual children. Action Man is an ensemble of commodities produced by a multinational conglomerate, and one of the nodes around which a web of commercial relationships and transactions is cemented.[4] It could be claimed that this structure of economic relationships is irrelevant to the specific form of Action Man as a heroic figure. From this point of view, the corporate structure of the toy industry is simply a kind of neutral medium through which Action Man passes. The problem with this approach (still common in studies of written texts, unfortunately) is that it neglects the power-relationships encoded in children's culture by the economic and political structure of production. Part of the cultural significance of Action Man as a heroic figure is his availability and comprehensibility to very large and very diverse groups of people around the world. Action Man is a heroic figure for children on a global scale. We can therefore argue that Action Man is himself a medium through which economic and ideological relationships are established. Through the medium of toys, individual human subjects are constituted as consumers of products and as consumers of ideas. This essay argues that Action Man is simultaneously a product and a communication, and that both these aspects of Action Man are significant in children's culture and in adult culture.

Children's knowledge of, and desire for, branded commodities like Action Man is part of their socialisation into consumer culture, a mark of "grown-up-ness" which Ellen Seiter has argued "signals a mastery of the principles of consumer culture, that is, the accurate perception by the child of a system of meaningful social categories embedded in commodities and sets of commodities." (Seiter 1993, p. 205) Two obvious examples of social categories which are embedded in toys are those of gender and age-group. Boys' toys are different from girls' toys, and toys themselves are differentiated as products for children and not adults, while also being differentiated into toys for older or younger children. Adults may tend to think of toys as a huge and relatively formless group of products, but for children toys belong to very specific categories with finely-distinguished social meanings, as any adult who has unknowingly given a 'wrong' toy as a present will be painfully aware. Children's consumer culture is closely parallel in form to adult consumer culture, for the same highly-structured commodity economy of products and their social meanings can be found in each.

Toys are as stratified and codified as adult products, but one reason that adults may not perceive the systems of meaning in toys at all is that toys constitute a children's world, some of whose value is that it is different and even inimical to the values of the adult world. Thus, for instance, trashyness, tastelessness, or violence can become valued qualities in children's toys and uses of toys, since these characteristics are what adults disapprove of. Inasmuch as they solidify and express social meanings for children, toys are therefore available as totemic objects around which children's difference from adults can be organised. Having and playing with toys partly constitutes childhood. Furthermore, the possession of particular toys differentiates children into peer groups, providing a common language and topic of interaction from which adults are usually excluded. Children themselves use exclusion as a mechanism to create peer groups focused around toys or types of toy. Boys are differentiated from girls in part by their toys, and Action Man toy collectors are differentiated from Batman toy collectors or Ghostbusters toy collectors. As consumers, children are both fickle and discriminating, which makes them a difficult market to sell to but also potentially loyal devotees of brands with a strong identity and peer desirability, like Action Man. Not to have the toys valued by their peers is a potential cause of exclusion from children's social networks, so there are good reasons for children's apparently insatiable and irrational desire for particular products.

ACTION MAN AND THE STRUGGLE FOR MASCULINITY

The targeting of male children as a specific market got under way in the 1850s with the publication of adventure books, and the segmentation of the toy market along gender lines is still very obvious. Ellen Seiter notes that

> children's toys and television characters copy themes of the adult culture but present them in exaggerated versions unacceptable to adults. Gender roles are a notorious example of this. Female characters are marked by exaggerated aesthetic codes: high-pitched voices, pastel colors, frills, endless quantities of hair, and an innate capacity for sympathy. Male characters appear as superheroes with enormous muscles, deep voices, and an earnest and unrelenting capacity for action and bravery. (Seiter 1993, pp. 10–11)

Action Man figures are muscular and equipped with a profusion of warlike accessories. Even details like Action Man's square jawline, stern facial expression, and short-cropped military haircut add to the multitude of signifiers of a particular version of masculinity. His very name signals that this archetypal man is defined by physical attributes and physical activities, with the military connotations of "Action" supporting the linkage of physical activity to aggression.

The repertoire of signifiers in the Action Man ensemble of products enables particular forms of play, which can serve a number of different functions for boys. One of these functions is to associate masculinity with action outside the familial and domestic sphere. In common with other heroic figures in boys' culture like spacemen, pirates, or explorers, Action Man characters' sphere of operation is exclusively outside the home. While Action Man can easily be played with indoors, the imaginary world in which play is set is an exterior and unfamilial world. Furthermore, this elides into a repudiation of the feminine since Action Man toys are explicitly differentiated from the doll figures, with their own accessories, vehicles, and playsets representing domestic spaces, which are marketed to girls. Despite the fact that Action Man is primarily a doll, this word never appears in toy packaging or promotional material. Action Man's role as a hero for boys depends on the characteristics which the toys possess, but equally on the characteristics which they do not possess or which are rendered invisible. The association of Action Man with heroic masculinity depends on his structural relationship to other toys and elements of the childhood world, as much as on the forms of Action Man toys in themselves.

As part of the staging of a version of the gender differences which structure the adult and childhood worlds, playing with Action Man is part of an internal psychic drama for children.[5] From a psychoanalytic perspective, children's play is a form of work. It is a set of activities which enables the child to explore, understand and master the external world, while simultaneously developing a sense of the self as a separate entity from what is external and other. One of the key features of play with toys is that toys can be used as symbols representing aspects of the child's mental life. In effect, toy play is like staging a drama in which the playing child is at once the director, all of the actors, and the audience. An Action Man toy figure can be used as a representative of what the child wishes to become, described as an "ego ideal." And since the child identifies with Action Man as this heroic ideal, the image of Action Man gives shape to the better self held internally. This internalised and wished-for self is the "ideal ego." But contrary to some adults' use of this theoretical model to condemn Action Man as a "bad" ego ideal, the process of identity formation described by psychoanalytic theorists stresses the ambiguity and internal contradictions thrown up by toys and play. It is not simply the case that Action Man persuades boys to want to be macho soldiers.

There are some features of Action Man which endow him with the capacity to signify male powerfulness, like his body-shape and his association with combat and masculine physical proficiency. Some of Action Man's equipment and accessories do things, so that the toy figure can become really active (causing guns to fire actual projectiles, for instance) as well as imaginarily active. For example, the very successful Action Man Rapid Fire figure is equipped with a missile-firing rifle which shoots small plastic bullets, and weapons like this enable combat to be staged with the figures. Thus masculinity can be associated in play with physical activity, with conflict, and with aggressiveness and violence. The rifle has to be operated by the child of course, requires him to stand in for Action Man to make the weapon work, and helps to secure an imaginary identification of the child with the Action Man character. At another level of this exchange of identities between child and toy, some Action Man equipment is scaled for the miniature toy world, but also works in the child's scale. For instance the Street Combat Action Man figure has a twin missile launcher mounted on his belt, but this belt is designed to fit around a child's wrist so that it becomes a kind of toy gun. Clearly the child "becomes" Action Man in a more direct exchange with the toy figure. Further, there are some Action Man branded toys made exclusively for the child's use (and not the figure's), like a dart gun or plastic hunting knife. Here, there is a leap from child to Action Man without the intervention of a physical surrogate in the form of the toy figure. These examples show that the range of Action Man toys, in their material form, allow for and supply tools for a variety of identificatory relationships with Action Man as an emblem of masculine activity and proficiency.

However, there are also features of Action Man which detract from or contradict this simple equation of the masculine powerfulness, signified in the toy's characteristics, with an imaginary masculine powerfulness for the child. For one thing, Action Man does not have genital organs. He cannot concretely represent a perfected adult male body for the child because he is castrated, or at least lacking a key signifier of sex. Because he is a toy, he is small, inanimate, breakable, and dumb. He can only be made to take part in fantasies of powerfulness with the help of the child, and although the toys enable aggressive play, they are only active when their potential is realised by the child. There are ways of playing with the figures which are not determined by, or consonant with, the heroic masculinity outlined here. For instance a boy could ask a parent to knit Action Man a jumper to keep him warm, or a child could make a bed for him out of a shoebox in the context of "feminine" caring play. By virtue of being a toy, Action Man is in the power of the child who plays with him, whether as the hero of fantasy play or as an object of the child's sadistic impulses, nurturing impulses, or whatever. It cannot be argued that Action Man himself creates masculine behaviours or models of masculinity for children. Instead Action Man borrows from, and attains meaning through, the masculinities existing in adult culture, together with the contradictions, resistances, and alternatives inherent in these adult forms of gender identity.

Action Man is a doll, but his desirability as a totem of masculinity depends on a rigid separation from the characteristics of femininity represented in dolls for girls. As a masculine hero he must be protected from the feminine and from effeminacy. Action Man, as an adventure hero, is always represented either alone or in the company of other adventuring heroes. The *Action Man Bumper 1996 Annual* ("Action Man Profile," p. 4) reports that one of his friends is "Natalie—also known as Action Woman—they work together, but she is not his girlfriend." Action Man may not want a girlfriend, but that must not mean he is like a girl himself, or that he wants a boyfriend. The dangerous slippage from excessive manliness to effeminacy to homosexuality is displaced onto Action Man's opponent, the evil Dr X, who functions as his negative mirror-image. Thanking Paul Strain (aged eight) for his letter to the "Ask Dr X" page of *Action Man* comic (no. 5, November 1995, p. 25) complimenting the Doctor on his hair, Dr X adds "As for my hair, it's done by a lovely minion called Clive, and he'll be thrilled to know you like it." The supposed narcissism of Dr X's attention to his hair, his use of the adjective "lovely" and even the rather un-macho name "Clive" all point to the use of Dr X as a repository of the dangerous effeminacy of an Action Man world without women, and with a highly defensive and unstable notion of masculine sexuality.

Action Man can represent an ideal of masculinity, but the feminine against which the masculine is defined must be located somewhere. Femininity does not disappear, but instead becomes part of the stigmatised otherness represented by Dr X. When Daniel Gifford (aged ten) asks Dr X in the same issue of *Action Man* comic, "Do you like girls, yes or no?" Dr X replies, "Some of my best friends are girls. We like to swop clothes and help each other with our hair." It is surely no accident that play involving haircare is one of the key features of the exaggeratedly feminine world of dolls like Sindy and Barbie. Just as Action Man is a hero and Dr X a villain, Action Man is manly while Dr X is girlish. But bodily adornment and fetishism of the body are not absent from Action Man figures. The Action Man Operation T.I.G.E.R. figure is supplied with decals which can be used as temporary tatoos on the toy's body or on the child's body. Indeed issue five of *Action Man* comic in which the homophobic and sexist remarks quoted above appear, comes with three child-sized stick-on tattoos as a free gift. There is a code of bodily adornment and narcissistic behaviour in the Action Man world, and this code stigmatises some activities as feminine while other quite similar activities are positively valued as masculine.

There is also a potential ambiguity about the desirability of Action Man's moral position. As described above, Action Man figures represent heroic identities like soldier, explorer, space warrior, and supporting texts make it clear that Action Man is a force for good. Beneath the title of *Action Man* comic the strapline "The Greatest Hero Of Them All" appears. The *Action Man Bumper 1996 Annual* ("Action Man Profile," p. 4) describes him as "a human superhero, fighting for the good of mankind," and narratives accompanying the toys support these messages. But as the letter about Dr X's hair showed, children are interested in Dr X as well as Action Man. Their identifications are not only with the good Action Man but also with the evil Dr X. The letters to Dr X in *Action Man* comic have already been mentioned, and apparently there are as many written to Dr X as to Action Man. Issue six of *Action Man* comic included a new page of artwork by readers ("Minions' Masterpieces," pp. 28–29), and of the nine pictures reproduced, two were of Dr X and one of a reader adopting the identity "X-Kick" as one of Dr X's minions (i.e., henchmen). Like identifying with Action Man, identifying with Dr X must also serve a number of functions for children.

As David Buckingham has pointed out, referring to the work of Lyn Segal (1990): "Learning masculinity is about learning a code—or at least learning to appear to others as though one conforms to a code—rather than simply being slotted into a pre-determined role."[6] The elaborate but relatively binary code of good and evil in the Action Man world, allows children to position themselves in relation to the code, but without having to remain in only one of its constituent identities. Fantasy play with Action Man toys, or using the identities of Action Man or Dr X in play, allows the child to belong in an environment of meanings in which it is possible to be either good or evil, and to move between the two without quitting the game. Even in its crudest form, Action Man play enables children to be either or both Action Man and Dr X, and to enjoy the possibilities of each within a structure provided by the toys and their accompanying texts. In other words, Action Man play enables children to learn and perfect coded identities and moral positionings in the social world, through a process of taking up and exchanging different identities which are given form by Action Man products.

This process is necessarily social, and as the reference to Lyn Segal above points out, it is crucially bound up with how the individual child relates to real others by using the coded representations of the play world. Action Man toys facilitate social interaction, particularly between boys. As Graham Dawson has argued, children project onto toys like Action Man, which become symbolic representatives of themselves. But when the child becomes Action Man, he can subsist in this identity only if other children (or adults) will accept him in this role:

> identities are imagined through projection directed at omnipotently controlled, purely symbolic objects, these social imaginings position real others, inviting approval and affirmation and running the risk of refusal and negation. At stake here is the winning and witholding of social recognition: "who I can imagine myself to be" becomes inseparable from "who they will recognise me as." (Dawson 1994, p. 261)

It is not open to a child playing with Action Man to maintain any desired imaginary identity whatsoever. Instead, identities are negotiated by the child's relationships with others, who can either recognise him in an imagined heroic role as Action Man, for instance, or refuse to do so.

In this kind of context, identifying with Dr X as the powerful alien outsider may be an identity which enables individual children to at least temporarily negotiate an effective position for themselves in relation to a social or family group. It may be a more powerful masculine role to be the evil outsider than the too-good-to-be-true Action Man in some play situations, which thus complicates the role of the hero in play. The role of the hero may not be the most desirable role for some children in some situations. It is difficult to pursue this issue without ethnographic research on children's play with Action Man toys, and this research does not at present exist. Instead, the following section returns to the toys and their accompanying textual materials, in order to demonstrate how the meanings of Action Man's heroism are related to the narrative scenarios in which the toys and other products are placed.

ACTION MAN IN NARRATIVES

Heroes cannot be heroes outside of a narrative context which positions them as heroes. Action Man is embedded in narrative scenarios in the packaging of the toys, in the comic based around the toy, and in a new television series. These texts, all more or less under the control of Hasbro-Bradley, owner of the Action Man brand, are intended to set limits to the meanings of Action Man in childrens' (and adults') culture. While this enterprise has an inevitable leakiness and uncertainty, the construction of narratives featuring Action Man as a heroic figure produces a cultural currency for his heroic significance, a normalisation of his meaning.

The central node of Action Man's heroism is conflict in which Action Man is good and Dr X is evil. Action Man's physical appearance and costumes draw on a history of real wars, military uniforms, masculine professions and the dress codes associated with these. His heroism comes partly from these references to heroic figures of British and Western propaganda, adventure narrative, and news reporting. His opponent Dr X derives his negative meanings from a quite different set of registers. His outlandish purple clothing alludes to the supervillains of American comics, and to the evil aliens of comics, cartoons, fantasy literature, television and cinema. His Mohican haircut combines resonances of barbarian-ness with rebelliousness and criminality by virtue of the style's association with youth gang subcultures. He has a mechanical hand, a laser eye, and a partly-exposed electronic brain, so that where Action Man looks human and familiar, Dr X is inhuman and other. The appearance and attributes of Action Man versus Dr X signal a very clearly coded opposition between a heroic figure and a demonised one.

Further ingredients which identify Action Man as a hero can also be outlined as the valued terms in a system of binary oppositions: Action Man is an adult, not a child. He represents a better self, not an equal. He works as a professional, and is never seen at leisure. He likes excitement, and does not play safe. He uses violence as a means, and does not negotiate. He uses technology effectively, rather than ineptly. He is a loner, not a member of a team, although both Action Man and Dr X belong to organisations. Usually Action Man works for the World Amalgamated Military Strike Squad, or for the police force, while Dr X leads a gang bent on world domination. This scenario of a continual battle between the forces of good and evil is very common in toy-based narratives, since it provides a structure for play with the toys, offers the possibility of introducing new toy figures, accessories, vehicles and playsets onto the market, and can be used as the repeated premise for episodes of toy-based television series.

Action Man toys are made to facilitate active play by offering ready-made narrative scenarios for the toys, and by demanding activity from the playing child in these fantasy and dramatic settings. The Action Man 4 × 4 Jeep, for instance, has big tyres and a swivelling gun, and its box has an illustration showing the jeep in action, jumping over rough jungle terrain with Action Man driving. Of course the Jeep requires a child to push it, to operate the gun, and to compose a narrative scenario for the Jeep's journey. The Action Man brand's colour signature of orange and green are used on the package illustration, and the illustration's dramatic comic-book action reinforces the coding of the Action Man world as parallel to action-adventure cinema, in effect showing the child the genre of narrative in which the toy should be placed. To take another example, the Action Man Ultimate Assault Gear accessory pack has the words: "For the hero who wants to hit the bad guys and hit them hard. . . . The Ultimate Assault Gear is just what today's Action Man combat soldier needs!" The pack includes various weapons and military equipment: machine-guns, pistols, knives, ninja sword, helmet, etc. The accessories are for use with Action Man figures in fantasy combat narratives where to "hit the bad guys" requires the child to animate Action Man in a play scenario, and thus to turn the "Action Man combat soldier" into a hero. The toy only has meaning in relation to the playing child who animates him in a narrative, and who merges his own identity with that of the toy's fantasised role.

All Action Man figure sets and large accessories are supplied with a Mission Profile containing small illustrations and text. These Mission Profiles set the toys and Action Man figures (sold separately) in an action-adventure narrative. The Action Man Dinghy for instance, a motorized navy-blue and yellow boat, is established in this setting:

> Message: Disabled oil tanker adrift in North Sea . . . Dangerously close to an oil rig in that area . . . all crew except for the captain have abandoned ship . . . Cause: Engine failure . . . collision would result in huge oil spillage . . . potential ecological disaster . . . Solution: Action Man must transfer to ship by dinghy . . . helicopter grounded due to poor visibility. Help captain to regain control. [ellipses in original]

As in many television programmes based on boys' toys (like *Teenage Mutant Ninja Turtles* or *Ghostbusters*), good technology must overcome bad polluting technology. The action is goal-directed, but the goal itself does not seem very exciting. Helping the Captain seems much less interesting than the suspense, danger and infinitely-extendable narrative process of getting Action Man from his ship to the stricken oil tanker.

Hasbro-Bradley announced their Christmas 1995 Action Man promotion by issuing press releases in the form of narratives very similar to the Mission Profiles supplied with the toys.[7] The press release for the Military range is titled "A Major Problem," and begins:

> A news blackout was declared as military chiefs led by Major Muscle held an emergency meeting to discuss the escalating hostage drama. A militant wing of the terrorist FPR group were responsible but all attempts to negotiate had faltered and there was no alternative but to draft in the special forces. There was only one man for the job—Action Man—but which guise should he adopt?

This scenario, where Action Man represents the forces of an obscure global army in a battle against disorder and crime, allows three Action Man figures and their accessories to be introduced: Special Forces, Rapid Fire, and Operation T.I.G.E.R. Rapid Fire Action Man is dressed in camouflage and carries more than twenty items with him, including rifle, pistol, dagger, rope, grappling hook, and communication backpack with microphone. " 'There would be no need to worry about Rapid Fire Action Man if it came to a shoot out,' thought the Major. 'He was the fastest draw in the Northern Hemisphere.' Special Forces Action Man is "the most agile soldier in the business. His forte was climbing and no edifice was too high or rough thanks to his strategic use of sucker pads. What goes up must come down and seeing Special Forces abseil down was sheer poetry." Action Man Operation T.I.G.E.R. is distinguished by his orange and black camouflage, but the Major speculates that his name may derive from his propensity to "be wild and savage." He has "a weakness for tatoos and seemed to change them on an almost daily basis," since the figure comes with a supply of adhesive decals, and the Major considers this "one of his endearing pastimes" which he "quite admired." The press release goes on to detail the contents of the figure sets and accessory packs in the Military range, with their current prices.

Some of the components of the narrative briefly outlined here are very conventionalised. The description of the terrorist threat is very unspecific about the identity of the terrorists and thus allows for no potential embarassments in the international marketing of the toys to different nations over a fairly extended time. Action Man is not individuated and, in fact, exists in three incarnations determined by the setting and functions of the character in the story. He is therefore a heroic archetype rather than a fictional person, befitting his multiple uses in children's play. Action Man is heroic partly because of his excellence in his narrative roles, but he is not high up in the military hierarchy. He can therefore be required to carry out dangerous active missions, but he is so good at them that his authoritative superiors are drawn to him in identificatory and homosocial terms. His personality is rather mysterious, but combines raw masculine energy with dedication and professionalism. This mix of characteristics is very familiar in children's heroes, and will not be discussed more fully here. The same features are evident in the illustrated stories of *Action Man* comic, and in the scenarios of DIC's new *Action Man* animated television series.

While toy packaging and toy advertising are significant shapers of play narratives, the recent creation of *Action Man* comic provides numerous play scenarios involving the toy range, and explicitly features new or currently promoted products. The form of the publication cannot be discussed in detail here, but is an amalgam of at least three different types of text.[8] In its settings and other war genre references, the comic is related to war comics like *Battle, Warlord,* and *Blazing Combat,* which are black-and-white A5-size booklets with action-adventure stories often based on the Second World War. *Action Man* comic's colour, style of drawing and layout, however, are reminiscent of the American superhero comics dominated by Marvel and DC. In its promotional content *Action Man* comic is also a variant on the more recent A4-size comic book featuring licenced characters (like the comics based on the toys and television characters Sonic the Hedgehog, Power Rangers, and X Men, for instance). *Action Man* comic narratives are propelled by plot progression and suspense, but individual incidents are arranged so that Action Man can show off his heroic attributes of bravery, daring, physical strength, resourcefulness, determination, professionalism, and commitment to the good.

The recent *Action Man* television series is another opportunity to produce narratives around the products and thus both to advertise them and to reinforce very similar heroic characteristics. The television *Action Man* concept was originally developed for Hasbro-Bradley by Scottish Television, which has considerable experience in live-action children's programming, and DIC Animation of Los Angeles. The programme was intended to be a live-action children's drama, but the format was changed to animated drama with a live-action introductory sequence, and at this point Scottish Television ceased to be involved. The animated series opened on American network television in September 1995, and was shown in Britain in 1996. Mark Griffin, who was the Gladiator Trojan in the British network television version of *Gladiators,* was cast as the live-action Action Man. Using a Gladiator for the role picks up elements of masculine gender codes including physical prowess, pride and bravado, the narrative functions which occur in doing battle (challenge, contest, and moral judgement for instance), in addition to a certain "barbarianness" which is tamed and to an extent feminised and ironised by the melodramatic sports and gameshow format. *Gladiators* is as excessive in its versions of masculinity as the Action Man toys. In addition to supporting the physical and combat-based narrative scenarios for Action Man provided by toy packaging and *Action Man* comic, the television series makes intertextual links with televised aggression and masculine role-models through *Gladiators.* The body, the clothing and the accessories of

Action man toy figures already encode relatively coherent meanings. But these material objects are enfolded in a diverse but coherent textual world, where play with the toys can be facilitated and extended by multiple narratives in several media.

THE MEANINGS OF ACTION MAN

The first section of this essay noted that Action Man toys are significant acquisitions for children, especially boys, and are desired possessions in children's consumer culture. For the adults at Hasbro-Bradley, Action Man is a successful commercial brand. For parents, Action Man is much more ambiguous. The toys are relatively expensive, and are accompanied by other toys in a large and expensive product range. Action Man is associated with warlikeness, aggressive play, the commercialisation of childhood, gender stereotyping, and Action Man does not fit in with contemporary advice on which toys parents should buy. The meanings of Action Man vary widely between generations, social groups, and discourses.

The use of Action Man as an anti-hero in a discourse addressed to adults can be exemplified by a Christmas 1995 television commercial for Early Learning Centre (ELC) shops, shown on Britain's Channel 4 network at around 8:30 PM. It features a stop-motion animated military figure dressed in combat gear with a machine-gun (i.e., Action Man) accompanied by a doll with long blonde hair, red dress, fur coat, high boots, and pearls (i.e., Barbie). He is presented as a blundering redneck, while she is a slovenly Bronx tart. They have somehow sneaked into an ELC shop, and are first seen hiding under a slide. No matter how hard they try, they cannot attract the attention of the happy toddlers in the store, who are playing with primary-coloured blocks, books and other educational toys. A male voice-over knowingly comments "Some toys will never get into Early Learning Centre, because we only have toys that make learning fun." While the children seem largely unaware of the figures' presence, an adult female hand picks up the Action Man figure and then we see the toys landing sprawled on the concourse of the shopping mall, literally thrown out of the shop. An adult female voice comments "When are you going to learn? You'll never get into Early Learning."

The advertisement ridicules both the toy figures and the mass-market toyshops like *Toys R Us* which sell them. It shows how Action Man (and Barbie) function as totemic figures for adults, giving a social value to the difference between the two types of toy and toy shop. The difference is equivalent to a distinction between two types of parent and two modes of parenting, with the educational outlook of ELC prioritised. For adults the positive connotations of ELC are clear, and are based on guilt and fear about their children's development. But child viewers may well read this advertisement in a quite different way. The doll characters are the active, comic ones, and their rebellious behaviour is attractive. Advertisements directed to children, especially on television, are entirely different to the ELC advertisement, as a recent Action Man commercial demonstrates.

This Action Man Heligun Maxicopter commercial was shown on GMTV's nationally networked children's Saturday morning schedule, which runs from 6:00 AM to 9:25 AM, in the run-up to Christmas 1995. It appeared first at 8:30 AM, before a double-bill of *Mighty Morphin' Power Rangers* episodes (featuring another very popular boys' toy brand). Like many boys' toy commercials it is based on the chase and shoot-out, shows no girls or adults, places the helicopter toy in a fantasy setting rather than in the child's home, and is characterised by a rapid editing rhythm paralleling the energetic play which is shown. Its total duration is only twenty seconds, but the time is packed with images and sounds which cannot be described fully here. The soundtrack features drums, a chorus of bass-voiced singers, firing and exploding noises, and an American-accented male voice-over. This commercial offers ways to play with Action Man products, it contains a narrative scenario in which the toys are set, and features a child using the toys. The advertisement's first shot is a quartered frame showing four close-ups of the Heligun toy's moving parts while a male chorus cries out "Get ready for action!" The toy has a flip-up gunsight, flip-out missile launchers, and a heavy machine-gun with a red light flashing in the barrel. It is at once a child-sized gun and a vehicle which accomodates Action Man. We might note the fetishisation of the toy through the close-ups on its special features, and the immediate association of the toy with "action" and with masculine warlike play. The toy is not just a desirable object, but also does something; it has moving and functioning parts which lend themselves to play scenarios.

The second sequence shows a live actor as Dr X with gritted-teeth and clenched fist. A voice-over informs us that "Doctor X destroys all from his Death Rigs," we cut to a shot of a blasted wasteland and an X-shaped craft. A song intones "Action Man—the hero of the hour," and we cut to Action Man in the Heligun cockpit. Here is a simple narrative constructing a play scenario: The conflict between Action Man and Dr X can be enacted by the child using the Heligun toy. The voice-over reports "But in swoops Action Man Heligun with real working rotors, machine-gun fire and twin flip-out missiles with awesome pump-action fire and electronic sound." We see a boy holding the Heligun as if it were a gun. A series of shots show the boy holding the Heligun, frowning and with gritted teeth as he enacts Action Man's Heligun attack on Dr X. A missile fires, then two more. The sequence aligns the viewer's with the boy's point of view, alludes to war-film action sequences and further fetishises the exciting functions of the Heligun. What is purchasable for "around £39" is not just the toy but a fantasy scenario under the apparent control of the child where the child becomes Action Man.

In contrast to the Early Learning Centre commercial, this advertisement promotes excitement, aggression, masculinity, technology, and American-ness. The action shifts between toy play engaged in by the child, to action seemingly carried out by the toys themselves, to a live-action dramatization of the toy play. The slippages between boy and Action Man, aggression and pleasure, consumption and pleasure, fantasy and realism, testify to exactly the kind of rebellion against the adult norms of quiet, educational, imaginative and social play which Early Learning Centre and its commercial represents. In the Heligun commercial, Action Man is heroic, and play with the toys is pleasurable, precisely because the play is neither playful nor childish but earnest, based on adult norms of masculine warlikeness, and unconnected to intellectual growth or social skill. To sum up crudely, a child watching the Early Learning Centre advertisement might be more attracted by the antics of the animated Action Man than by the educational advantages promised by the commentary. Similarly, a parent watching the Action Man Heligun commercial might be more disgusted by its blatant aggression and hard-sell than drawn into its fantasy scenario of adventure and power. But analysing Action Man as a heroic figure requires us to acknowledge the multiplicity of meanings which children's culture can carry, and the very different interests, needs and fantasies supported by the discourses of, and about, children's culture.

NOTES

1. The historical information here was kindly provided by the Public Relations Department of Hasbro-Bradley, the makers of Action Man.

2. Further information on soldier toy figures, their history and cultural significance, can be found in Graham Dawson, *Soldier Heroes: British Adventure, Empire and the Imagining of Masculinities.*

3. I have discussed the relationship between war toys, war play, and the representation of contemporary conflicts in "The Meanings of War Toys and War Games," in Ian Stewart and Susan Carruthers (eds.) *War, Culture and the Media.*

4. An excellent discussion of the interconnected system of children's products and media can be found in Marsha Kinder *Playing with Power in Movies, Television and Video Games: From Muppet Babies to Teenage Mutant Ninja Turtles.*

5. The psychoanalytic perspective on play, drawing mainly on the work of Melanie Klein, is discussed in detail in Dawson op. cit., especially pp. 27–52.

6. David Buckingham "Boy's Talk: Television and the Policing of Masculinity" in David Buckingham (ed.) *Reading Audiences: Young People and the Media.* He refers to Lyn Segal's, *Slow Motion: Changing Masculinities, Changing Men.*

7. Quotations which follow are from the Christmas 1995 press release kindly supplied by the Public Relations Department of Hasbro-Bradley. Toys in each of the four Action Man product ranges, plus Dr X, were advertised by mini-narratives like the one analysed here, under headlines like "Action Man to Hunt Man-Eating Beast" and "A Devil of a Job."

8. The classic work on comics is Martin Barker's *Comics: Ideology, Power and the Critics.* For a more recent study encompassing the promotion of a heroic multi-media character in comics, see Robert E Pearson and William Uricchio (eds.) *The Many Lives of the Batman: Critical Approaches to a Superhero and his Media.*

BIBLIOGRAPHY

The Action Man Bumper 1996. Annual. Exeter, U.K.: Pedigree Books, Ltd., 1996.

Barker, Martin. *Comics: Ideology, Power and the Critics.* Manchester: Manchester University Press, 1989.

Bignell, Jonathan. "The Meanings of War Toys and War Games." In *War, Culture and the Media,* eds. Ian Stewart & Susan Carruthers. Trowbridge: Flicks Books, 1996.

Buckingham, David. "Boys' Talk: Television and the Policing of Masculinity." In *Reading Audiences: Young People and the Media,* ed. David Buckingham. Manchester: Manchester University Press, 1993.

Dawson, Graham. *Soldier Heroes: British Adventure, Empire and the Imagining of Masculinities.* London: Routledge, 1994.

Kinder, Marsha. *Playing with Power in Movies, Television and Video Games: From Muppet Babies to Teenage Mutant Ninja Turtles.* Berkeley: University of California Press, 1991.

Pearson, Robert E. & William Uricchio, eds. *The Many Lives of the Batman: Critical Approaches to a Superhero and his Media.* London: Routledge, 1991.

Segal, Lyn. *Slow Motion: Changing Masculinities, Changing Men.* London: Virago, 1990.

Seiter, Ellen. *Sold Separately: Children and Parents in Consumer Culture.* New Brunswick, N.J.: Rutgers University Press.

Stewart, Ian & Susan Carruthers, eds. *War, Culture and the Media.* Trowbridge: Flicks Books, 1996.

Spider-Man
An Enduring Legend

C. M. STEPHENS

The first sighting of Spider-Man on the front cover of *Amazing Fantasy*: #15, August 1962, made a direct appeal to young, particularly male, readers. An anonymous, costumed figure is seen against a backdrop of high-rise city blocks. Nonchalantly "flying" with one hand on his web rope, he carries an incapacitated and terrified tough guy under the free arm. The musculature is impressive but not extraordinary. Lithe and strong, rather than over-developed, he represents an attainable goal. Not surprisingly there are three separate pages of advertising for body building courses in this issue.

Our initial impression is of a mysterious but clearly confident and capable crime fighter, secure in his superior strength and skill, utterly in command of the situation. How attractive as a projection of wish-fulfilment for any frustrated teenager, yearning for the freedom and power of adult independence, whilst still controlled by the dual authority of school and parents. Both Jules Feiffer and Modechai Richler vividly recall their personal identification with the early superheroes as a means of temporary escape from the restrictions of everyday life:

> With them we were able to roam free, disguised in costume, committing the greatest of feats and the worst of sins . . . Comic books were our booze. (Feiffer 1977, p. 189)

Richler makes the link between repressed teenage aggression and the explosive violence of the superheroes, who were "our champions; our revenge figures against what seemed like a gratuitously cruel adult world"

(Richler 1967, p. 300). The opening words of this first Spider-Man story demand an empathetic response. The unknown figure exults: "Though the world may mock Peter Parker, the timid teenager . . . it will soon marvel at the might of Spider-Man!". This impressive figure is miraculously like one of us; in his daily life, accustomed to ridicule, and feelings of insecurity and inadequacy but also, when victorious, prey to vanity and self-aggrandisement.

The arrival of Spider-Man marked a change in editorial policy, away from *Amazing Fantasy's* association with uncanny tales and an adult readership. It was customary to introduce new superheroes gradually, through guest appearances in established titles and Spider-Man's unusually high-profile introduction probably owes much to the fact that Stan Lee felt there was nothing to lose in a doomed title, marked for the axe. A direct appeal was made to teen-aged fans: "Perhaps if your letters request it, we will make his stories even longer, or have TWO Spider-Man stories per issue." In fact, the essential ingredients that have led to thirty-plus years of top-ranking sales were gathered together in these early days and the recipe has remained fundamentally unchanged since then. As early as the first tale (SM1), there are clues to Spider-Man's enduring appeal.

The opening caption stresses how different Spider-Man is from other costumed "long underwear characters," and for once this was more than clichéd hype. Benton honours Spider-Man as:

> perhaps the most truly original super-hero of the 1960s. His litany of personal problems—love, financial and family—made him unique among super-heroes and set the tone for dozens of Marvel super-heroes to come. (Benton 1989, pp. 179/180)

The first story begins with a sad and isolated figure. Peter Parker is puny, bespectacled, the butt of contemptuous jibes: "bookworm," "professional wallflower." His peers despise him for his over-neat collar-and-tie appearance, his intellectualism and his lack of "hip" interests. Even worse, he is adored by the establishment—his surrogate parents worship him and the staff at Midtown High admire this "clean-cut, hard-working, honor student!" (although the exclamation mark is a stylistic commonplace in these publications, here one suspects it is particularly ironic). These are hardly traits to endear him to his peers. Unlike Superman, who only *assumes* a meek alter-ego, or Batman, whose everyday identity is that of a rich, attractive playboy, Peter Parker is your all-American failure as a teenager, as seen from a youngster's point of view—unpopular, isolated, and rejected. No wonder that, by the second page of this initial story, he is hurt, angry, and seeking revenge: "Some day I'll show them—sob—some day they'll be sorry that they laughed at me."

However unlikely, it is his despised scholarship that leads to his accidental transformation; his interest in atomic science prompts him to attend a public experiment in radio-activity where he is bitten by a spider that has absorbed a "fantastic amount of radio-activity." Peter Parker acquires the strengths and skills of a spider and, with a mixture of intellect and imagination, constructs a simple device that enables him to make his own web and manoeuvre its tentacles. He rejoices in his ingenuity that, unlike Batman's utility belt purchased with the vast Bruce Wayne millions, has cost him virtually nothing: "So they laughed at me for being a bookworm eh! Well only a science major could have created a device like this" (SM1 p. 6). Like many contemporary superheroes, the origin story is linked to the mishandling of radiation, obviously a 1960s preoccupation and significantly different from the fairy-story paraphernalia first envisaged in which Peter Parker's literary ancestor, Tommy Troy, was to find a magic ring that released a genie and ensured the granting of one wish.

Peter Parker displays understandable petulance and a desire to be revenged on his tormentors. We can all relate to his ambition to "show them" and make his tormentors "sorry." And because his superhuman powers are not gained at the expense of becoming grotesque and inhuman like Toxic Avenger or Swamp Thing, he retains his humanity. He is not permanently or obviously mutated, nor is he the victim of uncontrollable transfigurations and, most importantly, he decides when to be Spider-Man. He can continue to live inconspicuously in normal society if he wishes to, but with the advantage of becoming an overnight "sensation." Previously he has only received contempt from people; now they are "awe-stricken," "incredulous," "amazed."

One can see why Spider-Man was so appealing to youngsters. The opportunities for empathy, identification and wish-fulfilment were obvious. Peter Parker was a teenager's nightmare vision of himself, an embodiment of typical youthful insecurity. An outsider from peer society, friendless, lonely, despised, his only talents were intellectual. Being admired by adults and the establishment does not bring him complete happiness, although he never rejects their affection. Significantly, he does not rebel but accidentally discovers a way to be powerful, feared, admired, and effective. Peter, the "swot" and "wimp," acquires a physical manifestation of the real him—the life force we all believe or hope is there beneath and beyond the flawed exterior upon which the world judges us. As Spider-Man he can be another self, freed by his special powers and secret identity to mentally, as well as physically, "fly" through the New York skyline. Whether loved or hated, he is no longer dismissed as a joke.

The first episode, however, does not conclude at this point. The fatal flaw that eventually caused the downfall of the superhero of Greek legend was hubris. Peter, rejoicing in his new-found superhuman powers and the media adulation they bring, selfishly refuses to assist a policeman in his attempt to capture a criminal: "I'm thru being pushed around by anyone! From now on I just look out for number One . . . that means . . . me!" (p. 8). The point here is, surely, that without the influence of his superhuman persona, Peter Parker would have been incapable of abrogating his civic responsibility in this way. Although Peter/Spider-Man's downfall for this act of hubris is indefinitely deferred, retribution is swift. The criminal he has allowed to escape later kills his beloved guardian (and foster father) Uncle Ben.

The early death or absence of the father (and sometimes both parents) is a familiar motif in superhero comics. As Reynolds points out, "Few superheroes enjoy uncomplicated relationships with parents who are regularly present in the narrative" (Reynolds 1992, p. 12). Peter Parker experiences the same recurring sense of guilt and responsibility for his "father's" death as Bruce Wayne who, when only a young child, has been forced to witness the killing of his parents by a hired killer. Wayne's guilt stems from his recognition that he was a "spoiled brat who threw his model trains at his mother" (Reynolds, p. 70). Though indirect, Parker's responsibility for Uncle Ben's death is clearly much greater than Wayne's for his parents' murder. Acknowledging that responsibility, he declares, "And now no matter what I do—no matter how great my super powers are, I can never undo that tragic mistake. I can never completely forgive myself. Sometimes I hate my Spider-Man powers! Sometimes I wish I were just like any normal teenager. If only it had never happened." (SM4 ,p. 6). This sense of the gift of superhuman powers being both liberating and empowering *and* an intolerable, inescapable burden is another familiar motif of the superhero narrative. It also allows the writer/illustrator to explore the theme of schizophrenia, with the "real-life" character frequently undergoing an identity crisis as he struggles to stop his superhuman alter-ego dominating his psyche.

Like Wayne/Batman, Parker/Spider-Man seeks to atone for his "sin" by dedicating his life to crime-fighting. A year after his uncle's death, he visits his grave and vows:

> "For whatever I am—whatever I've become—the good—whatever good I've done with the powers fate gave me—the best of me came from you! You didn't die in vain, Uncle Ben! You died that Spider-Man might be borne! It's not the way I would have chosen it to happen, but if your death is to have meaning—then I must rededicate myself to your faith that one day Peter Parker will do something to change this world . . . for the better!" (quoted in Palumbo 1983, p. 70)

The essential moral, stated in the final panel of the opening story, is that "in this world, with great power there must come . . . great responsibility!"—a saying that has acquired an almost proverbial resonance. One must also bear in mind that, for Peter, the loss of his foster father is further complicated by Aunt May's hostility to his alter-ego (she loathes and fears Spider-Man, describing him as a "menace to society") and by his encounters with a series of sinister father figures and father substitutes, such as J. Jonah Jameson and Doctor Octopus.

By the close of his first adventure, Spider-Man has an origin story and a motivation for his future actions as a superhero. A formula was established which was to remain fundamentally unchanged for the next thirty years. It was a formula that seemed designed to suit everyone: For developing adolescents, it provided opportunities for vicarious adventure and self-determination; for parents and teachers, an acceptable role model who upheld the right kind of moral values.

This careful balance is maintained and developed in the second story where Spider-Man, now the eponymous hero of *The Amazing Spider-Man* (apparently the change of title was due to huge popular demand, although the cynic might refer to the prophetic editorial quoted above) is working as a freelance photographer for *The Daily Bugle*. Its editor, J. Jonah Jameson, is one of Spider-Man's most persistent and effective enemies. Using photos of Spiderman taken by Parker, Jameson mounts a newspaper campaign to unjustly vilify Spider-Man. Voicing fears that children might try to copy Spider-Man's exploits (fears that, later in real life, were to be expressed about the popular TV cartoon series), Jameson warns, "Think what would happen if [children] make a hero out of this lawless, inhuman monster" (SM2, p. 5). This could be read as an obligatory warning to youngsters, designed to pre-empt establishment criticism and it has echoes of the moral panic generated in the 1950s around horror comics and reinforced by the publication of Dr. Frederic Wertham's *Seduction of the Innocent* (1954). The validity of Jameson's attack on Spider-Man is undermined, however, by the hyperbolic tone and the fact that, like some of the condemnation of horror comics in the 1950s, it is clearly inspired by ignorance and irrational prejudice.

Jameson's role here might be interpreted as reflecting the dark side of paternal authority and his narrative function is certainly to prevent Spider-Man wallowing in the fruits of success. Peter Parker does, after all, make the mistakes of a youthful, unformed morality: His first thoughts when he acquires his superhuman powers are to exploit them commercially for fame and fortune, especially when the latter is legitimised by the poverty resulting from his uncle's death and by the searing images of Aunt May pawning everything she has, to provide for his upkeep and education. The effects of guilt, poverty, and rejection by many of his peers, at times, leads to despair: One frame in SM2 (p.6) portrays Peter literally pounding his head against a brick wall. Clad in his "failure" clothes—the knitted slipover, collar and tie, and glasses—he represents archetypal youth: powerless and frustrated. Like so many actual youngsters, he is unable to earn a living officially; too young for a man's job, too old to be carefree and irresponsible, without the accompanying feelings of guilt. Once again, the realistic depiction of Peter Parker's everyday life encourages an empathic response from youthful readers.

Even in his Spider-Man role, Peter faces the same injustice many young people would recognise as their everyday lot. "It's not fair," he and they cry, as he is hounded by the police and feared by all, including the saintly Aunt May. By the end of the second issue, he has been universally rejected in both personas. Furthermore, the typical adolescent search for identity—which suggests a kinship between Peter Parker and film and literary cult heroes of the 1950s like James Dean and Holden Caulfield—is, in Peter's case, exaggerated and polarised by the character's dualism.

The possibility of a split personality had been there from the beginning. Page one of Amazing Fantasy #15 shows Peter Parker with the shadow of Spider-Man brooding behind and Ditko reflects the growing identity crisis by drawing split faces, half Spider-Man and half Peter Parker. By #12 (SM3, p. 124) Peter Parker dreams of being advised by his alter-ego and the psychological possibilities are further explored in #13 (SM3, p. 140): "Am I becoming a SPLIT PERSONALITY like Dr. Jekyll and Mr. Hyde? Perhaps . . . Perhaps I did it in my sleep without knowing ??!" Spider-Man even resorts to a psychiatrist (who recognises a money-spinner when he sees it) before realising that he can confide in no-one without revealing his secret identity. Palumbo suggests that Spider-Man's increasing sense of social alienation and bifurcated personality mark him out as an existentialist (anti) hero: "As is the case with nearly all existentialist characters, his most prominent trait is a crushing, encyclopedic alienation" (Palumbo 1983, p. 68). Young people, of course, found it easy to identify with this feeling of alienation. Comic Collector #7 1992 (Holland), suggests that: "Much of the reality and romance—and attraction—of Spider-Man was down to him being as ill-at-ease with situations as many of the young audience he was being read by" (p. 29), and adds significantly, "This character gained superpowers but retained the moods and attitudes of a teenager who feels his inadequacies keenly, whether real or imagined, [he was] an anti hero for the 60s" (p. 30).

Psychological analysis—often in the form of introspection—is a recurrent motif: "Sometimes it seems like I'm always running out on friends to become Spider-Man! Maybe I'm subconsciously afraid of friendship and I use ol' Spidey as an escape!" (SM6, p. 11). Some understanding or awareness of his problems by others is often a sign of a close relationship. For example, we see Betty Brant, his first girlfriend, pondering: "It's strange—although Peter seems so calm and easy-going, I get this feeling that he's like a smouldering volcano inside, just waiting to erupt" (SM3, p. 55). In 1964 his rejection of the Spider-Man identity causes temporary loss of powers and Peter is immediately confused, depressed, unable to function properly, even as his everyday self. He is aware of the irony that it is when those powers return that he is spiritually and physically transformed. Visually, a full page, action-packed panel celebrates the return of his life force.

A further attraction of the early issues was the art work of the legendary Steve Ditko. Chosen for his understated, realistic style and his skill in "depicting the average man in the street"(Lee, 1997 p.127), Ditko's contribution to Spider-Man's success has been acknowledged by Stan Lee:

> If ever there was a perfect artist and co-plotter for our amazing arachnid, it had to be the dazzling Mr. D! His layouts and drawings set the unique illustrative style for the strip, a style which made Spidey utterly distinctive among comic strip creations. His sense of pacing, his flair for action scenes, and his ability to make the most outlandish situations look totally believable after he had drawn them gave the early Spider-

Man stories an impetus which helped keep them rolling until this very day! (Benton 1989, p. 136)

Initially, the task of creating Spider-Man had been given to Jack Kirby by Stan Lee, who told him that the character "was not to be overly-heroic-looking . . . just an ordinary guy who happens to have a super power . . . not too handsome, not too glamorous, not too graceful, not too muscular" (Lee 1997, p. 126). Kirby's style, however, leaned more towards dramatic inflation, the grandiloquent and over-stated, so Lee decided that Ditko might be more suited to the job of portraying a Spider-Man who was a less heroic, essentially ordinary figure. He was to be "a character that had imperfections—a flawed hero of human proportions that was easier for Marvel's audience to relate to," declared (Comic Collector #7 (Holland 1992, p. 28). "Ditko generated an immense sense of the helplessness which exists within today's urban environment and the apparent inability of even a superhero to make good out of bad" (p. 31). Certainly the placing of Spider-Man in a real environment, the suburbs and inner city of New York, added to his essential humanity—this was our world, not Gotham City.

By the end of the second episode then, the crucial character components had all been established. Being Spider-Man does not solve all Peter Parker's problems at a stroke. Young people are dramatically reminded that being powerful, and mature, means taking responsibility for one's actions. I see the Spider-Man identity as a metaphor for adulthood, a desirable goal for most adolescents. However, in both the fantasy and the real world, growing up brings its own dilemmas. Choosing to do right is not always easy. Relationship problems are an intrinsic part of living as a social being. Teenagers can identify with the angst of Peter Parker and revel in "Spidey's" victories, whilst traditional moral and social values are reinforced through the details of Spider-Man's emotional and spiritual development.

Since 1962, society, genre conventions, and relevant technology have all changed dramatically and one must avoid making simplistic sweeping statements about the immutability of the Spider-Man character and universe. I will confine myself to examining areas of psychological and ideological interest that have sustained the series' enduring popularity.

Traditional family values are unquestioned and accorded priority status. The young Peter Parker suffers loneliness, as well as the emotional and practical difficulties of living a double life, in order to save Aunt May the pain of discovery. He faces the constant and, judging from the number of heart attacks she suffers, justified worry that the shock of exposure might kill her. The re-appearance of his lost parents added a new anxiety. Their somewhat implausible incarceration in a Russian prison for twenty-five years underlines the belief that in "Spidey's" world you must have a very good reason for deserting a child!

Peter wants to have girlfriends and, eventually, a wife. Western social norms of heterosexual pair-bonding and monogamy are, not, of course, interrogated by the comic. His early attempts at close relationships proved largely unsuccessful, which was, perhaps, reassuring to insecure adolescent readers. Even though his increased confidence makes him more popular with his peers, his desire for an emotionally supportive lover, friend, and confidante remained for many years unfulfilled. This was largely because of the special circumstances of his bizarre lifestyle and his chivalrous refusal to allow anyone else to share his danger: "Dare I allow another to share that kind of existence? . . . Am I doomed to always be alone?" (SM8, p. 17). He assumes the stereotypical male role of support to Aunt May and protection to Betty Brant. When he eventually marries Mary Jane Watson, he finds that combining his marital obligations with his Spider-Man crime-fighting crusade inevitably produces separations and tensions but also provides the opportunity for the comic to reinforce the concept of monogamy as a desirable ideal: "His eyes embrace the woman who makes his life worth living, the partner with whom he shares dreams, uncertainties.. everything" (SM9, p. 30). While Mary Jane becomes a highly attractive and successful television star, Peter remains deliberately boyish and not especially "sexy." She becomes progressively more glamorous and her admirers press heavily around her but his emotional vulnerability and his open adoration of her are rewarded by her fidelity. He draws attention to his ordinariness and resistibility with deliberately ironic references to his sexual attraction: "Ah, Peter Parker . . . Love-God! Have to drive them off with a stick! . . . Sigh" (SM10, p. 11). Is this a message to young male readers that even the boy next door can win the heart of the most beautiful and loving girl "on the block"? The comic, it should be noted, does eventually begin to reflect some modification of conventionally sexist attitudes—by 1992, for example, Felicia, the New Black Cat, is a worthy, comrade-in-arms (SM12), whereas fourteen years earlier, even the formidable Tigra was treated with paternalistic courtesy (SM5).

Spider-Man faces more than an ailing dependent relative, emotional problems and an endless supply of criminals: From the beginning he also must contend with the ironies that typically confront the existentialist hero. Palumbo points out that "Spider-Man is the persistent victim of more significant thematic and structural ironies as well as (general absurd Marvel universe) ironies that are an integral part of his existence" (Palumbo 1983, p. 71). Aunt May loves Peter Parker but hates Spider-Man, as does Betty Brant, who reveals her antagonism to Spider-Man just as Peter is preparing to confide in her. He has a complex, uneasy relationship with the media: Peter's desire for fame is presented in opposition to the approved aims of Super-Heroism, exemplified by the non-profitmaking work of The Fantastic Four Peter responds naively to the seductive wiles of media men, one of whom says: "Listen friend I'm a TV producer! With that Act of yours I can make you a fortune! And keep the mask angle . . . it's great showmanship!" (SM1, p. 6).

It would be wrong to suggest that Spider-Man's success—and his cultural importance—can simply be explained in terms of his reflecting the identity problems that typically afflict adolescents, and the anxieties surrounding personal appearance, social acceptance and relationships with significant others. There was also a political and ideological dimension to the character that found expression in his fight against crime and in the way he addressed a range of controversial social and political problems.

Although individual policemen defend Spider-Man's integrity and decency, he is often unfairly victimised by establishment figures, and in the 1970s he was a fugitive from the law, wrongly accused of murder. In fact, he always fights crime, usually in the style of the defender-of-the-weak. However, Spider-Man not only protects individuals from crime, but also America from its national enemies. The tensions of the Cold War era are represented, particularly during the first five years of Spider-Man's existence (1962–67), in his battles with Russian villains. In 1963, for example, he foils an "attempt to turn over secret documents from an American defense installation to the Communists" (Mondello 1976, p. 235).

But Spider-Man's influence is felt more importantly, argues Salvatore Mondello, in the way that, between 1967 and 1973, he addressed himself to every important issue confronting American society, and in his fight against "drug abuse and drug pushers, organised crime, pollution, and racial bigotry" (Mondello 1976, p. 236), he played an important part in educating America's young people. Since 1962, claims Mondello, *The Amazing Spider-Man* "helped to shape and reflect the American character" and deserved "special attention from students of American history because it . . . enjoyed a popularity and thus an influence second to no other comic book" (p. 237).

In 1971, Stan Lee declared he was neither a hippie nor a conservative and Spider-Man's (and Peter Parker's) own views, Mondello suggests, reflect the middle-of-the-road, political stance of their creator: They support many liberal causes and, though "worried by political extremism especially from the right" (p. 236), eschew involvement in militant action or protest movements. Peter Parker, for example, "believes in equal justice for black Americans, but he has never joined a protest movement to defend that principle. Like his fellow liberals, he feels that blacks will attain full social and political parity with whites by working in the system" (ibid.) In one story attacking racial prejudice, Lee portrays a security guard restraining a nervous colleague who has reached for his gun when confronted by black student protesters thus "showing that not all policemen were intent upon shooting young college protesters." Another story—which appeared "at the very moment America was experiencing the tragedy of Attica"—had Spider-Man making a television appearance to plead for improved living conditions in American prisons (p. 237).

Perhaps more daring still was Peter Parker's profound unease about American involvement in the Vietnam War:

> Like most middle-class young men, he never talked about it. But after saying farewell to his friend Flash Thompson, who is leaving for a tour of duty in Vietnam, Peter thinks to himself: "Which is worse . . . ? Staying behind while other guys are doing the fighting . . . ? Or fighting a war that nobody wants . . . against an enemy you don't even hate?" (*The Amazing Spider-Man,* April 1970, p. 10, in Mondello, p. 237)

Neither this engagement with controversial social and political issues nor the personal and psychological problems facing Spider-Man/Parker prevent the frequent surfacing of what might be described as a typically post-modernist ironic humour: Sometimes this is self-referential, sometimes it involves a puncturing of intellectual and artistic pretensions and it seems likely that this humour is one of the reasons for the comic-book's continuing popularity and appeal to a varied readership. Often the mundane, practical problems arising from Peter's dual identity are exploited for their comic potential even though, on occasions, they could have serious repercussions. For example, failure to rinse out his Spider-Man costume might result in shrinkage, and forgetting to close his bedroom curtains whilst changing might endanger his secret identity (SM7).

Humour in the comics is frequently used to convey some of the ironies previously identified. Aunt May, for example, compares our hero unfavourably with a long established opponent:

> "So, that's Spider-Man! What a perfectly ghastly outfit! He's so villainous looking! Not at all as pleasant as that well-mannered Dr. Octopus! I'm sure Dr. Octopus would never have entered that way without knocking!" (SM4, p. 39)

Peter smiles indulgently when May rebukes him for using slang such as "shook up," moments after his heroic alter-ego has saved her from the doubtful mercy of ruthless villains. Thus the teenage American male can patronise "female domestic tyranny" (see Hawkins, 1990 and Feiffer, 1965), whilst also experiencing the pleasure of knowing more than the Aunt May character.

The 1991 story, *The Web of Spiderman*, comments satirically upon current outlandish artistic fashions:

> He has faced unflinchingly both the most brutal supervillains our world has to offer and slavering terrors from realms beyond the physical universe. He has stood before creatures from the furthest reaches of Space and walked the sub-atomic lands of the Microverse.
>
> But none of his incredible experiences has prepared him for the sheer, unadulterated horror of . . .
>
> Performance Art? (SM11, p. 24)

In this way, writers can ridicule aspects of contemporary society (here artistic pretentiousness) and the typically high minded attitudes struck by morally didactic superheroes are undercut by bathos, reminding us that this is, after all, only entertainment.

*   *   *

All the statistical analyses demonstrate that since the 1940s there has beeen a dramatic change in readership. Benton tells us that twelve to fifteen million comic books were sold in 1942, 75 percent of them to children and that in 1946, 90 percent of American youngsters between eight and fifteen years old collectively spent $40,000,000 per month on 157 active titles. Parsons (1991) claims that less than 10 percent of American school children are regular comic readers and that the readership profile is older teens and young adult males. However, the actual number of children reading comics remains substantial and compares well with other texts read purely for leisure.

The last decade has brought dramatic changes to the entire comics industry—changes in technology, marketing, distribution and readership—but I contend that the fundamental "core character" (Uricchio and Pearson 1991, p. 185) of Peter Parker/Spider-Man has remained constant. Even though later series of the comic reveal what appear to be significant differences in themes, graphics and layout from the 1962 originals, one can see that in terms of Spider-Man's traits and attributes, the recurrent characters featured in the strip, the settings and iconography, important continuities have been maintained. For example, Tod McFarlane's *Spider-Man* (1991 launch) was heralded as a publishing milestone and his portrayal of the webbed hero was described by Stan Lee as "daringly different from all the [preceding]versions." Certainly under McFarlane's single artistic control, the story-lines and pictures commanded a cult following but the the essential qualities of the central character remained intact—Spider-Man was self-deprecating, lonely for Mary Jane and Peter Parker the same vulnerable, sensitive Peter of old. A year later, Spider-Man 2099 arrived. There was no official, "blood" link between this superhero and Peter Parker at all, but his fundamental compassion and sense of humour proclaimed his "spiritual" descendency.

Throughout his long history, Spider-Man has been the central character and focus of any issue bearing his name. He is the supreme Marvel Universe superhero, described by Lang and Trimble (1988) as "humanized" and subject to "demythification." As Reitburger and Fuchs point out, he endures "traumatic crises of identity and suffers from almost paranoiac attacks of self-doubt; but he never gives up . . . He is the most tenacious and absurdly heroic character of them all" (Reitberger and Fuchs 1972, p. 108). For young people, Spider-Man's archetypal insecurity encourages empathy and identification. His heroism is an inspiration and source of hope in gloomy times: "I saw Spider-Man in action up close. I saw a brave, tireless, selfless young man. A real honest-to-goodness hero! This world needs heroes, Peter . . . more than I need a Pulitzer Prize . . . A lot more" (SM7, p. 24). He can speak to and for modern teenagers because the problems of adolescence have not fundamentally changed. As Peter slowly aged, his worries have remained those of young people. Although his wife may now be emotionally centre-stage, rather than Aunt May, he continues to balance home life, study, work as a photographer, and crime fighting duties, as well as coping with everyday financial worries.

The appeal for older readers is largely that of nostalgia. In spite of other changes to the traditional comic format, "Spidey" is still recognisably the comrade of their own youth. A well-established rogues gallery ensures the periodic return of old foes—the Vulture is reborn in Spider-Man 2099, and Flash Thompson, Spidey's school-yard critic, also returns, as Felicia's boyfriend, in 1992 (SM12). Both first appeared in the earliest issues. Spider-Man may have been the voice of the liberal conscience but he is not, and never has been a rebel; he does not threaten the social conventions accepted by many as they grow older, and as the new millenium approaches, he continues to enjoy the loyalty of established fans.

BIBLIOGRAPHY

Spider-Man texts cited

SM1   August 1962 *Amazing Fantasy 15*
SM2   March 1963 *The Amazing Spider-Man 1*
SM3   September '63–March '64 *The Amazing Spider-Man 7–13* book form
SM4   1964 *Spider-Man Annual 1* reprint April '83
        plus Sinister Six Marvel Tales
SM5   March 1978 *Marvel Team-Up*
        (plus Tigra)
SM6   October 1981 *The Spectacular Spider-Man*
SM7   June 1983 *Marvel Team-Up*
        (plus the Scarlet Witch)
SM8   1983 *The Spectacular Spider-Man 83* reprint April '89
        plus The Punisher on Trial Marvel Tales
SM9   Late September 1990 *The Amazing Spider-Man*
SM10   February 1991 *The Amazing Spider-Man*
SM11   March 1991 *Web of Spider-Man*
SM12   Late December 1992 *The Amazing Spider-Man*

CRITICAL WORKS

Benton, M. *The Comic Book in America: An Illustrated History.* Dallas, Texas: Taylor Publishing Co., 1989.

Feiffer, J. *The Great Comic Book Heroes.* New York: The Dial Press, 1965.

Hawkins H. *Classics and Trash: Traditions and Taboos in High Literature and Popular Modern Genres.* Hemel Hempstead: Harvester Wheatsheaf, 1990.

Holland, S. ed. *Comic Collector:* # 7. Colchester, Essex: Aceville Publications Ltd,. 1992.

Lang, J. and Trimble, P. "Whatever Happened to the Man of Tomorrow? An Examination of the American Monomyth and the Comic Book Superhero," *Journal of Popular Culture* 22:3 (1988): 157–173

Lee, Stan. *Origins of Marvel Comics.* New York: Marvel Comics, 1997 (originally published 1974).

Palumbo, D. "The Marvel Comic Group's Spider-Man is an existentialist Super-Hero or 'Life Has No Meaning Without My Latest Marvels!' " *Journal of Popular Culture* 17:2 (1983): 67–81.

Parsons, P. "Batman and his Audience: The Dialectic of Culture," In *The Many Lives of Batman,* eds. R. Pearson and W. Uricchio. New York: Routledge, 1991.

Pearson, R. & Uricchio, W. "Notes from the Batcave: An Interview with Dennis O'Neill." In R. Pearson & W. Uricchio, eds. *The Many Lives of Batman,* USA: Routledge, 1991: 18–33.

Reynolds, Richard. *Superheroes.* London: Batsford, 1992.

Reitberger, R & Fuchs, W. *Comics: Anatomy of a Mass Medium.* London: Studio Vista Publishers (English Edition), 1972.

Richler, M. "The Great Comic Book Heroes," in *The Cool Web,* eds. Meek, Wharlow & Barton. London: Bodley Head, 1967.

Urichio, W. & Pearson, R. "I'm not Fooled by that Cheap Disguise," in *The Many Lives of the Batman,* eds. R. Pearson and W. Uricchio. New York: Routledge, 1991: 182–212.

Wertham, F. *Seduction of the Innocent.* New York: Rinehart & Co., 1954.

Children and Popular Culture
The Case of Turtle Power

DAVID LUSTED

"Turtles in a Hard Shell. Turtle Power." (Final line of the theme song over the credits to the television cartoon series *Teenage Mutant Hero Turtles*)

TURTLES ON TELEVISION

In the spring of 1990, the BBC (British Broadcasting Corporation) in its busy children's television schedule programmed an American cartoon series called *Teenage Mutant Ninja Turtles*. This was a time of political challenge to the future of the BBC and to the principle of funding by licence fee. The BBC needed to demonstrate to its political paymasters that it could continue to compete for audiences not only with commercial operators in the ITV (Independent Television) network, but also in the developing satellite and multi-media markets; the popularity of the Turtles seemed to offer a good bet.

The problem for the BBC was that the cartoon series' popularity made it a high profile target for attacks from various quarters. In America, for example, the Turtles were condemned by moralist lobbies in terms that prompted widespread media alarm, especially in the British press. News of the BBC decision became part of the media attention given to pressure groups who were offended by the Turtles' street language and activity with martial arts armoury, and anxious about actual or potential imitation, especially among a young audience that was considered impressionable. Another body of opinion more vocal in Britain was concerned about the range of commodities associated with the Turtles—

everything from pocket-money bubble gum to expensive toys (labelled "commoditoys" by detractors). The objection here was to a perceived financial exploitation of children and the commodification of children's culture. Programming the *Turtles* in the midst of such an emerging moral panic posed a problem for the BBC's role as a public service broadcaster.[1]

The BBC therefore needed to negotiate a difficult balance between conflicting commercial imperatives and public service responsibilities. In order to maximise audiences but minimise public concern, the BBC decided to change a word in the title of the series: Significantly, the term to go was "Ninja," and with it was lost not only feared military connotations of mercenary assassins and lethal weaponry, but also foreign and possibly exotic cultural associations. The term replacing it was "Hero"; so it was that the *Turtles* on British broadcast television became *Teenage Mutant Hero Turtles.*

The alteration to the title may seem trivial but much more than the treatment of the Turtles can be revealed by it—certainly, a great deal was at stake for the BBC. The outcome must have been everything the corporation hoped for: There was some public anxiety about the cartoon series for a time, but it was focused on the Turtles rather more than the BBC. Media attention fueled (and was, in turn, fueled by) a more general popular response, turning the Turtles into a cultural phenomenon for their limited life span. The BBC fed off this widespread attention and the cartoon series was massively popular among an even wider audience than the expected child audience. In time, the popularity of the Turtles waned and the drama over their retitling was forgotten. This was one campaign in the politics of the BBC that the institution won in its own interests. As a public relations exercise, the adjustment to the name of the Turtles appeared a socially responsible and minimal act of censorship.

WHAT KIND OF HERO?

What the BBC did to the Turtles may have been individual, but it also fits a familiar pattern of response in Britain to popular culture for children. In that context, the choice of the term "Hero" was surely calculated. The term "Ninja" connotes certain specifics of warrior activity rather than the generality of heroic deeds. Even so, its associations are wide: skills of combat inscribed in personal, professional, and national military and sporting cultures, the arts of martial arts and the belief systems of eastern religious traditions, professional and mercenary (i.e., monetary and self-)

interest. All this is antagonistic to an elite British culture that constructs its military ideal in quite alternative ideological terms of institutional regulation and professional soldiery, thereby divorcing it from the kinds of ethical, religious, and moral belief systems integral to Eastern philosophies. In British culture, "Hero" invokes very specific historical feats of national daring associated with the glory of Empire and Defenders of the Faith: the Charge of the Light Brigade, for instance, or the resistance at Rourke's Drift.[2] It also has associations of glory in defeat or disaster—Dunkirk and the sinking of the Titanic. There is also Heroism of a more mundane kind beloved by the tabloid press: the little ships at Dunkirk relate to headlines like "The Boy Who Saved His Sister From The Flames" or "The Mum Who Gave Up Her Job For Her Kids"—tales of denial as much as daring.

Heroes of national fiction fall into one of these categories too: either the glory of a Sherlock Holmes or the lovable roguery of a Just William. And if heroes must be foreign then they are invariably mythical; in the same figure, there are the Gods and mortals of Greek and Roman myth or the Dutch boy with a sacrificing finger in the dyke.

This string of associations is very British and bound up in deeply rooted conservative cultural choices. These are heroes who service ideas about a chauvinist national identity, which is not only descriptively distinct from others but also evaluatively better. The word "Hero" does ideological work, then, universalising a particular meaning by tearing particular acts from the reputations and disputes of the cultural periods and geographical contexts in which they took place. By using the term "Hero," the BBC were making the Turtles safe for British culture. In place of alien cultures and attitudes, the BBC called up a chain of cultural association drawing on romance histories and fictions of Nation and Empire, and oral traditions of pre-industrial common and folk cultures.

The act of renaming could be seen simply as a minor example of a wider ideological process through which bourgeois elites in England have used official mechanisms of the state throughout the twentieth century to universalise their own conservative cultural choices and marginalise competing ones. Towards the end of the century, the phenomenon has been particularly acute and widespread, connecting even with wider changes in the national culture: In education, for instance, the same process can be seen at work in national curriculum documents, where History becomes British History and Literature becomes a legitimised canon.

To be fair to the BBC, the use of the term "Hero" was more opportunist than propagandist, intended to utilise, rather than further, ideological notions of heroism. Yet the consequence was to reproduce the comfortable sanction of a British cultural conservatism. Certainly, the ideas of Hero that were no part of the BBC's calculation, were those like Tom Ripley or Dracula, Arnold Schwarzenneger or Turtles in a Half-Shell. The associations here are of darker figures of the baroque, parodic adventurers, heroes more by role than deed, even anti-heroes whose transgressive acts and desires undermine superficial notions of heroism. Then again, there is the absurdity of the notion of heroic *Turtles*.

NOT JUST TELEVISION TURTLES

For a short period between 1988 and 1992, the Turtles were very popular indeed. Although on television they were "Heroes," they were all over the media of the press, television, cinema, newspapers, comics, magazines, and music, and in advertising displays of merchandising in commercial sites, sometimes as "Hero," often as "Ninja." Their public ubiquity in both guises was ample testimony to the power of contemporary mass communications and capitalist forms of consumerism to create mass international demands.

It was not only the availability and display of the Turtles that made them a cultural phenomenon, however. At the same time, they also found an important place in the rituals and patterns of common life, in the consciousness and identities of individuals and groups in many, otherwise unlike, social and geographic locations. Parents and teachers were easily found by journalists eager to turn a phrase about the intensity of the Turtles' penetration into a children's culture of play, game and language. As a commercial phenomenon, the Turtles were created by their producers. But as a cultural phenomenon they were created as much by their consumers. The investment in "Turtles product" for its producers was a matter of profit; for its consumers, it was a means to buying into the Turtles fantasy.

This is a general feature of popular culture. It is widely available rather than imposed, chosen by consumers in relation to, rather than as a result of, their production. The Turtles were ubiquitous and popular but there is no easy cause and effect between availability and popularity. Availability itself is not enough to produce popularity; other phenomena available at the same time as the Turtles became nothing like as popular. Yet nothing can become popular without the media machinery that brings it to public attention.

The primary, though not exclusive, audience for the Turtles was children. The idea that children and commerce together made the Turtles popular is important as a corrective to common fears about the relation of children to the commercial production of popular culture. It is typical of very popular phenomena—what might be termed the supra-popular—that they attract particularly intense public movements of anxiety. The Turtles were such a phenomenon and no exception in the anxiety they attracted. In addition to fears of anti-social behaviour through imitation (especially violent behaviour, and especially among the young) and anxieties about the commercial exploitation of children, their fictions were rejected on aesthetic grounds, as pulp fiction and worse for the undiscriminating. Together, the moral panic formed an indicator of a more widespread fear of popular culture as cultural decline.

POPULAR CULTURE AND ITS DETRACTORS

The popularity of the Turtles and the moral panic over them is intimately linked. The popularity of the Turtles had meaning among its consumers in and of itself. For this group, popularity is associated with shared desires among a distinct group of consumers of, and participants in, the production of what popular culture means. And since popularity like this is invariably accompanied by moral panic, those involved in the creation of the panic also constitute a distinct and contrary group for whom the meaning of popular culture is bound up with desires resisted. The meaning of popular culture is therefore produced in the struggle between the two distinct groups.

This larger context figures in the recurring moral panics over children's popular culture. In this, the case of the Turtles is typical: It typifies the cyclical nature of supra-popular phenomena. They rise in popularity for a short period before they fall, to be replaced by another in a continuing cycle of popular cultural fashions. A few years ago, it was the Mighty Morphin Power Rangers—not unrelated to the Turtles—but before them, there were the despised Cabbage Patch Dolls, My Little Pony, Care Bears, and others stretching back over the years. Merchandising cultural production for children is at least as old as the twentieth century. Cinema-associated products alone have a lineage back through 1970's *Star Wars* to Walt Disney's Mickey Mouse character of the 1920s. As Perry and Aldridge note, the same goes for comic strip characters like Popeye in the 1930s, Felix the Cat in the 1920s, and Krazy Kat in the 1910s, all of whom were rendered into everything from bars of soap to fireworks in their time.[3] There are also phenomena with greater longevity: a regular if less spectacular profile for dolls like Barbie and Sindy or a range of earlier cartoon characters like Disney's Mickey Mouse or Warner's Bugs Bunny. But the supra-popularity of each of these also provoked a moral panic in its own time.[4]

The extent of penetration of the supra-popular into wider social cultures clearly depends on an international capitalist economic system with efficient relations between manufacture, distribution, and retail outlets. This in turn depends on large scales of investment finance to sustain advertising campaigns across integrated media ownership. But economic and structural arguments underpin only matters of display and availability. They explain how phenomena like the Turtles come to public attention; they do not explain why they are taken up so powerfully in the cultural imagination. If they did, every newly developed cultural feature would be equally popular and that is evidently not the case. For every successful campaign for characters like the Turtles, there are equally expensively promoted campaigns over characters that never quite make it—like the Pound Puppies—or never quite make it outside their own national culture—like the tribe of Magic Roundabout characters who made the transition from France to Britain but crossed no further national boundary.

To understand success on this scale, we have to attend to the meaning of the Turtles themselves. And that meaning will have to be complex in its range of multivocal, extensive, and intensive possibilities to explain its widespread popularity. The case of the Turtles exemplifies the nature of the relations in this recurrent pattern.

HOW THE TURTLES CAME TO BE

The Turtles began their fictional lives in an alternative comic strip for adults published on the cultural fringe in San Francisco in 1983. They were subversive figures of absurdity, satirical comments on fictional superheroes like Superman and Batman and on current political and social events in the nuclear and chemical industries, ecology movements and state politics. The Turtles were figures of paradox, both juvenile innocents and cyberpunks; they fought street crime and intergalactic war on skateboards, but also in more recent incarnations, surfed the Internet. Much was made of their tragic origin: Echoing current affairs stories of small reptiles flushed via the toilets of bored yuppie owners to grow into fierce monsters threatening the sewage system, these fictional baby turtles were accidently spilled into a drain and subsequently transformed by radioactive waste into knights errant.

But this scenario is only slightly less improbable than their subsequent transformation into the stuff of childhood fantasy. By the height of their popularity in 1990, their appearance had undergone several more changes. The first significant change came with their move into a nationally syndicated comic magazine: Archie, the action comics company with a history of superhero figures like Superman and Batman, commissioned the originators of the Turtles, Kevin Eastman and Peter Laird, to produce a comic series. In the process, redrafting and colour-processing transformed the Turtles into comic characters for a wider and younger, teenage audience. The graphic energy of their martial arts combat was toned down, their slit-eyed ethnic specificity was made into doe-eyed racial ambiguity and their cynical sneers softened into eager grins.

A television cartoon series produced by Mirage Studios followed in 1987 and was sold worldwide. The result was another transformation of the Turtles into more cuddly figures for the child market. The martial arts armoury was curtailed so that each of the four Turtles was identified by a colour-coded bandana mask and a single ninjitsu weapon. The series was further censored in Britain to edit out the use of the *numchukka,* a weapon comprising two short, hand-held sticks connected by a chain whose appearance in any film had been subject to censorship by the British Board of Film Classification (the film industry's censorship body since the late 1970s), following an incident in which a child had injured himself when playing with one.

A range of adult figures was developed, such as the motherly television journalist, April O'Neil, and the fatherly teacher, Master Splinter. It was in this guise that the Turtles were commercially exploited through merchandising agreements with Playmates Toys Inc. and other companies to produce a range of Turtles toys, clothing, bedding, food products and so forth.

This success further interacted with negotiations for the Turtles to appear in theatrical forms, with actors in costume, especially in the live performance of a Turtles pop record that topped the music charts in America, Britain, and Australia. Related to this, the Turtles appeared in two live-action films as "animatronic" figures (actors in costume again, but this time with electronic control of facial and skin features) in a process developed by The Muppets Company. The first film was released in 1989 in America, but its release in Britain was delayed until Christmas of 1990. It became the most profitable independent film at that time, co-produced by Golden Harvest (a Hong Kong studio associated with martial arts kung-fu films, most famously those featuring Bruce Lee) and a leading American independent company, New Line.

What this account demonstrates is that the Turtles were never singular. For the earliest adult readers of the comic strip, they were political satires; for the later youth readership of comic magazines, they were generic superheroes in a parodic spin on familiar figures of vengeance like Batman; for the final audiences of children, they were playful cartoon figures of fun. Yet the economy of transformation, like the chronology, is not even. At the same time as children were watching the television series and buying Hero soft toys in the supermarkets, they also were taken to see the Ninja film and bought the Ninja games, with parents left to account for the discrepancies.

Cumulatively, then, the Turtles were considerable intertextual figures, not uniform, available in distinctive styles across a wide range of media to overlapping audience groups. This meant that any one form targeted at a particular audience nonetheless carried vestiges, and thereby associations, of the complex range of the additional meanings of others. Any individual person meeting a Turtle in one of the variety of forms and contexts would respond in relation to the accrued meanings from earlier and wider experiences.

This explains how the Turtles could become the extensive popular phenomenon they were. The Turtles had potentially multivalent combinations of meanings for their notionally "mass" audience of many different identities. To find favour with the large numbers of people within as many of the sociological categories of age, class, gender, and ethnicity as they did, many people of many ages had to feel some large measures of investment in the Turtles phenomenon to watch, read, talk about, and buy their multifarious paraphernalia. All this on a global scale; not only in the wealthy industrial countries but in the Third World, too.[5]

TURTLES FOR CHILDREN

The Turtles were potentially meaningful for large numbers of people, then. But why were they popular with children? As generic superheroes, they were familiar fictional figures to children. There is a sense, also, in which they were institutionally familiar too, for the television cartoon series was scheduled in a slot in the BBC children's programming, which regularly featured 1980s superheroes like He-Man, Masters of the Universe, Thundercats, and Transformers in American and Japanese cartoon

series. These cartoon series were themselves developments of 1930s' superheroes like Superman, Batman, Spiderman, Wonderwoman, and other
creations of Marvel Comics, who also appeared in live-action film serials
and television series from the 1950s to the 1970s, and in cartoon series
from the 1980s. Expensive film blockbusters were made featuring Spider-
Man in the 1970s and Batman in the 1990s, the latter especially familiar
to children at the time of the Turtles. The familiarity of the superhero tradition thus provided a cultural and institutional context for the reception
of the Turtles.

However, the narrative structures of the episodic television series
owed more to what Ellen Seiter calls the "Let's get out of here!" adventure formula common to otherwise generically different cartoon series
like *Scooby Doo* and family films like *Ghostbusters*.[6] The Turtles were
familiar generic heroes operating in untypical yet equally familiar narrative fictions. Variation in repetition is crucial for supra-popularity. A
combination of familiar features with novelty bears out Steve Neale's
idea of how film genres remake themselves for new generations of audiences through patterns of similarity and difference.[7]

The absurd, parodic nature of the Turtles added novelty to the superhero genre. The Turtles were named after Renaissance artists Leonardo,
Donatello, Raphael, and Michaelangelo, yet spoke in a polyglot mixture
of sub-cultural and ethnic teenage street argot ("Party on dudes," "Radical," "Get a grip," "What a bummer") and postmodern poesy ("Holy
guacomole!" rather than the "Holy Catfish!" of Batman's Robin, and
"Mondo bizarro" rather than the laconic "Strange" of Superman). Some
occasional villains also evoked classical figures like Medusa, whose reptilian head of hair was commented upon reflexively: "Pity her hair-
dresser." Such post-modern play with names and language across high
art and street cultures provided different linguistic and rhythmic pleasures across age ranges and sub-cultures of audiences.

What the Turtles represented to children, however, can be seen as
much more substantial in connections to child identities. Take each of the
terms in their full title. The Turtles are only loosely "Teenage" in their
street language. In their group relations, they are more like children.
Their sibling rivalry and bickering is observed by a long-suffering par-
ent/teacher figure, Splinter. They can act with foolhardy cocksureness
one moment and irrational fear of the unknown at the next. Similarly,
they reason with strategic thinking on occasions yet with naive innocence at other times. As fantasy figures, then, they are sur-generational,
slipping in and out of emotional and behavioural characteristics of all

age groups. For younger age groups, they also promise both the difference and status in becoming a teenager along with the security of familiar behaviour in the childlike hopes and fears of Turtles who are therefore only notionally Teenage.

The Turtles are also "Mutant," a concept connoting not only mutation but also wider metamorphosis. Children at play adapt toys for the purposes of fantasy exploration and experiment.[8] Toy manufacturers recognise this and the 1980s' Transformer toys are only the most explicit incarnation of multi-function play toys. The Turtles are mutants, reptilian in shape but human in size and anthropomorphic in all other ways. Often in stories, their size is subject to change by villainy and they are either shrunk or placed in a giant environment. Ideas of mutation, transformation, and metamorphosis, then, operate as metaphors for the child's own physical growth, muturation and malleability, a point noted by Marsha Kinder.[9]

Transformation also operates as a metaphor for emotional and aspirational child relations to maturational development. Growing up is both an ideal and an anxiety for children, wanting to be like older others and yet fearing the loss of their own childhood identity. The Turtles are commonly placed in narrative situations that rehearse dramas of maturation. Their mentor, Splinter, demands caution and wisdom in their actions yet is often obliged to tolerate the opposite. He requires the difficult adoption of individual responsibility in collective action. Plots are often pretexts for testing out action within this moral framework and always climax with debates over learning. More than metaphors for physical maturation, therefore, Turtle stories are commonly—for children—cultural and psychic dramas of growing up.

Importantly, other teenage and adult figures are seen as subject to the same process of change. Splinter is a ninjitsu teacher sent in disgrace from Japan to America. Residing in the same sewer and caught in the same waste (called "mutating gell" in the cartoon series) as the Turtles, he mutates from human to rat. Shredder, the major antagonist of the Turtles' world, mutates two youths, Bebop and Rock Steady. And Krang, the "alien dude from Dimension X," is a brain-like shape lodged in the stomach space of a robot after his own body is taken as a punishment for extra-terrestrial war crimes. This range of generational body-changing operates as exemplars of maturation throughout the generations, functioning to caution children that maturational matters are universal and not just to do with growing up into adulthood.

Finally, mutation and transformation also is connected to role-play and disguise. A feature of superheroes is their dual role: "ordinary" Clark Kent transforms into Superman, and wealthy Bruce Wayne dons the guise of Batman. The ordinary identity is submerged into a fantasy of heroic action as the ego becomes an ego-ideal. Exceptionally, the Turtles can mutate at will into figures able to deal superheroically in tight corners with villainy. But this is not consistent with their central identity as figures whose drama is precisely that they cannot change who they are: They cannot go back to the real turtles of their origin and cannot be publicly accepted because of their scary appearance. Unlike Bruce Wayne, the Turtles live in poverty; unlike Clark Kent, they cannot transform themselves and adopt a more publicly acceptable persona. The Turtles can transform themselves, however, but only through disguise. They wear human clothing to disguise their appearance so they can walk unrecognised without causing alarm among a human world they wish to be a part of. This scenario taps into the Peter Pan complex of fear of maturation but also the importance of role-play for children, experimenting and "trying out for size" the different social roles observed around them.

Mutation also connects with the last term in their title. The Turtles are mutant reptiles—alongside insects, the members of the animal kingdom most despised in European and Asian cultures. Unlike crocodiles (*Peter Pan*), snakes, or spiders (*The Jungle Book*—though the spider Anansi's heroism spider in Afro-Caribbean cultures makes me cautious to universalise this principle), turtles may be exceptions to this rule. The henchmen to villain Shredder, Bebop and Rock Steady, are ugly mutant rhinocerous and wart-hog. The heroic Turtles are more likely associated with domestic pets; the slow motion of the tortoise (as in the story of the Tortoise and the Hare) makes an identification figure as improbable as the Turtles. These associations make the Turtles available as unlikely, but nonetheless novel, heroes of a children's fiction.

However, the Turtles' appearance is considered ugly by new arrivals to the fiction. Even April O'Neill, "ace reporter" for Channel Six News, who later functions as human friend and go-between for the Turtles, screams on their first appearance when they rescue her from street muggers. The general public fears them and denies their knight errant actions because of their alien appearance. What children look like is as important to their own sense of personal identity as it is to even the least style-conscious of adults. Yet children's anxieties are commonly unacknowledged by adults, even those in close relationship, such as parents and siblings.

The Turtles' Ugly Duckling scenario is therefore traditional and significant to child anxieties over size, physical development and the vagaries of individual appearance. Even more, in contemporary consumer cultures—where a premium is placed upon dress fashion and other modes of style, especially amongst child groups—what you look like can be regarded as a statement of what you are.

Children share similar anxieties about their good intentions being misunderstood; often what seems by their logic and choices to be reasonable action, is perceived by significant adults as bothersome misbehaviour, or stupidity. In such common conditions of childhood, being a child can in itself be experienced as socially deviant.

These symbolic congruences between the drama of the Turtles and the conditions of childhood—between the unstable child identity and social relations of the Turtles and their audience—confirm a more general relation between them. Children and Turtles alike are equally constituted on the margins of social power. The Turtles function as surrogate children, exploring, through fantasy, conditions that children experience in social relations with notable others around them such as parents, relatives, peers and teachers. Like the Turtles, children are subject to regulation by adults. The Turtles function as a peer group of siblings/friends. In relation to the Turtles, Splinter operates as good father/teacher, April as good mother, Shredder as bad father, Bebop and Rock Steady as school bullies. The main social group of "significant others" for both children and Turtles is the nurturing family in an unpredictable wider environment.

Also, like the Turtles, children can experience their conditions at times as beleaguered and constrained. The Turtles' underground home, remote from the everyday routines of a public going about their routine lives above them, pictures the psychic state of childhood when children are marginalised (as most children are) from adult spheres of operation and understandings of matters which nonetheless bear on their lives. Moreover, the state of anxiety in which the Turtles live—dependent on significant others, under imminent attack from villainy, and maligned by a generally hostile world—powerfully evokes the psychic state of a child dependency in ceding control to adult figures of authority. When the Turtles burst out of these confines to overcome villainy, they live out a fantasy of social power on behalf of—and thereby appealing to—the secret desires of children to undermine comparably oppressive parenting and adult regulation.

The Turtles were popular with children because in significant ways they could be perceived by them as living out, in fantasy, the social and psychic conditions of childhood, what being a child "feels" like. Through the mechanisms of fantasy, the Turtles tested out and resolved problems in the social relations and situations of childhood recognisable to children. It is in this sense that "Turtle Power" had force with children.

I don't mean to suggest that children were conscious of any of this, nor that the Turtles necessarily positioned a child audience as child subjects alone. But I do want to suggest that to understand the popularity of the Turtles among children requires attention to the general and particular characteristics of their popularity, to those social and psychic congruences at the level of representation and form that relate to social and generational experience and identity.

TURTLES FOR ELITES

How can this attempt to account for the popularity of the Turtles be related to understandings of the moral panic over them? Earlier, I sought to describe how the BBC's action over the Turtles is best seen as part of a much wider elite anxiety not only around the Turtles but concerning popular culture in general. Here, I want to examine adult anxiety over the Turtles as a case study of long-standing cultural attitudes that underpin such anxiety.

When the BBC sought to adjust a cultural product to mollify organised detractors, it typified the elite treatment of popular cultural phenomena in Britain. Though the BBC positioned itself at a distance from the wilder expressions of moralist disapproval, it nonetheless shared assumptions that the popular needs policing every bit as much as the serious needs promoting, and that the popular choices of the young require particularly alert forms of policing. Anna Home, the BBC's Head of Children's Programming at the time, was clear that the Turtles did not represent the best programming possible for children ("the best" was defined as home-produced drama), but was justifiable in terms of a mixed programming diet. Interestingly, Home's concerns centred on the issue of aesthetic quality and children's culture rather than concerns about copycat behaviour or commodification that dominated the moral panic.[10]

MODERNITY, CONSUMERISM AND AMERICANISATION

The elite agenda on popular culture is a complex of moral, social, and cultural fears. Nowhere is this better exposed than in attitudes to children's popular culture. These attitudes are deeply rooted and longstanding among British elite groups. In order to put them into perspective, they need to be understood as historical.

Elite anxieties about popular culture have their origin in the moment of modernity, the troubled moment associated with the massive social changes wrought by industrial manufacture, urbanisation and mass communications during the late nineteenth century.[11] That they are cultural attitudes bound up with the interests of elite groups is revealed by contrasting them with the attitudes and practises of non-elite groups who make their choices more centrally from amongst popular cultures and without the same anxiety. These are therefore also social assumptions, dividing and affirming subjective identities in conflicting social classes.

Popular culture is a product of modernity. Mass manufacture provided for a system of cheap reproduction: Where before a cultural product was an individual item, industrialisation enabled rapid replication and troubled the previous distinction between (valued) art and (devalued) craft; where before access to a cultural product was limited by its singularity and rarity, mass distribution meant common availability in a shorter time scale; where before a cultural product was rare enough to be an event in itself, the ubiquity of mass production required new systems of promotion to alert public attention to the latest in the multiple chain of product, hence, advertising; Finally, where before rarity guaranteed status, modernity equalised value and access, and everything mass produced became, at least notionally, available to all.

Modernity, then, promised a profound democracy; at the same time, however, it challenged powerful and strongly held views among elite groups about the value of art as rare and singular. Extension, wider availability, and access troubled the connections between elite values and elite controls. In the same way that modernity threatened traditional groups, forms, and ideas of elite power, popular cultures appeared to challenge those same groups, forms, and ideas of elite culture. The ways in which the challenge of modernity was embraced in the very forms of popular culture in America was particularly striking but was also to be observed on the continent in ways that initially were resisted in Britain. The skyscrapers of New York and Chicago championed modern styles like Art Deco that were rejected by the traditional tastes of British elites. Hollywood favoured a cinema of spectacle that was actively resisted by groups in Britain who preferred the challenge to British Cinema posed by the documentary realism of John Grierson[12]; Europe produced modernist art movements like surrealism and impressionism that were resisted in Britain until after World War II.

Popular culture is also a feature of consumerism, the emphasis on consumption rather than manufacture as an index of economic activity.[13] New cultural industries of cinema, broadcasting, comics, and magazine publications grew in intimate connection with other leisure activities, the fashion houses, cosmetics industries, and domestic cultures that characterised the social order of twentieth-century modernity. In 1920s and 1930s America, WASP (White Anglo-Saxon Protestant) outrage over a Hollywood cinema associated with working-class and migrant cultures led to censorship controls. The ostensible objections to moral offence clouded the mix of cultural anxiety over the conspicuous consumption of stars off-screen and socio-political suspicion of representations of social mobility on-screen.

In particular, in this period of Latin lovers and matinée idols, Hollywood was seen as a site of cultural change and moral challenge over the new woman of modernity.[14] Socially, the modern woman was newly visible on the streets and in the workplace, and available for unchaperoned relationships regardless of age and social class. Culturally, her independence was marked by a new relation to consumer culture and her representation on cinema screen and in the pages of new women's magazines. The body of the "American Woman" came to represent social and cultural change.

In England, elite fears about social invisibility and mobility were displaced less onto the body of the woman (though there is a case to answer here, too) and more onto the figure of the child and youth. Mass Observation[15] photographs of working-class children responding to a Western film, taken by cameras hidden under the cinema screen, testify to the social fears of Hollywood's popular culture in the same period. The recurrence of such fears has been the primary factor in subsequent censorship legislation throughout this century. Just two famous examples make this point: In the immediate post-war period, there was legislation to prohibit the import of horror comics—popular with GIs stationed in Britain during the war—and in the 1970s, campaigns against video nasties (exploitation horror films) led to legal restrictions on the burgeoning video outlets. In both instances, as Martin Barker argues, the rising moral panic centred on the effects of representations of violence on the young.[16]

The fear of popular culture and its effects has been particularly powerful in Britain because of the association of the popular with American culture, and fears of Americanisation as a form of cultural colonisation of British culture. Since the rise of Hollywood film in the 1920s, American popular cultural forms have been massively popular with British audiences and elite resistance in Britain to American popular culture has been articulated in a number of ways, from moral panics over particular films or comics to a range of regulatory controls and agencies such as the British Board of Film Censors. The public service foundation of the BBC in the 1920s was both a method of political control over the new broadcast technology and an ideology of national cultural value. Debate over the provision of a commercial channel with Independent Television in the 1950s saw fears of commercialisation (associated with American broadcasting's sponsorship system) answered by regulatory systems in favour of cultural protectionism in a mixed broadcasting economy. British cinema has been historically associated with middle-class values, even down to the famous Home Counties' accents, and the British film industry has never been able consistently to compete with American popular cinema. Equally, forms of popular music have historically been associated with American voices and accents such as (southern white) country-and-western, and (black) blues and jazz.[17]

The complex association of modernity, consumerism, and Americanisation with popular culture has taken particular shape and force this century in Britain. In all this, the sign of the child has been central: Over the sign of the child as the social group most in need of cultural protection, popular culture has been vilified as morally culpable, reflecting elite fears of cultural degeneracy through foreign incursion.

REALISM, PARODY AND THE BAROQUE

It is not only the relative status and modern history of popular culture that implicitly challenges elite attitudes to art and value. It is also in the representations and aesthetic forms of popular cultures that relations with their audiences are constructed. These tend also to be representations and forms that challenge a certain aesthetic as the standard by which not just art for children but all art is judged. The aesthetic deemed appropriate to the children's classic novel is even narrower, and one that combines a bowdlerised romance tradition with a particular form of social realism.

The dominant mode of romance for children is generically the fairy tale, nursery rhyme, and folk fable. The symbolic and mythic qualities of these traditional forms have been sustained even as retelling over time has censored their more baroque qualities of death and cruelty: Red Riding Hood's grandmother may still be eaten by the Wolf but the Woodsman no longer cuts open its body to release her; the Three Blind Mice now have their tails, rather than their throats, cut by the carving knife; the exploits of Disney's Pinocchio—though famously scary enough for most children—are as nothing to the truly terrifying metamorphoses of Collodi's literary original.

In contrast to the folk tradition, the dominant mode of literary fiction for children, the classic children's novel, is social realism, from the English National Curriculum's classics of *The Secret Garden, The Railway Children,* and *Black Beauty* to the modern fictions of Anne Fine. Interestingly, exceptions to this pattern such as the works of Roald Dahl have equally been subject to debate over their "suitability." The Turtles invoke, even more explicitly, alternative and contrary aesthetics to romance and realism. Though George H. Lewis is correct in locating the Turtles within an American tradition of heroic figures of romance,[18] the aesthetic modes within which I prefer to locate the Turtles are expressionism and melodrama.

The original Turtles strip depicted a dystopian city of nightmare, a frenzied design of line and movement spilling from each frame. The expressionist vision was retained in the first film of the series through a low key *noir* lighting style and grainy flashbacks. Much of the action took place in the sewers or on the streets at night. This is not the case so much with the softened television series for children, but enough of the original baroque conception survives in the delineation of setting and characters for traces of the original sensibility to remain. Krang, in particular, a manic face barking crazy orders from a stomach, is a surreal presence. Shredder's mask and the animal heads of his henchman are less visually unsettling but still retain a Gothic charge. Where the expressionist vision remains most, however, is in the background landscapes of slum tenements, car lots, and waste ground, which situate the romance dramas. Minor characters people the settings appropriately: Muggers and street vagrants constitute the lumpenproletariat of criminals and victims on the streets of the modern city, while in the high-rise blocks the nouveau riche and media professionals live out an ordered life style. If the scenes were set at night, as they largely are in the films, this would be the Gotham City of the reincarnated Batman in the graphic Dark Knight novels.[19]

The expressionist aesthetic imagines a fearful and irrational social world through visual styles. Characteristically, the style exaggerates and distorts natural shapes, expressing as abnormal and therefore open to change, a world conventionally offered as normal and unchangeable.

The political challenges of the expresionist aesthetic can disturb any conservative tendencies of romance and realism; the Gothic aesthetic relates to expressionism but its representations tend to darker realms of imagining where psychic disturbance expresses a wider social and political disturbance.

If the visual stylistics of the Turtles' world relates to an expressionist—even Gothic—aesthetic, the dramatic structures of their fictions come from melodrama. The underlying tragic irony of the Turtles is that, neither animal nor human, they have no subject by themselves against which to measure their futures. At a point in almost every story, on occasions at the climax, one or other Turtle will be alone—either through incarceration or voluntary exile—in existential musing over a troubled identity. These are always painful moments both for the Turtle and the audience, moments of melodrama's emotional excess of "tears and fears."[20] This is a product of the social position of the Turtles too, classic innocents of melodrama's struggle between the powerful and the powerless.

The Turtles' call to action, to put right the wrongs suffered by the innocent at the hands of villains, can therefore be understood as dramas of displacement, wherein their own unresolved psychic needs are played out in resolution for others. The Turtles become figures of tragedy, able to act only for others, never for self. As figures of melodrama and expressionism, the Turtles have a wide range of cultural antecedents from both "high" and "low" arts on which to draw: nineteenth-century melodrama theatre, silent cinema, women's romance fiction, French and German expressionism, Theatre of the Absurd, gothic melodrama, surrealism, the horror film, and so on. The eclectic range enables the Turtles not only to reference widely but also to provide new combinations in ways that can connect to new generations of audience and new social conditions.

The Turtles operate fantastically, parodically, in what is, nonetheless, a recognisably social world. Their fictional form is best described as baroque, a form of drama whose social reference is coded through an ornate and over-embellished *dramatis personae,* iconography, and fictional world. It is a mode of storytelling familiar in British culture through the Gothic novel and theatre, but a mode largely separated from legitimated cultures around the child.

This is not the case in America, where there is a greater cultural connection to variant aesthetics like the baroque. This is, in part, a product of America's history as a migrant nation, founding its moment of modernity in a populist fusion of cultural traditions from many national cultures. It is also a related product of cultural forms adapted to the new mass entertainments and communications technologies of the period at the turn of the century, cultural forms that expressed the interests of a plurality of social minorities whose tragic stories of displacement and oppression dramatised the conditions that new immigrant communities met in the WASP host nation.

This means that there is a far greater historical tolerance of the baroque in American cultures than in Britain. The tolerance extends to children's culture, too, which is less divisible from adult cultures. It is interesting, as David Pirie has noted, that the Hammer horror films of the 1950s, which were critically condemned for their baroque qualities at the time, were not initially considered adult fare in America where they were programmed as matinée material for children before their popularity grew.[21]

THE CASE OF THE TURTLES

> In order for something to become a big fad, it has to make mothers and
> fathers feel a little disgusted and a little uncomfortable.
> (Unattributed "expert," *TV Hits* no. 25, September 1990.)

The Case of the Turtles opens up questions about the cultural choices children make for themselves, from within the wide range potentially available to them, as distinct from those choices made for them by responsible adults like parents and regulators whose choices tend to be from within a far narrower aesthetic range. It also prompts questions about the role of popular cultures in children's lives and the organised adult elite resistances to moments of supra-popularity.

In order to account for their popularity among children, I have sought to show how the Turtles offer fantasy fiction that represents in complex ways an experience of childhood and maturation from a point of view with which children and significant others can identify. In the process, it becomes clear that much of the meaning of the Turtles reworks themes and concerns of elite-sanctioned classic children's fiction and literature. Nonetheless, the Turtles attracted moral panic: They were policed and controlled in ways that echo a typical and repeated pattern of elite cultural reception of popular cultural phenomena in Britain throughout this century.

A large part of that reaction needs to be seen as knee-jerk, a response not to the Turtles or any other particular example of the popular, but to the status and visibility of popular culture itself, its connection to modernity, consumerism, and Americanisation, and in relation to a British elite resistance to that complex.

But a substantial part of any resistance to the popular is a resistance to the far wider range of aesthetics and cultural forms, which is part of its common language. Rather than a narrow aesthetic, popular culture is extensive and substantial. In place of the restricted language of elite aesthetic choices and its related minority audiences, popular culture has a multi-vocal address that can nevertheless appeal to and address specific audiences.

There is a case to argue that the Turtles were popular with children for the same reasons that adults rejected them, but the relation is not transparently generational, nor necessarily causal. My claim would be that the Turtles spoke to children in ways that could not be heard or understood by dominant lobbies among elite social groups. The Turtles spoke to their audiences about matters that concerned them. In particular, they spoke powerfully to children who embraced their characters and fictions. It is in the nature of popular culture to construct visions that speak to many groups on the social margins at a particular moment. Some popular phenomena transcend their moment and even return in modernised guises for subsequent recycling. It is difficult to predict whether the Turtles will do that. What is more certain is that the commercial imperatives behind the production of popular culture will continue to provide a rich harvest from amongst which other supra-popular phenomena will emerge to speak for their social moments just as powerfully. The meaning of Turtle Power lies in the meanings of Popular Culture.

NOTES

1. For more extensive accounts of the Turtles, see John Langer, "Folk Devils in a Half-Shell," *Melbourne Report,* 1991 pp. 11–12, and David Lusted, "Turtle Power, Turtle Panic," *Monthly Film Bulletin* vol. 57, December 1990, pp. 345–47. On moral panics, see Stan Cohen, *Folk Devils and Moral Panics,* 1980.

2. Kathryn Castle, *Britannia's Children,* 1996, examines representations of empire in school text books.

3. See George Perry and Alan Aldridge, *The Penguin Book of Comics,* 1971.

4. See George Perry and Gerald Peary, *The American Animated Cartoon,* 1980.

5. On the global popularity of the Turtles, see Dermot Purgavie, "Cowabunga! We've all Turned Turtle," *You Magazine: Mail on Sunday,* 24 June 1990, pp. 38–43.

6. Ellen Seiter, *Sold Separately: Parents and Children in Consumer Culture,* 1995. See also Brian Dutton-Smith, *Toys as Culture,* 1986, for another valuable analysis of children and consumer culture.

7. Steve Neale, *Genre,* 1980.

8. On children and play, see Vivian Gussin Paley, *Boys and Girls: Super-heroes in the Doll Corner,* 1984. On the gender differences of children at play, see Carolyn Steadman, et al., *Language, Gender and Childhood,* 1985.

9. Marsha Kinder, *Playing with Power in Movies, Television and Video Games: From Muppet Babies to Teenage Mutant Ninja Turtles,* 1991.

10. Anna Home, interviewed in "Toys on Television," *Public Eye* series, transmitted BBC 2 Television, 14 December 1990. Much recent research has queried the generally suspicious relation between children and television culture. See Patricia Palmer, *The Lively Audience: A Study of Children Around the Television Set,* 1986; Robert Hodge and David Tripp, *Children and Television: A Semiotic Approach,* 1986; Cary Bazalgette and David Buckingham, eds., *In Front of the Children: Screen Entertainment and Young Audiences,* 1995.

11. Key texts on modernity and popular culture are Roland Marchand, *Advertising the American Dream: Making Way for Modernity 1920–1940,* 1985, and Barbara Ehrenreich, *The Hearts of Men: American Dreams and the Flight from Commitment,* 1983.

12. Julian Petley, "The Lost Continent," in Charles Barr, *All Our Yesterdays: 90 Years of British Cinema,* 1986: 98–119.

13. Colin Campbell, *The Romantic Ethic and the Spirit of Modern Consumerism,* 1987. See also Stuart Ewen, *Captains of Consciousness: Advertising and the Roots of Consumer Consciousness,* 1976.

14. Martin Pumphrey, "The Flapper, the Housewife and the Making of Modernity," *Cultural Studies,* Vol. 1, 2 May 1987, pp. 179–95. See also Mica Nava, "Consumerism and Contradictions," in *Changing Cultures: Feminism, Youth and Consumerism,* 1992.

15. Mass Observation was a social reporting organisation set up by the anthropologist Tom Harrison and the journalist Charles Madge in 1936. John Stevenson comments: "[Mass Observation] recruited observers to report on almost every aspect of daily life and social behaviour . . . Although a great deal of material was rather unsystematically collected, Mass Observation's studies of such things as drinking habits in *The Pub and the People,* published in 1943, added another dimension to social investigation , one which was co-opted by the government during the Second World War as a means of gauging civilian morale" (John Stevenson, *British Society 1914–1945,* 1984, p. 321).

16. Martin Barker, *A Haunt of Fears: The Strange History of the British Horror Comics Campaign,* 1984. See also Martin Barker, ed., *The Video Nasties: Freedom and Censorship in the Media,* 1984.

17. Dick Hebdige, "Towards a Cartography of Taste," in *Hiding in the Light,* 1988.

18. George H. Lewis, "From Common Dullness to Fleeting Wonder: The Manipulation of Cultural Meaning in the Teenage Mutant Ninja Turtles Saga," *Journal of Popular Culture,* Vol. 25:2, 1991, pp. 31–43.

19. Robert Pearson and William Uricchio, eds., *The Many Lives of the Batman: Critical Approaches to a Superhero and his Media,* 1991.

20. Christine Gledhill, *Home is Where the Heart Is: Studies in Melodrama and the Woman's Film,* 1987.

21. David Pirie, *A Heritage of Horror,* 1973.

BIBLIOGRAPHY

Barker, Martin. *A Haunt of Fears: The Strange History of the British Horror Comics Campaign.* London: Pluto, 1984.

Barker, Martin, ed. *The Video Nasties: Freedom and Censorship in the Movies.* London: Pluto, 1984.

Bazalgette, Cary and Buckingham, David, eds. *In Front of the Children: Screen Entertainment and Young Audiences.* London: British Film Institute, 1995.

Campbell, Colin. *The Romantic Ethic and the Spirit of Modern Consumerism.* Oxford: Basil Blackwell, 1987.

Castle, Kathryn. *Britannia's Children.* Manchester: Manchester University Press, 1996.

Cohen, Stan. *Folk Devils and Moral Panics.* Oxford: Martin Robertson, 1980.

Ehrenreich, Barbara. *The Hearts of Men: American Dreams and the Flight from Commitment.* London: Pluto, 1983.

Ewen, Stuart. *Captains of Consciousness: Advertising and the Roots of Consumer Consciousness.* New York: McGraw Hill, 1976.

Gledhill, Christine. *Home Is Where the Heart Is: Studies in Melodrama and the Women's Film.* London: British Film Institute, 1987.

Hebdige, Dick. *Hiding in the Light: On Images and Things.* London: Routledge, 1988.

Hodge, Robert and Tripp, David. *Children and Television: A Semiotic Approach.* Palo Alto: University of Stanford Press, 1986.

Kinder, Marsha. *Playing with Power in Movies, Television and Video Games: From Muppet Babies to Teenage Mutant Ninja Turtles.* Berkeley: University of California Press, 1991.

Lewis, George H., "From Common Dullness to Fleeting Wonder: The Manipulation of Cultural Meaning in the Teenage Mutant Ninja Turtles Saga," *Journal of Popular Culture.* Vol. 25: 2 (1991): 31–43.

Lusted, David. "Turtle Power, Turtle Panic," *Monthly Film Bulletin.* Vol. 57 no. 683 (1990): 345–347.

Marchand, Roland. *Advertising the American Dream: Making Way for Modernity.* Berkeley: University of California Press, 1985.

Nava, Mica. *Changing Cultures: Feminism, Youth and Consumerism.* London: Sage, 1992.

Neal, Steve. *Genre.* London: British Film Institute, 1980.

Paley, Vivian Gussin. *Boys and Girls: Superheroes in the Doll Corner.* Chicago: University of Chicago Press, 1984.

Palmer, Patricia. *The Lively Audience: A Study of Children Around the Television Set.* London: Allen and Unwin, 1986.

Pearson, R. and Uricchio, W., eds. *The Many Lives of Batman.* New York: Routledge, 1991.

Perry, George and Aldridge, Alan. *The Penguin Book of Comics.* Harmondsworth: Penguin, 1971.

Peary, D. and Peary, G., eds. *The American Animated Cartoon.* New York: Dutton, 1980.

Petley, Julian. "The Lost Continent," in *All Our Yesterdays: 90 Years of British Cinema,* ed. Charles Barr. London: British Film Institute, 1986: 98–119.

Pirie, David. *A Heritage of Horror.* London: Gordon Fraser, 1973.

Pumphrey, Martin. "The Flapper, the Housewife and the Making of Modernity," *Cultural Studies* Vol. 1: 2 (1987): 179–195.

Seiter, Ellen. *Sold Separately: Parents and Children in Consumer Culture.* New Brunswick, N.J.: Rutgers University Press, 1995.

Sutton-Smith, Brian. *Toys as Culture.* New York: Gardner, 1986.

Peter Pan
Flawed or Fledgling "Hero"?

CHRIS ROUTH

Although most adults and children are familiar with the characters from *Peter Pan*, if not with the essence of the story, relatively few will have read J. M. Barrie's original texts. The history of the story of *Peter Pan* is complex. It evolved out of games played with the Llewelyn Davies boys, first appearing as part of a novel (*The Little White Bird*, 1902) intended for adults, and later expanded into a play (*Peter Pan or The Boy Who Would Not Grow Up*, 1904), which was repeatedly revised by Barrie before its publication twenty-four years after the first performance. The relevant chapters from *The Little White Bird* were published separately in 1906 as *Peter Pan in Kensington Gardens*, with illustrations by Arthur Rackham. The story of the play, *Peter and Wendy*, followed in 1911. Other retellings appeared before and after Barrie's novel, which has now been published in many languages around the world.

Barrie also wrote a film scenario (1920), "based on the play and the book, but imagined and written expressly for the silent screen" (Green 1954, p. 164); however, to Barrie's disappointment, none of it was used for the first screen version (Paramount, 1924). When Walt Disney's animated version of *Peter Pan* was released nearly thirty years later in 1953, Hodder and Stoughton, who at that time held the exclusive rights to Barrie's text, published at least five different Disney editions of the story the same year, and innumerable versions have followed since. The appearance of Disney's film on video in 1992 coincided with a modern day live-action sequel, *Hook*, which also spawned a number of associated texts.[1]

There are regular revivals of the play, and *Peter Pan* continues to inspire new stories in the form of books, computer software, and a cartoon series for children's television with associated publications.² Intertextual references made by contemporary authors and illustrators confirm that the story has been absorbed into popular culture.³ Moreover, the fact that Peter Pan has been adopted as a trade name for a range of children's toys provides the source of inspiration for a British library supplier's decorated furniture for children's book-corners and libraries, and is used as a descriptor in the field of psychology, underlines the enduring appeal and significance of the story for children and adults alike. For children, perhaps, the most appealing elements are the possibility of a magical place where their own fantastic adventures might come true and the alluring character of Peter Pan himself. In Disney's version, John and Michael believe Peter Pan is a real person and make him the "hero" of their games even before he appears. Adults, on the other hand, no longer have access to this "world of childhood imagination, play and dream"; for them the immortal boy on an island represents "the irrecoverable power and autonomy of childhood play" (Hollindale 1993, pp. 158, 171).

Considered in its historical context, *Peter Pan* can be regarded as a progeny of Victorian adventure stories, in which, according to Kevin Carpenter (1986), young readers were often invited to:

> willingly suspend their disbelief and simply to accept their world of adventure as dream-world where games are played according to rules that did not obtain to the real world. (Carpenter 1986, n.p.)

Carpenter's survey of English adventure fiction to 1910, introduces a selection of stories about boyhood heroes that would have been exciting the imaginations of young readers around the turn of the century and that in some cases, as we will see, had an acknowledged influence on Barrie's own writing. Carpenter's discussion of *Treasure Island,* for example, highlights Stevenson's imaginative treatment of the confrontation scene between Jim and his captors—a scene, says Carpenter, "found in most boys' pirate yarns." Barrie uses the same convention in *Peter Pan* when Peter fights Captain Hook for the last time; and it is the intention of this chapter to explore aspects of Peter's heroism, with particular reference to illustrations of the confrontation scene in the context of the association of "man" with "the sword."⁴

Earlier in the novel, Wendy is watching over Peter and the Lost Boys while they doze after their midday meal. She senses approaching danger, but rather than rousing the children she stands over them "to let them have their sleep out" (*Peter Pan*, Viking Kestrel 1988, hereafter referred to as the novel, p. 98). In contrast to Wendy's passivity, Peter, the "hero," springs into action:

> It was well for those boys then that there was one amongst them who could sniff danger even in his sleep. Peter sprang erect, as wide wake at once as a dog, and with one warning cry he roused the others (the novel, p. 98).

In a discussion about violence as a learnt activity, Tony Eardley (1985) quotes Vic Seidler's explanation of how violence becomes encoded into boys' bodily stances:

> As boys we have to be constantly on the alert to either confront or avoid physical violence. We have to be ready to defend ourselves. We are constantly on our guard (p. 98).

While Jan Ormerod's portrait of Peter (Viking Kestrel, 1988), with legs akimbo and brandishing a wooden sword, captures this sense of physical alertness, it is also an allusion to Barrie's photographic records of games played with the Davies boys, which acknowledges the origins of *Peter Pan* and confirms that Peter's activities belong to the realm of imaginative play.

In fact, in 1901 Barrie privately published a book of photographs taken while playing with the Davies boys during a summer holiday at Black Lake "with a title and chapter headings reminiscent of previous great adventure stories."[5] Significantly, Robert Louis Stevenson (whose influence on Barrie was declared by the words "Dear Robert Louis Stevenson," which appeared on a drop-curtain sampler designed for an early production of the play) refers to one such adventure story, *Robinson Crusoe*, in an essay called "Child's play" in *Virginibus Puerisque* (first published in 1881):

> Crusoe was always at makeshifts and had, in so many words, to *play* at a great variety of professions; and then the book is all about tools, and there is nothing that delights a child so much. (Stevenson 1946, p. 132)

Stevenson goes on to explain how imaginative play contributes to a child's developing understanding of the world around him:

He is at the experimental stage; he is not sure how one would feel in certain circumstances; to make sure, he must come as near trying it as his
means permit. And so here is young heroism with a wooden sword, and
mothers practise their kind vocation over a bit of jointed stick. (ibid.)

The last sentence seems to provide a perfect metaphor for the "games" of
Neverland.

Both the play and the novel show Peter's "life" as a series of make-
believe adventure "games" in which he always takes the role of leader
and hero and which are quickly (if not heartlessly) forgotten. For Peter,
Neverland is a refuge from the real world and a guarantee that he can retain *puer aeternus*. His fear of mortal life is most poignantly revealed
when he seeks reassurance from Wendy that his role of father is only
"make-believe"/ "pretend" (the novel, p. 123/ *Peter Pan,* Hodder and
Stoughton, hereafter referred to as the play, p. 103). Kathleen Blake
(1977) refers to Peter as "a kind of embodiment of the play spirit, playing
at islands" (p. 170).

In his own preface to *The Coral Island* (1913), another of Barrie's
favourite novels, he wrote that "to be born is to be wrecked on an island";
and in the programme notes for the Royal Shakespeare Company's production of *Peter Pan* at the Barbican in 1983, Andrew Birkin points
out that:

> J. M. Barrie's classic adventure story evolved through his own experi-
> ences—both of literature and "being wrecked." The greatest pirate tale
> of all, Robert Louis Stevenson's *Treasure Island,* was his *starting
> point.* (n.p.)

This influence is visually acknowledged by Michael Foreman's "nods
and winks" in the direction of N. C. Wyeth's renowned illustrations for
an edition of *Treasure Island* published in 1911—coincidentally the
same year as the novel *Peter and Wendy.*[6] Barrie devoted a whole chapter
in *Margaret Ogilvy* (1896) to describing how his mother responded to
the novels of Robert Louis Stevenson, including *Treasure Island,* in
which she became particularly engrossed. He referred to Robert Louis
Stevenson as "the spirit of boyhood tugging at the skirts of this old world
of ours and compelling it to come back and play" (p. 143).

Coral Island and *Treasure Island* are two of the three island narratives used by Joseph Bristow (1991) in a study focusing on boys' adventure stories, to exemplify "the gradual permutations of the Crusoe

myth ... emerging at different points in the nineteenth century." Bristow suggests that:

> In children's literature, the island regularly serves as an appropriately diminutive world in which dangers can be experienced within safe boundaries. Boy heroes can act as the natural masters of these controllable environments. Islands provide an appositely "child-like" space which boys can easily circumnavigate without revealing any lack of manful maturity. (p. 94)

Moreover:

> the central character of this type of adventure had conspicuously moved from the ageing and isolated individual associated with Crusoe himself to the boy surrounded by threatening (cannibalistic) natives and ne'er-do-well men (usually pirates). Consequently, as attention is focused more and more closely on the boy's ability to take control of his fate, the issue of moral responsibility almost slips out of sight. There can be more adventure once a boy becomes the master of his fate and the captain of his soul. (p. 95)

The Neverland adventure contains all the ingredients of such island stories and is typical of the "masculine narrative" described by John Fiske (1987). Barrie avoids multiplicity of characters and plots by concentrating on a single adventure, chosen self-consciously by the author (the novel, p. 95), structured around the "main controlling figure" (Fiske 1987, p. 217) of Peter, and initially concerning the lagoon. Set in "the world out there" (Fiske p. 220), as opposed to the safe haven of home, it focuses on action rather than relationships, involving the rescue of Tiger Lily (and later Wendy) from Hook's clutches—the classic woman-as-victim (and later heroine-in-jeopardy) scene that provokes stereotypical responses from both Peter and Wendy (the novel, p. 101). The final confrontation between Peter and Hook is simultaneously the climactic scene of the Neverland adventure and the moment of narrative closure, signalling that the return home is now possible. Significantly, most editions of the novel contain at least one full-page illustration of this scene, while Wendy's first encounter with Peter is not always given the same space and sometimes not even represented. In such cases, emphasis is placed on the masculine narrative and it could be argued that the frozen image of Peter's victory has the same effect as the use of slow motion in action drama, which according to Fiske "is used to eroticize power, to extend the moment of climax" (1987, p. 219).

Fiske observes that "the word 'climax' is significant for it has both a sexual and narrative application" (1987, p. 215), and the sword is a common (although some would argue inappropriate) symbol of the male genitals and, perhaps more relevant here, of the violence and dominance equated with socially constructed masculinity.[7] Fiske refers to "the boy's fantasy of masculinity as physical strength (including its mechanical extension into guns, cars, and machinery)" (1987, p. 200). He also suggests that images of men making uncontrolled use of such "penile extenders" (p. 210) demonstrates the "natural wildness of masculinity" (p. 212). Like the author, who orchestrates the murder of a pirate for the sake of demonstrating "Hook's method" to the reader (the novel, p. 64), Peter is also capable of indiscriminate killing, which for him is merely part of yet another adventure (the novel, p. 92), being a little boy and having fun.

As Ormerod's portrait implies, Peter's actions are not based on sexual impulses. In fact it is *Peter* who is the object of desire, not only in the eyes of Wendy, Tiger Lily, and Tinkerbell, but also in the eyes of Hook, who is profoundly stirred by the sight of Peter sleeping, despite his hatred of Peter's cockiness (the novel, p. 148). Hook is the antithesis of Peter. According to Michael Egan (1982), he is "a highly sexual figure . . . replete with phallic symbolism" (p. 51), but, perhaps more importantly, a grown-up man for whom death is inevitable and therefore a disturbing reminder of mortality. Once again Robert Louis Stevenson—in a discussion about marriage in modern comedies in *Virginibus Puerisque*—supplies an appropriate comment when he links marriage (associated with Wendy in Barrie's story) and mortality (represented in *Peter* Pan by Hook). The heroes, says Stevenson:

> look forward to marriage much in the same way as they prepare themselves for death: each seems inevitable; each is a great Perhaps, and a leap into the dark, for which when a man is in the blue devils, he has to specially harden his heart. (pp. 9–10)

An earlier confrontation with Hook on Marooner's Rock brings Peter face to face with his own grown-up "potential . . . his despised manhood, which he feels he must eliminate" (Rotert 1990, p. 118). Most illustrators draw attention to Peter's antithetical relationship with Hook at this point in the narrative.

Many illustrations of the last meeting of Peter and Hook also accentuate the oppositional nature of their relationship while celebrating Peter's triumph. The composition of Michael Foreman's illustration (Pavilion, 1988) is a typical example. It depicts the moment after Hook has admitted defeat and thrown himself over the side of his ship towards the open jaws of the crocodile. The figures of Peter and Hook are virtually mirror images, with Peter standing erect, legs apart, his sword held high signalling victory and Hook falling head first towards death, his sword lost from his grip signalling defeat. The dominant feature of this picture is, however, the giant skull and its smaller companions that decorate the stern of the pirate ship. The viewer, whose eyes are drawn towards those of the skull, is invited to look Death in the face as a reminder of his/her own mortality, while Peter stands directly above the death's head, indisputably "the master of his fate and the captain of his soul" (Bristow 1991, p. 95) and the harbinger of Hook's demise. However, Foreman discourages the viewer from seeing the conflict as a simple matter of Good versus Evil by the mixed reaction to Hook's fate expressed by the skulls, for the reader knows that Hook is not a wholly unattractive or unheroic figure (the novel, pp. 64, 143, 176–77), and that Peter himself is far from perfect. According to Peter Hollindale (1993a), "he is heartless, possessive and scheming" (p. 29). Foreman's illustration works like a cinematic long shot, which distances the viewer from individual characters and accentuates the (symbolic) significance of the whole scene.

The effect of Jan Ormerod's version of the same moment, which shows Hook's falling body in close-up, is dramatically different. The viewer cannot avoid the grotesque expression of terror on Hook's face, only inches away from the crocodile's grinning jaws, while on the bows of the ship above, Peter's comparatively small figure is silhouetted against a full moon, sword and dagger held aloft victoriously, a wide grin the only facial detail. The implied link between Peter and the crocodile is appropriate. Michael Egan (1982) draws attention to the fact that the crocodile is "chronology personified" and when his clock stops running, "we know then that Hook is doomed" (pp. 51–52). As Peter boards the ship he unconsciously imitates the ticking sound and "Barrie allows all the deadly temporal meanings associated with the crocodile to gather around his hero. Peter thus becomes both Time and Fate" (p. 52). Time itself is apparently on the child's side and is, as Michael Foreman's cover illustration suggests, the *real* enemy of Hook. Ormerod invites the viewer to relate to the personal drama of the scene and contemplate Hook—caught between the devil and the deep blue sea—with a degree of sympathy.

Ormerod also depicts an earlier moment of the fight on the page immediately preceding. The picture is striking for several reasons. Hook's malevolent expression recalls something of George Du Maurier's stage portrayal, which, according to his daughter Daphne, had children screaming in the stalls. Ormerod's portrait suggests "that ashen face, those blood-red lips, the long dank, greasy curls" described by Daphne Du Maurier (in Lancelyn Green 1954, p. 91) and, like F. D. Bedford, the first illustrator of the novel whose Hook is truly terrifying, Ormerod makes Hook's hate-filled eyes a major focal point of the illustration. Furthermore, by depicting Hook with bloodstained clothes, Ormerod does not baulk the violence of the situation and stresses the pirate's mortality. A strong sense of movement is conveyed by the composition due to an "invisible" circle linking Peter's body and rapier with Hook's arm and sword, completed by the ropes hanging behind. It is a perfect complement to the text:

> He fought now like a human flail, and every sweep of the terrible sword would have severed in twain any man or boy who obstructed it; but Peter fluttered around him as if the very wind it made blew him out of the danger zone. And again and again he darted in and pricked. (the novel, p. 176)

Unlike Hook's massive figure that fills two-thirds of the frame, Peter's tiny translucent body, gracefully flying before his adversary, appears as light as a feather. A comparison is invited between Hook's "terrible sword," so large that it cuts through the frame of the picture, and Peter's rapier, "a light and slender sword"[8] used in the *sport* of fencing. The concentrated violence of Hook's actions is counterbalanced by the boy's lightness of touch. Hook demonstrates the "natural wildness of masculinity" referred to by Fiske (1987), which is, however, ineffectual against Peter. Young audience members or readers who associate both Hook (the archetypal villain) and Mr Darling (the stereotypical patriarch) with adult/parental power/authority, probably find Peter's victory particularly satisfying. And yet, despite the textual hints and the theatrical convention of casting the same actor in both roles,[9] illustrators of the book do not seem inclined to suggest the same link between the characters. They generally choose to simply represent two extreme examples of masculinity, which in Hook's case is clearly rooted in swashbuckling adventure stories.

To contrast with Hook's substantial presence, both Jan Ormerod and Paula Rego (who was commissioned to illustrate a new edition of the play for the Folio Society) give Peter an unearthly appearance. The unnatural yellow tint of Peter's skin results in an ethereal quality that supports Peter's own declaration that he is "youth . . . joy . . . a little bird that has broken out of the egg" (the novel, p. 176/ the play, p. 141), and acknowledges Barrie's comment that "he is less like a boy than a mote of dust dancing in the sun" (the play, p. 140). These illustrations endorse Barrie's description of Peter as "only half human" (Barrie 1986, p. 22) and make possible an interpretation of Peter as "Trickster," which Joseph L. Henderson (1978) describes as "the first rudimentary stage in the development of the hero myth, in which the hero is instinctual, uninhibited, and often childish" (p. 104).

Using the example of the stories told by the North American tribe of Winnebago Indians, Henderson demonstrates how the image of the hero evolves through four cycles that reflect the stages of development of the human personality. He quotes Dr. Paul Radin's suggestion that the evolution of the hero myth "represents our efforts to deal with the problem of growing up, aided by the illusion of an eternal fiction" (p. 103). Peter seems to possess several characteristics of the Trickster stage—his ability to fly, for example, corresponds with the Trickster's semi-divine or semi-magical powers; he is even linked by name with a mythological god. Henderson's own description of the Trickster certainly brings Peter to mind:

> Lacking any purpose beyond the gratification of his primary needs, he is cruel, cynical and unfeeling . . . This figure, which at the outset assumes the form of an animal, passes from one mischievous exploit to another. But, as he does so, a change comes over him. At the end of his rogue's progress he is beginning to take on the physical likeness of a grown man. (p. 104)

Following Hook's death, Peter adopts the role of "Captain Pan" and, wearing a suit made out of

> some of Hook's wickedest garments . . . he sat long in the cabin with Hook's cigar-holder in his mouth and one hand clenched, all but the

forefinger, which he bent and held threateningly aloft like a hook. (the
novel, p. 181)

Elisa Trimby (Puffin, 1986) draws attention to this unattractive phase,
while Michael Hague (Methuen, 1988) shows Peter surrounded by an
array of weaponry/ mechanical extensions of masculinity. However, unlike Wendy and her brothers, Peter fails to progress to the second stage of
development described by Henderson, in which the "irresponsibility of
childhood gives way to a period of socialization" (p. 110). Confirmation
that, for Peter, nothing has changed, comes in the concluding chapter of
the novel when he returns for Wendy a year later and has no recollection
of Hook as "new adventures had crowded the old ones from his mind"
(p. 196).

Although Peter savours the power that accompanies pirate captaincy, he rejects the role in favour of *puer aeternus*. As many critics and
biographers have pointed out, Peter seems to reflect Barrie's own inability (if not refusal) to grow up, both emotionally (in terms of his relationship with his own mother and his unusual friendship with the Davies
family) and physically (in terms of his unfulfilled marriage to Mary
Ansell). After the tragic death of Michael Llewelyn Davies in 1921, he
wrote: "It is as if long after writing 'P. Pan' its true meaning came to
me—Desperate attempt to grow up but can't" (quoted in Carpenter 1987,
p. 187). The equally tragic death of Barrie's older brother David and its
effect on Barrie's relationship with his mother has often been cited; however, it seems to me that, as unreliable as biographical explanation may
be, Barrie's relationship with his father also should be considered.

In *Absent Fathers, Lost Sons: The Search for Masculine Identity*
(1991), Guy Corneau suggests that the quality of the relationship between a father and his son is of crucial importance to the development of
the son's masculine identity. That very little is known about Barrie's relationship with his own father might be significant—a brief mention in
Margaret Ogilvy suggests that David Barrie was regarded with respect
from a distance, rather than with the warmth that develops from a close
association; she referred to him as "one who proved a most loving as he
was always a well-loved husband, a man I am proud to call my father"
(1896, p. 31). As David Barrie does not figure in his son's accounts of
everyday family life it is possible that he was, in effect, an "absent father," which could explain Barrie's own fragile masculine identity, personified by the asexual character of Peter, forever in search of a mother
figure. In this context, it could be conjectured that the fight between Peter

and Hook represents the author defending himself against the aggressive aspect of his own masculinity.

Indeed, the visual interpretations of this scene show Peter resisting the violent power symbolised by Hook's "terrible sword," emphasise his desire to remain eternally youthful (Ormerod) and celebrate his victory over death (Foreman); but they also hint at the limitations of his heroism (Ormerod and Rego). Peter's sword is more of an accoutrement for a game than a symbolic instrument of justice, for even though he refers to himself as "Peter Pan the avenger," his ego thrives on the outcome of the confrontation and he happily takes the place of his rival. Furthermore, it is only when Peter returns to Neverland as a grown-up in Steven Spielberg's recent film sequel *Hook*, that the sword is clearly meant to symbolise leadership.[10] As R. D. S. Jack (1991) points out, Peter "endures as a stage of life artificially held, not as All-Life mirroring the ages of man" (p. 195), and death is "the one adventure that he does not dare to face" (p. 196). Even "the Notes confirm the intention to present Pan as the flawed 'hero'; indeed on occasions, they suggest that he might have vied more obviously with Hook in villainy" (p. 196).

Is it to Wendy then, that we should really be looking for our hero figure? As Natalie Babbitt (Harrison & Maguire, 1987) suggests, in the context of Wendy's story, Peter Pan fits Joseph Campbell's description of the herald who "summons the hero to cross a threshold—from the real world into mystery, from life into death, from waking state into dream" (p. 150). He is also the protector who helps Wendy, John, and Michael to "survive a succession of trials" (p. 150) before they return home. As the only character who maintains a strong grip on "reality" throughout their adventures, Wendy plays an important part in defining the Neverland adventures as "fantasy"; and as the child who regards the Neverland as a diversion rather than an escape from the unavoidable business of growing up, she is the reader's touchstone for recognising the significance of Peter's desire for eternal youth. Although there is no denying that Wendy is a typical example of the culturally constructed female, whose place is in the home in a nurturing and caring role, defined in terms of her relationships with others, she is not entirely passive. It is Wendy, after all, who initiates the children's departure from Neverland and their subsequent return home.

As I have already suggested, in the context of the Neverland adventure, Peter is the "hero" of a typically masculine narrative which rejects women, marriage, work, and even death. Not surprisingly, commentators have noted that the story seems to lack a positive, let alone ideal, male role model. According to Penelope Scambly Schott, when all the excitement has subsided, "the story has little to say to boys" (1974, pp. 24–25). However, Jack Zipes (1990) suggests that *Peter Pan* offers an implicit critique of "the gender roles designated for men" (p. 143) at a time when England was the major industrial power in the world. He argues that "instead of viewing Peter Pan merely as an escapist figure, the eternal adolescent, the unfulfilled son," he is also "a rebel who consciously rejects the role of adulthood in conventional society" (p. 142). Furthermore, Barrie's own penchant for participating in (if not initiating) imaginative games with his young companions reflects the same "theory of mothering and responsibility valid for both males and females" that Zipes perceives in his work. Unlike Kenneth Grahame's Olympians who "spent the best part of their time stuffily indoors" (Avery 1986, p. 178), Barrie apparently possessed an imagination equal to that of any healthy child. He *also* refused to "become a pirate"[11]; and in this context the sword could be seen to signify the individual's fight for independence in spite of the pressure to conform. Although Peter's self-centredness undoubtedly sours his heroism, there is nothing of the racial arrogance, aggressive nationalism, or class bigotry that characterises other fictional boyhood heroes of the time (Carpenter 1986). Consequently, the Neverland adventure is refreshingly free of the kind of didacticism typical of a large number of nineteenth-century adventure stories. Perhaps this accounts, to some extent, for the lasting appeal of *Peter Pan*.

In Beryl Bainbridge's novel, *An Awfully Big Adventure* (Penguin, 1991), which focuses on a group of thespians rehearsing for a Christmas production of *Peter Pan,* the director, Meredith, declares:

> There are numerous books on the meaning behind this particular play . . . I've read most of them and am of the opinion they do the author a disservice. I'm not qualified to judge whether the grief his mother felt on the death of his elder brother had an adverse effect on Mr. Barrie's emotional development, nor do I care one way or the other. We all have our crosses to bear. Sufficient to say that I regard the play as pure make-believe. I don't want any truck with symbolic interpretations. (p. 99)

The "make-believe" of *Peter Pan* has continued to delight children and adults alike. Letters sent to Eva Embury, who played Peter for several years on tour in England during World War I, demonstrate young audience members' particular fascination with Peter's ability to fly.[12] However, as we have seen, the superhuman powers that allow Peter to defy both gravity and death are combined with less endearing (and recognisably human) features. I would like to suggest that it is this element of "truth" in Barrie's portrayal of Peter, which simultaneously invites children to empathise with the boy hero and adults to sympathise with him. F. D. Bedford's illustration of the Mermaids' Lagoon, which teems with life, acts as a complete contrast to the illustration at the end of the same chapter. Entitled "To die would be an awfully big adventure," it shows Peter standing totally alone on Marooner's Rock, looking out across the calm, moonlit sea. Considered together, the two illustrations summarise the nature of Peter's existence and are charged with emotional content. On the one hand his life is full of excitement and pleasure, on the other it is lonely and unfulfilled—is this the price of heroism?

NOTES

1. Peter Hollindale discusses the publications associated with Spielberg's film in "Peter Pan, Captain Hook and the Book of the Video", *Signal,* Number 72 (1993), pp. 152–75.

2. For example, Gilbert Adair, *Peter Pan and the Only Children* (Macmillan, 1987); Keith Faulkner, *Peter Pan Adventure Game* (Hodder & Stoughton, 1984); and *Fox's Peter Pan and the Pirates* (Fox Children's Productions, 1992).

3. In Bill Gillham's *Cinderella Doesn't Live Here Any More* (Methuen, London, 1988), one of a series of paired reading storybooks, an intertextual reference to Hook and the crocodile assumes that the young reader is as familiar with these characters as he/she is with Cinderella and Little Red Riding Hood. Similarly, Judy Blume assumes that her (albeit more junior) audience has a basic knowledge of the play, in *Otherwise Known as Sheila the Great* (Bodley Head, London, 1979). More recently, *Amazing Grace* (Frances Lincoln, 1991), a picture book by Mary Hoffman, features a young black girl who wants to play the part of Peter Pan in the school production.

4. In a discussion about the visual representation of women in the nineteenth century, Griselda Pollock (1988) quotes from Tennyson's poem, *The Princess,* to demonstrate how the absoluteness of gender difference was one of the key features in mid-nineteenth century discourses on masculinity and femininity:

> Man for the Field and Woman for the Hearth:
> Man for the Sword and for the Needle She:
> Man for the Head and Woman with the Heart:
> Man to command and Woman to obey;
> All else confusion (p122).

5. A reference to *The Boy Castaways of Black Lake Island* in the programme for the Royal Shakespeare Company's production of *Peter Pan* at the Barbican Theatre, London, 1982 and 1983.

6. This reference to Wyeth's illustrations was confirmed by Michael Foreman in correspondence:

> Your observations about Mabel Lucie Attwell and N. C. Wyeth are correct. In my work there are occasionally nods and winks in the direction of other artists, double takes, optical illusions and sexual allusions. I like to think that my books work on different levels. (20 September 1992)

7. For example, Richard Dyer argues that although in the context of cinematic images of sexual arousal:

> a hard gleaming weapon is at once understood to be like a penis . . . even erect the penis and testicles are not hard, tough, weapon-like. The penis cannot stab and do all the other violent things it is evoked as being capable of . . . (p. 31)

> "Male Sexuality in the Media," in *The Sexuality of Men,* eds. Andy Metcalf and Martin Humphries, pp. 28–43.

In *The Chalice and the Blade: Our History, Our Future* (1990), Riane Eisler points out that:

> For millennia men have fought wars and the Blade has been a male symbol. But this does not mean men are inevitably violent and warlike . . . The underlying problem is not man as a sex. The root of the problem lies in the social system in which the power of the Blade is idealized—in which both men and women are taught to equate true masculinity with violence and dominance and to see men who do not conform to this ideal as "too soft" or "effeminate" (p. xviii).

8. The *Concise Oxford Dictionary*, 1990.

9. According to Roger Lancelyn Green (1954), Gerald Du Maurier was engaged for the first production of the play "doubling Mr. Darling with Hook, and thus setting a fashion that many famous actors were to follow" (p. 91). The link is hinted at by the scenes that involve medicine. Michael Egan (1982) suggests that Hook "is thus literally Wendy's father in elaborate disguise. When she takes his arm, therefore, and Peter rushes hotly in pursuit vowing vengeance, the archetypal Freudian triad (Oedipal Father-Mother-Oedipal Son) is complete" (p. 51).

10. In Steven Spielberg's film sequel *Hook* (1991), the sword becomes a powerful symbol of leadership, which the Lost Boys' new leader, Ruffio, returns

to Peter as a sign of acceptance, and which Peter uses to indicate his successor when he is ready to return to London with his own children.

11. Terry Brooks, *Hook* (1992), p. 29. In this book of the screenplay (as in the screenplay), Wendy uses the term metaphorically to describe a corporate raider—the grown-up Peter:

> Wendy broke from the children and came back to him, tucking his arm firmly under her own, wheeling him toward the living room. "Important businessman, are you? And just what are you doing these days that is so terribly important, Peter?"
>
> Her bright eyes fixed and held him once more, mesmerizing, depthless. He found himself squirming to find a reply. "Well, you see, I, I, well . . ." He gave up and spat it out. "I'm doing acquisitions and mergers, and recently I've been dabbling in land development, ah, and . . ."
>
> Behind him Jack made a sound like a cannon being fired. "Yeah, Dad blows them out of the water."
>
> Wendy glanced down at the boy, then smiled at Peter. "So, Peter," she said softly, and her eyes were almost sad, "you've become a pirate."

12. Catherine Haill, *Dear Peter Pan* (Theatre Museum/Victoria and Albert Museum, London, 1983).

BIBLIOGRAPHY

Primary Sources

Adair, G. *Peter Pan and the Only Children*. London and Basingstoke: Macmillan Children's Books, 1987.

Bainbridge, B. *An Awfully Big Adventure*. Harmondsworth: Penguin, 1991.

Ballantyne, R. M. *The Coral Island: A Tale of the Pacific Ocean*. Preface by J. M. Barrie, illus. Septimus E. Scott. London: Nesbit, 1913 [1857].

Barrie, J. M. *Margaret Ogilvy by Her Son*. London: Hodder and Stoughton, 1896.

———. *The Little White Bird*. London, New York, Toronto: Hodder and Stoughton, 1902.

———. *Peter and Wendy*. Illus. F. D. Bedford. London: Hodder and Stoughton, 1911.

———. *Peter Pan or the Boy Who Would Not Grow Up* (The Plays of J. M. Barrie). London: Hodder and Stoughton, 1928.

———. *Peter Pan*. Illus. Elisa Trimby. Harmondsworth: Puffin/Penguin, 1986.

——. *Peter Pan in Kensington Gardens.* Illus. Arthur Rackham. London, Sydney, Aukland, Toronto: Hodder and Stoughton, 1986 [1906].

——. *Peter Pan.* Illus. Michael Hague. London: Methuen, 1988.

——. *Peter Pan.* Illus. Jan Ormerod. Harmondsworth: Viking Kestrel/Penguin, 1988.

——. *Peter and Wendy.* Illus. Michael Foreman. London: Pavilion, 1988.

——. *Peter Pan.* Illus. Paula Rego. London: Folio Society, 1993.

Blume, J. *Otherwise Known as Sheila the Great.* London: The Bodley Head, 1979.

Brooks, T. *Hook.* London: Arrow Books, 1992.

Disney, W. *Peter Pan.* Walt Disney Company. Directed by Hamilton Luske, Clyde Geronimo & Wilfred Jackson, 1953. [Feature length animation.]

Faulkner, K. *Peter Pan Adventure Game.* London: Hodder and Stoughton, 1985. [Computer software.]

Fox Children's Productions. *Fox's Peter Pan and the Pirates: Peter Saves the Unicorn.* Horsham, West Sussex: Ravette Books, 1992. [Based an animated television series.]

Gillham, E. *Cinderella Doesn't Live Here Anymore.* Illus. Margaret Chamberlain. London: Methuen Children's Books, 1988.

Haill, C. *Dear Peter Pan . . .* Exhibition at the Theatre Museum/Victoria and Albert Museum, London, 1983.

Hoffman, M. *Amazing Grace.* Illus. Caroline Binch. London: Frances Lincoln. 1991.

Spielberg, S. (Dir.) *Hook.* Tri-Star Pictures Inc. 1991.

Stevenson, R. L. *Treasure Island.* Illus. N. C. Wyeth. London: Gollancz Children's Paperbacks, 1990 [1883].

——. *Virginbus Puerisque and Other Papers.* Harmondsworth: Penguin, 1946 [1881].

Secondary Sources

Avery, G. "The Cult of Peter Pan," *Word and Image.* Vol. 2 No. 2 (1986): 173–184.

Babbitt, N. "Fantasy and the Classic Hero," in *Innocence and Experience: Essays and Conversations on Children's Literature,* eds. B. Harrison and G. Maguire. New York: Lothrop, Lee & Shepard, 1987.

Blake, K. "The Sea-Dream: *Peter Pan* and *Treasure Island,*" *Children's Literature,* Vol. 6 (1977): 164–81.

Bristow, J. *Empire Boys: Adventures in a Man's World.* London: Harper Collins Academic, 1991.

Carpenter, H. *Secret Gardens: A Study of the Golden Age of Children's Literature.* London and Sydney: Unwin, 1987 [1985].

Carpenter, K. *Boyhood Heroes.* London: Bethnal Green Museum of Childhood. [Booklet to accompany the exhibition *The World of Adventure* (1986).]

Corneau, G. *Absent Fathers, Lost Sons.* Boston and London: Shambhala, 1991.

Dyer, R. "Male Sexuality in the Media," in *The Sexuality of Men,* eds. Andy Metcalf and Martin Humphries. London and Concord, Mass.: Pluto Press, 1990: 28–43.

Eardly, T. "Violence and Sexuality," in *The Sexuality of Men,* eds. Andy Metcalf and Martin Humphries. London and Concord, Mass.: Pluto Press, 1990: 86–109.

Egan, M. (1982) "The Neverland of Id: Barrie, *Peter Pan* and Freud," *Children's Literature,* Vol. 10 (1982): 37–55.

Eisler, R. *The Chalice and the Blade: Our History, Our Future.* London, Boston, Sydney, Wellington: Unwin, 1990.

Fiske, J. *Television Culture.* London and New York: Routledge, 1987.

Goodman, E, ed. *Programme for J. M. Barrie's Peter Pan or the Boy Who Wouldn't Grow Up.* London: The Royal Shakespeare Theatre, 1983.

Green, R. L. *Fifty Years of Peter Pan.* London: Peter Davies, 1954.

Henderson, J. L. "Ancient Myths and Modern Man," in *Man and his Symbols,* ed. Carl Jung. London: Aldus Books, 1964.

Hollindale, P. "Peter Pan, Captain Hook and the Book of the Video." *Signal* 72 (1993): 152–75.

———. "Peter Pan: The Text and the Myth," *Children's Literature in Education,* Vol. 24 No. 1 (1993a): 19–30.

Jack, R. D. S. *The Road to the Never Land: A Reassessment of J. M. Barrie's Dramatic Art.* Aberdeen: Aberdeen University Press, 1991.

Rotert, R. "The Kiss in a Box," *Children's Literature* 18 (1990): 114–23.

Schott, P. S. "The Many Mothers of Peter Pan: An Exploration and Lamentation" *Research Studies,* Vol. 42 No. 1 (1974): 1–10. (Quoted in *Children's Literature Review,* Vol. 16: 24–27.)

Zipes, J. (1990) "Negating History and Male Fantasies Through Psychoanalytic Criticism," *Children's Literature,* Vol. 18 (1990): 141–43.

Dahl, The Marvellous Boy

CATRIONA NICHOLSON

In his lifetime, Roald Dahl enjoyed extraordinary acclaim as a writer. The success of his children's books made him the world's most successful living author and his name has established a publishing phenomenon. By the end of his life, it was estimated that one in three British children acquired a Dahl book every year. In 1997, seven years after his death, a poll organised by BBC television's *Bookworm* programme firmly endorsed Roald Dahl's continuing position as the favourite author of books for children. His popularity is such that young readers in the United Kingdom and their parents regard him as "the master" when it comes to tickling children's literary fancies, and most adults acknowledge that his consummate gift is the blend of humour, subversion, and violence that characterises his stories and which exerts a magnetic spell on young readers. The *Times* newspaper, reporting on the runaway success of his books in this survey, suggested that "children have elevated Dahl as their literary cult hero." The presenter of the *Bookworm* programme, with Dahlesque extravagance, declared "I predict that Roald Dahl will take over the world eventually."[1] Quentin Blake, Honorary President of the Roald Dahl Internet Club, whose distinctive drawings have become instantly recognisable signifiers of the Dahl phenomenon wants "the heritage that Roald has left to last forever." In its first year of operation, the Roald Dahl Children's Gallery housed in the museum near his Buckinghamshire home, has received more than eighty thousand people from Britain and around the world.

The litany of memorable book titles can be recalled by most children and through their extraordinary feats and superhuman qualities,

well-known characters like Charlie, James, Danny, and Matilda have se-
cured iconic status for their author. In his lifetime, Dahl found the overwhelming evidence of his popularity as the supremely successful
children's writer profoundly satisfying:

> What makes me feel good is having this enormous audience of chil-
> dren. I suppose I could knock on the door of any house where there
> was a child—whether it was the U.S., Britain, Holland, West Germany,
> France—and say: "My car's run out of petrol. Could you give me a cup
> of tea?" and they'd know me. That does make me feel good.[2]

Such recognition was the essential impetus that powered his continuing
commitment to his readers. Dahl would be gratified to know that eighteen years after making this claim, his books remain best sellers.

Many children are addictive in their reading and writers like Dahl,
who enjoy great popularity, achieve acclaim through their instinctive
awareness of the themes, incidents, and language that generate complicit
understanding between author and reader. Such writers are able to sound
chords of remembrance from their own childhood, which find responsive
echoes in their readers. Dahl himself, when invited to comment on the
way in which his stories appeal to children, suggested that he himself remained a child.[3] Preserving links with his own distant childhood enabled
Dahl to make connections with young readers like Rachel, who are able
to identify the essence and nature of his popularity. Ten-year-old Rachel
perceptively encapsulates his appeal using her own creative language:

> Roald Dahl has a very special touch and uses a *magical ingredetion*
> [sic]. I think that the things children look for in his books are the rude-
> ness, the types of words he uses, the sense of humour, the fast-moving
> stories, the way you get into the plot quickly and the short sentences.
> The main character is normally a child and children like reading about
> the danger the child gets into. I think the important point about his
> books is that a child is always the centre of attention and wins over
> adults in the end.[4]

Dahl's powerful imagination enabled him to write for all ages from infancy upwards and his books reveal contrasting moods and styles. However, the controversial nature of his status as a children's writer, which
lies at the heart of his appeal to young readers, is signified by adult critics
whose discussions of his work include captious terms and titles like "re-
gression," "grotesque," "subversion," "Is it Suitable?," "Is he a BF?," "A

Question of Taste," "Dangerous Fictions," "Wish Fulfilment," "Bewitch-
ing the Boys." Such a pejorative dossier of commentary militates against
the more esteemed critical reputation he would have desired.

Dahl's account of his own early life, his family history, and his
schooldays is chronicled in *Boy, Tales of Childhood* (1986). In a foreword to the reader, he explains that "an autobiography is usually full of
all sorts of boring details," emphatically declaring that *his* book is "not
an autobiography," for he would never write a history of himself. However, he seems to counter that claim by attributing autobiographical ve-
racity to the tales, stressing that, "Some are funny. Some are painful.
Some are unpleasant. I suppose that is why I have always remembered
them so vividly" (Dahl 1986, n.p.).

A complicity with the reader is forged when he reveals that a "number of things which happened" to him have left "a tremendous impression" on his mind; childhood incidents and encounters remain "seared"
on his memory; he had only to "skim them off the top of consciousness"
in order to write the book. This sort of confidential adult declaration acts
as a seductive bait, tempting the expectations of child readers. Once
hooked into the magic net of story by the teller's skill, most children are
willing to believe in his reliability as a narrator. Sealing the authenticity
of the tales within his own bond to the reader, Dahl concludes his brief
foreword in ardent style with the pledge: "All are true. R.D."

The confidential voice of Dahl, the big, friendly, child-wooing author continues to preside within the text through a recurring device
which is both assuring and pedantic. As if in vindication of his "all are
true" guarantee, the endorsement of "I promise you," or "I must tell you"
used at strategic intervals throughout the book, serves as an interpella-
tory device to hail and alert the reader. Each confiding phrase usually
precedes or emphasises the disclosure of a significant "secret," or it provides a further endorsement to revelations of how Dahl, the playful boy-
trickster, and his friends managed to outwit a hostile grown-up or some
adult in authority. Through direct textual interjections his insistent voice
intones familiar mantras of persuasion such as "it is worth reminding the
reader," "do not forget," "I tell you my friends," "you should know," "by
the way," "you cannot imagine," thereby endorsing and validating the
"truth" of remembered experience. "Truth," Dahl declares "is more important than modesty" (*Boy* p. 25). The truth of remembrance is the currency Dahl trades in as he peddles his tales of youthful daring, shrewdly
casting himself thereby in the hero role. Towards the end of the book,
Dahl allows his young readers to glimpse his inner frailty and his dread
of failure as a writer:

> The life of a writer is absolute hell . . . if he is a writer of fiction he lives
> in a world of fear. Each new day demands new ideas and he can never
> be sure whether he is going to come up with them or not . . . A person
> is a fool to become a writer. His only compensation is absolute free-
> dom. He has no master except his own soul and that, I am sure, is why
> he does it. (*Boy* p. 171)

Such an admission of apparent vulnerability from the most popular
writer in the world cannot fail to touch the heart of the individual reader.

The overriding theme of *Boy* is of a young hero confronting and bat-
tling with the often cruel and oppressive domination of the grown-ups
who peopled his world of home and school. Clearly the theme provokes
sympathetic responses in young readers who recognise aspects of their
own, more recent, childhood confrontations with adult power and authority. The book clearly reveals how incidents and influences in the
young Dahl's life are reworked into the themes and beliefs he reiterates
with disturbing frequency in many of his stories. There is nothing new in
this idea of the creative artist writing (or re-writing) his own autobiography through the veil of fiction. In his paper, "Creative Writers and Day-
dreaming," Freud's basic assumption that "connections exist between the
life of the writer and his works" (Lodge 1972, p. 41), has provided scholars of children's literature with fertile research fields that continue to be
well ploughed. David Krause argues that autobiography "is the art of
supreme fabrication . . . most fiction is autobiographical and most autobiography is fictional" (Hodgson 1993, p. 17).

Roni Natov, discussing how this strand of autobiographical writing
features in contemporary novels for children, points out that alongside the
"literary and formal patterns," which constitute the great traditions of a
culture—the stories of its marvellous heroes—there should be an awareness of the lesser tradition: the autobiographical stories of common lives,

> which are created out of the childhoods of those who became writers,
> those who found the ability to express in words what ordinary people,
> like themselves, feel, think, live, and dream. (Natov 1986, p. 112)

Although episodic in structure and therefore lacking the sustained page-
turning suspense of his more distinctive stories for readers of all ages,
Dahl's *Boy* can be read as a "companion" volume of intertextual reference for most of his children's books. In suggesting that "autobiography
tends to be anecdotal with chronically determined plots that summarise

how the hero got to do, be, overcome something" (Natov, p. 113) and that "fictionalising tends to intensify storytelling with the novelist's use of distilled memory" (p. 112), Natov nicely identifies the embedded interface that exists between this particular author's recollections of his childhood and the capricious way they are woven into the fabric of his fiction. Dahl, in these boyish *Tales of Childhood*, exemplifies Natov's suggestion that contemporary writers "tell the truth about what was tragic in the hopes of revealing the truth about what it means to be heroic for ordinary people" (p. 114). Furthermore, the stories also disclose not only the author's acquaintance with pain, but his own heroic resilience in the face of its impact. He conveys how "out of that pain something important is salvaged" (p. 114).

Children are captivated by the subtly instructive and pedantic tone of Dahl's authorial voice assuring them of the "truth" behind the recollections of pain or the moments of glory. His direct addressing of the implied young reader enables him to project his own bad memories into his narratives of "distilled" experience. Freud argues that the creative artist, like the neurotic, is oppressed by unusually powerful instinctual needs, which lead him to turn away from reality to fantasy. Accordingly, he suggests that, like a child in play, the creative writer, "rearranges the things of the world in a new way which pleases him" (Lodge 1972, p. 36). By performing just that literary manoeuvre, Dahl re-presents the experiences of his childhood in a form and sequence that nurtures his adult well-being. And readers of both his "autobiographical" work and his other fictions celebrate this Pied Piper as the hero author who plays the subversive tune they love to hear: stories of small triumphing over huge, weak over strong, good over bad, child over adult. It is also clear that Dahl the "creative writer" is also the "daydreamer" whose stories of how victims become victors and underdogs become heroes, cast him in a traditional storyteller mould described by Freud:

> One feature above all cannot fail to strike us about the creations of these storytellers: each of them has a hero who is the centre of interest, for whom the writer tries to win our sympathy by every possible means and whom he seems to place under the protection of a special providence . . . All the characters in the story are sharply divided into good or bad in defiance of the variety of human characters that are to be observed in real life. The "good" ones are the helpers while the "bad" ones are the enemies and rivals of the ego which has become the hero of the story. (Lodge 1972, p. 40)

Returning to a world of fantasy is a means by which a writer (and reader) can conceptualise experiences of desire or pain. Developmental psychology indicates that "the retreat to a fantasy world is common amongst those who cannot control their environment . . . fantasising becomes a necessary stepping-stone to try to cope with real situations" (Landau 1972, p. 292).

In Dahl's books of fantasy, a small hero or heroine, in the face of grim starting odds, and after unbelievably adventurous exploits, emerges victorious. Such reversal of fortunes is the axis upon which the oppositional structures of "good" and "bad" are established. The unswervingly delivered pattern is recognised, learned, and predicted by child readers. Here is eleven-year-old Anthony, who, having read all the books, is aware of the reassuring pattern that seals the bond between author and reader:

> You can always be sure of a Roald Dahl book being a good one because really they are all the same thing wrapped up in a different way. I noticed that in *Danny,* the awful teacher who caned him was called Captain Lancaster and in *Boy* he is caned by a man called Sergeant Hardcastle . . . He nearly always has a child in his story and this child always comes out on top and the bad person ends up losing. This bad person is nearly always bad to children and that gives the child a good enough reason to get back.

Dahl's repeating patterns of transmutation are seen in the physically weak triumphing over the strong (Sophie over the child-devouring giants in the *BFG*); the innocent and vulnerable gaining ascendancy over the venal and grotesque (Matilda over Miss Trunchbull; James over his aunts; the un-named boy/mouse over the witches); the humble and meek over the prosperous and domineering (Danny over Mr Victor Hazell). This theme of regeneration through endurance and suffering is a persistent motif in mythology, traditional tale, and legend. Joseph Campbell (1975) illustrates how heroic figures of myth and traditional tale encounter a series of challenging trials. Such trials or tests of endurance represent a struggle, a confrontation with inner confusions, terrors, and painful experiences. In overcoming and achieving mastery of these fears, individuals can live freely and with honour in the real world. Tales of young gods and mortals overcoming adversity and oppression have offered messages of hope for the powerless and downtrodden in any culture and to the poor and ordinary growing up in any generation. Moses and Pharaoh, David and Goliath, Snow White and her stepmother, Tom Thumb and the gruesome giant, many of Aesop's Fables, are variants of the paradigm. Dahl extends, enlarges and obsessively repeats the model and achieves his phenomenal success as a writer primarily through his ability to align himself with the child in an adult world. In his own "rearrangement of the world," he fits his towering adult stature to the dimensions and psychological needs of the young reader.

In *Boy,* which hovers between autobiography, tall-tale, and Freudian case book, the structural pivot upon which Freud's model rests is located in the good/bad tensions signified by home and school. Dahl must have had his imagination fired by the contrast between the two extremes. Although home was where his mother Sofie, "a young Norwegian in a foreign land . . . lost a daughter and a husband all in the space of a few weeks," it was also where the young, fatherless Dahl was surrounded by a household of loving females: sisters (four are mentioned in the dedication), adoring mother, and nanny. Dahl conveys the lingering magic of his childhood summers through the happy times when the family returned to the homeland of Norway: "All my summer holidays, from when I was four years old to when I was seventeen . . . were totally idyllic." Fresh food, wonderful picnics, benignly ancient grandparents, swimming off deserted beaches, sailing through "narrow channels with rocky islands," playing among "wooden skeletons of shipwrecked boats . . . big white bones, wild raspberries and mussels clinging to the rocks" (*Boy,* pp. 53–67).

School was where Dahl suffered intense homesickness; where looming adult figures menaced the well-being of pupils, and where older boys practised the mendacity and sadism modelled by those in authority. Dahl's remembrance of his first headmaster provides him with a grotesque prototype for a succession of authoritarian male characters, often referred to as giants, who appear in his books:

> His name was Mr Coombes and I have a picture in my mind of a giant of a man with a face like a ham and a mass of rusty coloured hair that sprouted in a tangle all over the top of his head. All grown-ups appear as giants to small children. But headmasters (and policemen) are the biggest giants of all and acquire a marvellously exaggerated stature . . . I sat there small and frightened, and to me at that moment the Headmaster, with his black gown draped over his shoulders, was like a judge at a murder trial. (*Boy,* p. 41)

The recurring motif of the small and frightened pitted against the huge and powerful is clearly conveyed through such descriptions. Dahl and his school friends became, similarly, the victims of tyrannical "boazers" or prefects, who forced these small fags to warm lavatory seats on freezing mornings and who habitually beat them until they bled. Writing in The *Times,* George Hill examines and expands upon this familiar theme in Dahl's work, suggesting that "the triumph of the underdog" is Dahl's abiding theme and "it is stamped on his mind that children are generically victims and adults generically tyrants"(Hill 1998, p. 12). Ernest Jones, in his paper "Psychoanalysis and Folklore," suggested that:

> The conception of giants, with their clumsy stupidity and their alternations of kindliness and ogrish devouring of children is a projection of various infantile thoughts about grown-ups. (Tucker 1982, p. 85)

Interestingly, Dahl himself was well in excess of six feet tall, and he describes his paternal grandfather as "an amiable giant nearly seven foot tall" (*Boy,* p. 13). Most of his small heroes, like some fairy-tale characters, begin fictional life under threat from adults, in dire adversity, or as suddenly orphaned. James Henry Trotter, in *James and the Giant Peach,* whose parents were eaten by a rhinoceros, "finds himself alone in a vast unfriendly world" (Dahl 1973, p. 7), before his misery is further compounded by being sent to live at the home of two unspeakably inhumane aunts where his room is "bare as a prison cell" (p. 8). In *The BFG* (Dahl 1984), Sophie, whose parents both died when she was a baby, lives in a comfortless orphanage under a punishing regime, which includes being "locked in the dark cellar for a day and a night without anything to eat or drink" (p. 39). The child narrator in *The Witches* (Dahl 1983) is left an orphan at seven after his parents' car skids on a road, killing them both. Charlie Bucket enjoys familial affection but lives in abject poverty (Dahl 1973). Danny's mother died when he was four months old (Dahl 1975). Matilda Wormwood's parents look forward to the time when they can "flick her away" (Dahl 1989, p. 10).

Campbell (1975) explains that the hero journey from adversity to fulfilment or resolution must be undertaken without symbolic parental representation, for parents belong to the world of reality; in the process of venturing forth and thereby crossing the threshold from the ordinary world into a realm of wonders, or a dream landscape, the hero must single-handedly confront and overcome the evil forces that beset him, assisted only by a protective figure, a supernatural helper. Campbell describes the standard pattern of the hero's adventure as a formula represented in the rites of passage: separation-initiation-return.

Several of Dahl's stories begin with what Campbell describes as "the call to adventure," which initiates the departure theme—the separation from home or family. *The BFG, James and the Giant Peach, The Witches,* and both *Charlie* books depict protagonists who leave what serves as home, and enter a realm of fantasy. The personification of the benign, protecting power of their destiny is the helper or the supernatural aid who accompanies them. Thus, they are placed under what Freud earlier described as the "protection of special providence" (Lodge 1972, p. 40).

Sophie has the big friendly giant; James has the community of residents inside the peach; the boy narrator of *The Witches* has his grandmother; Charlie has Mr Willy Wonka. In more domestically centred books such as *Danny the Champion of the World* and *Matilda,* the child hero is similarly befriended by a protective adult: Danny by his father and Matilda by Miss Honey. The real-life Dahl was a man who relished his role as head of his household and who greatly enjoyed the weekly occasions when he could preside over the extended family gatherings.[5] Dahl's male protectors, in their different ways, bear strong resemblances to the writer. In his early books, which began life as bedtime stories for his own children, there is a strong sense of a benign, paternalistic Dahl cast in the role of helper to the young hero. With his long, stooped stature and fatherly benevolence, his love of language (albeit confused), the BFG can be regarded as a self portrait of the writer. Dahl's inspiration for the long, thin, dream-blowing trumpet must surely be the pipe "made of meerschaum clay [with] a flexible stem about three feet long" (*Boy,* p. 56) smoked by his Norwegian grandfather. According to his daughter,[6] when Dahl first told the story to his family he would creep around the house enacting the BFG role, pretending to blow dreams through open windows. By the final pages of the book, his big friendly giant of a child-protector not only receives letters by the million from admiring children but has begun to write "essays about his own past life." But, being "a modest giant he couldn't put his name on it. He used someone else's name instead."

Mr Willy Wonka, though small and mercurial is, like Dahl, an inventor. He upholds his creator's declared values in hating ugliness, adoring chocolate, and believing that dire punishments should be inflicted on ill-behaved, spoilt children. Wonka, like Dahl, remains a child at heart declaring, "I don't want to be a grown-up person at all. A grown-up won't listen to me; he won't learn. He will try to do things his own way and not mine" (p. 185).

In *Danny the Champion of the World,* we see a sensitively drawn cameo of a protective and wholly loving father. In *Boy,* Dahl tells the reader about the two tragedies of his infant life. He describes how his sister died at seven and how his father, grief-stricken with loss, refused to fight a sudden bout of pneumonia, and died when the writer was three years old. Clearly the absence of his father as a friend and a role model was keenly felt by the young Dahl, who speaks with intense admiration throughout *Boy* about the way his mother took on the role of both parents. However, the gap in life must surely have influenced his developing perceptions and observations of adult behaviour. Freud was insistent about a child's need of a father, declaring, "I cannot think of any need in childhood as strong as the need for a father's protection" (Rutherford 1996, p. 142) His view was that a child should be shielded from the overwhelming excesses of maternal love (Dahl's dependence, as an only boy, upon the sole love of his mother, raises interesting issues that relate to his ambivalent and polarised depictions of women in his books). In a perfect world, it is claimed, a boy's first idealised hero will be his father for later, as adults,

> we become aware of our incompleteness. The myth of idealism, the desire inherent in hero-worship, is a belief in the possibility of our own completeness. It is a dream of becoming the idealised father, escaping our mothers and our need. (Rutherford, pp. 142/3)

Danny is given the idealised father that the author never had but would liked to have been himself. Significantly, Dahl dedicates this, his most realistic book, to his wife and children. Accompanying illustrations depict a tall, Dahl-like man, and the reader is told that Danny's father was "a marvellous storyteller [who] used to make up bedtime stories every single night." Danny's "wildly funny . . . marvellous and exciting father" with his brilliant blue flashing eyes tells him the story of the BFG. For the sleepy child, the most wonderful feeling was the knowledge that "when I went to sleep, my father would still be there, very close to me" (*Danny,* p. 11).

The setting for the book is a specific area of the Chilterns where Dahl lived and where a gypsy caravan, clearly the inspiration for Danny's home, remains in the writer's garden. Members of the family remember Dahl's ingenious attempts at pheasant poisoning and attest to his quirky sense of humour, his love of practical jokes, his memorable bedtime story telling sessions.[7]

The devastating losses and family tragedies that continued to mark Dahl's life have been well documented. In his fantasies for children it is tempting to propose that by creating extravagant scenarios within which child protagonists, helped often by superhuman characters, could achieve recognition as young heroes, the writer was resolving battles with his own remaining giants, or with malignant forces, which troubled his adult well-being. Most of Dahl's books for children are tales of fantasy, and in their recurring themes and subliminal issues they rework many incidents, encounters, and experiences in the writer's life. According to Freud, such tales can be interpreted as "unsatisfied wishes and every single fantasy is the fulfilment of a wish, a correction of unsatisfying reality" (Lodge 1972, p. 38). Joseph Campbell believes that regressive tendencies can come into play during the rite-of-passage from childhood to maturity and that accordingly, some adults, "remain fixated to the unexorcised images of [their] infancy" (Campbell 1975, p. 19).

It is evident in reading *Boy* that the extreme cruelty, injustice, and adult hypocrisy that Dahl claims were his schoolboy experience have become fertile wellsprings of inspiration for his writing. His sense of scholarly inadequacy, an apparent lack of recognition, and the gradual diminution of self-esteem are clearly conveyed to the reader. His most bitter and intense declaration of outrage and injustice is reserved for the chapter detailing the pleasure that another headmaster, who he claims was later to become the Archbishop of Canterbury, seemed to take in flogging the boys in his care:

> I would sit in the dim light of the school chapel and listen to him preaching about Mercy and Forgiveness and my young mind would become totally confused. I knew very well that only the night before, this preacher had shown neither Forgiveness or Mercy in flogging some small boy who had broken the rules . . . All through my school life I was appalled by the fact that masters and senior boys were literally allowed to wound other boys. I couldn't get over it. I never have got over it. (*Boy*, p. 146)

Not surprisingly, child readers may experience the pleasurable echo of Dahl's masterful coup within their own consciousness. His wish to triumph over what he remembered as the supreme flogging giant of his schooldays is fulfilled as he, the now celebrated author, unmasks the revered archbishop, and thereby exposes an aspect of adult duplicity.

The themes and conflicts made manifest in Dahl's *Tales of Childhood* prefigure the forces for good and evil in his tales of fantasy. Characterised by brave children, malevolent adults, and magical possibilities, they replicate the structure of fairy tales where fortunes are reversed, the ordinary becomes fabulous, and native cunning outwits pompous stupidity. In most of the books a child ultimately gains control over adult power and as Dahl elevates his protagonist to the heights of heroism or acclaimed popularity, his persistent theme of "deferred revenge" (Wood 1979), the genesis of which forms the ground bass accompaniment to *Boy,* is sweetly reiterated. The adult writer's insatiable need to repudiate the sufferings (and delights) of his childhood finds expression in his retreats to the world of fantasy where, in control of his fictional environment, the burden of his obsessive song is replayed through recurring structural motifs.

Children are quick to recognise his adversarial themes that depict children under threat:

> Roald Dahl's books are about bad adults and good children. At the beginning something awful always happens to children. (Mark, nine years old)
>
> Just about every one of his books are about children getting hurt or ill treated. (Jenny, ten years old)
>
> Dahl's books are about hurting or eating or trying to kill children. (Emma, ten years old)
>
> I like Dahl's books because the adults and children are always having a war and the children always win in the end. (Paul, ten years old)

Dahl readers who have been safely frightened by gigantic and child-devouring depictions in such fantasies as *The Enormous Crocodile* or *The BFG* are familiar, by the time they meet the true-life giants in *Boy,* with the element of fear that the author delights in inducing. At the age of ten, Rachel recognises that fear plays a seductive role within texts for children and she speculates how "some children might *like* the fear, the fear of being eaten and the gruesome feeling. Others might like the fantasy."

Dahl knows well how good the feeling of triumph in the face of tribulation can be. At the end of "The Great Mouse Plot" in *Boy,* his triumph is clear as he, the small undervalued schoolboy, invests himself with hero status: "We all have our moments of brilliance and glory and this was mine. . . . I felt like a hero. I was a hero. It was marvellous to be so popular" (pp. 35–37). In these telling words, there is a sense in which his memory looks forward to the proven acclaim of his adulthood. The boy Dahl's "daring mouse plot" is replicated in *Matilda,* when the heroine constructs a daring newt plot in order to subdue a grown-up predator. The adult Dahl is familiar with her longing "to do something truly heroic . . . It would be her turn now to become a heroine if only she could come up with a brilliant plot" (*Matilda*, p. 136). The child reader can also, as Norman Holland suggests, "recreate himself, his own psychological processes" (Holland 1975, p. 40). Children, we understand, often experience feelings of powerlessness but through vicarious identification with a fictional child hero, the reader can play at being powerful:

> In a battle of wills, parents often take care to make it seem that they have won even though the child has carried the day . . . Playing at being powerful . . . redresses the feeling of powerlessness and makes the child's limitations tolerable. (Newsom 1979, p. 106)

Bruno Bettelheim endorses and develops this theme when he discusses the ways in which identification with fairy-tale heroes enables a child to experience feelings of omnipotence:

> The fairy tale hero has a body which can perform miraculous deeds. By identifying with him, any child can compensate in fantasy for . . . all the inadequacies, real or imagined of his own body. He can fantasise that he too, like the hero, can climb into the sky, defeat giants, change his appearance, become the most powerful person, the most beautiful person. (Bettelheim 1978, p. 57)

Quentin Blake believes that Dahl's tales "are fairy stories at bottom . . . even the real people are ogres and giants" (Hill 1988, p. 12). Reluctant to be drawn on the meaning of his work, Dahl in an interview declared: "I am a fantasist. I make up stories. That is my trade" (Wood 1979, p. 22). The two storytelling modes are closely related and each enables writer and reader, through different processes, to suspend disbelief and to enter a world of imaginative possibilities. Bruno Bettleheim's definition of fairy tales as being "condensed metaphors of human conflict," and Italo Calvino's proposal that fantasy is not an escape from reality but "a way of looking inside ourselves and our own problems," clearly articulate how an underlying psychological dimension is common to both modes of storytelling. Each offers, through metaphor, symbol, archetype, and the conflicting play of oppositional forces, a way of understanding or reconciling complexities of the real world.

Dahl's books portray archetypal characters from traditional tales and, more significantly, they feature elements of the supernatural and extraordinary with which Norwegian folktales and myths abound. These stories tell of giants, ogres, witches, and humans with supernatural powers. Dahl's gift as a storyteller was clearly inspired by the stories he heard told by his grandmother[8] as a child during the summers in Norway, and his more grotesque and tyrannical adult characters fuse the fantastic with the real. The "Going to Norway" chapter in *Boy* is retraced in part by the child narrator at the beginning of *The Witches*. Although Dahl asserts that the book is "not a fairytale . . . it is about REAL WITCHES," he clearly identifies the influential source of his inspiration for the story:

> My grandmother was Norwegian. The Norwegians know all about witches, for Norway, with its black forests and icy mountains, is where the first witches came from . . . my grandmother . . . was a wonderful story teller. (*The Witches*, pp. 12/14)

Children identify and understand other strategies their hero uses to entice his readers into reading and buying his books. Dahl's particular predilection for including large doses of "rumbustious rudery" (Townsend 1965, p. 251) in his books is to be found in the form of lewd humour, suggestive symbolism, and gratuitous scatological reference. Whether or not adults like it, young readers consider this excessive "rudery" to be an essential ingredient of Roald Dahl's success and what sets him apart from other writers. James, at the age of ten is in no doubt of its efficacy:

> Roald Dahl is popular because he writes things no other author would dream of writing like "the children ran off smiling with their buttocks shining in the sun." No other book for children that I've read has something as rude as that written in it. The fact is that Roald Dahl is thinking, "if I write rude things in my books then that will make children laugh and they will buy more of my books."

Similarly, Sophie is judiciously aware of how Dahl's strategy achieves its effect:

> I think Roald Dahl is on top because he is disgusting. If you delve into our minds you must find something somewhere that is disgusting and we think disgusting things are funny. I am not saying that I am rude but to read a Roald Dahl book you can get away with a little bit of rudeness and that will make me laugh.

As she goes on to discuss a much quoted couplet in *Revolting Rhymes,* this discerning child recognises the extent to which Dahl contrives to shock or manufacture laughter:

> In Red Riding Hood he writes:
>> Once again her eyelid flickers
>> She whips a pistol from her knickers
> I mean really! He *could* have written:
>> Her mind was racing like a rocket
>> She whipped a pistol from her pocket

These child critics have pinpointed some of the reasons for Dahl's popularity. Besides appearing to be on the side of the child reader, he shamelessly exploits the notion that a particular form of pleasure is to be found in risqué humour and juvenile reference to bodily functions. Through the validating agency of fiction, children conspire with Dahl and delight in his subversive glimpses of the unrespectable. Elizabeth Wright explains how readers in general are pleasurably diverted by texts which fulfil our unconscious desires:

> What draws us as readers to a text is the secret desire to hear, much as we protest we do not. The disguise must be good enough to fool the censor into thinking that the text is respectable, but bad enough to allow the unconscious to glimpse the unrespectable. (Jefferson and Robey 1988, p. 149)

Dahl has asserted that the writer for children must "keep them interested and make them laugh." By exploiting certain juvenile tastes, which to some adults appear deplorable, Dahl has achieved overwhelming success with child readers. The humour, like that of folk tales, is richly spread and takes several forms: base toilet humour, comically grotesque depictions of adults in authority, and ludicrous situations. Sid Fleischman reminds us that literature and folklore present the mask of laughter in order to cover subliminal pain. "Comedy," he submits, "is alchemy. The base metal is always tragedy" (Heins 1977, p. 201). Dahl's own tragedies and struggles, which lurk beneath the comic surface of his books, can be detected in the trials his young heroes undergo, in the punishment meted out for his domineering adults, and in the underlying streak of cruelty that pervades every story. Child readers as we have seen, aligned alongside the young victim, recognise the element of cruelty inherent in Dahl's writing. Most note its presence but some, like the perspicacious Sophie, speculate about the psyche of the writer. Her thoughts take on a Dahlesque quality as she considers the possibility that this popular children's author may not actually *like* children: "In *Boy* he has got this obsession with canes. He writes the book as though it is hurting with every stroke of the pen but I think its a weapon to hurt children with."

Dahl's ability to combine within each story his distinctive brand of humour, fantastic adventure and strong measures of adult ridicule or exposure is a winning formula. His books offer children (and many adults) a unique reading experience for through the exuberant optimism, extravagant literary devices, and the child-centred gratification of common desires, Dahl establishes a binding rapport with his readers. His need for recognition was channelled through the triumphs of his heroes and heroines who "inspire children with the discovery of how remarkably heroic, ordinary people like themselves can be" (Natov 1986, p. 124). Such tales of triumph signify children's capacity for self-preservation in the face of adult threat and show that boys and girls can overcome adult oppression. Fleischman identifies three narrative elements that betray our unconscious rather than our formal literary taste:

> The supernatural; hero tales; and writ especially large, HUMOR. And these are the delights of childhood. To be safely frightened. To identify with larger-than-life heroes. To laugh. (Heins 1977, p. 203)

Roald Dahl, it would seem, has exploited these elements to the full.

NOTES

1. *Bookmark,* BBC2 Television Programme, 1986.

2. Interview with Elizabeth Dunn, *The Sunday Times Magazine* 25 May 1982, p. 46.

3. *Bookmark,* BBC2, 1986.

4. Rachel, and other young readers cited in this chapter, discussed their responses to Roald Dahl's writing during a series of booktalk sessions. Tapes were made of their conversations and I have included selections from the transcripted material. They also responded in written form to the question: "What do you feel are the particular reasons for Roald Dahl's popularity?"

5. Members of the family spoke to me about their remembrances of the writer. They were able to confirm or clarify points I raised about events and influences in Dahl's life.

6. In *An Awfully Big Adventure: The Making of Modern Children's Literature*, a BBC2 Television Documentary, 7 March 1998.

7. Family members recalled Dahl's attempt to sedate pheasants using sultanas laced with sleep inducing powders. Other adventures in the locality were also recounted and memorable if frightening bedtime story sessions recalled. Dahl stated on several occasions that he believed children enjoyed being frightened.

8. Dahl's Norwegian grandmother was remembered by the family as being a wonderful story teller who told younger members of the family, traditional stories from her homeland.

BIBLIOGRAPHY

Primary Texts

Dahl, Roald *Boy, Tales of Childhood*. Harmondsworth, England: Puffin, 1986. [orig. pub. 1984]

———. *The BFG*. Harmondsworth, England: Puffin, 1984. [orig. pub. 1982]

———. *Charlie and the Chocolate Factory*. Harmondsworth, England: Puffin, 1973. [orig. pub. 1964]

———. *Charlie and the Great Glass Elevator*. Harmondsworth, England: Puffin, 1975.

———. *Danny the Champion of the World*. Harmondsworth, England: Puffin, 1982. [orig. pub. 1975]

———. *James and the Giant Peach*. Harmondsworth, England: Puffin, 1973. [orig. pub. 1961]

———. *Matilda*. Harmondsworth, England: Puffin, 1989. [orig. pub. 1988]

———. *The Witches*. Harmondsworth, England: Puffin, 1985. [orig. pub. 1983]

Secondary Texts

Bettelheim, Bruno. *The Uses of Enchantment: The Meaning and Importance of Fairy Tales*. Harmondsworth, England: Penguin Books, 1978.

Campbell, Joseph. *The Hero with a Thousand Faces*. London: Sphere Books, 1975.

Dahl, Roald. Interview with Elizabeth Dunn, in *The Sunday Times Magazine*, 25 May 1982: 46.

Heins, P. (ed.). *Crosscurrents of Criticism: Horn Book Essays 1968–1977*. Boston, Mass.: Horn Book Inc., 1977.

Hill, George. "Dahl: Pied Piper with a Magic Pen," *The Times*, 21 April 1988: 12.

Hodgson, John. *The Search for the Self: Childhood in Autobiography and Fiction since 1940*. Sheffield: Sheffield Academic Press, 1993.

Holland, Norman. *5 Readers Reading*. New Haven: Yale University Press, 1975.

Jefferson, A. and Robey, D. *Modern Literary Theory*. London: B. T. Batsford Ltd., 1988.

Landau, E. D., et al., (eds.). *Child Development Through Literature*. Englewood Cliffs, N.J.: Prentice-Hall, 1972.

Lodge, David. (ed.). *20th Century Literary Criticism*. London: Longmans, 1985.

Natov, Roni. "The Truth of Ordinary Lives," *Children's Literature in Education*, 1986, Vol. 17: 112–14.

Rutherford, Jonathan. "Heroes and Mother's Boys," *Soundings* 3 (1996): 137–44.

Townsend, John Rowe. *Written for Children*. London: J. G. Miller, 1965.

Tucker, Nicholas. *The Child and the Book*. Cambridge, U.K.: Cambridge University Press, 1982.

Wood, Michael. "The Confidence Man," *New Society*, Dec. 1979: 20–27.

Television Programmes

BBC2 *Bookmark: Roald Dahl*. 13 September 1986.

BBC1 *Bookworm: The Nation's Favourite Children's Author*. 31 August 1997.

BBC2 Documentary Programme: *An Awfully Big Adventure: The Making of Modern Children's Literature: Roald Dahl*. 7 March 1998.

Visionary Children and Child-like Heroes
Steven Spielberg's "Primal Sympathy"

DOUGLAS BRODE

Judged simply in terms of box-office receipts, Steven Spielberg is probably the most successful director in the history of American cinema. What distinguishes the work of Spielberg from other celebrated and popular auteurs like John Ford, Howard Hawks, or Alfred Hitchcock, is the recurrent preoccupation with issues surrounding childhood and the fact that many of his films feature children or adolescents in principal roles. One has only to think of Barry in *Close Encounters of the Third Kind*, Elliott (and friends) in *E.T.*, Short Round in *Indiana Jones and the Temple of Doom*, and Jim in *Empire of the Sun* to appreciate the importance of children in Spielberg's work. Spielberg's "fascination and identification with children and the child's point of view" identified by the critic Peter Wollen as a "key characteristic in his work" (Wollen 1993, p. 9) meant that his eventual decision to adapt Sir James Barrie's *Peter Pan* for the screen came as no surprise to those who knew him well.

In the films cited above, the child characters are either cast in heroic roles themselves, or they adopt men such as Indiana Jones or Basie (in *Empire of the Sun*) as heroic models. This chapter explores the way heroism is depicted in the Spielbergian canon, examining what constitutes heroic action both for child heroes, and for adults acting as heroic (and sometimes flawed) mentors to children. However, whilst Spielberg is generally associated in the public mind with "family entertainment" and adventure movies, some of his movies have included scenes so disturbing and violent that they have led to a change in the certification of films for a young audience. I want to begin by outlining the background to that change.

In the early 1980s, America's ratings system—put into effect in 1967, when such films as Arthur Penn's graphically violent *Bonnie and Clyde* and Mike Nichols's sexually explicit *The Graduate* had rendered the old Production Code irrelevant—came under attack by concerned parents. Fifteen years of movie ratings had made it abundantly clear that the system was not working; it was influenced more by the status of a film's production company and the millions of dollars invested in it than by its content. Not surprisingly, Jack Valenti, the man in charge of the ratings system, had been deluged by letters from anxious parents, who pointed out that a system designed to make their job of selecting films easier had instead made it virtually impossible (Brode 1995, p. 144).

Some suggested a new, fifth rating ought to be established for classifying films that fell somewhere between the "PG" and adult-oriented "R" certificates. Nevertheless, Valenti publicly insisted throughout early June 1984 (with the year's major moviegoing season about to get under way), there would no revision (ibid.). He turned out to be a real-life counterpart of Vaughn, Amity's mayor in *Jaws* (1975). Having initially insisted that, despite shark scares, the beaches would not be closed (because this would mean jeopardizing the tourist season), Vaughn (Murray Hamilton) reverses his decision only after a child perishes. Two weeks after Valenti's pronouncement, the PG-13 rating (the intermediate rating parents had been requesting) was quietly slipped into place.

What occurred in between was the release of *Indiana Jones and The Temple of Doom.* This was the second in the trilogy of nostalgic action-adventure films, directed by Steven Spielberg, which simultaneously paid homage to, and parodied, 1930s and 1940s movie cliff-hanger serials such as *Flash Gordon Conquers the Universe.* These serials were the standard fare of the Saturday matinée programs he and George Lucas, the film's producer, remembered with such affection from their own childhood (McBride 1997, p. 312). The film, featuring scenes in which dinner guests consume jellied monkey brains at a native feast, and sacrificial rites where the victim's heart is torn from his chest, brought small children to tears. Ironically, the catalyst for the radical change to the ratings system was the filmmaker who had established himself as "the new Disney," thanks to *E.T.*, a heart-warming film, which everyone agreed merited its PG certificate. One critic described *E.T. The Extra-Terrestrial* (1982) as "the best Disney film ever made by anyone other than Disney" (Brode 1995, p. 122); not surprisingly, Spielberg had initially hoped to set up that project at the post-Walt, pre-Eisner Disney studio.

Significantly, however, *Temple Of Doom* was not Spielberg's only out-of-character shocker. That same summer during which *E.T.* charmed audiences, Spielberg offered another feature, *Poltergeist:* "It's nice I can release two sides of my personality so close to each other," the still-emerging auteur admitted. "*E.T.* is what I love; *Poltergeist* is what I fear" (Brode, p. 100). This gruesome ghost story's presentation of horrific images—a steak turns to worms, a scientist's face disintegrates—intensified the pressure for a fifth rating. The situation became critical in May 1982, when Spielberg and MGM chairman Frank Rosenfelt flew to New York after learning that the CARA chairman Richard D. Heffner had decided the "cumulative effect" of cadavers and "intensity" of images in *Poltergeist* necessitated an R rating. Nevertheless, *Poltergeist* was eventually released as a PG film, absurd though that decision might seem today. "I don't make R movies" (Brode, p. 113), Spielberg (who in fact favored a fifth designation) told anxious reporters as he left the now infamous meeting. Still, it is worth noting that Spielberg barely blinked in 1993 when *Schindler's List* received an R rating. Of course, the Steven Spielberg of 1993 was a very different film maker from the one who, some ten years earlier, uttered those words. During the intervening decade, he had faced his first negative reviews (*The Color Purple*, 1985), box-office disappointment (*Empire of the Sun*, 1987), and dealt with the deaths of actor Vic Morrow and two children on the set of *Twilight Zone—the Movie*, as well as that film's painful legal aftermath. And he had gone through an ugly divorce requested by his wife, actress Amy Irving, which led to the loss of immediate contact with his son, Max. Spielberg survived, starting a second family (with Kate Capshaw, the actress who played Willie in *Temple of Doom*), and moving ahead with his movie career.

In essence, as the harsh subject matter of *Schindler's List* made clear, he had grown up. How intriguing to note, then, that *Growing Up* had been the working title for *E.T.* during the early stages of the film's evolution. While still struggling with John Milius on the harmless, heartless mega-budget comedy *1941*, Spielberg began wondering if his harshest critics might not be correct: That he and Lucas were mere makers of popcorn entertainment movies—the best at what they did, yet hardly in a class with serious cinematic contemporaries such as Francis Coppola and Martin Scorsese, whose films reflected the European arthouse tradition of personal expression and indifference towards commercial considerations. Spielberg, having recently turned thirty, pondered whether his birthday might be a watershed, suggesting that it was time to move on to more mature matters.

But it proved difficult, if not impossible, for Spielberg to escape the issue of childhood. It was, after all, such a natural subject to him. In *Close Encounters of the Third Kind* (ostensibly a 1950s sci-fi flying saucer movie, produced with 1970s state-of-the-art special effects), Spielberg had presented an early incarnation of a recurring type in his gallery of heroic figures: an out-of-place New Yorker, Roy Neary (Richard Dreyfuss). Apparently Jewish, Neary lives in a middle-American suburb with his ultra-typical family. His entire life-experience, like that of the writer-director who created him, has been marked by attempts to deny his essential difference from everyone else—to be "average" and "ordinary" or, at least, appear so to those around him. Similarly, in *Jaws,* Sheriff Brody (Roy Scheider) a born-and-bred Amity native in Benchley's book (Benchley 1974) is converted by Spielberg into a misplaced New Yorker, hoping to "fit in."

Brody strives to gain acceptance from the community in which he has settled. The film wisely dispenses with Benchley's sub-plot of the sheriff sailing out to prove himself to a straying wife, preferring instead to celebrate family values. Neary's situation in *Close Encounters* is somewhat different: While for years he has chosen to ignore Thoreau's "different drummer" within him, the music—however muted—plays on, and eventually he loses his conventional family to find his unconventional self. What transforms Neary into the first full-blooded Spielbergian hero is his "close encounter" of the title.

From the moment Neary sees a UFO, and attempts to convince others of its existence, his sanity is called into question. When his wife and children leave him because of what they believe are his fantasies, his conformist side is ready to deny the truth he knows, if this will bring them back. What spurs him on—and allows him to emerge not only as the author's alter-ego but also as a true "hero-figure" (rising to epic stature while under extraordinary pressure)—is his psychic connection with a child. Barry (Carry Guffey) shares Neary's visions of a magical mountain, which eventually leads them both to Devil's Tower, where friendly aliens will land.

By that point, Neary and Barry have become what Joseph Conrad once termed "secret-sharers": characters who, though apart, share a single vision (Conrad 1910). The heroic element of Spielberg's oeuvre, however contemporary its presentation, harkens back to the "natural" philosophies of nineteenth-century Romantic poets: "The child," William Wordsworth wrote, "is father of the man." (Wordsworth 1959, p. 98)

Barry, unsullied by civilization's educating process, is intellectually and emotionally free, open to visions from beyond. Neary, though an adult, is one of the "elect"—as Wordsworth expresses it, one of those rare individuals able to "find/ Strength in what remains behind; In the primal sympathy/ Which having been must ever be" (Wordsworth, p. 100)—that being, of course, the spark of youth, so easily buried when one assumes adult responsibilities. Patricia Read Russell, in tracing connections between *E.T.* and Barrie's classic play *Peter Pan* (which Spielberg would later go on to film), also invokes Wordsworth's "visionary gleam" and refers to the "romantic view of childhood [which] conceives of the child because he is close to nature, as capable of clearer vision than the socialised adult. The child's mind accepts and integrates rather than excludes, the strange and the wonderful" (Russell 1989, p. 30).

Contact, physical and/or psychic, with Barry inspires Neary to cast off the conformity of civilized life; in so doing, Neary "grows," and finally enters the spacecraft to embark on his hero's journey. In fact, he has already completed an inner journey toward self-knowledge. Little Barry must remain behind, in the arms of his mother (Melinda Dillon); Barry serves as catalyst, allowing Neary the man to accept, and then embrace, his inner child. Essential in helping Neary is Lacombe, a unique government employee, who has both an analytic mind and an understanding heart. Lacombe represents the perfect adult who shares Neery and Barry's primal sympathy, and is able to balance a grown-up's grasp of science with a youngster's unsullied spirituality. Such an ideal is at the heart of this movie, as well as the Spielbergian canon.

It was no coincidence that Spielberg cast one of France's leading "nouvelle vague" directors, Francois Truffaut, in the key role of Lacombe. While Spielberg's contemporaries respected Truffaut's artistry, Spielberg responded to the fact that alone among New Wave artists, Truffaut crafted "serious" films about childhood, including *The 400 Blows* (1959) and *The Wise Child* (1969) (Cook 1996, pp. 571–579). In these and other works, Truffaut detailed the painful but necessary process of growing up. Spielberg wondered if he might likewise "grow up" (as a film maker) by making a movie based on his experiences during formative years he had spent in Scottsdale, Arizona. Always isolated by being the single Jewish kid in a "whitebread" neighborhood, young Steven watched helplessly as his parents moved inexorably toward divorce. Scorsese had made a film based on his early life, *Mean Streets* (1973) and Lucas did the same with *American Graffiti*. Spielberg might yet, with the film-in-progress he then referred to as *A Boy's Life,* emerge as America's Truffaut rather than a latter-day Disney. The movie, eventually known as *E.T.,* emerged as an odd (if curiously satisfying) combination of the two.

Hollywood executives were begging for a sequel to *Close Encounters,* but that didn't interest a creative person like Spielberg. Then, in 1980, while filming *Raiders of the Lost Ark,* Spielberg—far from home and the comfort of family—had grown lonely, and fantasised an imaginary friend (as he had when equally isolated as a child). This fantasy-figure eventually took the shape of a *Close Encounters* alien, the "little guy who was left behind" (Spielberg's own words) when the mother ship ascended (Brode 1995, p. 115). Like its predecessor, the new film would balance Hitchcock-like suspense with heartwarming Disney emotion, the alien now assuming centre stage. The emotions of childhood could be "seriously" explored within the context of an "escapist" film: "It's a personal movie for me," the filmmaker explained, "closer to my heart than any movie I've made before" (ibid.). Actually, it created the model for Spielberg's personal style, forging an unspoken "contract" with the audience. It provided them with the agreeable entertainment they desired, whilst incorporating enough personal material to allow for self-expression.

Audiences would probably have cared little if they had known that the monster-tree outside little Robbie's room in *Poltergeist* was drawn from Spielberg's childhood memories of an identical tree outside his bedroom window in New Jersey (Brode, p. 107). They got what they came for: a contemporary ghost story with stunning effects. If *Poltergeist* scared moviegoers, *E.T.* made them love the very sort of beautiful-ugly creature this director adored. *E.T.* also provided audiences with a religious epiphany, neatly disguised as secular entertainment. The mother (Dee Wallace) who takes in E.T. (he descends from on-high) is named Mary and there is no sexual partner sleeping by her side. "It's essentially the Christ story," Ted Koppel insisted on ABC's Nightline. "Christ was the ultimate extraterrestrial" (Brode, p. 127).

Rabbi Harold S. Kushner concurred: "Like religion, *E.T.* is real, even though it is not history. Real, because it tells us something that's true about the human spirit. It gives us a mythology that offers hope and comfort" (ibid.). Marta Tarbells of *McCall's* added that "Like Christ, E.T. can heal the sick and perform miracles; he also dies, is resurrected, and leaves earth for home (somewhere above). It is a familiar story . . . however new the form in which it is told" (ibid.). That, of course, fits Joseph Campbell's notion of popular films as our current equivalent of ancient myth. We hunger for recurring story patterns, responding when old tales are effectively presented in a modern guise (Campbell, 1989). So Luke Skywalker in *Star Wars* is our Arthur (the young man living in humble surroundings, gradually discovering he's of royal birth, born for greatness) and *E.T.* embodies a late twentieth-century retelling of the story of Jesus, something Spielberg's idol, John Ford, did in *The Fugitive* (1947) and *The Three Godfathers* (1948).

"That sounds like the atonement," observed Dr. Phil Lineberger—Pastor at the Metropolitan Baptist Church in Wichita, Kansas—during *E.T.*'s "death scene." "In the gospel, Christ died for our sins so that we might live, just as E.T. was doing. When E.T. was resurrected, and then at the end when he was ascending, (he was) watched by all his (own) disciples" (Brode, p. 127). Spielberg's masterpiece presented parable as paradox, a secular, apparently escapist entertainment but with strong, if implicit, spiritual values, which offered children contemporary heroes modelled on archetypes of the past, and parents something magical from their own youth, long repressed but not entirely lost.

Spielberg has risen to enormous levels of influence—in 1997, *Entertainment Weekly* named him as the most powerful person in Hollywood (Brode, p. 24). He supplied the public with regular doses of simple emotion and near-religious elevation. In fact, he had accomplished this before *E.T.* with *Raiders of the Lost Ark,* and (in collaboration with Lucas) would do so again in the sequels to that film. Each "Indy" (Indiana) film opens as an engaging diversion: a seemingly "new" kind of action film for those children unfamiliar with old adventure movies, and tongue-in-cheek nostalgia for adults who have come to reclaim their own lost youth. Then, as each instalment in the trilogy progresses, it gradually transforms into an ever more allegorical experience, conveying a conservative, even reactionary, agenda. Indy (who is "born again" in each movie) initially scoffs, with pseudo-sophisticated glibness, at the religious element of whatever artefact he's seeking, whether it's the Hebrew's Lost Ark of the Covenant or the Christian's Holy Grail; similarly, in *The Temple of Doom,* he initially has little patience with the Indian Holy Man's loving talk of Shiva or his fearful words about that good god's evil counterpart, Kali.

But like Brody and Neery before him, Indy will have to take an inner, spiritual journey, paralleling his outward, physical one. In *Raiders of the Lost Ark,* he and Marion Ravenwood (Karen Allen) survive the summoning of the Ark's spirits by sincerely believing, which takes the form of closing their eyes as God has commanded. In *Temple of Doom,*

he comes to see that the old shaman's vision is a legitimate way of looking at what he, the sceptical realist, first perceived as an accidental down-
ing of his plane. In *The Last Crusade,* Indy must reconcile his love for
his estranged father (Sean Connery) with belief in the God Indy had deserted. "Our Father, who art in heaven," he prays; in so doing, Indy saves
his earthly father's life. Miracles occur in Spielberg movies, even as they
did in the old Disney films for children, and in a number of John Ford's
supposedly adult-oriented pictures.

Critic Michael Marsden once referred to Alan Ladd's character in
Shane, George Stevens's seminal western, as a "saviour in the saddle"—
an uncommitted man who transforms before the eyes of audience and the
child/visual-narrator into an allegorical figure, able to defeat not merely
a gunfighter and a rancher, but evil incarnate. Shane is the white knight,
an avenging angel shrouding himself in cowboy's garb. Whatever soldier
of fortune guise Indy and other Spielberg's heroes adopt, the outcome
(good conquers evil) is much the same—as is the hero's "conversion"
from cynical, disbelieving modern man to old-fashioned true believer.
This is as true of one of Spielberg's most "realistic" pictures to date,
Schindler's List, as it was of his more fanciful, earlier projects.

Indy is first encountered as Professor Jones, stern archaeology professor. In a mature manner, Jones assures college students there's no romance or glamour in his chosen profession. Then, to escape the rigours
of office appointments, he leaps out a side window, swiftly transforming
into Indy—every child (or child man's) adventure hero come gloriously
to life. The grown-up in glasses and tweeds, we realize, was but a pose;
the real man is not Professor Jones but Indy, reinforcing Spielberg's conception. The person we encounter, employed in some humdrum job, is
not the "real" person, only the conventional role he or she has been
forced to play by society. The real person can be found in fantasies,
whether they remain imaginary as in movies such as this or, in rare cases,
lived out as Indy does in the movie.

Then again, one way of interpreting the Indy films is as a Walter
Mitty-esque fantasy: the great adventures take place only in Professor
Jones's mind. That would explain (and justify) why the stories resemble
tales in old movies; if Jones (like Spielberg) never experienced such excitement in the actual world, then in the privacy of his imagination (made
public via the movie), he would perceive them in the form of films—our
shared daydreams which Jones, like Spielberg himself, caught at some
matinée long ago.

Spielberg's basic assumption is that like him, we have never really strayed far from the image of the world as presented in Disney and Ford films, despite our national flirtation with *Easy Rider*-style radicalism in the late 1960s. This helps explain why adults, even former hippies, love to take their children to Disney theme parks and why Universal Studios added attractions in their parks based on recent Spielberg films, which play to the public in much the same way. *Jurassic Park,* a movie about a theme park, is now . . . a feature in a theme park. Indeed, Universal Studios in Florida and California are well on their way to becoming "Spielbergland."

In fact, as far back as 1991, Spielberg himself attempted to convince Universal they ought to use leftover sets for *Hook* as the basis for a park attraction. The disappointing critical and public reaction to that film, however, militated against such plans—ironically because the film's failure derived, in part, from the obvious fact that the on-screen pirate ship and Lost Boys hideaway looked less like true movie sets than theme park approximations. Whatever the film's failings (and they are many), *Hook* is perhaps the most significant work for any discussion of Spielberg as an artist who speaks to both the oncoming man in any child viewer and the lost boy hidden deep inside the adult. Originally, *Hook* was to have been a virtual remake of Walt Disney's animated *Peter Pan* (1953). For years, Spielberg planned to tell the story of a little boy who refused to grow up, using live actors and George Lucas's wondrous special effects. He even considered casting Michael Jackson (truly a little boy who never grew up) as the lead. Many believed it was the film Steven Spielberg had been born to make; he was, after all, largely written off as the Peter Pan of movie directors, talented but immature.

Then, as Spielberg grew, not only older but also up, his desire to do this project nearly died, with the film maker at one point insisting he'd never do a Peter Pan movie. It was time to move on; *Schindler's List* was just around the corner. Still, Spielberg could not deny his own "primal sympathy." So the project resurfaced, taking an entirely different, difficult direction, leading to a fascinating if less than successful film. Brian D. Johnson of *Maclean*'s commented at the time of *Hook*'s release: "Spielberg has made a movie that is less about Peter Pan than the Peter Pan syndrome" (Brode, p. 199).

Spielberg's Peter Banning (Robin Williams), unlike Barrie's Peter Pan, did indeed grow older and up, living to regret it. Described by his son as a corporate raider (which provokes Grandma Wendy's comment,

"Oh Peter, you've become a pirate"), Peter must eventually recall his long-repressed identity as leader of the Lost Boys if he is to rescue his own children; in the process, he rediscovers the lost joys of youth. This is a difficult process: Neery's "adult" existence was only a single step beyond childhood, making it relatively easy for him to revert; Banning is far removed from such innocence, which makes his eventual learning curve all the more impressive. Audiences complained about *Hook* as a work of popular entertainment, insisting it was too dark for children, too childlike for adults. Unwittingly, they accurately described the tension existing not only within this film—a transition piece from the children's entertainment preceding it to the adult art that, in *Schindler's List,* followed—but also within the heart and soul of its film maker.

For Spielberg, like Peter, still feels Wordsworth's "primal sympathy." In *Schindler's List,* it is the saving of innocent children that Spielberg emphasizes; in Thomas Kenneally's book, the children and adult Jewish prisoners received equal emphasis (Keneally, 1982). Spielberg's Schindler shares that man's name, but is, after all, a grown-up's version of the child-saving "man in the hat" we encountered in *Temple of Doom* and *Jurassic Park.* No wonder, then, that while greeting a visitor to the Poland location, actor Liam Neeson grinned when the man noted his fedora, insisting: "Please, no Indiana Jones jokes!" (Brode, p. 235) The Schindler we encounter in the film is the Schindler of Steven Spielberg's imagination, just as his Nazis are not all that different from the sharks, Thuggees, and dinosaurs populating his other pictures. After all, evil is—in the end—evil, whatever guise it wears. Nevertheless, in the movie that would at last win him an Academy Award as Best Director, Spielberg attempted something more complex: The villain Goethe (Ralph Fiennes) emerges as a human being, however flawed.

"I wanted this to be my first film without referencing," Spielberg said on the eve of Schindler's release, setting it apart from earlier homages to beloved movies. In fact, *Schindler's List* is full of filmic references, though they are less apparent than in previous pictures. The doomed child's red dress, in an otherwise black-and-white film, represented, by Spielberg's own admission, his "Rosebud" (Welles's recurring motif in *Citizen Kane*) approach to Schindler's unknowable personality (Brode, p. 231); the black-and-white film stock was not that of contemporary movies, but was chosen to give the impression of an old World War II documentary, through which Spielberg—and others of his generation—"know" the war years; the Jewish child with glasses resembles little Sabine in Truffaut's *Jules and Jim;* even the Gestapo's shower for their Jewish captives is shot in a manner that uneasily recalls Alfred Hitchcock's famous *Psycho* shower sequence.

Schindler's List was, however, the first film in which Spielberg at last managed to distance himself stylistically from the sensibility of a child's adventure tale. Such a reductive approach had diminished the potential power of his earlier *Empire of the Sun,* based on J. G. Ballard's grim autobiographical novel. In Spielberg's hands, the material played as a grand if dangerous romp for a courageous little boy (Christian Bale). Even Basie, Jim's three-dimensional mentor in the novel, emerged as a caricature; John Malkovich, ordinarily an actor from whom audiences expect complexity, delivered a simplistic rendering of a seductively charming-villain out of some conventional nineteenth-century piece of boys' fiction: Long John Silver of Robert Louis Stevenson's *Treasure Island,* with a touch of Fagin from Charles Dickens' *Oliver Twist.*

In the film, Jim—separated from his own father—adopts Basie as a surrogate father-figure. Thus the filmmaker personalized the tale, making it one more variation of the key theme running through his work: How to survive in the world without a father present. If Jim turns to Basie, then Elliot turns to E.T., who—as a Christ figure—becomes the perfect father. Neery, in *Close Encounters,* loses his own children and compensates by becoming substitute father to little Barry; it is not long, however, before Neery is learning spiritual wisdom from the boy; once again, "The child is father of the man."

Hook, coming at a later point in the auteur's development, also reworks the thematic preoccupation with surrogate fathers. Peter Banning, one-time free spirit, has completely conformed to the "Yuppified" L.A. lifestyle, with the result that he can no longer recall his former life as a "wild" child. Peter has become so distanced from his son Jack that, once in Neverland, the boy temporarily accepts the wicked Captain Hook (Dustin Hoffman) as surrogate father. In the film's most deeply felt moment, Banning watches helplessly as Hook plays baseball with Jack, something Peter failed to do with the boy. However, in this magical place, not unlike Shakespeare's Green World forest from *A Midsummer Night's Dream,* Banning's primal sympathy—so long repressed—is revived; at one with the Lost Boys, this born-again Pan is a true Spielbergian figure: half man, half child, complete hero.

But as the film maker matures, he can no longer present the old simplicities, at least not without revision: Though Banning saves his own boy, he does so at a terrible price, allowing another child (Rufio, now dependent on Banning as surrogate father) to die. The message seems to be that heroes—especially heroes who are fathers or surrogate fathers—can be deeply flawed. Clearly this applies to a villain like Hook but what makes him such a disturbing and complex figure (in both Barrie's text and the film) is that he embodies those anti-heroic qualities that lurk within Peter Banning: to some extent he is Banning's alter-ego, his dark side.

The preoccupation with fatherhood recurs in *Jurassic Park*. Spielberg has the palaeontologist, Dr Alan Grant (Sam Neill) overcoming his arrested-adolescent repulsion towards children and taking on the responsibilities of foster-father to children threatened by the rampaging dinosaurs. The film charts Grant's moral education as he comes to understand what every male hero in Spielberg's later films must grasp: there is no greater reward than parenting, however limiting or exhausting it sometimes seems and however much the hero recoils from the constraints of parental duties. Reviewing the film in *Sight and Sound,* Henry Sheehan commented on Spielberg's "continuing obsession between fathers treading the line between life-giver and life-destroyer" (Sheehan, 1993, p. 10).

The same tension is evident in *The Temple of Doom.* Although Indy at first shuns adult responsibility, he gradually accepts the role of surrogate father to the orphan child, Short Round (Ke Huy Quan). With the help of the unlikely mother-figure Willie (Kate Capshaw), Indy becomes saviour to the children enslaved by the Thuggees, as well as long-awaited religious Deliverer in the eyes of the Indian village whose children had been abducted. He re-unites the children with their parents and returns the religious stones that protected the village from evil and misfortune. Before these heroic feats are accomplished, however, the father as both "life-giver and life-destroyer" re-emerges in the movie's disturbing and macabre climax. In the cave of the Thuggees, Indy has been drugged by the High Priest to obey his commands and sacrifice Willie. She tries to pull him out of the spell but fails. However, when Short Round, ignoring Indy's vicious rejection of him, cries, "I love you, Indy," the father figure is able to snap out of his catatonic state to resume his life-giving role and rescue Willie, Short Round, and the imprisoned children:

> In the world according to Spielberg, the parent-child bond is a more basic, potent positive than the man-woman bond. Like Roy Neary and a half-dozen other Spielberg heroes, Indy discovers that there is more

he can learn from the child than he can ever teach him. (Brode 1995, p. 143)

Each of the Indiana Jones films exhibits the racist and sexist attitudes so inherent in the old-fashioned boys' adventure stories that inspired the Spielberg/Lucas trilogy. But what makes *The Temple of Doom* much more disturbing than the other two films is the prominent role of children in it, especially that of Short Round, who clearly idolises Indy and sees him as a father. What kind of heroic model is being offered to Short Round and the child viewer? And what kind of values are being espoused?

George Lucas, who once declared, "If I could be a dream figure, I'd be Indy," seemed unaware of the ideological implications of the archaeologist cum-soldier-of-fortune (McBride 1997, p. 312). They were certainly not lost upon the Indian government officials who, before filming began on *The Temple of Doom*, had refused permission to shoot location scenes in India because they regarded the storyline as "racist." "With its stereotypical Indian villains," says McBride, "and its lurid relish in depicting bloodthirsty Thuggee rituals, *Temple of Doom* went far beyond the casual racism of *Raiders of the Lost Ark*, paying mindless homage to the worst aspects of *Gunga Din* and other past examples of cultural imperialism" (McBride 1997, p. 354).

It troubles us when Spielberg revives not only the narrative formulas of old films, but also their repellent racist ideology. Equally offensive is the sexist representation of Willie. Leaving aside her high pitched screams (evoking memories of Fay Wray in *King Kong*), which regularly punctuate the film, and her excessive alarm over broken finger-nails, it is impossible to defend scenes in which she is subjected to a symbolic/actual violation by spiders, and later—as sacrificial victim—spreadeagled on a frame and lowered into a fiery pit. This was a particularly disturbing scene because the pose and her diaphanous clothing emphasised her sexual vulnerability.[1]

The outcry provoked by the film, which predictably focused on its violence rather than its racist and sexist representations, led to the speedy adoption of a PG-13 rating. Even Spielberg admitted that he would put his hand over the eyes of a ten-year-old child during the scene depicting torture and human sacrifice. Perhaps the most out-spoken criticism came from the film critic of *People* magazine, who denounced it as "an astonishing violation of the trust" audiences placed in Spielberg and Lucas as makers of family entertainment adding that, "No parent should allow a young child to see this traumatising movie; it would be a cinematic form of child abuse" (in McBride 1997, p. 357).

The effect of films like *The Temple of Doom* was to blur the line between films containing material more appropriate for an adult audience and those intended for children. It also had the effect of creating an immature audience, whatever its age. Spielberg may not have been the first or the only film maker to propel the American motion picture in this direction, but he is unquestionably the most successful and, as such, came to be seen as the spearhead of this "dumbing-down" tendency. Influential critic, Pauline Kael described this process as the "infantilization of popular culture" (Brode, p. 25).

When Andrew Sarris observed that, "E.T. is every childish fantasy we never outgrew," he could have been speaking of the Spielberg's oeuvre as well as this character. Sarris went on to claim, "E.T. is the eternal child in all of us" (Brode, p. 127), thus providing a perfect explanation for Spielberg's popularity. Tellingly, Spielberg's favorite actor and close friend Richard Dreyfuss once noted: "He's a big kid who at twelve years old decided to make movies," adding that on some level, "he's still twelve years old" (Brode, p. 24). But only on some level. If he were still a child, existing in a man's body, he would make G and PG films; if he were an adult who had forsaken the inner child, he would make R and NC-17 films. As Steven Spielberg—still in touch with that twelve-year-old within himself—he inspired the PG-13 rating, which had to be created to designate those films that bridge the gap between child and adult.

Spielberg would understand what Wordsworth meant when he wrote: "Though nothing can bring back the hour/ of splendour in the grass, of glory in the flower;/We will grieve not, rather find/Strength in what remains behind" (Wordsworth, p. 98). What remains behind is, of course, the ghost of the child that exists within every adult woman and man, the primal sympathy waiting to be rekindled. So we—adults who now attend movies with our children—respond to Steven Spielberg films because his primal sympathy mirrors our own.

NOTE

1. For an extended critique of the film's racism and sexism, see also "*Indiana Jones and the Temple of Doom*—The return of the repressed" by Moishe Postone and Elizabeth Traube, in *Jump Cut,* 1985, March, Vol. 30, pp. 12–14.

REFERENCES

Benchley, Peter. *Jaws.* New York: Bantam, 1975 [1974].

Brode, Douglas. *The Films of Steven Spielberg.* New York: Citadel Press, 1995

Campbell, Joseph with Bill Moyers. *The Power of Myth.* New York: London: Doubleday, 1989.

Conrad, Joseph. *Heart of Darkness and The Secret Sharer.* New York: New American Library, 1971 [1912].

Cook, David. *A History of Narrative Film.* New York: Norton, 1996.

Keneally, Thomas. *Schindler's Ark.* London: Hodder and Stoughton, 1982.

McBride, Joseph. *Steven Spielberg.* New York: Simon and Schuster, 1997.

Russell, Patricia Read. "Parallel Romantic Fantasies: Barrie's *Peter Pan* and Spielberg's *E.T.: The Extraterrestrial, Children's Literature Association Quarterly.* Vol. 8 No. 4, 1983: 28–30.

Sheehan, Henry. "The Fears of Children," *Sight and Sound,* July 1993. p. 10.

Wollen, Peter. "Theme Park and Variations," *Sight and Sound,* July 1993. pp. 7–9.

Wordsworth, William. *Major British Writers,* ed. George B. Harrison. New York: Harcourt Brace Jovanovich, 1959 [1888].

Unbronzing the Aussie
Heroes and SNAGs in Fiction and Television for Australian Adolescents

ROBYN McCALLUM AND JOHN STEPHENS

For half a century after 1921, the most recognizable hero in Australian popular culture was a comic strip character named Ginger Meggs, a small boy inhabiting an imaginary middle-ground Australia—neither middle class nor working class, neither urban nor rural—and exhibiting traits often (then) assumed to be quintessentially Australian: He was a low-key hero and was, among other things, apt to be a likeable larrikin, anti-authoritarian, generally anti-intellectual, always ready for a game of backyard cricket or to miss school to go fishing, prone to violence (often implicitly homophobic in its direction), and reflexively racist because of assumptions about Australian social homogeneity. In his history of this character, Barry Andrews points to three factors which led to a waning in his popularity during the 1970s: wide acceptance that Australian society is multicultural; the impact of television (not introduced into Australia until 1956) in disseminating global culture and creating new international heroes; and the influence of feminism, which interrogates the assumptions of that imaginary Australia (Andrews, 1982). *Ginger Meggs* survived the 1970s, and still presents a society in which "men must work and women must weep or nag, and boys will be boys with black eyes, and little girls will be demure and feminine" (Andrews 1982, p. 228), but Ginger's attributes as a male hero have become increasingly anachronistic in a constantly transforming society.

Various macho male images still endure in Australian popular culture, and the "bronzed Aussie" still appears on television advertizing breakfast cereals for "iron men," but narrative fictions which target a contemporary Australian adolescent audience now characteristically eschew any kind of traditional male heroic image, and the only international hero figures to be found are the anti-hero and the sensitive guy. This observation applies equally to television narratives, soap operas, popular fiction and "high culture" fiction, and the effect is accentuated by the absence of either an indigenous comic book industry or locally produced animated cartoons for television. Furthermore, the representation of alternative masculine role models is often clearly a conscious attempt to comment on or intervene in a culture where there is a widespread recognition that so-called traditional models of masculinity are socially and personally destructive, and are increasingly seen to be a central factor in the increasing gap between the academic performance of girls and boys in secondary schooling: In the 1994 New South Wales Higher School Certificate examination (the Year Twelve examination which concludes secondary schooling) girls outperformed boys in every single subject, including "traditional" boys' fields such as the hard sciences. This outcome sparked extensive public anxiety around the question: How are we failing our boys? But, as Richard Fletcher argues, the crucial issues for boys go well beyond tertiary entrance scores. Where boys do outperform girls, he reminds us, is "at suicides, . . . at drownings, low literacy, drug offences, serious assaults, expulsions from school, alcohol abuse, reading difficulties, work injuries, attention deficit disorder and head injuries" (1995, p. 208). To begin to even try to change this situation, society needs to address both the images widely disseminated through popular culture and the question of the kinds of masculinity which might be privileged.

Narrative fictions in literature and television directed at Australian adolescents were, as elsewhere in the world, exploring and advocating alternative masculine schemata long before the need to do so became a transitory media issue.[1] Such alternative constructions, it must be acknowledged at the outset, reach only a minority audience, and their impact is probably more to reassure members of the audience that they have viable choices than to induce change. After all, these texts are only a small part of a total social context. Also, in the absence of social consensus about desirable masculinities, the texts themselves, often overtly or implicitly, present ambivalent or shifting points of view, or their implied audience is female and the textual objective is to influence girls to contribute to changing images of masculinity by showing preference for males who are, for example, communicative, intellectually and emotionally sensitive, and whose relationships with females are based on friendliness, companionability, empathy, and equality. A common textual strategy in the literature for adolescents is thus to construct a dialogic relationship between differing masculine schemata which are co-present in the everyday world, but because some schemata are affirmed rather than others, they are presented as discourses consistently oriented as a form of social advocacy rather than reflection.

Our purpose in this article is to examine the masculine schemata and the modes of representation in a sample of Australian texts produced during the 1980s and early 1990s. We will begin with *His Master's Ghost,* a short telemovie produced by the Australian Children's Television Foundation in their "Winners" series and subsequently published as a novelization, and we will go on to make some comparisons with *Quest Beyond Time,* an earlier production in the "Winners" series, and several novels written within popular or series genres. The novelizations of the two telemovies conform with genres common in Australian children's fiction: respectively, they are a contemporary realist and a post-disaster dystopian fiction. The film versions of *His Master's Ghost* and *Quest Beyond Time* are predominantly narrative in form, driven by story, action and character types. Film is, of course, limited in its techniques for depicting character introspection, and is dependent on the use of visual and verbal cues to indicate character point of view. The film versions of the two texts utilize visual generic conventions, camera angles and cutting techniques to evoke and explore the masculine schemata which shape the texts. Whereas the differences between the novelistic and film versions of *His Master's Ghost* are minimal, the novelistic version of *Quest Beyond Time* capitalises on narrative strategies which allow access to character thought and is hence much more introspective and reflective in its approach. The book of *His Master's Ghost,* like other fictions of this kind, maintains the illusion that the actual world is being re-presented by using narrative strategies which conceal the status of the text as fiction, and especially by the manipulation of narrative voice. A contemporary realistic children's novel is characteristically narrated by one of the main characters and this often has the effect of rendering experience more immediately, since there is no impersonal or anonymous narrator to mediate between events and readers. There is an implication that narrator and implied readers share the same language, attitudes and values. The equivalent strategy in *His Master's Ghost* is a narration which frequently addresses an implied reader with assertions that characters and events being described are familiar and part of a common shared experience. The illusion that a text is unmediated can also be effected in third person narration, as when, for example, in Tim Winton's *Lockie Leonard,*

Human Torpedo, the narrating voice and the main character's speech and thought processes employ a very similar language, sharing vocabulary—especially slang and idiomatic expressions—and sentence structures. Thus the slippage between the conceptual point of view of the narrator and the register characteristic of the protagonist is virtually unmarked in a passage such as: "Ah, you should have seen them there, holding hands like there was no tomorrow. I don't know if you've ever been in love or not, but I tell you, when you are in love, you might as well have your brain sealed up in a jam jar until it's all over" (p. 52).

His Master's Ghost is a useful starting point because, although its story-line seems redolent of a "high culture" text, its narrative processes are playfully and parodically affiliated with popular genres—horror fiction, the country house mystery, school story, and soap opera—and its masculine images are constructed out of a patterned interrelationship of common schematic stereotypes. The story tells of a group of young, talented music students attending a Summer Camp held at Monsalvat, an old Gothic building on the outskirts of Melbourne, and centers around the rehearsal and performance of an avant-garde composition by one of the students, Jason. A second strand deals with Colin, known as "Flea," the practical joker of the group, and his developing fascination with the property's caretaker, a strange old man who in some sense re-embodies the ghost of Beethoven. The setting is itself significant, because of course there are rumours of ghosts and there are spooky places for the boys to explore after lights out. The movie includes some important female roles, but these are seldom more than necessary functions, and the story interest is focused on the males, especially Flea. This is underlined by the camera-work and, in the novelization, by the distribution of the minimal amount of character focalization between males and females. It is most evident, though, in the patterning of masculine models in a way not parallelled by the female characters. That is, there are six central male characters, three adults and three adolescents, each of which represents a different type.

The adults roughly conform with the categories Helen Townsend suggests are often characteristic male types in Australian-made soaps: "decent bloke, wimp, or psychopath" (1994, p. 131). Mike, the composition teacher, is quintessentially the "decent bloke": he dresses casually, relates with the students in a friendly and informal manner, is even boyish in his tolerance of pranks, and acts on his belief that people should be given a chance to prove themselves. The novel emphasizes his approachability by usually designating him by his first name, "Mike." Mr Gwynne, conductor of the orchestra, is the "wimp": He always dresses in grey suit and tie, and his appearance, speech, and body language suggest such descriptors as "inhibited," "affected," "querulous" and "self-important"; his relationship with the students is paternalistic and often sarcastic, but he has little real authority; his musical tastes seem conservative and unadventurous (he dismisses Jason's concerto as a "decomposition" and contrasts it with "the sanity and sanctity of Beethoven"). In the novel, the narrative always refers to him as "Mr Gwynne," and crucial actual descriptors are "thin, flustered, prim, patronizing, petulant." This is a problematic representation, especially in the novel, because it too often slips into the trap of implicitly pejorating the character as not-masculine by using descriptors, many of which have a semantic history as pejorative terms applied to women. The problem here is the other side of a more pervasive problem of representation in which "masculine" tends to be defined as "not being feminine" (see Franklin, 1988, p. 2). Third, the caretaker is initially constructed as psychopath by Flea's genred interpretation of appearance and setting, and by long camera shots of him at night appearing, at least to Flea and his friend Martin, mysterious and dishevelled. The viewing audience, however, seeing both the caretaker and the boys, always has another perspective, and is invited to collude in moments of allusive playfulness, as when the shadow of the caretaker bringing his axe to lop a tree-branch becomes a direct borrowing from an (in)famous moment in *Nosferatu*. This process of construction and reconstruction enables the character of the caretaker to disclose capacities for caring and empathy and for creativity. His "madness" is the madness of Beethoven, "a weirdo. Ranging and raving around the place . . . as mad as a meat axe" as Flea describes the Beethoven he reads about in *Immortal Beloved* (novel, p. 57).

The example of older males who may serve as role models is a significant element in the process whereby young males explore male sex roles, whether within the family, in educational institutions, or in other social settings which function as contexts where men negotiate masculinity (cf. Franklin, 1988, p. 121). In *His Master's Ghost,* the Music Camp combines some of these possibilities by bringing together the presence of potential adult role models, single-sex dormitories, and the possibilities of male-female peer interactions. As with the adults, the three young male characters represent different ways of being male. Martin, as the novel puts it, is "a bit of a spunk . . . really good looking." He is popular and sociable, and the only one of the three with an overt interest in the girls and enough self-assurance to act on this: he and Sarah, the most outgoing of the girls, quickly become an item. One day Martin will grow up to be very like Mike. Flea, at the outset of the story, has a little of Ginger Meggs about him, in that he is also a likeable larrikin, anti-authoritarian, openly anti-intellectual, full of mischief. He is not the forever prepubescent hero, however, but a boy genuinely open to growth and change. Jason epitomizes the pubescent creative male, self-conscious and defensive about his work, able to relate quite confidently with adults but awkward with people his own age, especially girls. There is no clearly definable, convenient masculine schema into which Jason might be slotted, and both movie and novel work to find some accommodation with a SNAG (Sensitive New Age Guy) schema.

In broad terms, the representation of Martin is a shorthand version of the Sensitive New Age Guy schema which grounds all of the positive masculine schemata employed or advocated in Australian popular fiction, more usually as the product of character growth or narrative disclosure. Texts such as *Lockie Leonard* or the majority of *Dolly* (later *Paradise Point*) fictions, a series of Australian teen romances launched in 1988, share a process whereby males who seem at first somewhat unpromising are inducted into self-awareness and sensitivity. At one point in Francis's *Heartbreak City* (*Dolly* No. 71, 1991) the main female character asks herself, thinking about the young man she's been trying to have a relationship with, "Who is this guy? Is he the rude, self-centered meathead I met at the first tai chi class? Is he the complex sensitive guy I got to know over the following months? Or is he a mixture of both?" (p. 72) In a *Dolly*, if he's going to finish up with the girl at the end, he will have to be, or even better, become, the second, "the complex sensitive guy." *Dolly*-fiction offers the clearest examples of attempts to construct female perspectives on masculinity, to influence girls' expectations, and, indirectly, to help shape male sex roles by encouraging girls to reject macho forms of masculinity.

Lockie Leonard, like *His Master's Ghost,* incorporates adult male role models. The main male characters, who are usually just ordinary people, tend to be distributed so that they represent various masculine social types. All of these types—bordering, at times, on stereotypes—are laden with moral values grounded in social ideology, and it is largely Winton's organisation and representation of that ideology which determines how as readers we weigh one against another. Winton's technique is to pair characters so that the valorized masculine type, the "decent bloke," is juxtaposed against a range of pejorated male types, including "the wimp," "the wally," the car salesman, the tyrannical teacher, and the Bogan.[2] The Sarge (Lockie's father) and John East, the guidance counsellor, are both "decent blokes." Both are characterized as "boys at heart": the Sarge "peeled out of the bus zone like one of the Dukes of Hazzard" (1990, p. 20) when he picked Lockie up from school in the police patrol car; and John East surfs and uses colloquial "adolescent" language. Surfing has a conventional association with male adolescence and in *Lockie Leonard* it is associated, via Lockie and East, with a valorized construction of masculinity. The trajectory of maturation that the novel offers for Lockie (the "decent" adolescent bloke) involves a return to the boyish behaviour exemplified by his father. Another stereotype that is implicitly evoked via the counsellor, East, is that of the ineffectual older male who appropriates adolescent culture and language. In the first interview between Lockie and John East, both characters are sizing the other up, so when East asks Lockie what kind of board he has, "Lockie smiled. He's trying to get in with me, the wally, he thought. He wouldn't know a damn thing about it" (p. 34) and Lockie forecloses the conversation by asking if he can leave. What is at issue here is the idea of cultural ownership, and East's right, as a teacher and an older male, to address Lockie as an equal and to implicitly identify himself with Lockie. Later East and Lockie meet surfing, and it emerges that East had also doubted Lockie's ability to surf—"You little prick! . . . You *can* surf." (p. 37). Likewise, East's ability to surf proves his status as "decent bloke" for Lockie.

The character of Lockie is also worked out through oppositions to Vicki, his girlfriend. The story charts the progress of Lockie's and Vicki's relationship—before, during, and after. He is the poor, but good-hearted boy; she is the rich, but unhappy girl. He is in no hurry to grow up, while she is only too ready to grow up. A problematic aspect of Winton's attempt to construct Lockie according to a sensitive adolescent male schema is that Vicki becomes a foil for Lockie and is slotted into a stereotyped, and conventionally pejorated feminine role—the active, sexually precocious female. Conventional romances depict females as occupying passive roles while males occupy more active roles. However, in *Lockie Leonard,* it is the more experienced female who initiates the relationship and who pressures the less experienced male into a more sexual relationship. By placing Lockie in the more passive role, Winton constructs a role for Vicki which is conventionally seen as deviant for females—this is accentuated through Vicki's association with the "bogans" (the devalued male stereotype). It is also clear in the foreword of the novel: "Lockie Leonard fell in love last term. No one in school knew who the hell he was before it all happened . . . Vicki Streeton . . . she's always been known in this town" (p. 1) where, through the associations of being "known in this town," the terms "knew" and "known" mean quite differently for males and females. Winton is using Lockie to affirm childhood against Vicki's desire to throw off childhood. And the novel closes with Lockie and his younger brother, Philip, riding their bikes down the street doing wheelies, in a scene which nicely echoes the earlier scene of the Sarge picking Lockie up from his first day at school. Winton's solution to the problem of what type of male role model to aspire to is for Lockie to remain a boy for as long as possible.

The Lockies, John Easts, Mikes and Martins of the world present an image of amiable, sensitive masculinity, but it is also far from definitive. The range of possibilities is extended through the representations of the other characters in *His Master's Ghost*. Jason, the composer, could in another context be a boy at risk of being victimized by other boys, and the male dormitory situation is used to express this possibility a little more sharply in the novel than in the movie. In both narratives, he obsessively works on his concerto in the dormitory rather than attempting to socialize, and when he complains to the others about their noise, "he immediately cops the sort of response you'd imagine such a remark to receive" (novel, p. 15); in the novel, Martin has already short-sheeted his bed, while in the movie, in a socially more complex incident, Flea tricks him by offering to shake hands and in doing so administers an electric shock. These incidents seem to allude to ways in which boys' peer groups regulate membership and, in doing so, police masculinity. Such behavior is a continuing focus in popular narrative fictions. For example, many of the stories by Paul Jennings—Australia's most successful author of popular adolescent fiction—pivot around acts of victimization which are an implicit questioning of a boy's sexuality. In "Just Like Me" and "Pubic Hare" (from *Uncovered!* 1995), the narrators are outsiders who do not conform to the current "masculine" paradigm, and are thus objects of victimization by other boys who establish their own group solidarity and masculinity by processes of exclusion and physical violence. The narrator of "Just Like Me" is "skinny, dorky," freckled, artistic and sensitive; that of "Pubic Hare" is a "skinny wimp." Both are made to suffer, but the stories are also characteristic in depicting outcomes which empower the outsider, and hence serve to reject the masculine schema of the group and, presumably, to offer reassurance to readers whose own experiences are in some way analogous with those of the narrators.

Other short story writers have gone further in overtly thematizing issues of masculinity. Two pertinent examples are Allan Baillie's "The Champion" (in Wheatley, 1993) and Peter McFarlane's "Coober" (in *Lovebird*, 1993). "The Champion," about a boy whose desire to excel over others leads to loss of integrity and self-respect, presents another straightforward image by linking masculinity with the notion of winning at any cost, and then undermines it by introducing an opponent who clearly has a different kind of masculinity and a young admirer who witnesses the misdeed that enables the victory and so loses his respect. This story demonstrates how some discourses are so pervasive in the literature that they can be evoked by absence or inference. The belief that selfhood should be intersubjective, for example, has clear implications for representations of masculinity. As we have suggested, the civilizing of the male is an outcome depicted in a wide range of texts, and Baillie evokes this by what is a virtual list of traits which Lee, the "champion" of the title, derisively identifies in Watson, his opponent: "Floppy hair, owl glasses, looks like a scarecrow . . . He's a student, studies Ancient Greece, Literature . . ." (p. 72). From Lee's perspective, Watson is marked as "not-masculine." Lee is a character who attracts a reader's contempt, and by telling the story with Lee as focalizer, and Watson as a shadowy figure seen almost entirely in terms of Lee's perceptions, Baillie successfully pejorates Lee's version of masculinity. The story clearly illustrates how a dialogic relationship between two versions of masculinity might be organized as discourses consistently oriented as a form of advocacy rather than reflection.

Like *His Master's Ghost*, McFarlane's "Coober" situates its dialogue between versions of masculinity from within a context which empowers a masculinity that does not conform with traditional male sex roles: this is done by having the story narrated by Vincenzo, a seventeen-year-old dance student. Hospitalized because of a knee injury, he forms a friendship with a fellow patient of the same age suffering from a similar injury. Gary, however, is a footballer and a carpenter by trade. To pass the time before either can return to training, they decide to bicycle from Adelaide to the inland, opal-mining town of Coober Pedy, a distance of 860 kilometers. The story's schematic conjunction of apparent opposites enables McFarlane to work with familiar stereotypes, though these are shaped by Vincenzo's narration in order to produce the re-hierarchization of masculinities we are concerned with. Gary thus makes the conventional macho assumption that an interest in the arts signifies that a man is possibly gay, and cannot even consider Vincenzo's counter-claim that "there are more gay guys playing footy than doing ballet" (1993, p. 5). We have pointed to another version of this assumption in Baillie's story, in Lee's pejorative "student, [who] studies Ancient Greece, Literature," and it seems to hover around Flea's ambivalence towards classical music in *His Master's Ghost.* Gary also sums up the attitude when declining Vincenzo's offer of tapes for his Walkman: "He snorted. 'Listen to your classical shit? Hell, no.' " (1993, p. 14). The presence of this assumption in Australian classrooms has been documented by Wayne Martino from his survey of the attitudes of 249 senior secondary students towards English as a subject for study (1995, p. 126–130). In their extended responses the boys expressed dislike for a subject which they considered to be feminine (p. 127), and described it as boring, much less interesting than football, and difficult to engage with because of its concern with feelings and ideas. The extreme response—"it's not the way guys think . . . most guys who like English are faggots" (p. 129)—does not come as any surprise, as the kind of texts we are discussing here have already been chipping away at this cliché of masculine culture for many years.

The idea of a male subjectivity being formed and shaped within specifically masculine domains—sporting activities, relation to physical landscape—also occurs in *Lockie Leonard* in repeated descriptions of surfing. Surfing functions metonymically in this novel to construct quite a complex schema for male adolescence and for the formation of masculine subjectivity. In the interview with John East, Lockie suggests that his best subject is probably English and claims to hate all sport; by "sport" he means team sports and competitive sports. In rejecting competitive sport, and liking English, Lockie is also rejecting the traditional "macho" construction of masculinity. In valorizing surfing, a pastime which one does for "fun" and for oneself, Winton also valorizes a construction of masculinity as individualistic, and as sensitive and cooperative. There are four key surfing episodes in the novel—these occur at crucial moments in the narrative. In two episodes Lockie surfs alone; in the other two episodes he surfs with another surfer. Descriptions of Lockie surfing alone depict his experience as a moment of pure feeling, as a total immersion in the physical action and of interaction with the physical landscape. In these scenes, Winton is using surfing as an element in the story, as an aspect of Lockie's character, and as a metonym for moments of essential being when Lockie is most intensely himself, independent of the social relations and forces which surround him. For example, Lockie's lone surf after a scene with Vicki has echoes of the late seventies cult surfing movie *Big Wednesday,* wherein the act of surfing a big swell represents an intense personal confrontation with "nature" and a moment of transcendence, as in "and then came this great green thing hissing out of nowhere and Lockie knew he'd either ride it or drink it, so he turned and went for it and felt it power him out forward as though he'd been shot from a cannon. . . . He was swallowed up . . . And then he shot out the end into the light" (p. 123–124). This is reminiscent of traditional images in Australian texts wherein the conflict between an individual and the physical landscape is metonymic of spiritual growth, but Winton's narrative strategies blur the distinction between the focalising subject and the fictive landscape. This dismantling of the boundary between self and world implies a masculine subjectivity which is formed through both interaction with, and dissolution within, the natural world. However, Lockie does not always surf alone. Surfing is also a highly codified social activity which is ordered according to rules determined by age and ability, and as the following quote indicates, the surf becomes a vehicle with which to work out hierarchical social relationships based on competitive behaviour: "Lockie dropped into a crouch, held an edge and came powering down the line, getting speed from each hit at the wave's lip . . . as he closed on the other kid . . ." (p. 12).

One ideological implication of the way that surfing is being used metonymically in the novel is an implicit refusal of the "bronzed Aussie" surfer-hero figure and of the gendered social configurations that this figure evokes. Lockie is a grommet (a young surfer) and, according to the codes of surfing, his actions when other surfers "drop in" on him are socially inappropriate—"he pulled a big re-entry and came floating down right across the guy's leg-rope. Twang!" (p. 12). The episode implicitly re-asserts social hierarchies and codes for competitive masculine behaviour that Lockie has breached. However, in a later episode where Lockie and East surf together, a similar sequence of events serves to imply a non-competitive cooperative equality between the two characters as surfers—"Lockie stayed in behind as this drop-in made a whole pile of radical moves, turning with real power . . . Lockie worked up high . . ." (p. 37). While Lockie does help to form a surfing club at the school, he is reluctant to do so, thereby implicitly refusing to be complicit in the construction of the surfer as hero. Likewise many of his actions, such as starting a fire with a joint, undercut the conventional associations of surfing as a group activity. Finally, by implicitly rejecting the stereotyped figure of the surfer as hero, Winton also rejects equally stereotyped images of female characters as "surfie chicks." Vicki, Lockie's girlfriend, is well aware of the way in which the construction of Lockie as "bronzed surfer" positions her: "You won't expect me to sit on the beach like some dumb adoring surf-chick, will you?" Her refusal of this role conversely emphasizes the narrative construction of Lockie as the sensitive, marginally incompetent, but likeable and "boyish" guy: "Now don't go thinking you're a real spunk, or anything. I can't stand male pride. You're still Lockie Leonard who can't get out of his wetsuit and has obviously never been kissed by anyone but his mum before"(45).

   Lockie Leonard consistently valorizes cooperation over competition. Obsessive competitiveness, a compulsion to turn everything into a competition, is another masculine stereotype evinced in most of the texts we are considering, and it is invariably represented as undesirable and destructive. In "The Champion," Lee must win at any cost, whereas Watson just runs—"No training, no coaching, no real reason for it all" (1991, p. 72). In "Coober," Gary tries to turn the ride to Coober Pedy into a race, but Vincenzo refuses to compete: "I wasn't going to degrade him or me by doing that. . . . Dancers strive to be the best in themselves, not to beat their friends" (1993, p. 11). Finally, one of the caretaker's portentous utterances in *His Master's Ghost* discloses how such behaviors are also metonyms for being-in-the-world: "a great musician wins the audience with his genius. He doesn't grovel for approval. He doesn't need it" (p. 62). While this statement is primarily about creativity, implicit in it is a redefinition of how Flea is to relate to the world. As an assertive individual, a prankster, self-taught and undisciplined, Flea has the makings of a conventional male hero: "Everything about Flea tells you he is a percussion instrument" (p. 19). To develop a different male schema, he has to learn the virtues of cooperation, and these come through work in the orchestra, because an orchestra builds power by mutual cooperation and working as a group. At the first rehearsal (pp. 19–20) Flea proves incapable of entering at the right moment (he is at first a bar late, and then a bar early, but either way completely disables the performance). The obvious reason for his failures is that he can't read music, but that is not the significance of the episode. Rather, the significance is elicited as a metonymic effect when, in a moment of masculine camaraderie, Martin gives him "a timpani thump" on the shoulder, and exclaims, "Stick to your guns, mate. You're an individual" (p. 21): both the sentiment, and the verbal and physical language used to express it, evoke the assertive "individuality" of the macho male schema. What Martin's action here evidences is a capacity for code-switching between masculine schemata, a capacity rarely seen amongst the males of these texts, who are more apt to illustrate permanent schema transformations. At this point, Flea immediately reasserts the urge to stand apart from the group by pretending to eat a spider sandwich. Under the mysterious influence of the caretaker, however, Flea is subsequently enabled to perform brilliantly in accord with the group and experiences a new sense of wonder at the drama, richness and amplitude in the cooperative process. Audiences also become aware—as was flagged at the outset by an insight of Greta's—that Flea's disruptive behavior actually signifies a desire to be liked. Part of the reconstruction of Flea's masculine identity thus involves a dismantling of his self-destructive habit, common amongst young males, of drawing attention to himself in alienating ways. An obvious part of this process is the number of times other characters turn his pranks back against him. In the novel this is done by Martin and Sarah, but in the movie the caretaker also recycles one of his props, and even Jason, in the movie's final minutes, plays out a reprise of the electric shock gag as part of a scene in which Jason and Flea are each seen to have gained a larger range of masculine attributes.

Another strategy used in many texts to enable a reconfiguration of male schemata is a quest undertaken in the form of a journey. In "Coober," the two young men undertake a journey from a coastal city into a desert, and like most journeys this one is redolent of a quest. As is conventional in many quest narratives, the significance of the journey is different from its ostensible purpose, and only emerges in the outcome. The journey in "Coober" thus turns out to be an adventure on which one of the questers, Gary, experiences a profound loss of self-definition—when he damages his bike through his insistently macho behavior, he has to hitch a ride with a truck driver and experiences for the first time a sexual overture from another male. The outcome—Gary is more disconcerted by his failure to feel revulsion than by the overture itself—is rather factitious, but its point is consonant with other representations of masculinity in adolescent texts: Gary is finally left confused about his sexual orientation and hence his masculinity because all the macho assumptions which grounded it, have been rendered invalid.

In earlier Australian fictions, a journey/quest had a conventional rite of passage function whereby a young male was exposed to hardship and danger and emerged from this testing as a man. Colin Thiele's long short story "The Water Trolley" (in *The Rim of the Morning*, 1974) can be taken as the epitome of such narratives. The idea that a crucial rite of passage takes place in confrontations between the individual and the frontier, the outback, the bush, is well established in Australian literature, and

Australian narrative has often displayed, as Turner says, a pattern of representation in which the harshness and indifference of the land is compensated by its natural beauty and by the discovery of a certain spirituality in communion with it (1993, p. 28). Comparable and parallel developments in children's literature have been described by Brenda Niall, especially ways in which the "bush tradition"—as exemplified by, say, Mary Grant Bruce—was modified by writers such as Thiele, Nan Chauncy, and Joan Phipson in the 1950s and beyond (1988, p. 552). In "The Water Trolley," Paul, a twelve-year-old boy, pits himself against the elements in an attempt to haul water to the homestead from a bore five miles away, and although he is defeated in his physical purpose he comes through spiritually triumphant. His "Pyrrhic victory" (1974, p. 68) marks his development into adult masculinity through his relation to and against the land, a conclusion drawn explicitly in the perceptions of his mother during the close of the story: "he had gone out confident and strong and came back stumbling and ashamed; he had gone out a boy, but he was a boy no longer. For a whole day a continent had hurled itself at him, and he had beaten it back" (p. 68). The ideological formation that Thiele is evoking here has its complexity, in its configuration of physical and spiritual, but it remains nevertheless an account of a paradigmatic *masculine* experience. *Quest Beyond Time* attempts to deconstruct and reconstruct this ideological formation, a purpose that becomes self-consciously present in the closing moments of both movie and book when, as Mike is leaving, his quest completed, the gruff warrior Fergus runs out:

> "The boy," he roared. "I want to farewell the boy!"
> "There is no boy." Simon pointed to the sky. "The man is there."
> (*Quest Beyond Time*, p. 160)

The signifying gap between the two sentences of Simon's reply here—that is, that the quest has again been a rite of passage—is made explicit in the movie, where he instead says, "The boy has passed the test. The man has gone."

Quest Beyond Time is a futuristic time-shift post-disaster narrative. It uses the traditional male quest-narrative to explore two opposing masculine schemata: on the one hand, a 1980s construction of the adolescent male hero as the "sensitive guy"; and, on the other, a more traditional conception of the hero as warrior—that is, as competitive, aggressive, quick to take offense, quick to have recourse to violence. The former schema is difficult to embody within quest narrative because of a propensity for genred discourses to evoke gender stereotypes. That is, characters are involved with events that tend to have gendered forms and outcomes. Quests, in particular, are characteristically built around a male career pattern which follows a structure of anxiety, doubt, conflict, challenge, temporary setback, then final success and triumph (Stephens, 1996), and this clearly applies to the hero of *Quest Beyond Time*.

The story tells of a young man, Mike, who, while hang-gliding, is transported through a "temporal discontinuity" from 1985 into a post-nuclear future of 2457, into a society which has reverted to a more traditional hierarchical and "barbaric" form of social organization comprising a number of small social groups or Clans, based on family, religion and "race." The opening of the film depicts the Clan Murray[3] performing a sacrifice to their gods because a fatal illness is afflicting the clan, and they need someone who can fly in order to obtain a cure from an offshore island inhabited by Christian nuns who have preserved medical knowledge and skill. When Mike arrives, they conclude he has been sent from the gods, and he reluctantly undertakes the quest in company with Katrin, the clan chieftain's young warrior daughter, and her uncle, Fergus.

Mike's quest corresponds with a conception typical of Australian fiction, whereby masculine identity is shaped through an interaction with a hostile physical and social landscape, as in "The Water Trolley." It is also modelled on a more traditional quest, the Quest for the Holy Grail, in that the objective is to cure a blighted land and the questers need to prove their own worthiness. Most significantly, however, this rite of passage reverses the "civilizing of the male" outcome we have pointed to in other contemporary Australian texts, insofar as Mike is being socialized within a heroic warrior society. But this is not straight reversal. Mike's initial male schema is essentially the SNAG, marked by such qualities as his sense of humour, genuine self-deprecation, aversion to violence, and the overt declaration "I'm really not the hero type" (p. 38). The needs and standards of a different society highlight deficiencies in this schema: he is ineffectual, lacks a sense of adventure, is unwilling to get involved, and lacks a sense of empathy with and responsibility for others. A strong implication here is that modern individualism constructs solipsistic subjects, and this condition disables the SNAG schema from the outset. The solution is to layer in sub-schematic elements from the other construction of masculinity, so that the objective of his rite of passage becomes the humanizing of the civilized male. The argument would not be much advanced if Mike were apprenticed to a traditional hero, however, and

Morphett gets around the problem by attributing the traditionally masculine role and behavior to Katrin, the young female warrior. As seen from Mike's perspective in the novel, Katrin was "the most aggravating young woman he had ever met. She could out-run him, she was trained with weapons, and he suspected that she was just as strong as he was" (p. 76). The point is that Mike doesn't need to acquire these attributes, but the best aspects of the ideology that underpins them. Indeed, by the end of the narrative he can cheerfully and affectionately acknowledge Katrin's physical superiority, and an encounter with another clan, the River Vikings (even less subtly, "River Yobbies" in the novel), functions to assert the repugnance of an unmodified macho schema.[4] These men, all too familiar in our own time, are physically overbearing, not very bright, and (in the movie) communicate mainly through grunts. The novel is explicit in identifying this schema, when Katrin and Mike spy on their evening meal:

> They slurped, let the drink dribble down their chins, wiped their hairy mouths on the backs of their hairy hands, and belched gently to show polite appreciation. They reminded Mike of his father's friends at backyard barbecues.
>
> He pondered wryly on the fact that even a nuclear holocaust could not wipe out one great Australian tradition. (*Quest Beyond Time*, p. 77)

The future/archaic warrior society of *Quest Beyond Time* organizes social relationships, and hence its masculine schemata, through the linked concepts of "kinship" and "covenant." These are humanistic concepts, based on a notion of an essential humanity which links the various clans and can also embrace the outsiders (the mutants who are *de rigeur* in a post-disaster narrative). The world in 2457 is very relativistic in its diversity of cultural practices, but the codes of kinship and covenant are universals which mediate elements of human similarity and difference. Mike's coming-of-age entails an acceptance of these codes, and both narratives—but especially the novel—use them to indicate a sense of lack in twentieth-century society. As Mike explains to the Mother Superior of the convent, "You live in a group here. You belong. I come from a time when everyone's solo. All single units" (p. 135). Mike thus returns to his own time with an acute sense of loss, and a longing for a social world which is ordered and has meaning, in contrast with a late twentieth-century world perceived to lack common values and to be confused about roles and behavior. But he also returns with assurances—

"Promises that he could find in his own time the things he had grown to value in the future" (p. 161)—and an insight which is the standard outcome of post-disaster narratives, namely, that finding those missing values is the way to shape the present so as to avoid a disastrous future.

Mike's participation in the quest in future time transforms him from a boy into a man, but more particularly it redefines the masculine schema he exemplified at the beginning of his adventure. This tends to be more evident in the novel, both because of additional episodes not included in the movie and because constant focalization from Mike's perspective enables actions to be reinterpreted subjectively. An audience is thus more aware of the incremental layering of attributes which augment the schema, and which enrich it with qualities such as bravery, patience, compassion, kindness, generosity, and the capacity to be other-focused.

An examination of a considerable range and variety of popular texts creates the impression that authors and film-makers share a broad consensus about the kind of SNAG schema that is desirable for Australian society and the kinds of strategies that might be useful for implementing it. This does not mean, however, that there is an actual corresponding social consensus. On the contrary, studies of Australian boyhood seem to reveal that alternative schemata have as yet made little impact on the lives of many boys. The intensity of the advocacy we have seen may rather indicate a sense that the SNAG schema has as yet attained only limited currency in society, and that it is most likely to be found within the social groups who write books and make films. Even here, gender correctness seems fragile when texts such as *His Master's Ghost* or *Lockie Leonard* use language and motifs which conventionally disparage females in order to define the desired masculine schema. In part, this happens because that schema is being defined too restrictively, and characters are not enabled to engage in the kind of code-switching between schemata which many males in actual world social interaction may commonly practise. On the other hand, the strategies of over-layering attributes to redefine a schema, of redefining schemata in ways that women and girls can approve, and of assuring girls and boys that they have choices in this area of their lives, are, at least in potential, very affirmative strategies.

NOTES

1. We are using *schema* here as Bem defines it: "A schema is a cognitive structure, a network of associations that organizes and guides an individual's

perception. A schema functions as an anticipatory structure, a readiness to search for and to assimilate incoming information in schema-relevant terms" (1981, p. 355).

2. Bogan refers to a male youth belonging to a subcultural group whose members wear "black T-shirts, ripple-sole desert boots, grimy jeans" (Winton, 1990, p. 93), drive souped-up Holdens and listen to heavy metal music. Otherwise known as Petrolheads, Sumpheads, Bogs, or Westies.

3. As their name and their predeliction for tartan suggests, the Clan Murray is primarily based on the ancient Scottish social structure, but the name also incorporates a pun on *Murri*, the general name now used by Aboriginal inhabitants of Queensland. Neither the movie nor the novel addresses Katrin's racial origins, but she is a woman of colour; her people's practice of control-burning the landscape is linked with Aboriginal practice before European settlement; and although events take place in the Sydney region, the Clan is said to have migrated there from the North. Such cultural hybridity, or perhaps just pastiche, is typical in post-disaster narratives.

4. *Yobby* is here an alternative form of *yobbo*, a term designating a male schema marked for such "anti-social" traits as loutish behavior, lack of consideration for others, noisiness, drunkenness, misogyny, and an overwhelming absence of any social graces. The "tradition" in the passage quoted refers as much to the "yobbo" behavior as to the Australian penchant for barbecues.

BIBLIOGRAPHY

Andrews, Barry. (1982) "Ginger Meggs: His Story," pages 211–233 in Dermody, Susan, Docker, John, and Modjeska, Drusilla (eds.) *Nellie Melba, Ginger Meggs and Friends: Essays in Australian Cultural History.* Malmsbury, Victoria: Kibble Books, 1982: 211–233.

Bem, Sandra Lipsitz. "Gender Schema Theory: A Cognitive Account of Sex Typingo *Psychological Review* 88, 4, 1981: 354–371.

——. "Gender Schema Theory and Its Implications for Child Development: Raising Gender-aschematic Children in a Gender-schematic Society," *Signs: Journal of Women in Culture and Society* 8, 4, 1983: 598–616.

Browne, Rollo and Fletcher, Richard, eds. *Boys in Schools.* Sydney: Finch Publishing, 1995.

Fletcher, Richard. "Changing the lives of boys" in Browne and Fletcher, *Boys in Schools.* 1995: 202–211.

Francis, Jaye. *Heartbreak City.* Sydney: Pan, 1991.

Franklin, Clyde W. II. *Men and Society.* Chicago: Nelson Hall, 1998.

Jennings, Paul. *Uncovered!* Ringwood: Penguin, 1995.

Martino, Wayne. "It's not the way guys think!," in Browne and Fletcher, *Boys in Schools*. 1995: 124–139.

McFarlane, Peter. *Lovebird*. Ringwood: Penguin, 1993.

Morphett, Tony. *Quest Beyond Time*. Ringwood: McPhee Gribble/Penguin, 1985.

Niall, Brenda. "Children's Literature" in *The Penguin New Literary History of Australia* ed. Laurie Hergenhan. Melbourne: Penguin, 1988: 547–559.

Townsend, Helen. *Real Men*. Pymble, Sydney: HarperCollins, 1994.

Shapcott, Tom and Simpson, Roger. *His Master's Ghost*. Ringwood: McPhee Gribble/Penguin, 1990.

Stephens, John. "Gender, Genre and Children's Literature," *Signal* 79, 1996: 1–14.

Thiele, Colin. *The Rim of the Morning*. Adelaide: Rigby, 1974 (orig. 1966)

Turner, Graeme. *National Fictions: Literature, Film and the Construction of Australian Narrative*. 2nd edition. Sydney: Allen and Unwin, 1993.

Wheatley, Nadia ed. *Landmark*. Ringwood: Penguin, 1993 (orig. 1991)

Winton, Tim *Lockie Leonard, Human Torpedo*. South Yarra, Victoria: McPhee Gribble, 1990.

Producing the National Imaginary
Doctor Who, Text and Genre

JOHN TULLOCH

[A] cultural subject is always a multiple thing, framed around gender, ethnic, racial, economic, class, political, and ideological antagonisms and interests. Cultural practices, the representations, languages, and customs of any specific historical society, interact in the production of a national popular culture. It is within this national popular culture that the major ideologies of a culture are played out in daily discourse and in the local and national media. (Norman Denzin)[1]

In the national media, the major "antagonisms" of a culture are played out in terms of a debate of texts and genres. In this chapter, I will discuss the science fiction series, *Doctor Who*, in the light of *its* engagement with British popular culture and British nationalism at a time of major economic conflict—the 1974 miners' strike against the Health Conservative government. This will involve analyzing *Doctor Who* in terms of:

- the national imaginary;
- institutional and societal orders of discourse;
- text and genre;
- textual analysis of an episode;
- audience response.

Nationalism is, as Benedict Anderson argues, always a cultural artifact, an "imagined political community":

It is *imagined* because the members of even the smallest nation will
never know most of their fellow members, meet them, or even hear of
them, yet in the minds of each lives the image of their communion. . . .
Communities are to be distinguished, not by their falsity/genuineness,
but by the style in which they are imagined.[2]

Furthermore, the nation is imagined as a *community,* because, regardless
of the actual inequality and exploitation that may prevail, the nation is always conceived as a "deep, horizontal comradeship".[3] Despite, then, the
social "antagonisms" that Denzin refers to—of gender, class, race, ethnicity, and (I would add) age—nationalism is a powerful imaginary in
the construction of solidarity, hope, aspiration, and utopian thinking. For
instance, Clyde Taylor, analyzing *Star Wars,* is interested in the construction of a utopian imaginary in the United States, which actually draws on
its continuing context of racism;[4] and similarly, in this chapter, I will discuss the way in which *Doctor Who* draws on "antagonisms" of gender
and class to construct its own idealised "welfarist" ideal.

But comparing popular media texts across a broad historical period
(as Taylor does from *Birth of a Nation* to *Star Wars*) also raises another
issue: that national imaginaries themselves shift and change. In Taylor's
analysis, the Asian (Japanese) economic threat to the United States by
the late 1970s in some ways replicated the socio-economic grounds of
Birth of a Nation, thus replicating, too, the condition of the earlier film's
racism. This is to emphasise the continuities across, rather than the historical particularities of, specific national imaginaries. In this chapter, I
will examine a particular *Doctor Who* episode, "The Monster of
Peladon" (1974), to suggest that the *particular* "imagined communities"
in one nation (Britain) at one time (the 1970s/1980s) are themselves a
matter of contestation. The 1970s mark a point of transition in British national culture between a welfarist and a Thatcherite imaginary in which
popular cultural forms were active.

Roger Bromley, for instance, analyses the construction of
Thatcherite "romantic nationalism" as contesting an earlier British imaginary by means of narrative fictions, autobiographical writings and television productions, which foreground the period in Britain between the
two world wars. Bromley draws on the Barthesian notion of myth as the
narrative resolution of social contradictions, to argue that a major
achievement of the Thatcher government was that it emphasised (as
though not contradictory) *both* the sovereignty of the world multinational economy *and* the power of a resurgent Britain:

So, to reimagine the "national" in the face of this contradiction, involves drawing on "popular memories" of the unified nation during World War Two symbolized in numerous national allegories. . . . Thatcherism is a contradictory ideological exercise, and it has required the *cultural* construction of narratives which resolve the contradictions and synthesize the competing images, symbols and meanings into a "popular" and unitary form of consciousness. This ideological unity does not depend upon logical consistency, but a process of symbolic transference in which a narrative of the past "stands in" for the present and sediments itself in "popular memories."[5]

Popular culture contains a large range of generic repertoires that can work mythically to resolve cultural and economic contradictions: Taylor, for instance, looks to the future narratives of science fiction, while Bromley finds narratives of "organized forgetting" in popular memories of the past. There are close similarities between Bromley's kind of analysis and a number of critical theorists of science fiction[6] in terms of myth and the contradictions of managed capitalism; but a valuable addition in Bromley's account is his notion of the shift in the "imagined community" of Britain from the consensus of social welfarism (the period from the post-1945 Labor government up to the early 1970s) to the new consensus of nationalism, which was to find its symbolic apotheosis in Thatcher's construction of the Falklands War.

Bromley describes the way in which a genre of "nostalgic returns" to the earlier period of class conflict in the 1920s and 1930s helped establish the myth that "in absolute terms, there is no poverty now and therefore no need for such a vast welfare apparatus".[7] Representing poverty as a succession of lovingly detailed "photographs" of a time definitively "past", and emphasizing the dominant image of the survivors ("figures who 'made it' despite demoralizing conditions, and have lived to 'write' the tale"[8]), a succession of works of "organized forgetting" extracted the period between the wars from its history of class exploitation.

Golding and Middleton argue in *Images of Welfare* that notions of "efficiency, morality (of the work ethic and self-sufficiency) and pathology (of individual inadequacy as the cause of poverty)"[9] have been fixed in popular consciousness at certain key moments in British history; and Bromley identifies one of these moments as the decade of the late 1970s and 1980s with its prevailing discourse of "scroungerphobia" and the "retreat from 'welfare' characteristic of the 'new Right' ."[10] This also was the time when these works of "organized forgetting" became popular.

A central generalisation in this genre is, Bromley observes,

> that the family did not manage its household budget well, incurred un-
> wise hire-purchase commitments and were thriftless, and that the suc-
> cess of the writer showed the social structure to be openly mobile,
> relatively egalitarian.[11]

My point is that a central generalisation of the imagined community of
capitalist *welfarism,* which Thatcherism replaced, was that the *national*
family did not manage its household budget well, and that state intervention was needed precisely to establish the notion that the social structure
was openly mobile and relatively egalitarian.

Bromley is interested in particular popular genres that emerge to
help mobilize shifts in national imaginary at specific historical moments.
But one of the interesting features of a very long-running television series like *Doctor Who* (which began life in 1963 and in 1996 was introducing its eighth Doctor in a new Fox/Universal television/film venture)
is that it spans these shifts in British national imaginaries that Bromley
describes. For example, the fan writer, Gary Hopkins, notes that the 1974
Doctor Who story, "The Monster of Peladon,"

> dares to touch a political nerve with its depiction of a miners' revolt
> and a class system not unlike those that existed in the UK in 1974 . . .
> However . . . a decade later "The Monster of Peladon" might well have
> been censored for blatant anti-conservatism.[12]

As Denzin says, debates within national popular culture are "played
out in daily discourse and in the . . . national media." Consequently, one
interesting project would be to examine changing readings of the long-
running series by, say, 1970s, 1980s, and 1990s audiences. Certainly,
leading fans became very hostile to the more cynical and violent (and
much less "welfarist") Doctor of the mid-1980s. Another project would
be to examine the readings of a *Doctor Who* episode situated within one
national imaginary (for instance, the "welfarist" "The Monster of Peladon") by different readerships situated in a different period. For instance,
would different age groups and different constituencies of young people
in the 1980s all read "The Monster of Peladon" in the same way as fan
Gary Hopkins, who says that "such radical posturing does not become
Doctor Who"?

"THE MONSTER OF PELADON" AS IMAGINED COMMUNITY

Doctor Who began life in 1963, at a time when the BBC was first feeling the impact of commercial television on its traditional audiences.[13] The science fiction+education formula of the early *Doctor Who* (which alternated between "bug-eyed-monster" Dalek-type stories and "educational" historical narratives, which had school teachers praising the BBC for the accuracy of its Aztec, Marco Polo, or French Revolution stories) reflected its own multiple subjectivity as a program begun in the new era of commercial competition. As a series designed to help win audiences back from commercial television, it adopted genres, producers, and writers *from* commercial TV, while attempting at the same time to retain a BBC "seriousness." And though it was a program designed in part for children, it came out of the drama department and not the more conservative, "classics" oriented children's programming section of the BBC. *Doctor Who*'s first producer, Verity Lambert, commented:

> Although the kids liked it, and still do, it also—which I happened to think was a plus—got in a much older audience of 18 to 25 to 30 year olds . . . There was no pressure on me from the drama department to do that. I had no children . . . It's perhaps because I *had* no knowledge of kids that . . . made it span those two groups.[14]

Eleven years later, when producer Barry Letts made "The Monster of Peladon," some of *Doctor Who*'s early child/adult "educational" focus was still retained, hence narratives about big business and the environment, "women's lib," class conflict, and other issues of modernity were not unusual. In "The Monster of Peladon," the Doctor returns to a planet that he has already helped (in the earlier "The Curse of Peladon") to move out of backwardness by joining a galactic federation. Peladon has been a feudal society ruled by a king and high priest dedicated to the "ancient ways." But the planet is rich in the rare mineral, tricilicate, which has been found in only one other place in the galaxy. So, by encouraging Peladon's king to join the Federation, the Doctor is promoting modern entrepreneurial activity that will have the effect of creating a new social order. The tricilicate needs to be mined in huge quantities, with the corollary of a growth of a new working class on the planet. The new wealth will need to be managed, requiring new functions of the state. Moreover, as a "one crop" economy with a total lack of technology, Peladon will risk military or economic exploitation by the Federation and other galaxies as a "Third World" planet.

This is, in fact, the scenario of "The Monster of Peladon," where the planet is trapped in a struggle for the tricilicate between two much more advanced forces, the Federation and Galaxy Five. "The Monster of Peladon" is the story of a patriarchal society where a young Queen rules in the shadow of her chancellor, Ortron. In this narrative, gender difference is one marker of the divide between the feudal (since the sexist Ortron is still fundamentally dedicated to idol worship and the "ancient ways") and the modern. Hence, in one key scene, the Doctor advises his female assistant, Sarah Jane Smith, to counsel the Queen about "Women's Lib." Another marker of modernity in the text is class power: The miners of Peladon are on the point of armed rebellion against Ortron and his aristocratic friends who are keeping all the wealth from the rare mineral, tricilicate, for themselves. A further twist of "modernity" in the plot is that Eckersley (an engineer sent from Earth to bring Peladon up to date with the latest laser mining technology) has his own plans of controlling the mineral wealth of the planet. He is in collusion with a Galaxy Five group of Ice Warriors from Mars (the only other planet in the galaxy which has tricilicate), who are posing as Federation troops. Control of Peladon will give the Martians economic and military power in the "superpower" conflict, while Eckersley plans to use the wealth in his own quest for power on Earth. So, as well as generating new areas of gender and class conflict, Peladon's shift into modernity also raises the issue of multi-planetary corporations, super-power conflict, inter-planetary racial conflict and the "development of underdevelopment." On the other hand, by promoting modern entrepreneurialism within the Federation, and by encouraging the Queen to take action to ensure that the new wealth is shared by all classes, the Doctor is promoting state welfarism and a new, mobile social order.

My view is that, written in 1974 (when genres of what Bromley calls "organized forgetting" were already beginning to circulate in mass forms), "The Monster of Peladon" needs to be understood as operating at a particular moment of contestation and reconfiguration of the British "imagined community." It represents a late stage of the consensus of state welfarism, binding together in its narrative the exploiters and exploited (at a key moment Ortron and the miners combine against the exploiting Ice Warriors), on behalf of greater equality and national security. The year 1974 was also the time of major political confrontation between the Heath Conservative government and the British miners, while the debate over joining the Common Market continued—so these were extra political readings available to many who watched the programme. However, beyond these specific events, it is the state welfarist inflection of modernity that seems fundamental to "The Monster of Peladon."

"The Monster of Peladon" does not simply "reflect" the miners' strike and class system of 1974. A national imaginary has to be worked for, via the construction and reconstruction of narrative, myth, and genre. As Denzin says, a national popular culture at any specific historical moment consists of the interaction of many cultural practices, representations, languages, and customs. Important practices and representations in the case of "The Monster of Peladon" include those of both the makers and the audiences of the program; and, in particular, their production of the narratives, texts, and genres by means of which they understand *Doctor Who*.

PRODUCING SCIENCE FICTION: SHIFTING INSTITUTIONAL AND SOCIETAL ORDERS OF DISCOURSE

Doctor Who has had an audience following for over thirty years. This has been a period marked by distinct shifts in the British national imaginary, with related changes in the position of its producer, the BBC. To understand more fully the ideological project of a particular *Doctor Who* text—"The Monster of Peladon," for example—we need to look more closely at the relationship between the program's institutional orders of discourse (in this case strongly influenced by the self-image of the BBC) and the shifting societal orders of discourse in Britain during the 1970s. Unless we look both at historically and institutionally located audiences (as in the case of fans) and at historically and institutionally located producers (as in the case of the 1974 BBC producers of *Doctor Who*), we are moving too quickly from the economic (the class conflict of 1974) to the cultural (the narratives of Peladon). As Featherstone says, many critical theorists move too quickly from textual analysis to political economy: "we need not just to read the signs but look at how the signs are used by figurations of people in their day-to-day practices."[15] This means that we must inquire into the role of the producers and transmitters of new popular cultural forms; and, of course, look at the schemas, conventions and practices of their differentiated consumers.

Critical media theory has emphasised the one-sidedness of television discourse, which differentiates it, for example, from the face-to-face communication of fans. As Norman Fairclough notes, "In face-to-face interaction, participants alternate between being the producers and the interpreters of text, but in media discourse . . . there is a sharp divide between producers and interpreters—or since the media 'product' takes on some of the nature of a commodity, between producers and 'consumers'."[16] Furthermore, since all discourse producers must produce with *some* interpreters in mind, what media producers do is address an *ideal* subject, be it viewer, or listener, or reader. Media discourse has built into it a subject position for an ideal subject, and actual viewers or listeners or readers have to negotiate a relationship with the ideal subject.[17]

What many critical theorists are concerned about is the producers' construction of "ideal subjects" in science fiction and other popular genres according to a technocratic and "managerial" ideology of scientism, "a closed universe of discourse, where alternatives to prevailing societal arrangements are automatically dismissed by restricting definitions of reality to the existing factual order."[18] Nevertheless, as most current audience analysts insist, actual viewers do *negotiate* a relationship with this "ideal subject." In other words, audiences are not simply "positioned as ideal subjects" by the science fiction text; and the same holds true of producers negotiating the science fiction genre. They also "read" it in terms of their own social experience. Furthermore, *"ideal subjects" are themselves never unitary.* Quite apart from their other subjectivities, they are also constructed at the level of both societal and institutional orders of discourse.

At the level of *societal* orders of discourse[19] the producer of a TV science fiction text will incorporate ideas that, as *Doctor Who* script editor Terrance Dicks said, are "in the air." Speaking about the *Doctor Who* story "The Monster of Peladon," Dicks said:

> You can't just do a kind of old imperial story whereby the galactic federation is coming to Peladon and is bringing the simple natives the benefits of civilization, like Sanders of the River bringing law and order to Africa. This isn't how people think any more, and you can't do a story like that, even with a children's adventure story or a family adventure serial. We are all well aware now that what happens when an advanced race meets a primitive race is not always to the benefit of the primitives.[20]

Most often, the "ideal subject" is constructed at this level, outside the individual intentionality of the producer.[21] In other words, although Terrance Dicks' intention was to achieve "realism" and show "the kind of thing that now happens in real life," his view (just as much as the imperialistic "Sanders of the River" one that he rejected) was an ideological one, based on a "BBC" liberal consensus that I will look at later in this section. This is not to say that this level of ideological operation cannot be *brought* to the level of consciousness.

At the level of *institutional* orders of discourse (for instance, the professional common sense of TV producers) that mask of "realism" operates more consciously. There, the ideal subject is consciously constituted in terms of naturalistic intentions, which are often so demanding and punctilious that they go beyond what the "ordinary viewer" is likely to notice. In that case the ideal subject can be constituted in terms of the values and stock of knowledge of *other TV professionals*. But *other* ideal subjects from the more general audience are consciously constituted as well: "bedrock" audiences who "want" the action-adventure in *Doctor Who;* and "bonus" audiences who, as the late-1970s producer of *Doctor Who,* Graham Williams said, "spot" the inter-textual references in the show.

In that very conscious way, then, the producer of *Doctor Who* was constructing an "ideal BBC reader" with particular inter-textual preferences and experiences; and, as Tulloch and Jenkins show in *Science Fiction Audiences,* particular audiences do "read" the text and gain pleasure from these "bonus" and "bedrock" textual constructions. At the same time, it is *always* important in this construction of ideal subjects that the producers of *Doctor Who* remember the child audience. Verity Lambert's notion of her "ideal subject" as bifurcated between children and adults was still adopted twenty years later by *Doctor Who* script editor Eric Saward, who said of "Kinda":

> We are attempting to appeal to a very broad audience of all ages . . . All the Buddhist stuff . . . all the symbolism and so on—it's there if you can get it . . . But when children are sitting there, they want a bit of something that will help them along too.[22]

So at one level (of societal orders of discourse) producers operate "invisibly" (often non-consciously) to construct "ideal subjects" in relation to the "real." But at another level (of institutional orders of discourse) producers operate visibly (and usually quite consciously) to construct ideal subjects both naturalistically and inter-textually. Given that TV serials depend for their survival on broad demographics, the ideal subject in contemporary popular texts is likely to be constituted—at the societal and the institutional levels—in several different ways.

As we have seen, the producer of "The Monster of Peladon," Barry Letts, identified himself with the "left-liberal" consensus. Similarly, the script editor of "The Monster of Peladon," Terrance Dicks, argued that:

> It is a kind of general liberal consensus that in any strike there are rights and wrongs on both sides. . . . It is never heroic capitalist against strikers, and it is never heroic strikers against evil capitalists.[23]

But just a few years later, during Thatcher's victory over the miners in the early 1980s, the popular media *did* represent "heroic capitalists against strikers"; and the 1980s generally was a period when the representation of "heroic capitalists" (in Australia, for instance, media magnates like Bond, Murdoch, Skase, etc.) profoundly influenced banking practices and the economy.

As Tulloch and Alvarado argue in *Doctor Who: The Unfolding Text,* "The Monster of Peladon" (and other *Doctor Who* episodes) represents the BBC's own adaptation to the break-down of the *previous* "national consensus" of cultural (and class) leadership embodied in the guiding BBC philosophy of Lord Reith,[24] and, of course, there are residual elements of the Reithian "uplifting" philosophy in the new, 1963 science fiction series, *Doctor Who,* which was to have its "serious" elements of history and education. But by the 1960s, the dominating metaphor was for the BBC to act as "a theatre in the middle of a town", airing voices of "Right" and "Left" without ever standing *for* these positions. Its professionally "neutral" stance was often represented by a general populism as a new generation of skeptical and aggressive interviewers took the position of the "man in the street" against "militant" unions or against "unscrupulous" big business. Homologously, the Doctor too adopted that "professional, neutral" stance, at least until the end of the 1970s.

> He has consistently adopted exactly that liberal-populist role in criticizing "sectionalist" forces of "Left" and "Right", and in rebuking the "official" and the powerful, whether in big business, the military, government or "militant" unions. That is possibly why the first producer, Verity Lambert, intuitively was uneasy with the third Doctor who lost his "anti-establishment" character and was at risk of becoming identified with the needs of the military and government.[25]

But even with Jon Pertwee's (third) Doctor in "The Monster of Peladon," the typical narrative position was, as Terrance Dicks said, to "step back" from the conflict—as between the miners and aristocracy. Like the BBC itself, the Doctor operates a professional "theatre in the middle of town," accessing the voices of liberal welfarism in one community after another. It is in this precise sense that *Doctor Who* worked in the 1970s out of what senior Australian fan Tony Howe called "the Left-wing liberal tradition" of the BBC.[26] It was, however, the national imaginary of welfarism which accounts for "The Monster of Peladon," and not, as Howe argued, "socialist bias at the BBC."

"Realism"—of the kind that Terrance Dicks speaks about—lies in the dramatic juxtaposition of opposing "points of view," with the Doctor functioning to *access* these viewpoints (that "the miners have grievances your Majesty") in "BBC" fashion. In this way institutional orders of discourse (the "neutral" BBC ethos) work to maintain or reposition the national imaginary. It was, of course, precisely the BBC's self-positioning within the myth of the "neutral professional" mediator that got it into trouble with Thatcher's new nationalist consensus over its reporting of the Falklands War.

It is this particular imagined community (situated between the earlier Reithian one of imperial/cultural leadership and the later one of Thatcherite nationalism) that Australian audiences that we interviewed readily recognized as "very English." Indeed, one group of communication professionals studying for a Masters at Macquarie University *equated* "Pomminess" *with* the self image of the BBC in that period:

> *Doctor Who* seems to have a real BBC ethos sort of guiding it all the way—like the discussions about the striking miners I was amused by, because it really reminded me of the sorts of ways that political and class issues are usually handled by sixties British drama. The kind of almost patronizing sort of reasonableness and the way that everything can be put into a very stable view of society, with people knowing their place. That's right, with no real confrontation being expected. Whereas, with *Star Trek* they tend to have a much more patriotic and nationalistic and democratic kind of political sort of thing underlying it all the time, where there are wars and there are conflicts and nationalism. . . . *Star Trek* mentions the moral at the end of every story.
>
> "The Monster of Peladon" was "small-l liberal"—the attitudes were very "small-l liberal" . . . the way something like women's lib.

is presented in a way which is not confronting but accepted as a very reasonable and just attitude to have. The way the Queen really wants to meet with the miners and treat them equitably. She doesn't want to exploit them. The way that the lead miner does want to resolve it for the good of the people. There isn't a sense of dominant force winning—it's a matter of resolving things so that we can all live and continue things in a fair way.[27]

As Bromley points out, ". . . small-l liberals"

naturally gravitate towards the middle ground in politics from which they seek to mediate between competing claims of capital and labor . . . [They] proclaim the merits of private enterprise yet renounce class privilege . . . seek to extend material security and cultural opportunities to the poor but refuse to identify themselves fully with any particular section of society.[28]

It is this "small-l" liberalism that the Doctor and his producers are conveying in 1974. So, "The Monster of Peladon" is indeed very English—but a particular imaginary of Englishness, as carried during the national consensus of welfarism by the ("liberal/left of center" yet "neutral") positioning of "intelligent, creative people" at the BBC.

What the Australian students seem to be contrasting is what science fiction writer Joanna Russ has called American first-year college civics' "need for a community and morality" in *Star Trek* with *Doctor Who*'s "BBC atmosphere of reasonableness," where "it's a matter of resolving things so that we can all live and continue things in a fair way." Both these long-term science fiction series represent modernist "grand narratives" of enlightenment, truth, and morality, but they are recognisably different in their positioning within different national popular cultures. In Britain, in the mid-1970s, there were circulating in popular culture representations of two different imagined communities: On the one hand, there was the relationship between British industrial conflicts, feminism, and the consensus of welfarism, as mediated by the "professionalism" of the BBC; on the other hand, the beginnings of the emergent "populist" nationalist consensus which came to be known as "Thatcherism."

Precisely because, as Norman Fairclough argues, the social identities of consumerism and technocratic/bureaucratic welfarism are so "ersatz," the imagined communities of national identity have become a potent source of "utopian longing." Indeed, as Fairclough also notes, popular anti-bureaucratic feeling could be incorporated in Thatcher's new nationalism as a critique of the *welfare* state and its version of "being British." One (Thatcherite) imagined community was becoming dominant by focusing, precisely, on the "patronising reasonableness" at the heart of its predecessor.

What Bromley says of "the 'generic' retrospectives" he analyses, is as true of the "end-of-feudalism" histories of science fiction:

> One important strategy that has been used to maintain power at a symbolic level is to attempt to "colonize" people's memory of the past, to obliterate dreams and ambitions other than those which correspond with a particular set of ideological definitions. Thatcherism has created an empty space in people's lives, filled it with public images of a privileged national past *and* of people building their own lives in their own way, while actually taking the past away from them in some respects.[29]

An important part of that "past" was the myth of post-war consensus—of full employment, the welfare state, and a benignly controlling public sector. *That,* it seems to me, was the imagined community of "The Monster of Peladon." It is from within *that* particular national imaginary that the future-story "liberation" of feudal society by state capitalist enterprise was represented in the text.

The public, Bromley insists, "are not 'dupes' of the ruling class or of the mass media,"[30] but they must, nonetheless, "make 'coherent' lives out of the existing stock of symbolism and metaphor."[31] Popular cultural texts (including science fiction) are important purveyors of that shifting stock of symbolism and metaphor as they compete for control of the national imaginary. In the next section, I will examine how "The Monster of Peladon" works at synthesizing narratively and visually the contradictions thrown up by its assemblage and the national/ideological project. This will involve looking at the textual relations between its "utopianism," its project of state-led modernity, and its version of the national imaginary.

TEXT AND GENRE

An apparent contradiction operating across the texts of *Doctor Who* during the Pertwee/Letts/Dicks period (1970–74) was between, on the one hand, the ideology of scientism and gadgetry (with its intended "James Bond" inflection tying the Doctor into an organizational and technocratic world), and, on the other, its ideology of "welfare consensus" (carried by the "liberal-left" politics of its producer). Were industry needs (cashing in on the market recently produced by James Bond films and novels) in contradiction with the national imaginary contained in the text?

In fact, this was not a contradiction in any fundamental sense. As Bennett and Woollacott note, the James Bond image operated "as a hero of modernisation,"[32] reorienting imaginaries of "Englishness." As a "meritocratic" and "professional" hero, Bond was working against the self-same imperialist imaginary as the BBC, in its "professional theatre in the middle of town" era. Whereas earlier heroes of British spy fiction achieved effortlessly a "superiority which is naturally, rightly and indisputably theirs" as a result of being English gentlemen,[33] Bond had to work harder at it. "Required to vindicate a myth of Englishness which has been put into question by the tide of history . . . he does so not by sheer force of personality or by means of naturally acquired aptitudes; instead he relies on the assistance of technological gadgetry, does regular target practice, and trains for physical fitness."[34] Bond's significance, in relation to readers formed within the earlier "imperialist" fictions, was "to promote a certain ideological shift in facilitating an adjustment from one mythic representation of Britain's ruling elite to another, and from one mythic conception of Englishness to another."[35]

Like Bond, Pertwee's Doctor (unlike any of the other Doctors) was physically trained for aggression when needed, and utilized technological gadgetry. This shift in popular fiction from a "natural-aristocratic" to a "meritocratic" national imaginary was perfectly compatible with the values of "welfare statism" and the "professional" values of the BBC in this period. Consequently, the overlay of the Bondian image and welfarism in "The Monster of Peladon" was not really dissonant.

To analyze popular fiction in this way is to examine genre historically (working at the fault lines of society) as well as formally. According to this view, far from simply reflecting social change as producers see it, genre actually engages in change, acting, in Bennett and Woollacott's words "as a catalyst enabling other ideological forms to be rearticulated in a new configuration."[36] But this approach to genre is also limiting if it does not, at the same time, focus on tensions and contradictions *within* specific genres. As Steve Neale points out,[37] the narratives of particular genres do not simply develop in a linear way from equilibrium through disturbance to new equilibrium, as argued by the classic narrative theorists. Rather, the narrative process within any one genre simultaneously inscribes a number of discourses. Narrative equilibrium/disequilibrium is thus a function of relations of *coherence and contradiction* between the discourses involved. Differences generated by social change are then mediated by production values.

According to this theory of genre and narrative, there are certain core values that prevent the genre splitting apart. In science fiction, this would include the emphasis on "human" values as part of the assemblage. The "human" is encoded according to a particular set of oppositions: intuitive intelligence versus rationalistic intelligence ("good" science versus "bad" science), organic versus robotic, fragility versus strength, purity versus defilement, garden versus wilderness, and so on.[38] In *Doctor Who,* for instance, the very *definition* of "villainy" (as in the Doctor's major enemy, the Cybermen) is the progression from intuitive, organic, fragile beings to rationalistic and machine-like robots. But, at the same time, the tension between positivist science and Romantic Gothic within the genre allows a long-running series like *Doctor Who* to play between the "good" (reasonable, liberating, welfarist) and the "villainous" (alien, evil scientist) doppleganger within the Doctor's own persona.[39] In the "liberal-left" period of Pertwee and Letts (1970–74), the reasonable, issues-oriented, welfarist Doctor prevailed, whereas in the following period (1974–78), with Tom Baker as the Doctor and the Gothic-oriented Philip Hinchcliffe as producer, the Doctor/doppleganger tension began to be articulated more clearly.

The successive developments within a genre can then be seen as a playing out of relations of contradiction and coherence between core values, generic tensions, and new social discourses, as these are appropriated by professional production values within a particular national culture. In *Doctor Who,* as a long-running series, the discourses of the "liberating" and the "alien doppleganger" scientist are both available, to contest and contend and be inflected by other social discourses (welfarism, feminism, Thatcherism, re-emergent militarism, etc.). Thus, in "The Monster of Peladon," the feudal-minded Ortron is "villain" only in the context of the modernity/welfarist discourse. In contrast to the Doctor's future-science doppleganger, the Ice Warriors, Ortron becomes a hero of state consensus, and dies, accordingly, a noble death.

In addition, in 1974 a core *institutional* discourse is the "stepping back" positioning of the Doctor himself as the "professional in the middle of town." As such, the Doctor performs a similar role in accessing "voices of Left and Right" as the presenters of current affairs television—a genre that was developing at the same time, and for some of the same reasons,[40] as the new TV series, *Doctor Who.* Consequently, his "professional" discourse is marked by the same sequence of narrative strategies which Brunsdon and Morley found in the presenters of current affairs television, namely, Linking, Framing, Focusing, Nominating, and Summing-up.[41] It is via this sequence of narrative strategies that "The Monster of Peladon" works to inscribe potential tensions and discursive contradictions, such as the full implications of feminism for this profoundly patriarchal text. It is indeed "the man that counts." Despite the structural motif of regenerating the Doctor in a number of very different personae, the Doctor has never become a woman—and it is clear, speaking with producers of the show, that it is unlikely he ever will. Similarly, for British super-fan Ian Levine, "you could never imagine a woman Doctor."[42] Consequently, institutional orders of discourse (the "theatre in the middle of town" liberal welfarism of the Doctor/BBC) contradict societal orders of discourse (the greater currency of feminism in the 1970s), generating potential tensions in the text.

"THE MONSTER OF PELADON": TEXTUAL ANALYSIS

Elsewhere, I have looked at how *Doctor Who* fans negotiate the textual ambiguity of "feminism" in this patriarchal series-text.[43] Here I will examine how the narrative of "The Monster of Peladon" works by examining textually a significant moment of "women's liberation" (and therefore of potential discursive tension) in "The Monster of Peladon." This occurs in the sequence where Sarah "innovates" by devising a plan for getting rid of the Ice Warriors. The scene is prepared for by two earlier sequences: first, where the Doctor accesses the miners' grievances and Sarah's "women's lib" discourse; and, second, where Ortron and the Queen (who is emboldened by Sarah's "women's lib" speech) argue over the arrest of the Doctor. Ortron reasserts his power over the Queen:

ORTRON: The Doctor will remain imprisoned where he can do no further harm and I shall give orders for the arrest of his female companion.
QUEEN: No Ortron, *that* you will not. The girl Sarah will remain at liberty.
ORTRON: As your majesty wishes. Since she is only a female her activities are of little importance.

The scene between Ortron and the Queen is marked by the Queen's growing resolution (as woman) to resist her Chancellor, but only (at this stage) on behalf of another *woman*. In fact, this "psychologically real" aspect of character development acts as a textual alibi, ensuring that the Doctor stays in prison and so is absented from the narrative at the moment of Sarah's "innovation." The Doctor's conventional "stepping back" role has already accessed Sarah's "women's lib" discourse verbally; now his imprisoning will enable it narratively. The Doctor has framed, focused, and nominated this "innovative" moment, and the camera marks it stylistically. Fiske says of the camera work in *Doctor Who* that it "exemplifies Kristeva's hidden productive work of the closed text . . . there are no dissolves, fades or wipes. Every cut is motivated by the dialogue or action."[44] In this scene, as in the series generally, the camera style and editing are naturalistic—a series of shot/reverse shot and establishing shot/three-shot/close-up mixes that promote the action rather than draw attention to the text. Yet Sarah's innovation *is* marked stylistically.

As Fiske argues, in *Doctor Who* "connoting, and therefore value-laden, camera work is subtle enough to escape conscious notice on first viewing, but nonetheless signifies on the ideological level. The author . . . may be invisible but he is not absent. Discourses are visual as well as verbal, and ideology is the framework of meaning that holds the discourses together."[45] In this third episode of "The Monster of Peladon," for example, the slow zoom is used as a marker of an "authentic" response from the "good" characters (the Queen, Gebek, Sarah) who are *subordinate* to the Doctor—often as recognition dawns for them of an idea the Doctor has accessed.

"The Monster of Peladon" text must mark out Sarah's "modern" nationalism (the freedom of Peladon from foreign troops) compared with Ortron's pre-modern isolationism. It does this by camera style, gesture, and clothing. Sarah's camera-marked "feminism" is in fact a conventional *Doctor Who* call for the liberation of oppressed, primitive, and feudal peoples. However, this "feminist" intervention in the narrative is *enabled* by the absence of the two dominant "modern" males (hero and villain); and *encoded* in terms of the series-text's conventional, liberal "liberationist/modernity" discourse. In *Doctor Who,* the "girl" acts, not as an object of desire as in Bond, but as the secondary part of a team in which women's emancipation is a process that accesses "welfarist" discourses of modernity, mobility and meritocracy to feudal regimes (as in "The Monster of Peladon").

This accessing is, however, only enabled narratively by the "stepping back" role of the Doctor. Thus the Doctor accesses Sarah, then steps back and withdraws while *she* tells the Queen about "women's lib." In the recurring *Doctor Who* narratives of feudal liberation, this "stepping back" recurs systematically, as each story ends with the Doctor stepping back into the Tardis and dematerializing, so leaving each liberated society to its own process of self-management and meritocracy. Textually, then, "The Monster of Peladon" works to inscribe the modernist "utopian" (miners' rights, feminism) within a meritocratic welfare-capitalist ideology by way of the Doctor's "stepping back."

Like any popular cultural narrative, "The Monster of Peladon" is an "ambiguous text."[46] Anne Cranney-Francis, for example, explores the relationship in popular fiction between reading position (the textually inscribed audience position from which the text reads coherently and intelligibly) and new subject positions (for instance, the feminist subject position constructed by feminist discourse outside the text). The texts of *Doctor Who* were especially marked in the mid-1970s by the discourses of state welfarism, feminism and "progressive" liberalism. However (to draw on Cranney-Francis' distinction),[47] these new subject positions did not seriously challenge the conventional reading position of the patriarchal text. The state, the BBC, and the (male) Doctor worked homologously within the British imaginary of social welfarism to re-inscribe the "patronizing sense of reasonableness" of "The Monster of Peladon." What I have tried to illustrate here is how the text works to control these ambiguities between patriarchal reading position and alternative (e.g., feminist) subject position within its conventional quest/liberation narrative.

ACTUAL AUDIENCES: INFANT, PRIMARY AND SECONDARY SCHOOLCHILDREN RESPOND TO *DOCTOR WHO*

There is no space in this chapter to go very far into audience responses. Elsewhere, I have examined secondary school students' responses to "The Monster of Peladon," focusing, in particular, on generic mediations of gendered responses to the text.[48] In focus group discussions, girls debated *Doctor Who* via a contest of soap opera versus fantasy readings; boys liked or disliked the show in terms of "hard" versus "ideas" science fiction. Underpinning some of this analysis is David Morley's contention that television audiences are already constructed in linked gender/genre relations:

> Soap opera presumes, or requires, a viewer competent in the codes of personal relations in the domestic sphere. The viewer is required to have a particular kind of cultural capital—in this case in the form of the

ability to predict the range of possible consequences attendant upon
actions in the spheres of the domestic/familial.[49]

In Morley's view girls acquire a cultural competence in the domestic familial, which enables them to read assumptions/frameworks of meaning
in soap operas that are often no more than implicit in the text. Similarly
other genres like current affairs or kung-fu violence "fit" (according to
class background) with the acquired cultural competence of boys.

While my analysis of secondary students does support Morley's argument—and extends his simple gender/genre relation to a more Bahk-
tinian dialogic *negotiation* of genres within gender groups—his analysis
also needs to be re-thought in two important ways. First, are the viewers
of *Doctor Who* who are younger than secondary level able to read it via
genre competencies? Second, Morley's sense of the reading formation of
young people is primarily based on TV/media genres. But there clearly
are other institutionalized orders of discourse that work to establish reading formations, not least schools and "secondary" media texts like magazines and fanzines. In the remainder of this chapter, I will look briefly at
these two areas of young people and audience readings.

To give some sense of how actual audiences of children responded to
the gender representations of heroic figures in "The Monster of Peladon,"
I will draw upon group interviews that were conducted during our *Doctor
Who* audience project. While the *Doctor Who* narrative draws on historically changing conceptions of heroism (as between, for example, the state
welfarism of the third Doctor and the more violent "Doctor Whooligan"
that many fans disliked in the later, mid-1980s "Thatcherite" sixth Doctor), there are also other long-lasting "scripts" and generic narratives that
children adopt to read these texts.

We conducted focus group interviews with two classes of infant students in Sydney, after screening the "women's lib" episode of "The Monster of Peladon" that I have been discussing in this article. Forty-six
seven- to eight-year-olds (twenty-two girls and twenty-four boys) were
interviewed in focus groups, where the interviewer began with a "did
you like it? what did you like?" set of questions. Unlike the secondary
students, who were interviewed the same way, the infant children responded throughout with a "I liked it because . . ." format; and there was
a general consensus with the response that "I liked all of it."

Like other analysts of young children's response to stories, we noticed a significant gender difference in the responses. It was the boys
who liked violence:

CLAYTON: I liked it when the man hit the man in the face.
MIKE: I liked the bit when he was talking and the man got shot and he
   disappeared because the rays were melting his body.
PHILIP: I liked it when the man attacked the other man.

In her analysis of Sydney primary children's writing, Cate Poynton notes
that "Boys write about . . . physical activities . . . Boys' fantasy worlds
are inhabited by creatures from outer space, assorted monsters (prefer-
ably of the kind that kill people unexpectedly and messily, with lots of
blood)."[50] In contrast, on the rare occasion when a girl in our infant
groups says she liked a violent incident, she immediately adds, "I don't
like people getting killed." The only other time when a girl says she likes
a violent incident (during fifty minutes of focus group discussion), she
positions her comment in a familiar script of home and school:

PASCOLENA: I liked it when that monster came magically out . . . because
   it killed those naughty people that weren't listening to that other
   man, and they weren't going to do what they were told.

"Doing what you are told" is a familiar script for these young children,
learnt daily at home and school. Collins has shown that the kind of implicit and inferential information that, for Morley, underlies a knowledge
of genre is not comprehended by young children.[51] Even when younger
children are able to remember the central information in a plot, they are
less able than older children to infer the connections between key elements, especially concerning motives. Instead of interconnecting narrative by a process of motivational inference, Collins found that younger
children generally relied on general action scripts. Such scripts represent
the young child's knowledge of everyday activities as regular behavioral
sequences, such as "going shopping" or "police catching criminals." An
encoding of common action patterns (and not the goals or motives underlying them) provides a fragile basis for understanding the unusual and
complex events that are often central to television narratives. Collins indicates the difficulty, for example, that a story involving plain-clothes
policemen poses for younger viewers, given that the uniform is an identifying feature of a police script. Here an incident of television violence is
understood via evoking schemas and scripts from the child's existing
world knowledge.
   In "The Monster of Peladon," the "monsters" are visually and be-
haviorally "baddies," but the changing position of Ortron, the differentia-

tion between "good" and "bad" miners (who are dressed identically), the articulated gender positioning of the "heroes," and the role of the soldiers (which varies between being jailers of the Doctor, and supporters of the ambiguous Ortron), do create considerable narrative complexity for young viewers. In fact, the "naughty people that . . . weren't going to do what they were told" were the "radical" element among the miners. In a typically "small-l liberal" consensualist discourse, "The Monster of Peladon" (via the Doctor) distinguishes between good ("moderate") miners like Gebek who is reasonable (and deferent to the Queen) and bad ("young hothead") miners who seek to overthrow the whole system by violence. In Pascolena's reading, this issue of political motivation is converted into the "naughty people that weren't listening" behavioral sequence of a "parent/teacher" script.

Girls, then, generally located the few violent terms they used in qualifying clauses and home/school scripts, while boys had an almost total monopoly of violent transitives, for example, "kill," "hit," "punch," "drag," "bump," "shout," "attack." Rather than emphasise the violent action aspects of the science fiction narrative, girls tended to focus more often than boys on the visual: color, costumes, sets, and striking props:

ROSALYN: I liked the different colours on their heads.
CLARE: I liked the green thing with one eye.
KATE: I liked it when the green thing came out . . . with the one eye—the green monster . . . that had brown . . . wiggly lines . . . in his hair.

One girl liked the "wiggly lines" on the Ambassador's green head because "it was like a map"; another girl likened the green head to a shower cap. Pascolena liked the "coloured lights that were in it"; Jackie liked the "King's" (Ortron's) "orange and white hair"; Cassandra liked the colours in the Queen's costume. Again, this is typical of young children's response to narratives: as Rule and Ferguson note,[52] salient visual and auditory features enable young children to attend selectively to and thus infer (or "understand") narrative content. But in our interviews it was the girls (perhaps already being enculturated within the domestic) who focused on colours and clothes.

CASSANDRA: I liked the Queen's costume because she had . . . a kind of mauve-violet cape and her crown was silver and it had a stroke up here and it was all blue and then it had a white dot and a red dot and then another white dot.

It was the girls who commented on costumes (the Queen's costume; the guards' "Roman skirts"), sets (the way the tunnels were glistening; the curtain the Doctor opened), and props (the wine cups).

In comparison with the boys' preoccupation with behavioral/action events, these young girls could be extremely observant of visual details that no other groups noticed. Whereas an adult audience group might read the horn-shaped cups at the Queen's court as generic "medieval" props (appropriate to Peladon's feudal mores and dress), Kirsty constructed her own narrative memory by linking the shape of the cups to "the monster's horn" in the previous sequence. This was instead of understanding the more complex political discussion about miners' rights and Ortron's class-based control of mineral wealth, which the Doctor raises while he and Sarah eat and drink with the Queen. In this case, the infant child "understood" the television text via inferences evoked by the television medium itself.

The secondary school girls also did not read a clear, class-based political message in "The Monster of Peladon," for example: "The miners were rebelling. I'm not quite sure why." But whereas the secondary girls then negotiated whatever politics they did recognise (e.g., Sarah's "women's lib" speech) via genre categories, and whereas the secondary girls embedded their reading of costumes also in genre semiotics: ("I knew he was a baddie, he was dressed in black. . . ."), the infant children responded differently in both areas. Whereas the secondary girls seemed more worried by the embedding of "women's lib" in a science fiction genre than by its ineffectiveness as feminist discourse (which is how university-level female students responded to it), the infants re-read the political speeches in "The Monster of Peladon" via localized image/narrative connections and via the intertextuality of general action scripts.

Both boys and girls liked the "tricks" and "magic" in the episode:

KATE: I liked it when the man did the trick.
INT: That's Doctor Who, isn't it? What was the trick that you liked?
KATE: When he put the money, the coin, on his head and it came out of his teeth.
INT: Good, that was nice. Does Doctor Who do lots of tricks?
KATE: Yes . . .
NATHAN: Good tricks.
INT: Good tricks, why are they good tricks?
NATHAN: Because they are funny ones . . . And they are mysterious.

So, whereas generic intertexts position secondary students' reading of the political messages and the images of "The Monster of Peladon," infant children draw intertextually on action scripts of "tricks" in understanding the overall plot line. "Tricks" are understandable as regular behavioral sequences: the Doctor does tricks "because they are funny." Under pressure from the interviewer, some children can extend the Doctor's "escape trick" to his "helping the miners," and "trying to set them free from the other people that are trying to kill them." But even here it is the trick of "opening that box . . . it didn't touch the box" that the children remember. What this particular trick is *for* in the narrative, the children misunderstand, since the Doctor is not opening the door to help the miners, "so they don't have to work anymore for the soldiers." We should note also that in the infants' analysis, it is the soldiers and not Ortron's aristocratic group that is oppressing the miners.

So the infant children do not understand the class or the "women's lib" messages of "The Monster of Peladon." Rather, further "home" scripts are used to understand Ortron and Sarah's "women's lib" speech to the Queen:

CHILD: The Queen was trying to do what Doctor Who was saying, but she had to do what the other man said.

INT: Why did she have to do that?

CHILD: Because, you see, that was her husband . . . And she was always doing what he said, but that time she was trying to do what Doctor Who said.

INT: Why did she want to do what Doctor Who said and wanted?

CHILD: Because she wanted Doctor Who to be on her side and then she was on Doctor Who's side.

INT: What was he asking her to do? What was he trying to do?

CHILD: He was trying, he was telling her secrets, like he told Sarah a secret and then she went to tell it to the other man with all brown hair and stripes on his head [Gebek] . . . and then when she got there and she goes "I've got to tell you something" and he wouldn't listen to her.

INT: So Doctor Who was trying to tell the Queen secrets, is that what you're saying?

CHILD: Yes.

INT: And he was telling Sarah to tell her secrets was he?

CHILD: Yes.

INT: So what sort of secret was he trying to tell her?
CHILD: I don't know.

Like the "tricks" script, "secrets" is a script that allows these infants to understand the narrative where they are unable to follow its inferences of motivation. There *are* secrets here: The Doctor/Sarah/Queen have to keep their negotiation with Gebek and the miners a secret from Ortron. But this simple narrative device is embedded in the "miners' rights/women's lib" discourse that the Doctor "tells" (Sarah to tell) the Queen:

QUEEN: Ortron says it is wrong to give in to the miners, that they will want more and more.
SARAH: But don't you see, your Majesty, Ortron just wants to see that the benefits of joining the Federation go to him and his aristocratic friends.
DOCTOR: You've got to convince your people that the Federation means a better way of life for everybody, not just for a few nobles at court.
QUEEN: I will try your plan, Doctor. Can you get a message to Gebek for me. Tell him to come to the citadel and meet with me in secret. I will hear the grievances of his people and try to remedy them . . .
DOCTOR: (as he and Sarah turn to go) Sarah, why don't you have a few words to the Queen. I have an idea you could give her some good advice. (leaves)
QUEEN: What advice did the Doctor mean?
SARAH: Well, it's going to be rather difficult to explain, but I think he was referring to women's lib.
QUEEN: And what's that?
SARAH: Women's Liberation, your Majesty. On Earth it means, well very simply, it means that we women don't let men push us around.

It is at this cultural/political level that the infants "don't know." Instead, the "Queen trying to do what the Doctor was saying" is embedded in scripts of domestic relations: "Because, you see, that was her husband . . . she was always doing what he said." Just prior to this, Ortron is described as "the King or something." Either as husband or king, Ortron's role in the class relations of the text is occluded.

Family life, then, as visible (sexist) hierarchy and controller of daily scripts, was the embedded source of decoding here; and explanations drawn from other familiar scripts ("tricks," "secrets," "escape from jail") were used to understand the overall plot. The Doctor "helps" people by "tricks" and "secrets":

INT: What ways does he help people, how does he help people?
KATE: When he was in the dungeon, when he was in jail he tries to get the keys to open it so that he could get them out.
PASCOLENA: He does kind of magic to get them out of jail.

And so the Queen needs to be "on his side" in order to be given the "secret" to "make peace with the soldiers and the creatures and the miners."

The text of "The Monster of Peladon" is, of course, itself ambiguous in its politics, as these University of New South Wales students make clear when discussing the same "women's lib" sequence:

PHIL: I couldn't figure that one out because what they were saying didn't seem to coincide with what, like, Sarah was so obviously beneath Doctor Who.

Phil was pointing out (as many adult groups did), the contradiction between what Sarah is given to say (about "women's lib") and what the narrative gives her to do. Nevertheless, there are the occasional moments in the text, such as the one we have discussed, and another noticed by a female student responding to Phil, that make its politics more ambiguous:

JANE: Yeah, but she also, like, had some ideas and she said, you know, that "I think something's down there in that refinery" and [the Doctor] considered it and said "Right-oh, I'll act on it."
INT: There's actually one time when she had the opinion, wasn't there?
JANE: That's right, yeah. But I think she—what I thought was bad about it was that when she was supposed to give some advice about Women's Lib, she didn't really do it very well . . . They had an opportunity there to really spout a few theories or something about feminism . . . but she just said, "Oh, you just can't let them do that."[53]

What the infant students notice is the trick the Doctor uses to open the refinery door without touching it, not the fact that it was Sarah who sent him there, or what he went there to do. In contrast, the university student Jane is arguing for the kind of reworking of a patriarchal text (and genre) via a feminist authorial practice and feminist reading position that Anne Cranney-Francis discovers in some science fiction.

But this kind of negotiation of a text's formal ambiguities was not offered by "Monster of Peladon" writer, Brian Hayles. Indeed, it is arguable that the infant children understood the text better than the writer. Despite his (and his producer's) belief that he was writing positive women's roles here, the children are in an important sense, right to say that "the Queen was trying to do what Doctor Who was saying but she had to do what the other man said." Either way, the women (the Queen, Sarah) were being positioned in the narrative by men. My point is not simply that the infant students were cognitively unable to deal with the formal operations of political discourse—although that may be part of it, in so far as both the children's "I liked it when . . . I liked it when . . ." responses to the interviewer and their emphasis on behavioral sequence scripts and visual details rather than conceptual transformations, indicated a paratactic (string of individual messages) rather than higher level hypotactic structuring of their viewing.[54]

But my main point is that the text did not offer them a reading position from which a feminist reading *could* be intelligible and coherent. In the interstices of reading an already ambiguous text, the infants reached for conventional scripts just as the secondary students reached for genres, and university students reached for feminist intertexts to *make* it mean. And as Gilbert and Taylor have pointed out, so many of the conventional scripts and texts that are available to girls in the classroom and the home offer the dominant reading position of a male (even misogynist) persona: "it may be the only persona whose textual construction seems *known* and *natural.*"[55] The *Doctor* holds the authorship of "tricks" and "secrets"; small wonder, then, that the girls note Sarah when she "got a fright" and not when she was being (marginally) innovative in the narrative.

NATIONAL POPULAR CULTURE
AND READING FORMATION

Next to sex and religion, party-politics has normally been something of a taboo subject in *Doctor Who;* and yet "The Monster of Peladon" dares to touch a political nerve with its depiction of a miners' revolt and a class system not unlike those that existed in the UK in 1974. It is interesting to speculate that writer Brian Hayles may have been avenging [his earlier] "The Curse of Peladon" . . . which, as a result of another miners' strike, had become a casualty of power cuts and blank TV screens two year earlier. However, such radical posturing does not become *Doctor Who* and a decade later "The Monster of Peladon" might well have been censored for blatant anti-Conservatism (Hopkins (n.d.), p. 5).[63]

Two things are evident in these comments on "The Monster of Peladon" by British *Doctor Who* fan Gary Hopkins. First, there is the perception that *Doctor Who* shifted its ground as between this 1974 "class system" story and the Thatcherite 1980s. Hopkins is talking here about a national popular culture, and the historical shifts within it. Second, though, he is writing in an official fan club publication; and familiar protocols of the reading formation of fandom are evident. In particular, there is the fans' familiar *intra*-textual reference, so that Brian Hayles' motivation in writing a "miners' strike" story is worked through his earlier *Doctor Who* story, "The Curse of Peladon."

Hopkins' reading of the episode's "feminism" is, likewise, intratextual. As in some other readings of this episode, Hopkins believes that Sarah does "steal" some scenes from the Doctor. However, this is *in spite* "of her Women's Lib temperament." Hopkins' reading of Sarah's "independence" seems contradictory, certainly, from a feminist subject position, But it is less so within his own as part of the reading formation of *Doctor Who* fandom (and as such, his similarity with Australian fans about the "anti-conservative bias" of this 1970s *Doctor Who* text is not idiosyncratic).

CONCLUSION

Reading formations, as Bennett and Woollacott argue,

> establish definite relations of reading composed, in the main, of those apparatuses—schools, the press, critical reviews, fanzines—within and between which the socially dominant forms for the superintendence of meaning are both constructed and contested.[57]

In this chapter, I have related "socially dominant forms" to historically changing national imaginaries, as mediated by genre and by institutionalized discourses at the BBC. But *viewers/readers* of "The Monster of Peladon," whether in schools or in fanzines, are themselves constructing and contesting these already ambiguous textual meanings. As Bennett and Woollacott point out, reading formations work by way of intertextual bids and counterbids; and so the "class" or "feminist" politics of "The

Monster of Peladon" are read in terms of their coherence and relevance in relation to these intertexts.

Norman Fairclough has argued that "the interpretation of inter-textual context is a matter of deciding which series a text belongs to."[58] For the University of New South Wales student, Jane, the series it belongs to should include feminist texts. For Gary Hopkins, it belongs to the series *Doctor Who,* and within that to the Peladon series of stories. For the infant students, it belongs to a series of scripts of "tricks" and "secrets." Our secondary school students "bid and counterbid" with soap opera and fantasy, "hard" and "soft" science fiction; while another group of boys from an academic high school located the "best" *Doctor Who* in the "twists" it gave to school history.[59] Different age groups and different reading formations determine which "series" "The Monster of Peladon" is assigned to. As Fairclough says, it is because texts are always in inter-textual relation with other series of texts that they are always dialogic. Sometimes the choice of dialogic relationship depends on other dominant media forms, as in the case of the infants' frequent reference to the aliens as "dragons," or in the case of the secondary schoolgirls' choice of soap opera (or the fans' use of the history of *Doctor Who* itself). At other times, the inter-textual relationship works within the reading formation of the school (or home): the infants' "naughty people that weren't listening" and "weren't going to do what they were told," or the academic schoolboys' reference to school history. The schoolgirls' strong emphasis on fantasy also was, in part, formed within the school, with an English teacher (who was present at the interview) strongly emphasising in class the creative qualities of fantasy in contrast to what she saw as the media-determined "realism" and "failure of imagination" of girls of this age.

As Denzin remarks (see the opening quotation) a national popular culture is played out both "in daily discourse and . . . in the national media." While I have emphasised the importance of the national media texts and interests in this chapter, we must not underestimate its construction and contestation in daily discourse (including that of the family and the school).

NOTES

1. Denzin, 1992, p. 117.
2. Anderson, 1991, p. 15.
3. Ibid., p. 16.

4. Taylor, 1988, pp. 100, 101–2.

5. Bromley, 1988, pp. 4, 22.

6. Tulloch, and Jenkins, 1995, Ch. 2.

7. Bromley, 1988.

8. Ibid., p. 29.

9. Ibid., p. 50.

10. Ibid., p. 50.

11. Ibid., pp. 51–2.

12. Hopkins, n.d., p. 5.

13. Tulloch, and Alvarado, 1983, pp. 38ff.

14. Interview with Verity Lambert, August 1981.

15. Featherstone, 1991, p. 63.

16. Fairclough, 1989, p. 49.

17. Ibid., p. 49.

18. Dunn, 1979, p. 344.

19. For an elaboration of the relationship between societal and institutional orders of discourse, see Fairclough, 1989, Ch. 2, 8.

20. Interview with Terence Dicks and Barry Letts, August 1981.

21. See Morley, 1981, p. 4.

22. Interview with Eric Saward, August 1981.

23. Interview with Dicks and Letts, August 1981.

24. Tulloch and Alvarado, 1983, pp. 50–2.

25. Ibid., p. 52.

26. See Tulloch and Jenkins, 1995, Ch. 8.

27. Discussion with Masters Communication students, Macquarie University, March 1990.

28. Bromley, 1988, pp. 110–11.

29. Ibid., p. 189.

30. Ibid., p. 159.

31. Ibid., p. 160.

32. Bennett, and Woolacott, 1987, p. 141.

33. Ibid., p. 110.

34. Ibid., pp. 110–11.

35. Ibid., pp. 112–13.

36. Ibid., p. 282.

37. Neale, 1980. See also Tulloch, 1990, pp. 72–73.

38. Tulloch and Alvarado, 1983, pp. 71ff.

39. Ibid., pp. 127ff.

40. Ibid., p. 38.

41. Brunsdon and Morley, 1978, pp. 58–61.

42. Interview with Ian Levine, November 1981.

43. Tulloch and Jenkins 1995, Ch. 6.

44. Fiske, 1983, p. 94.

45. Ibid., p. 94.

46. See Buxton, 1990, pp. 15–19, 62–66; Cranny-Francis, 1990, pp. 20ff.; Tulloch and Jenkins, 1995, Ch. 2.

47. Cranney-Francis, 1990, p. 43.

48. Tulloch and Jenkins, 1995, Ch. 5.

49. Morley, 1981, p. 12.

50. Poynton, 1985, p. 35.

51. Collins, 1983, pp. 110–133.

52. Rule and Ferguson, 1986, pp. 29–50.

53. Focus group interview with General Studies "Sociology of Mass Communication" students, University of New South Wales, 17 March 1982; for an analysis of this group's reading of "The Monster of Peladon," see Tulloch and Jenkins, 1995, Ch. 7.

54. Hodge and Tripp, 1986, Chapters 1 and 3.

55. Gilbert and Taylor, 1991, p. 121.

56. Hopkins, n.d., p. 5.

57. Bennett and Woollacott, 1987, pp. 64–65.

58. Fairclough, 1989, p. 152.

59. Focus group interview with five boys from Sydney Boys High School, July 1981.

REFERENCES

Anderson, B. *Imagined Communities: Reflections on the Origin and Spread of Nationalism.* London: Verso, 1991.

Bennett, T. and Woolacott, J. *Bond and Beyond.* Basingstoke: Macmillan, 1987.

Bromley, R. *Lost Narratives: Popular Fictions, Politics and Recent History.* London: Routledge, 1988.

Brunsdon, C. and Morley, D. *Everyday Television: 'Nationwide.'* London: British Film Institute, 1978.

Buxton, D. *From The Avengers to Miami Vice: Form and Ideology in Television Series.* Manchester: Manchester University Press, 1990.

Cranny-Francis, A. *Feminist Fiction: Feminist Uses of Generic Fiction.* Cambridge, U.K.: Polity, 1990.

Collins, W. A. "Social antecedents, cognitive processing, and comprehension of social portrayals on television," in E. T. Higgens, D. N. Ruble, and W. W.

Hartrup, eds., *Social Cognition and Social Development: A Sociocultural Perspective*. Cambridge, U.K.: Cambridge University Press, 1983: 110–33.

Denzin, N. K. *Symbolic Interactionism and Cultural Studies: The Politics of Interpretation*. Oxford: Blackwell, 1992.

Dunn, R. "Science, Technology and Bureaucratic Domination: Television and the Ideology of Scientism," *Media, Culture and Society* 1, 1979: 343–54.

Fairclough, N. *Language and Power.* London: Longman, 1989.

Featherstone, M. *Consumer Culture and Postmodernism*. London: Sage, 1991.

Gilbert, P. and Taylor, S. *Fashioning the Feminine: Girls, Popular Culture and Schooling*. Sydney: Allen and Unwin, 1991.

Hopkins, G. *The Monster of Peladon. Doctor Who: An Adventure in Space and Time*. London: Cybermark Services, n.d.

Morley, D. " 'The Nationwide Audience'—A Critical Postscript," *Screen Education* 39, 1981: 3–14.

Neale, S. *Genre.* London: British Film Institute, 1980.

Poynton, C. *Language and Gender: Making the Difference*. Geelong: Deakin University Press, 1985.

Rule, B. G. and Ferguson, T. J. "The Effects of Media Violence on Attitudes, Emotions, and Cognitions." *Journal of Social Issues* 42:3, 1986: 29–50.

Taylor C. "The Mastertext and Jeddi Doctrine," *Screen* 29:4, 1988: 96–104.

Tulloch, J. and Alvarado, M. *Doctor Who: The Unfolding Text*. London: Macmillan, 1983.

Tulloch, J. and Jenkins, H. *Science Fiction Audiences Watching Doctor Who and Star Trek*. London: Routledge, 1995.

Tulloch, J. *Television Drama: Agency, Audience and Myth*. London: Routledge, 1990.

Contributors

Jonathan Bignell is Senior Lecturer and Director of Undergraduate Studies at the Media Arts Centre, Royal Holloway University of London, U.K.

J. S. Bratton is Professor and Joint Head of Department of Drama, Theatre, and Media Studies at Royal Holloway College, University of London, U.K.

Douglas Brode teaches in, and is coordinator of, the cinema studies programs at Syracuse University, U.S.A.

Dennis Butts is retired but teaches part time in the M.A. in Children's Literature program at the University of Reading, U.K.

Linda K. Christian-Smith is Associate Professor of Curriculum and Instruction, College of Education and Human Services, University of Wisconsin, U.S.A.

Alison Haymonds is a freelance writer and journalist.

Dudley Jones is Lecturer in English and Education, University of Reading, U.K.

David Lusted is Lecturer in Film Studies and Director of the Film Studies Program at the Southampton Institute, U.K.

Robyn McCallum is Lecturer in Children's Literature at Macquarie University, Australia.

Nina Mikkelsen has taught at universities in Florida, North Carolina, and Pennsylvania and has published over 20 articles in the field of children's literature.

Catriona Nicholson is Lecturer in English and Education, University of Reading, U.K.

Deborah Philips is Lecturer in the Arts Faculty, Brunel University, U.K.

Chris Routh is Resources Officer in the Reading and Language Information Centre, University of Reading, U.K.

Christine Stephens is Head of English Department, Ashmead Community School, Reading, U.K.

John Stephens is Professor of English at Macquarie University, Australia.

Alan Tomlinson is Professor of Sport and Leisure Studies at the University of Brighton, U.K.

John Tulloch is Professor of Media Communications and Head of the School of Journalism, Media and Cultural Studies, University of Cardiff, Wales, U.K.

Tony Watkins is Senior Lecturer in English, Director of the M.A. in Children's Literature program, and Director of the Centre for International Research in Childhood: Literature Culture Media (CIRCL), at the University of Reading, U.K.

Christopher Young is Lecturer in German, University of Cambridge, U.K.

Index